# Physiology

# Physiology

## All you need to know about how your body works

GENERAL EDITOR

*Professor Peter Abrahams*

amber
BOOKS

This edition published in 2007 by
Amber Books Ltd
Bradley's Close
74–77 White Lion Street
London N1 9PF
www.amberbooks.co.uk

The material featured in this book previously appeared in the partwork
*Inside the Human Body*.

ISBN-13: 978-1-905704-64-4

Contributors: Claire Cross
Project Editor: Michael Spilling
Design: Hawes Design


Printed in Thailand supervised by Kyodo Printing Co (S'pore) Pte Ltd

# CONTENTS

# Introduction

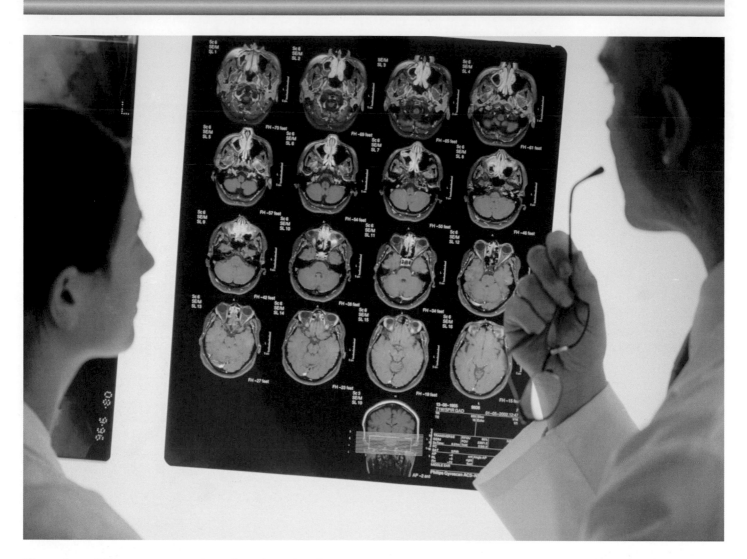

Throughout history mankind has endeavoured to understand exactly how our bodies work, using this knowledge to develop an arsenal of weapons to fight disease and prolong human life.

The convoluted history of human physiology, the study of how our bodies function when healthy, is chronicled through a series of false leads and the occasional brilliant breakthrough. It is a science that has preoccupied many great minds, at the same time inviting a fair degree of 'pseudo-science' and quackery. Ultimately, knowledge about our bodies and why we succumb to disease has led to modern-day scientists developing increasingly sophisticated treatments for illnesses, and cures for diseases once considered untreatable.

## EARLY MEDICINE

One of the earliest recorded uses of medicine is witnessed in European cave paintings where plants are depicted as crude healing agents. In Ancient Egypt, preserved papyruses record how detailed anatomical observations were carried out during the embalming of dead bodies, and one of the most renowned medical names of the ancient world, Hippocrates, born in Greece 460 BC, proclaimed the importance of clinical observation, recording symptoms and remedies.

Although some of these practices seem ahead of their time, they were based on little accurate knowledge. The accepted wisdom in ancient Greece was that the body contained four humours:

Doctors compare a variety of brain scans taken from four distinct angles.

phlegm, blood, red bile and yellow bile, an imbalance of which caused disease.

This belief held sway until the Middle Ages, a time of stagnation, when the church, a hugely influential force, taught that disease was punishment from God, a just desert for sinners. Few chose to argue with this powerful lobby and medical practices evolved into an incongruous mix of superstition and secular beliefs.

## ENLIGHTENED ATTITUDES

The Renaissance saw the return of a more enlightened approach, bringing a period of medical investigation. As well as Leonardo da Vinci's well-documented forays into human dissection, other pioneering figures included Andreas Vesalius and William Harvey, who challenged accepted folklore with scientific evidence. Vesalius revealed the differences between human and animal anatomies, while Harvey made the incredible discovery of how the heart pumped blood around the body.

Despite a greater understanding of physiology, with a lack of effective drugs there was little direct benefit to the general health of the populace. However, from the eighteenth century, advancements in chemistry and laboratory techniques led to the beginning of the science of bacteriology.

Louis Pasteur and Robert Koch definitively confirmed the germ theory, linking microorganisms with disease, culminating in Pasteur developing vaccines for rabies and anthrax.

Other fundamental discoveries had an enduring impact. In 1842, Crawford Long performed the first surgical operation using anaesthesia; in 1867, Joseph Lister highlighted the beneficial use of antiseptic in hospitals and consequently cut mortality

This angiogram shows human kidneys, outlined in purple. The orange area is the ureter, which carries urine to the bladder.

rates. Wilhelm Rontgen invented the X-ray machine in 1896, and in 1901 Karl Landsteiner revealed the human blood groups. These were all monumentally important, laying the foundations for the transformation of diagnosis and surgery in the twentieth century.

## MODERN TECHNOLOGY

With the twentieth century came the advent of evidence-based medicine, using scientific method to answer clinical questions. Advances in technology gathered such a pace that, for the first time in history, knowledge and science combined to produce an unparalleled number of breakthroughs in all areas of medicine.

In 1928, bacteriologist Alexander Fleming made one of the most significant finds of the century when he 'accidentally' discovered penicillin from a mould that developed a bacteria-

free circle around itself. Fleming's discovery marked the start of the antibiotic revolution. Further advances in pharmacology meant the development of more vaccines, enabling childhood diseases such as polio, measles and rubella to be virtually eradicated in the developed world. Today pharmacology is a multi-million pound industry with new drugs constantly developed. Sophisticated technology

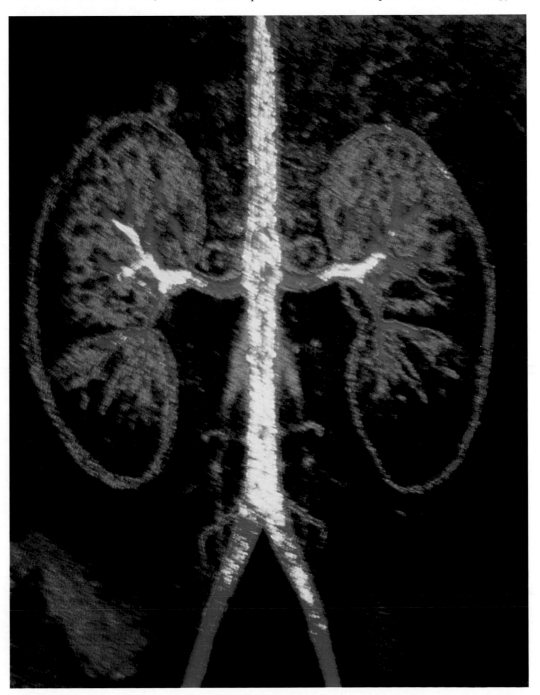

and screening devices have enabled scientists to view the human body as never before. As well as sustained improvements in X-rays, a diverse range of imaging techniques, such as ultrasound scans, magnetic resonance imaging (MRI), computed tomography (CT) scans, angiographies and endoscopies, has revolutionised diagnostic medicine, providing physicians with incredibly detailed pictures of internal structures, enabling earlier diagnosis and better treatment options.

## POWERFUL TOOLS

As well as scanning devices, powerful electron microscopes have enabled modern-day scientists to view body structures in minute detail. A fundamental research and diagnostic tool, electron microscopes are an integral part of any laboratory, commonly utilised in biopsies and the examination of microorganisms and cells.

Surgical procedures have become increasingly complex, with operations carried out today that would have been unimaginable just 50 years ago. From Christian Bernard's first successful heart transplant in 1967, a series of groundbreaking transplant operations has followed.

Keyhole and micro-surgery have transformed many procedures, dramatically cutting recovery rates and enabling operations to be carried out on minute tissues. One of the most awesome predictions is the possibility, using microsurgery, of performing complex operations on unborn babies. Some major diseases continue to challenge medical science. Cures for heart disease and cancer, two of the biggest killers in the developed world, have so far eluded scientists, although advances in treatments continue unabated.

New 'smart' drugs allow precision targeting of cancer cells, avoiding the destruction of surrounding healthy tissues and enabling higher, more powerful doses to be delivered with fewer of the unpleasant side effects traditionally associated with chemotherapy. Similarly, radiation therapy has been refined, with rays concentrated more precisely on cancer cells. One of the most exciting developments is the link between viruses and cancer and consequently the development of a vaccine against cervical cancer. The prediction is that many more cancers will be linked to viruses with the possibility of a new wave of protective vaccines.

Similarly, the treatment of heart disease has witnessed great leaps forward. The latest high-tech imaging techniques for observing clots and the emergence of robotic surgery for bypass operations hint at dramatically improved survival rates in the future.

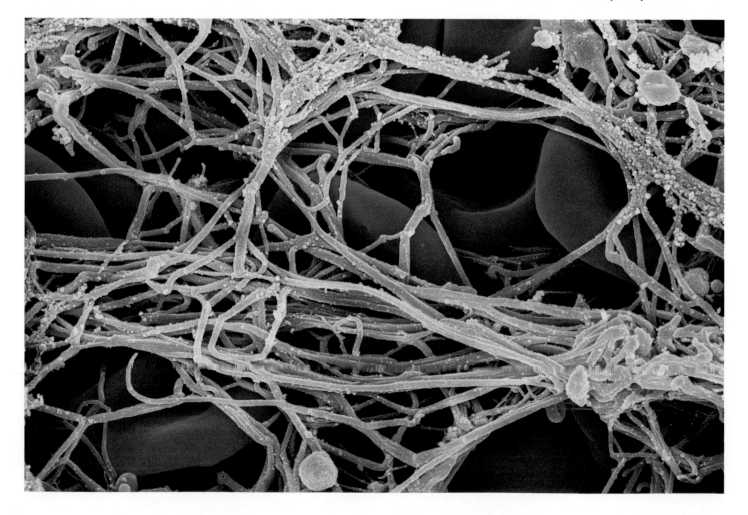

This microscopic image of a blood clot shows fibrin surrounding trapped red blood cells, or erythrocytes.

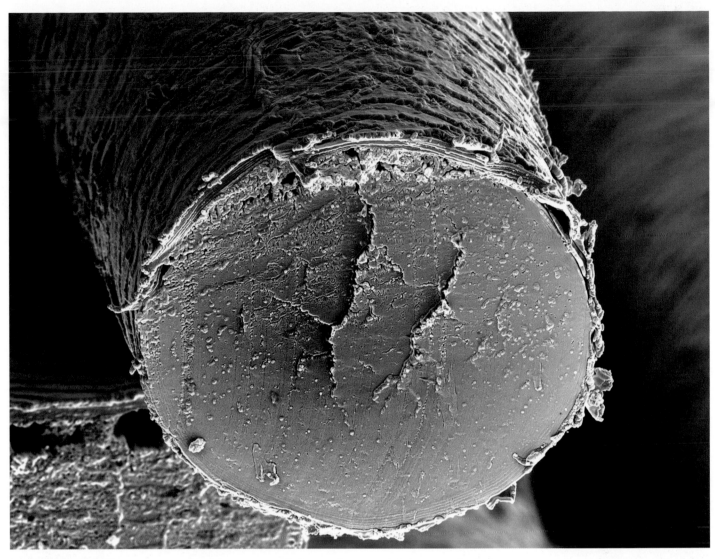

## NEW RESEARCH

Two of the most extraordinary, and contentious, developments in the medical world are gene therapy and stem cell research. These two areas offer unbelievable opportunities for fighting disease. The discovery in 1953 by James Watson and Francis Crick of the structure of human DNA began an incredible journey that led to the launch of the human genome project in 1990, an international venture to discover the 25,000 genes in human DNA. Completed in 2003, the project meant scientists could consider the possibility of replacing 'diseased' genes with healthy ones and the introduction of genetic profiling, alerting individuals to potential health problems. As each person's DNA is unique, DNA analysis, or genetic 'fingerprinting' has also been used in medicine to identify potential organ donors and establish paternity. Meanwhile, stem cell research uses 'blank' cells from early-stage embryos, cultured into specialised cell types, such as nerves, and used to replace diseased tissues. This offers hope in conditions such as Parkinson's and raises the almost miraculous possibility of treating conditions such as spinal cord injury, replacing damaged tissue with healthy renewable tissue. Despite the understandable excitement, both areas are controversial, raising ethical and practical issues; there are many obstacles to be overcome before either becomes standard medical practice.

In the face of all this science, new medical challenges continue to arise. Rising levels of obesity in the West have led to forecasts of unprecedented levels of disease affecting the young, while the misuse of antibiotics has led to the alarming development of a new raft of antibiotic-resistant superbugs.

A section of an Asian hair shows its scales and characteristic oval section. Different racial groups can be identified through hair analysis.

## ABOUT THIS BOOK

*Physiology* offers the reader an indepth insight into exactly how our bodies work. The book illustrates not just how body systems operate, but goes a step further, answering such intriguing questions as what is the link between smell and memory, how do we experience emotions, and how do our bodies react to stress? Arranged in thematic sections exploring the major body systems, *Physiology* takes the reader on a voyage of discovery like no other.

# How bones are formed

Bones are living tissue, and are in a constant state of renewal. They form the basis of the skeleton, and are responsible for locomotion as well as containing bone marrow and vital minerals.

Bones are the rigid body tissues that are the basis of the human skeleton. They are a living tissue, constantly being renewed and shaped by the process of growth and reabsorption.

### BONE MATRIX
Bone is composed of a calcified matrix in which bone cells are embedded. The matrix is made up of flexible collagen fibres in which crystals of hydroxyapatite (a calcium salt) are deposited. Three principal bone cell types are found within this matrix:

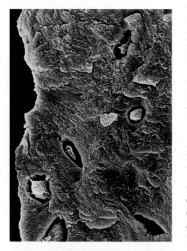

■ Osteoblasts – cells responsible for forming bone
■ Osteoclasts – bone-eating cells
■ Osteocytes – bone cells that have fully matured.
   Bone-forming and bone-eating cells permit the constant turnover of bone matrix that occurs throughout life.

### SKELETAL SUPPORT
Linked together at joints by ligaments and moved by attached muscles, bones form levers vital to locomotion.
   The intricate arrangement of the bones making up the skeleton provides cages which protect the soft, delicate parts of the body, while still allowing for great flexibility and movement.
   In addition, bones contain bone marrow, the soft fatty substance that produces most of the body's blood cells.
   Bones also act as a reservoir for the minerals calcium and phosphorus, vital to many body processes.

*Osteoblasts are bone-forming cells. This micrograph shows osteoblast cells (irregular ovals) surrounded by the bone matrix they have created.*

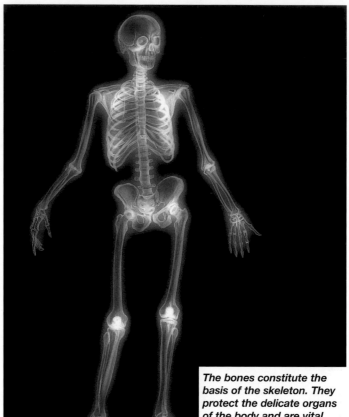

*The bones constitute the basis of the skeleton. They protect the delicate organs of the body and are vital for movement.*

## Structure of bone tissue

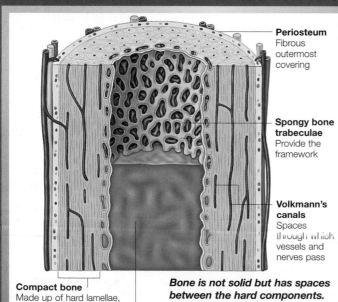

**Periosteum**
Fibrous outermost covering

**Spongy bone trabeculae**
Provide the framework

**Volkmann's canals**
Spaces through which vessels and nerves pass

**Compact bone**
Made up of hard lamellae, interspersed with lacunae

**Medullary cavity**
Filled with bone marrow

*Bone is not solid but has spaces between the hard components. The size and distribution of these spaces dictates whether bone is compact or spongy.*

Bone tissue exists in two forms: compact (or cortical) bone and spongy (or cancellous) bone.

**Compact bone**
Compact bone makes up the outer covering of all bones and is thickest in the places that receive the greatest stress. It is made up of a series of canals and passageways; these provide a route for the nerves, blood vessels and lymphatic vessels that extend through each bone.
   The structural units of compact bones (osteons) are elongated cylinders which lie parallel to the long axis of the bone. Osteons are composed of a group of lamellae (hollow tubes) of bone matrix arranged concentrically.
   The lamellae are organized in such a way that the collagen fibres in adjacent lamellae run in opposite directions; this is intended to reinforce the bone against twisting forces. Each

osteon is nourished by blood vessels and served by nerve fibres which run throughout its centre, known as the Haversian canal.
   The Volkmann's canals connect the blood vessels and nerve supplies of the periosteum (membrane around the bone) to those in the central canals and medullary cavity (which contains bone marrow).
   Mature bone cells (osteocytes) are located in the small cavities (lacunae) between each lamella.

**Spongy bone**
Spongy bone makes up the inner part of most bones and is much lighter and less dense than compact bone. This is due to the fact that it contains a number of cavities which are filled with marrow. Spongy bone is strengthened by a criss-cross network of boney supports, known as trabeculae.

# Formation of bone

Bone formation begins in the embryo and continues throughout the first 20 years of life. Development takes place from a number of ossification centres and, once these are fully calcified, no further elongation can occur.

The skeleton is made up of a variety of different bones, ranging from the flat bones found in the skull to the long bones of the limbs. Each bone is designed for a different function.

### LONG BONES
The longest bones within the body are those of the upper and lower limbs. Each long bone consists of three main components:
■ Diaphysis – a hollow shaft, composed of compact bone
■ Epiphysis – at each end of the bone; site of articulation between bones
■ Epiphyseal (growth) plate – composed of spongy bone and the site of bone elongation.

### PROTECTIVE MEMBRANE
The entire bone is covered by the two-layered periosteum.

The outer layer of this membrane consists of fibrous connective tissue. The inner layer of the periosteum contains osteoblasts and osteoclasts, the cells that are responsible for the constant replenishment of the bone.

*The humerus, a typical 'long bone', is found in the upper arm. The bone is divided into a diaphysis (shaft), with epiphyses (heads) at either end.*

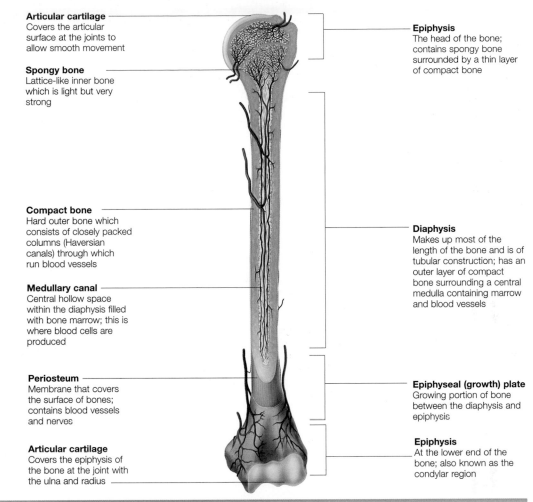

**Articular cartilage**
Covers the articular surface at the joints to allow smooth movement

**Spongy bone**
Lattice-like inner bone which is light but very strong

**Compact bone**
Hard outer bone which consists of closely packed columns (Haversian canals) through which run blood vessels

**Medullary canal**
Central hollow space within the diaphysis filled with bone marrow; this is where blood cells are produced

**Periosteum**
Membrane that covers the surface of bones; contains blood vessels and nerves

**Articular cartilage**
Covers the epiphysis of the bone at the joint with the ulna and radius

**Epiphysis**
The head of the bone; contains spongy bone surrounded by a thin layer of compact bone

**Diaphysis**
Makes up most of the length of the bone and is of tubular construction; has an outer layer of compact bone surrounding a central medulla containing marrow and blood vessels

**Epiphyseal (growth) plate**
Growing portion of bone between the diaphysis and epiphysis

**Epiphysis**
At the lower end of the bone; also known as the condylar region

## Bone development

### Long bone of a newborn

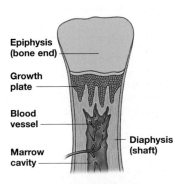

Epiphysis (bone end)

Growth plate

Blood vessel

Marrow cavity

*In a newborn baby, the shaft is mostly bone, while the bone ends consist of cartilage. In a child, new bone forms from secondary ossification centres in the bone ends.*

### Long bone of a child

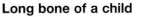
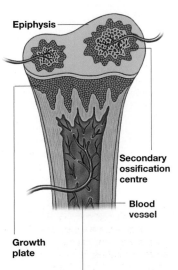

Epiphysis

Secondary ossification centre

Blood vessel

Growth plate

Marrow cavity

Skeletal development begins in the embryo and continues for around two decades. It is a complex process under genetic control, and is modulated by endocrine, physical and biological processes.

A template of the skeleton forms in the embryo from the primitive embryonic tissue. As the embryo develops, this tissue becomes recognisable as cartilage (soft, elastic connective tissue) and individual 'bones' begin to be seen.

### OSSIFICATION
Normal bone then forms within these templates by a process known as ossification. This takes place either directly around the early bone-forming cells of the fetus (intramembranous ossification) or by replacing a cartilage model with bone (endochondral ossification).

The formation of compact bone commences at sites in the bone shafts known as primary ossification centres. Osteoblasts within the cartilage secrete a gelatinous substance called osteoid, which is hardened by mineral salts to form bone. The cartilage cells die and are replaced by further osteoblasts.

Ossification of long bones continues until only a thin strip of cartilage remains at either end. This cartilage (the epiphyseal plate) is the site of secondary bone growth up to late adolescence.

The sequence of formation of ossification centres follows a prescribed pattern, allowing experts to age skeletons by the extent of ossification.

### MATURE BONE
Once the bone has reached full length, the shaft, growth plate and epiphyses are all ossified and fuse to form continuous bone. No further elongation can take place after this time.

# How bone repairs itself

Although bones cease to grow after late adolescence, bone is a very dynamic tissue. Bone is continually being reabsorbed and regenerated as its structure is constantly changing.

One of the most amazing features of bone is its ability to reshape itself. This process, known as remodelling, occurs during growth and continues throughout life.

### BONE REMODELLING
During bone formation, bone is deposited in a random pattern by a process known as ossification. Remodelling continually occurs, organizing the bone into orderly units that enable the bone mass to best withstand mechanical forces. Old bone is removed by osteoclasts (bone-eating cells), and osteoblasts (bone-forming cells) deposit new bone.

### BONE REABSORPTION
Osteoclasts secrete enzymes that break down the bone matrix, as well as acids which convert the resulting calcium salts into a soluble form (which can enter the bloodstream).

Osteoclast activity takes place behind the epiphyseal growth zone to reduce expanded ends to the width of the lengthening shaft. Osteoclasts also act within the bone in order to clear the long tubular spaces that will accommodate bone marrow.

### HORMONAL REGULATION
While the osteoclasts reabsorb bone, osteoblasts make new bone to maintain the skeletal structure. This process is regulated by hormones, growth factors and vitamin D.

During childhood, bone formation outweighs bone destruction, resulting in gradual growth. After skeletal maturity has been reached, however, the two processes occur in equilibrium so that growth proceeds more gradually.

### LONG BONES
The process of remodelling is especially important for the long bones which support the limbs. These are wider at each end than in the middle, providing extra strength at the joint.

As osteoclasts destroy the old epiphyseal swellings of the bone, osteoblasts within the growth zone create a new epiphysis.

Within each of the tubular spaces cleared by osteoclasts inside the bone, the osteoblasts follow along, laying down a layer of new bone.

### RATES OF REMODELLING
Bone remodelling is not a uniform process; it takes place at different rates throughout the skeleton. Bone formation tends to take place in areas where the bone undergoes the greatest stress. This means that bones which receive the most stress are subject to much remodelling. The femur for example (one of the load-bearing bones of the leg), is effectively replaced every five to six months.

A bone that is under-used, such as a leg that is immobilized after injury, will be prone to reabsorption however, as bone destruction outweighs formation.

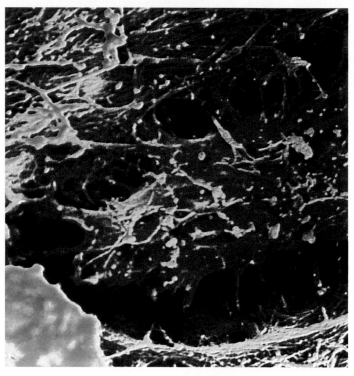

*Osteoblasts (the orange cell pictured) secrete a substance called osteoid which hardens to become bone. This bone may be reabsorbed by osteoclasts as remodelling occurs.*

*Bone that is subject to increased stress is constantly remodelled. The femur, for example, is effectively replaced every six months.*

*Remodelling gives rise to the distinctive shape of the long bones. These are wider at each end than in the middle.*

## Calcium regulation

Bone remodelling not only alters the structure of the bone, but also helps to regulate the levels of calcium ions in the blood. Calcium is necessary for healthy nerve transmission, the formation of cellular membranes and the ability of the blood to clot.

Bone contains about 99 per cent of the body's calcium. When body fluid calcium levels fall too low, parathyroid hormone stimulates osteoclast activity and calcium is released into the bloodstream. When body fluid calcium levels become too high, calcitonin hormone inhibits reabsorption, restricting the release of calcium from the bones.

# Bone repair

If bone is subjected to a force beyond its strength it will fracture. New bone must be formed and remodelled for the fracture to heal.

One of the processes which is dependent on the remodelling of bone is the repair mechanism that takes place after a fracture.

### BONE FRACTURES
Fractures occur when a bone experiences a force greater than its resistance or strength.

These can occur as the result of a spontaneous force, or after years of continued stress upon a bone. Bones are particularly susceptible to fractures later in life when they are less elastic and bone mineral density declines. Bone repair takes place in four main stages.

*A plaster cast aids the healing of fractured bone by immobilizing the limb. This is important to ensure that the ends of the broken bone realign correctly.*

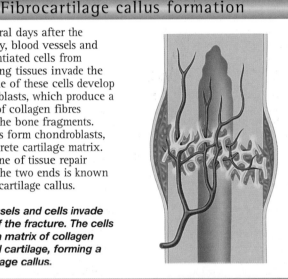

## Blood clot formation

**1** A fracture of the bone causes the blood vessels in the area (mainly those of the periosteum, the protective covering of the bone) to rupture.

As these vessels bleed, a clot is formed at the site of the fracture giving rise to the characteristic swelling that often accompanies a broken bone. Very soon, bone cells deprived of nutrition begin to die and the site becomes extremely painful.

*Blood vessels at the site of the fracture rupture, causing a blood clot to form. The nerves lining the periosteum are also severed, causing much pain.*

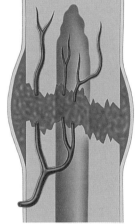

## Fibrocartilage callus formation

**2** Several days after the injury, blood vessels and undifferentiated cells from surrounding tissues invade the area. Some of these cells develop into fibroblasts, which produce a network of collagen fibres between the bone fragments. Other cells form chondroblasts, which secrete cartilage matrix.

This zone of tissue repair between the two ends is known as a fibrocartilage callus.

*Blood vessels and cells invade the site of the fracture. The cells produce a matrix of collagen fibres and cartilage, forming a fibrocartilage callus.*

## Bony callus formation

**3** Osteoblasts and osteoclasts migrate towards the affected area multiplying rapidly within the fibrocartilage callus.

Osteoblasts within the callus secrete osteoid, converting it into a bony callus.

This bony callus is composed of two portions: an external callus located around the outside of the fracture and an internal callus located between the broken bone fragments.

*Osteoblasts and osteoclasts multiply within the fibrous callus. Osteoblasts secrete a substance known as osteoid, which hardens, forming a bony callus.*

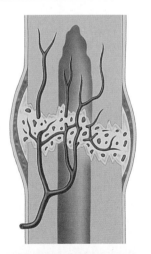

## Bone remodelling

**4** Bone formation is usually complete within four to six weeks of injury.

Once the new bone has been formed it will slowly be remodelled to form compact and spongy bone.

Total healing may require up to several months depending on the nature of the fracture and the specific function of the limb – weight-bearing limbs take longer to repair.

*As the new bone is formed it is remodelled by osteoclasts. In this way the bony callus is smoothed out, and the bone regains its original structure.*

## Bone injury

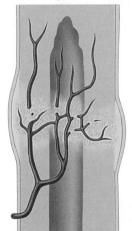

In some cases the extent of a fracture can be so severe that the normal process by which the

*In cases where damage to the bone is very severe it may fail to heal. The use of orthopaedic pins to hold the bone in place may therefore be necessary.*

bone repairs itself cannot occur.

Examples include shattered bones, or fractures in which fragments of bone are lost, so that the gap between severed ends is too great to heal.

The bones may need to be fixed in place with the use of orthopaedic screws, pins, plates

or wires, in order to encourage the bone's repair mechanisms to to take place.

Bone chips can be transplanted from other parts of the patient's skeleton in order to aid bone formation. In cases where there is massive injury, amputation may be necessary.

# How muscles contract

Muscle tissue accounts for about half of the body's total mass, and is constantly at work, whether articulating the skeleton, enabling the heart to beat or passing food through the gut.

Muscle is tissue that is capable of contracting. The two main types of muscle are voluntary and involuntary muscle. The contraction of voluntary – or skeletal – muscle can be consciously controlled, and this type of muscle is linked to parts of the skeleton to produce physical movement.

### INVOLUNTARY MUSCLE

Involuntary muscle is not under the brain's conscious control. It is controlled automatically by a special part of the nervous system and is found in non-skeletal parts of the body. The heart, for example, is made up of involuntary muscle, beating without conscious effort.

### VOLUNTARY MUSCLE

Muscle that moves bones is known as striated muscle due to its striped appearance under the microscope. It consists of bundles of fibres bound tightly together, with each fibre made up of a single long, multi-nucleated cell that stretches from one end of the muscle to the other. Each fibre consists of many long thin strands, known as myofibrils. These are made up of two kinds of tiny, overlapping protein filaments made of actin and myosin, giving the myofibril a banded appearance. The bands of neighbouring myofibrils line up so that the whole fibre appears to be striped.

## Muscle structure

*Muscles consist of many individual muscle cells. Cells are arranged in bundles called fascicles, and each fibre further subdivides into myofibrils. A segment of myofibrils is a sarcomere, which is the contractile unit, and the smallest functional unit of a muscle. This illustration shows the structure of skeletal muscle from the visible to the microscopic level.*

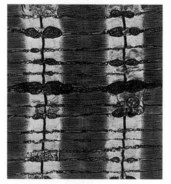

*This coloured electron micrograph shows the structure of skeletal muscle. The thick red lines separate the sarcomeres – the units of contraction. These are composed of sliding filaments: myosin (pink) and actin (yellow).*

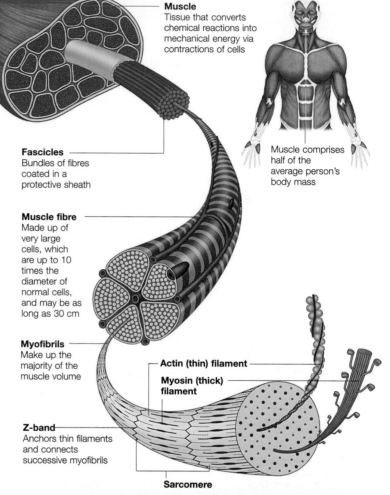

**Muscle**
Tissue that converts chemical reactions into mechanical energy via contractions of cells

Muscle comprises half of the average person's body mass

**Fascicles**
Bundles of fibres coated in a protective sheath

**Muscle fibre**
Made up of very large cells, which are up to 10 times the diameter of normal cells, and may be as long as 30 cm

**Myofibrils**
Make up the majority of the muscle volume

**Actin (thin) filament**

**Myosin (thick) filament**

**Z-band**
Anchors thin filaments and connects successive myofibrils

**Sarcomere**

## Muscle contraction

A muscle contracts when it is stimulated by a nerve impulse, which causes complex chemical changes to take place in the muscle fibres. Each group of filaments lies in a small chamber (sarcomere) in which the thin actin filaments are attached to each end. The thick myosin filaments lie between the actin filaments in the middle of the sarcomere.

When provided with energy – usually obtained from glycogen ('animal starch') stored in the muscle – they form chemical bonds with the actin filaments, and these bonds are repeatedly broken and remade further along. In this way, the myosin filaments work their way along the actin filaments like ratchets, with the result that the whole sarcomere becomes shorter and fatter.

When the muscle is no longer being stimulated, the chemical action ceases. The bonds between the filaments are no longer formed and the muscle relaxes.

Contraction of an opposing muscle stretches the filaments apart, and this is triggered by a chemical called acetylcholine, which is released by the nerve endings and alights on special receptive areas in the muscle. As long as acetylcholine is present in these areas, the muscle remains contracted.

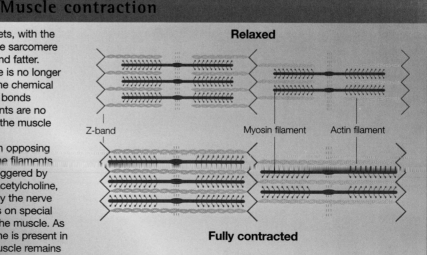

**Relaxed**

Z-band

Myosin filament    Actin filament

**Fully contracted**

*Contraction is achieved by myosin fibres rapidly breaking and reforming bonds with the actin fibres, in a ratchet-like manner.*

# How involuntary muscles move

The body contains two types of involuntary muscle (muscle not under the conscious control of the brain). Smooth muscle can focus the eye and pass food along the digestive tract; cardiac muscle causes the heart to beat.

## Smooth muscle

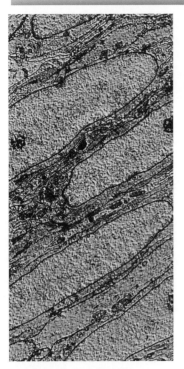

*The smooth muscle cells enclosing the inner wall of the uterus are shown in this false coloured electron micrograph. They are responsible for muscular contractions during labour and childbirth.*

Smooth muscle and cardiac muscle are both able to contract involuntarily, without conscious control. They are controlled by nerve impulses from the autonomic (unconscious) nervous system.

Smooth muscle is found in many parts of the body, notably the gut, but also in such places as the lungs, bladder and sex organs. It consists of spindle-shaped cells, whose average length is only a fraction of a millimetre.

### CELL ARRANGEMENT

The cells are tapered at both ends, have single nuclei and are arranged in bundles held together by a substance that acts as a cement. These bundles are grouped into larger bundles or flattened bands, held together by connective tissue. The arrangement of the cells is much looser than the regular pattern found in striped muscle, but the contraction of smooth muscle still results from the movement of filaments, which are found in the walls of the cells.

Contraction of smooth muscle is generally slower than that of striated muscle, and contraction does not necessarily take place throughout the whole muscle.

An action typical of smooth muscle is found in the intestines, where a band of muscle usually contracts over a certain part of its length, then relaxes while another part contracts, thus producing waves of contraction down the muscle, called peristalsis. This enables food to be passed down the digestive tract, into the stomach and through the intestines.

*Smooth muscle surrounds hollow body structures, such as the oesophagus, bladder, uterus and blood vessels. The rate of contraction of its cells is relatively slow, but they are more energy-efficient and able to maintain contraction for a longer time.*

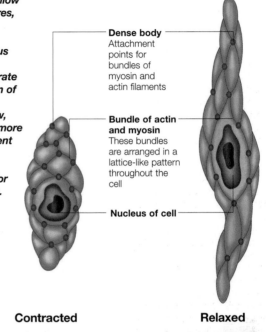

**Dense body**
Attachment points for bundles of myosin and actin filaments

**Bundle of actin and myosin**
These bundles are arranged in a lattice-like pattern throughout the cell

**Nucleus of cell**

**Contracted**      **Relaxed**

## Cardiac muscle

Cardiac muscle is only found in the heart, and its structure is somewhere between that of striated muscle and smooth muscle. It has a striped appearance when viewed through a microscope, but the cells of which it is made are shorter and more box-shaped than striated muscle fibres. Most of the cells are divided at the ends, and the subdivisions form connections with cells that lie alongside. In this way, a resilient network of fibres is formed with the ability to act in unison, and it is this structure that gives heart muscle its toughness.

Cardiac muscle has to be immensely strong for the demanding job it has to do. In an average lifetime, the heart beats over two billion times and pumps some 550,000 tonnes of blood. In order to keep the heart contracting steadily and regularly throughout this time, the heartbeat is controlled by electrical impulses.

*Cardiac muscle cells are less elongated than skeletal muscle. Adjacent cells are closely attached to each other by proteins called intercalated discs. Structures called desmosomes form junctions, allowing electrical signals to be transmitted between cells.*

**Sliding filaments**
Thick and thin filaments of actin and myosin

**Cardiac cell**

**Intercalated disc**
Connects cardiac cells together, both physically and electrically

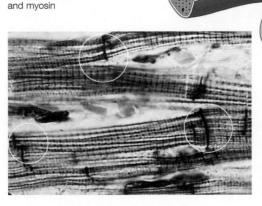

*This light micrograph shows the individual fibres which make up cardiac muscle. The round bodies are cell nuclei and the dark lines (circled) at right angles to the fibres are intercalated discs. These have a low electrical resistance which allows contractions to spread rapidly throughout the muscle.*

# How reflexes work

Bodily actions that can occur independently of conscious control are called reflexes. They are especially important when a rapid involuntary response is required.

The central nervous system is able to perform highly complex tasks, and not all of these require conscious thought. Those actions that are involuntary in nature are called reflexes, pre-programmed and predictable responses to a specific sensory stimulus.

### SOMATIC REFLEXES
Somatic reflexes result in the movement of a muscle, or the secretion of a chemical from a gland.

For example, if you were to touch a hot oven, pain receptors in your hand would send nerve impulses to neurones in the spinal cord. These in turn would communicate with the appropriate muscles in your arm telling them to withdraw the hand instantly. Only after the hand was withdrawn, however, would your brain become aware of what had happened.

### AUTONOMIC REFLEXES
We are not conscious of the outcome of all the reflexes that occur in our bodies. For example, the baroreceptor reflex corrects a rise in arterial blood pressure without us being aware that it is doing so.

## A simple reflex arc

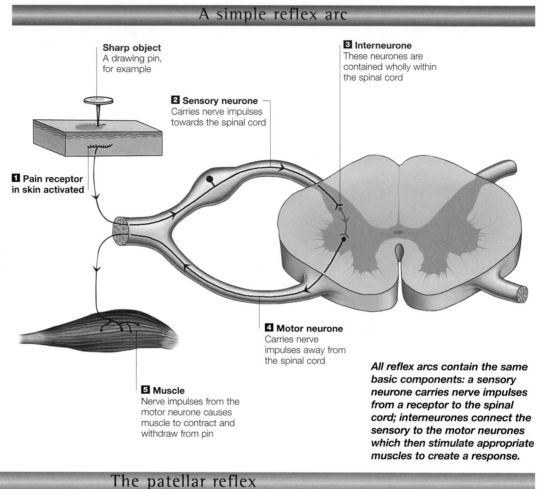

**Sharp object**
A drawing pin, for example

**2 Sensory neurone**
Carries nerve impulses towards the spinal cord

**3 Interneurone**
These neurones are contained wholly within the spinal cord

**1 Pain receptor in skin activated**

**4 Motor neurone**
Carries nerve impulses away from the spinal cord

**5 Muscle**
Nerve impulses from the motor neurone causes muscle to contract and withdraw from pin

*All reflex arcs contain the same basic components: a sensory neurone carries nerve impulses from a receptor to the spinal cord; interneurones connect the sensory to the motor neurones which then stimulate appropriate muscles to create a response.*

## The patellar reflex

**1 Sensory neurone**
Carries nerve impulses from the muscle spindles to the spinal cord

**3 Quadriceps**
This extensor muscle contracts in response to nervous stimulation

**2 Inhibitory interneurone**
This neurone inhibits the activity of the motor neurone which innervates the flexor muscle

**4 Hamstring**
This flexor muscle relaxes in response to nervous innervation

*The patellar reflex is tested by doctors after a patient has suffered a traumatic injury to determine whether their lower spine has been damaged.*

*Babies up to about one year old exhibit the Babinski reflex when the sole of the foot is rubbed. This disappears as their nervous system develops.*

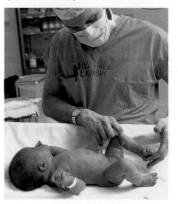

Clinicians often use the 'patellar reflex' to test the integrity of a patient's lower spine. The patient sits high up so that the legs hang freely. The doctor then lightly taps the patellar tendon (situated just below the knee-cap) and looks for a response.

### MUSCLE SPINDLES
In a healthy person, the knock to the tendon stretches the quadriceps muscle. This stretch is detected by structures in the muscle called muscle spindles. These send nervous signals to neurones in the spinal cord,

which in turn send impulses to the quadriceps muscle telling it to contract (to counteract the initial stretch). This causes the foot to spring forward. At the same time the antagonistic muscle, the hamstrings, are inhibited.

# Complex reflexes

Although some spinal reflexes, such as the patellar reflex, are relatively simple
and involve only a few nerve cells, the spinal cord is capable of carrying out more
complicated functions without needing to involve the brain.

If you were to step on a sharp object, such as a drawing pin, with your right foot, a complex reflex (the crossed extensor reflex) would be initiated in order to withdraw the foot and to shift the body's weight onto the left leg.

Initially, the drawing pin stimulates pain receptors in the skin of the right foot, causing them to send nerve impulses, via afferent nerve fibres (from the Latin 'afferre' – to carry towards), to the right hand side of the spinal cord. Neurones in this half of the spinal cord send nerve signals away from the cord via efferent nerve fibres to tell the extensor muscles to relax and the flexors to contract.

### TRANSFER OF WEIGHT

These events result in the injured leg being moved away from the drawing pin. However, unless the body's weight is transferred to the other leg, you will fall over.

Thus neurones from the right-hand side of the spinal cord cross over to the left-hand side and synapse with motor neurones which innervate muscles in the left leg. These motor neurones inform the extensor muscles in the left leg to contract and the flexors to relax, causing the leg to be extended so that it can carry the body's weight.

*When a bare foot treads on a sharp object, it is rapidly withdrawn and the body's weight is transferred to the other leg.*

## The crossed extensor reflex

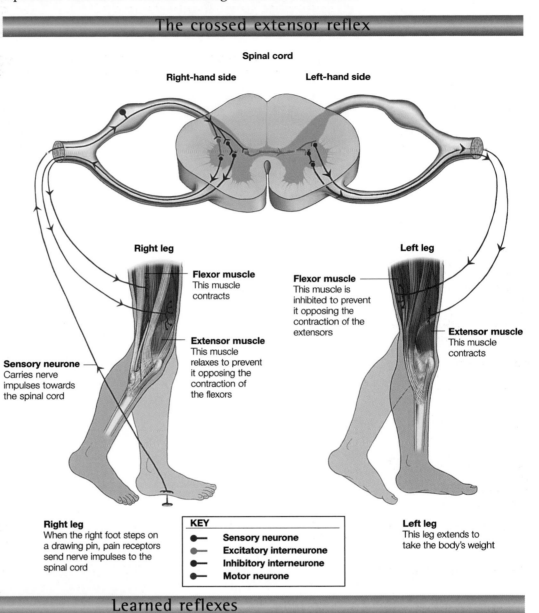

**Spinal cord**

**Right-hand side**    **Left-hand side**

**Right leg**

**Flexor muscle**
This muscle contracts

**Extensor muscle**
This muscle relaxes to prevent it opposing the contraction of the flexors

**Sensory neurone**
Carries nerve impulses towards the spinal cord

**Left leg**

**Flexor muscle**
This muscle is inhibited to prevent it opposing the contraction of the extensors

**Extensor muscle**
This muscle contracts

**Right leg**
When the right foot steps on a drawing pin, pain receptors send nerve impulses to the spinal cord

**KEY**
- ● ━ Sensory neurone
- ● ━ Excitatory interneurone
- ● ━ Inhibitory interneurone
- ● ━ Motor neurone

**Left leg**
This leg extends to take the body's weight

## Learned reflexes

The reflexes that have been discussed so far are 'hard-wired' into the nervous system.

However, while babies are born with the innate ability to learn how to walk, we have to make a conscious effort to learn to drive a car, ride a bicycle or play the piano.

With time, new movements can become as automatic as walking. For example, although learning to drive is a relatively difficult experience for most people, after a while the

*Pianists are able to read music and then play the appropriate note without thinking about what they are doing. This is an example of a learned reflex.*

movements become automatic and the driver no longer has to consciously think what he or she is doing.

Similarly, touch-typists do not need to think where their fingers are on a keyboard, and as a result many can type at up to 80 words per minute. Assuming that the average word contains around six letters, a fast typist can make up to eight keystrokes every second!

It is thought that during the learning process the neurones involved in controlling the movement change the way that they are connected to each other. Important connections between cells are reinforced and unnecessary synapses are lost.

# How teeth develop

Teeth are the body's toughest and most durable organs. They play a vital role in the digestion of food by helping to break it down into smaller fragments by biting and mastication (chewing).

The teeth are used to chew and grind food into smaller pieces. The action of chewing increases the surface area of food exposed to digestive enzymes, thus speeding up the process of digestion.

Teeth also play an important role in speech – the teeth, lips and tongue allow the formation of words by controlling airflow through the mouth. In addition, teeth provide structural support for muscles in the face as well as helping to form the smile.

## ANATOMY OF THE TEETH
Each tooth is composed of the crown and the root. The crown is the visible part of the tooth which emerges from the gingiva or gum (which helps to hold the tooth firmly in place). The crown of each premolar and molar includes projections or cusps which facilitate the chewing and grinding of food.

*Teeth provide structural support for the muscles of the face. In addition, they play an important role in speech, and help to form the smile.*

The root is the portion of the tooth embedded in the jawbone.

## STRUCTURE
Teeth are composed of four distinct types of tissue:
■ Enamel – the clear outer layer and the hardest substance in the body. Composed of a densely packed structure, heavily mineralized with calcium salts, this layer helps to protect the inner layers of the teeth from harmful bacteria, and changes in temperature caused by hot or cold food and drink
■ Dentine – encloses and protects the inner core of the tooth, and is similar in composition to bone. It is composed of odontoblast cells, which secrete and maintain dentine throughout adult life
■ Pulp – contains blood vessels which supply the tooth with oxygen and nutrients. It also contains nerves responsible for the transmission of pain and temperature sensations to the brain
■ Cementum - covers the outer surface of the root. It is a calcium-containing connective tissue that attaches the tooth to the periodontal ligament, which anchors the tooth firmly in the tooth socket (alveolus) located in the jawbone.

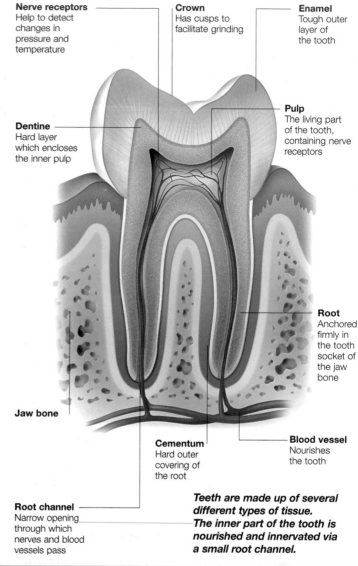

**Nerve receptors**
Help to detect changes in pressure and temperature

**Crown**
Has cusps to facilitate grinding

**Enamel**
Tough outer layer of the tooth

**Dentine**
Hard layer which encloses the inner pulp

**Pulp**
The living part of the tooth, containing nerve receptors

**Root**
Anchored firmly in the tooth socket of the jaw bone

**Jaw bone**

**Cementum**
Hard outer covering of the root

**Blood vessel**
Nourishes the tooth

**Root channel**
Narrow opening through which nerves and blood vessels pass

*Teeth are made up of several different types of tissue. The inner part of the tooth is nourished and innervated via a small root channel.*

## Development of milk teeth

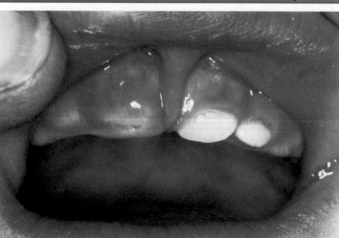

Humans develop two sets of teeth during their lives. The first set, known as the deciduous or milk teeth, starts developing in the fetus at around two months after conception and will consist of 20 teeth in total.

### STAGES OF DEVELOPMENT
The dentine of these teeth forms while the fetus is still in the uterus. After birth, the tooth enamel develops in stages.

*Tooth enamel begins to develop soon after birth. The milk teeth emerge in stages, with the front teeth erupting first and the second molars last.*

Front tooth enamel develops first and is usually complete at around one month after birth, while the enamel on the second (back) molars is not completely developed until a year and a half later.

Once the enamel is fully developed the tooth begins to emerge (erupt). Front teeth usually erupt at between six and 12 months of age, while second molars emerge between 13 and 19 months and canines at 19 months or older. The final stage of root development is root completion, a slow process that continues until the child is over three years old.

# Development of permanent teeth

Over several years, the milk teeth are replaced by a set of permanent adult teeth. There are 32 adult teeth, including the third molars, or wisdom teeth.

Around the age of six, the roots of the deciduous teeth are slowly eroded by the pressure of erupting permanent teeth and by the action of specialized bone cells in the jaws. This process, called resorption, allows the permanent teeth to emerge from beneath. If a permanent tooth is missing – a relatively common condition, the corresponding milk tooth is retained.

### COMPLETE SET
As the milk teeth are replaced, the mouth and jaw lose their childhood shape and take on a more pronounced and adult appearance. Adult teeth are usually darker in colour and differ in size and proportion from the milk teeth. A full complement of permanent teeth is generally present by the end of adolescence, with the exception of the third molars (wisdom teeth) which tend to emerge at around 18–25 years.

*By the age of six most children have begun to lose their milk teeth. These become loose and are eventually replaced by the permanent teeth.*

## Types of teeth

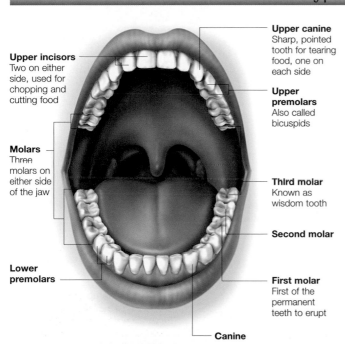

**Upper incisors**
Two on either side, used for chopping and cutting food

**Molars**
Three molars on either side of the jaw

**Lower premolars**

**Upper canine**
Sharp, pointed tooth for tearing food, one on each side

**Upper premolars**
Also called bicuspids

**Third molar**
Known as wisdom tooth

**Second molar**

**First molar**
First of the permanent teeth to erupt

**Canine**

Adults generally have 32 teeth – 16 on the upper jaw and 16 on the lower – which fit together to bite and chew food. Humans are referred to as heterodonts as they have a variety of different tooth types, with a specific size, shape and function:
■ Incisors – adults have eight incisors located at the front of the mouth – four in the upper jaw, and four in the lower jaw. Incisors have a sharp edge used to cut up food
■ Canines – on either side of the incisors are the canines, so-called because of their resemblance to the sharp fangs of dogs. There are two canines on each jaw, and their primary

*Humans are heterodonts – that is, their teeth are not of a uniform size or shape. The various types of teeth are formed differently to fulfil specific roles.*

role is to pierce and tear food
■ Bicuspids – also known as premolars, these are flat teeth with pronounced cusps that grind and mash food. There are four bicuspids in each jaw
■ Molars – behind the bicuspids are the molars, where the most vigorous chewing occurs. There are twelve molars, referred to as the first, second and third molars. Third molars are commonly called wisdom teeth.

### WISDOM TEETH
Wisdom teeth are remnants from thousands of years ago when the human diet consisted of raw foods that required the extra chewing and grinding power of a third set of molars. Today, wisdom teeth are not required for chewing and, as they can crowd other teeth and cause them to become impacted, they are often removed by dentists.

## Chewing

The muscles of the jaws allow the teeth to close together (occlude) and open in a vertical plane, and also to slide over one another in a horizontal plane. The former action is necessary in biting through food, the latter in grinding.

**Pressure sensors**
The periodontal ligament of each tooth contains sensory nerve receptors that protect the teeth and supporting tissues from excessive chewing and biting forces, which can cause damage. These nerve receptors transmit impulses to the central nervous system in response to sensation

and stimulation and give information about jaw movement and position, and pressure being exerted on the teeth.

**Brain control**
The brain responds by sending nerve impulses which control the position of the jaw and attached muscles (and thus the position of the tooth) allowing the process of chewing (mastication) to occur in an appropriate manner.

*Nerve receptors in each tooth convey information to the brain about the position of the jaw. The brain then transmits nerve impulses, controlling the jaw.*

# Hair

There are two main types of human hair: vellus and terminal. Only terminal hair, which is found mainly on men, has a central core or medulla and responds to the male sex hormone, testosterone.

The surface of the human body is covered with millions of hairs. They are most noticeable on the head, around the external genitalia and under the arm. The only regions of the body without hairs are the lips, nipples, parts of the external genitalia, the palms of the hands and the soles of the feet.

Although hair does not really serve to keep us warm, as it does in other mammals, it has a number of other functions:
■ Sensing small objects or insects that approach the skin
■ Protecting/insulating the head
■ Shielding the eyes
■ Sexual signalling.

### STRUCTURE OF A HAIR
Hair is composed of flexible strands of the hard protein, keratin. It is produced by hair follicles within the dermis (the inner layer of the skin) but arises from an 'inpouching' of the epidermis (the outer layer).

Each hair follicle has an expanded end – the hair bulb – which receives a knot of capillaries to nourish the root of the growing hair shaft. The shape of the hair shaft determines whether the hair is straight or curly: the rounder the shaft in cross section, the straighter the hair.

Each hair is made up of three concentric layers:
■ The medulla
■ The cortex
■ The cuticle.

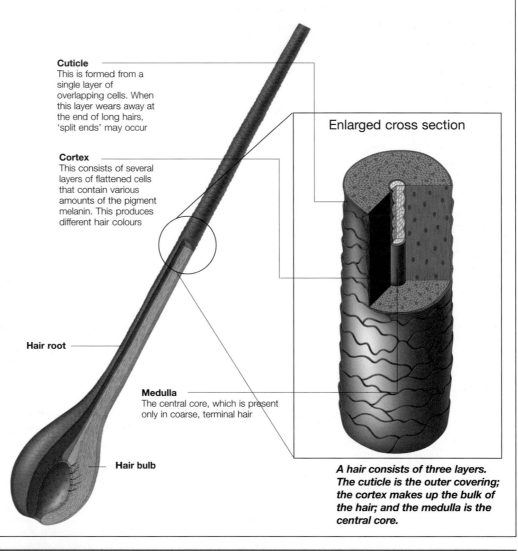

**Cuticle**
This is formed from a single layer of overlapping cells. When this layer wears away at the end of long hairs, 'split ends' may occur

**Cortex**
This consists of several layers of flattened cells that contain various amounts of the pigment melanin. This produces different hair colours

**Hair root**

**Medulla**
The central core, which is present only in coarse, terminal hair

**Hair bulb**

Enlarged cross section

*A hair consists of three layers. The cuticle is the outer covering; the cortex makes up the bulk of the hair; and the medulla is the central core.*

## Types of hair and their distribution

Although it seems as though there are many different types of human hair, it can be divided into just two main groups:
■ Vellus hair
■ Terminal hair.

### VELLUS HAIR
Vellus hair is the name given to the soft hair that covers most of the body in women and children. It is short, fine and usually light in colour, making it much less noticeable than

*Eyelashes are one of the few examples of terminal hair to be found on men, women and children. They prevent foreign bodies from entering the eye.*

terminal hair. Vellus hair shafts do not have a central medulla.

### TERMINAL HAIR
Terminal hair is much coarser than vellus hair. It occurs on top of the head, as eyelashes and eyebrows, as pubic and axillary (armpit) hair, and it makes up most of the body hair of adult men. Terminal hair does have a central medulla within its shaft.

Terminal hairs develop and grow in response to the presence of male sex hormones, such as testosterone. In medical conditions where women have too much of these hormones, unwanted male pattern hair growth (hirsutism) occurs.

# The hair follicle

Hairs are produced within hair follicles, which are present on most of the skin surface. A number of other structures are associated with these follicles, including sebaceous glands, nerve endings and tiny muscles that pull the hair erect.

Sebaceous, or oil, glands lie alongside hair follicles wherever they are on the surface of the body. They produce an oily substance, known as sebum, which drains out of the gland through a sebaceous duct into the hair follicle. The sebum then passes out around the emerging hair shaft to reach the surface of the body.

The amount of sebum produced depends upon the size of the sebaceous gland, which in turn depends upon the levels of circulating hormones, especially androgens (male sex hormones). The largest sebaceous glands are found on the head, neck, and back and front of the chest.

The function of sebum is to soften and lubricate the skin and hair, and to prevent the skin from drying out. It also contains substances that kill bacteria, which might otherwise cause infection of the skin and hair follicle.

### NERVE ENDINGS

A network of tiny nerve endings lie around the bulb of the hair follicle. These nerves are stimulated by any movement of the base of the hair. If the hair is bent by pressure somewhere along its shaft, these nerve

*The root of each hair sits in a follicle and is buried about 4–5 mm in the skin. Hair is kept lubricated with oil produced in the sebaceous glands.*

Hair shaft

Arrector pili muscle

Sebaceous gland

Hyaline membrane

Connective tissue of hair follicle

Hair bulb

Melanocytes

Hair matrix
Hair papilla

endings will fire, sending signals to the brain. This is what happens, for instance, when an insect alights on the skin; the slight bending of hairs it causes sets off a chain of events, resulting in a reflex action to remove it before it stings. In this way hair contributes to our sense of touch.

### ARRECTOR PILI MUSCLE

Each hair follicle is attached to a tiny muscle called an arrector pili, which literally means 'raiser of hair'. When this muscle contracts, it causes the hair to move from its normal, angled position to a vertically erect one.

When this occurs within many hair follicles, we see (and feel)

the condition known as goosepimples, which is commonly stimulated by either cold or fear.

The action of these muscles is more important in furry mammals, as it allows them to trap a large amount of air within their fur for insulation from the cold.

## Hair thinning and baldness

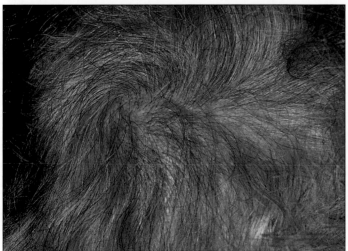

*After the age of around 40, hair follicles start to age and hair is not replaced as quickly as it falls out. Thicker terminal hair is also replaced by thinner vellus hair.*

Hair growth is fastest between childhood and early adulthood. After about the age of 40 this high rate of growth starts to fall as the hair follicles begin to age.

Hairs are not replaced as rapidly when they fall out, leading to general thinning, and some degree of baldness in both men and women. Thinning of the hair is also caused by the replacing of coarse terminal hairs with less noticeable, softer vellus hair.

### ONSET OF BALDNESS

True baldness, which is usually known as male pattern baldness, is a different condition, linked to a number of factors. These include:
■ Family history
■ Levels of androgens (male sex hormones)
■ Increasing age.

It is believed to be due to a gene that only 'switches on' in adult life and somehow alters the response of the hair follicle to circulating hormones.

Abnormal hair thinning or loss may also be linked to a wide variety of medical conditions and treatments of which doctors should be aware.

# How hair grows

Hair is a derivative of the skin, and is composed of keratin – a strong structural protein. Hair plays an important role in protecting the body, particularly the scalp, where it is most dense.

Hair is a distinguishing characteristic of mammals and in humans plays a role in the protection of the body from trauma, heat loss and sunlight.

### HAIR STRUCTURE

Hair is a complex structure comprised of keratin fibres – keratin is a strong structural protein also found in the nails and outer layer of the skin.

Each hair is made up of three concentric (circular) layers of dead keratinized (keratin-containing) cells: the medulla, cortex and cuticle.

The medulla (the central core) consists of large cells containing soft keratin, partially separated by air spaces. The cortex, the bulky layer surrounding the medulla, consists of several layers of flattened, hard keratin-containing cells.

### PROTECTIVE LAYER

The cuticle is the outermost layer, and is composed of a single layer of hard keratin cells that overlap one another like roof tiles.

This outer layer of the hair contains the most keratin, and strengthens and protects the hair, helping to keep the inner layers compacted. The cuticle tends to wear away as the hair becomes older or is damaged, allowing the keratin fibrils, or small fibres, in the cortex and medulla to escape, giving rise to the common phenomenon of 'split ends'.

**Erector muscle**
Pulls the hair into an upright position in response to cold or emotional stimulus

**Hair follicle**
Composed of two parts: an outer connective tissue root sheath and an inner epithelial root sheath

*Hair is made up of the shaft, which protrudes from the skin and the root, which is embedded in the skin within a hair follicle, the deep end of which is expanded, forming a hair bulb.*

**Hair shaft**
The visible part of the hair above the skin

**Sebaceous gland**
Secretes sebum, an oily substance, into the hair follicle via a small duct

### Cross-section through hair

**Cuticle**

**Cortex**

**Medulla**

**Hair root**
Lies embedded within the skin

**Hair bulb**
Contains the matrix – the growing part of the hair

## What causes hair to grow?

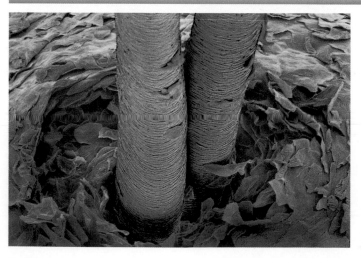

*This electron micrograph shows hairs on the scalp. There are two shafts of hair emerging from follicles located in the epidermis of in the skin.*

Each hair is divided into the shaft (the visible part) and the root. The root of each hair is enclosed within a hair follicle, below the surface of the skin. At its base the hair follicle is expanded to form the hair bulb.

### PRODUCTION OF HAIR

The hair bulb encloses a mass of undifferentiated epithelial cells (the hair matrix), which divide to produce hair. The hair bulb is nourished by a dense network of capillaries which are supplied by the dermal papilla (a projection of the dermis).

### STIMULATION OF GROWTH

Chemical signals from the papilla stimulate the adjacent matrix cells to divide and produce hair. As new hair cells are produced by the matrix, the older cells are pushed upwards and fuse together. They become increasingly keratinized and die. Thus the hair that extends from the scalp is no longer living, but due to the active cell division at its root, grows at a rate of around 0.3 mm every day.

# Stages of growth

Hair is produced in different stages. Any factors, such as stress or certain drugs, that upset this balance can lead to hair thinning and baldness.

Hair is produced in cycles that involve a growth phase, and a resting phase. During the growth phase the hair is formed and extends as cells are added at the base of the root. This phase can last from around two to six years. As hair grows approximately 10 cm a year, any individual hair is unlikely to grow more than one metre long.

### RESTING PHASE
Eventually, cell division pauses (the resting phase) and growth of the hair stops. The hair follicle shrinks to one sixth of its normal length, and the dermal papilla, responsible for the nourishment of new hair cells, breaks away from the root bulb. During this phase the dead hair is held in place. It is these hairs which seem to come out in handfuls when hair is washed or brushed. Eventually a new cycle begins, and the hair is shed from the hair follicle as the production of a new hair begins.

### DIFFERENT HAIR TYPES
The length of each phase depends on the type of body hair: scalp hairs tend to grow for a period of three years and rest for one or two years, while eyelash hair, which is much shorter, will grow for around 30 days, and rest for 105 days before being shed. At any one time around 90 per cent of scalp hairs will be in the growing stage, and there is a normal loss of around 100 scalp hairs per day.

*Hair does not grow at a constant rate; individual hairs pass through a growth phase and a resting phases, before falling out and being replaced.*

## Hair loss

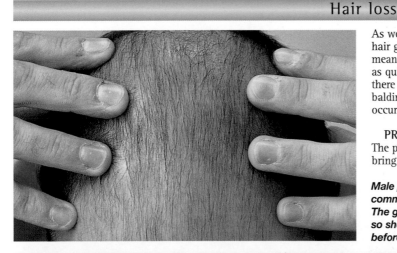

As we age the rate at which our hair grows declines. This can mean that hairs are not replaced as quickly as they are shed and there is an overall thinning, with balding in places (alopecia) often occurring, especially in men.

### PREMATURE HAIR LOSS
The physiological changes which bring about male pattern

*Male pattern baldness is a common hereditary condition. The growth stage of each hair is so short that they are shed before emerging from the scalp.*

baldness are different to those occurring with alopecia. Male pattern baldness is a genetically determined condition and is thought to be caused by changes in the response of the hair follicles to testosterone. The growth cycles of each hair follicle become so short that many hairs never emerge from their follicles before they are shed, and those that do are only very fine.

Hair thinning and loss may also result from factors such as stress that upset the normal hair loss and replacement cycle.

## Hair colour and texture

The colour of hair depends upon the presence of the pigment melanin, produced by melanocytes in the bulb of the hair follicle, and then transferred to the cortex.

Dark hair contains true melanin like that found in the skin, while blond and red hair results from types of melanin that contain sulphur and iron. Grey or white hair results from decreased melanin production (genetically triggered) and from the replacement of melanin by air bubbles in the shaft.

Adults have around 120,000 hairs on their head. Redheads tend to have fewer hairs, while blonds have more.

The exact composition of the keratin produced by the body is determined by our genes and differs among individuals. Since keratin is responsible for the texture of the hair shaft, this can vary greatly.

A smooth, cylindrical hair shaft will produce straight hair, while an oval hair shaft will produce wavy hair. A hair shaft that has a kidney-shaped appearance will produce curly hair.

*Hair colour and texture are genetically determined and can vary greatly. Colour is determined by melanin content while texture depends upon the exact composition of keratin.*

# How nails grow

The nails are extensions of the outer skin layer, and grow continuously throughout life. Apart from their protective function, they can also give a good indication of a person's state of health.

Like the hair, the nails are a derivative of skin, and form part of the outer covering of the body. Each nail is a scale-like extension of the epidermis (outer layer of skin) that covers the end of the finger and toe.

### ANATOMY OF THE NAIL

The nails are flattened, elastic structures that begin to grow on the upper surface of the tips of the fingers and toes in the third month of fetal development.

Each nail consists of the following parts:
■ Body – otherwise known as the nail plate. This is the main, exposed part of the nail
■ Free edge – this is the part of the nail that tends to grow beyond the fingertip
■ Lateral nail fold – this is the bulge of skin that grows either side of the nail. Folds arise at the boundary of the epidermis and nail because the epidermal cells divide more quickly than those of the nail and cause the skin to bulge over the nail
■ Eponychium (cuticle) – this is

a fold of cornified (dead) skin that partially covers the nail and also protects the growing area of the nail
■ Lunula – this is the slightly opaque area of the nail, which is crescent shaped (lunula means 'little moon' in Latin). This area of the nail may be partially obscured by the cuticle
■ Hyponchium – this is the area of skin attached just below the free border of the nail. The hyponchium has a very rich nerve supply, which is why it can be very painful if foreign bodies such as a splinter of wood penetrate it
■ Root – otherwise known as the matrix, this is the proximal part of the nail (closest to the skin) and is implanted in a groove beneath the cuticle
■ Nail bed – this is the area underlying the entire nail.

*The nails consist of curved plates of hard keratin. Beneath the lunula area lies the nail matrix – this is responsible for the growth of the nail.*

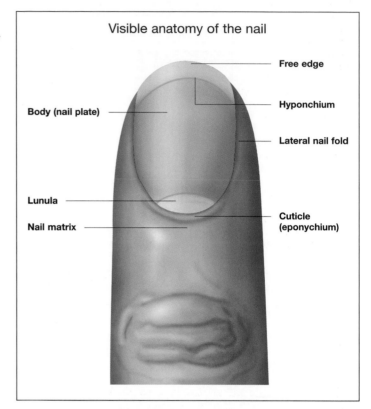

Visible anatomy of the nail

Free edge

Hyponchium

Body (nail plate)

Lateral nail fold

Lunula

Nail matrix

Cuticle (eponychium)

## The role of nails

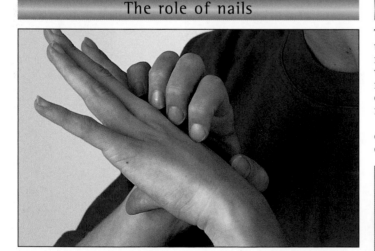

Despite the fact that the nails are not as strong as those of our ancestors, they still serve a number of important roles.

### PROTECTIVE ROLE

Like skin and hair, the nails are composed of keratin, a tough protein. This acts as a shock absorber, protecting the tips of the fingers and toes.

In addition, the fingernails are useful tools for tasks such as undoing a shoelace, picking up

*The nails are well designed for enhancing the movements of the fingers, such as scratching. They also protect the sensitive tips of the fingers and toes.*

small objects or scratching an itch.

Despite the fact that the nails lack nerves, they also serve as excellent 'antennae', since they are embedded in sensitive tissue that detects any impact when the nail touches an object.

## Brittle nails

The nails are very porous and they can hold up to 100 times as much water as the equivalent weight of skin. In this way, the nails limit the amount of water entering the tissues of the fingertips.

Water taken up by the nails is eventually lost through evaporation as they dry out and

resume their normal size.

Frequent immersion in water and then drying can cause the structure of the nail to become weakened, resulting in nails becoming brittle and splitting.

In addition, the use of nail varnish, and its removal with solvents, can cause the nails to become brittle.

## After death

It is a common misconception that the fingernails continue to grow for a short time after death.

It is understandable how this myth came to be believed, however, since after death the skin surrounding the nails dries up and shrivels away from the nail plates. This phenomenon creates the impression that the nails have actually grown in length, in the same way that pushing the cuticles back makes the nails seem longer.

In reality, however, every cell in the body ceases to grow after death, including those of the nails.

*It is often suggested that nails and hair continue to grow after death. Once death has occurred, however, every cell in the body ceases to function.*

# Growth rate of nails

It can take up to six months for a nail to grow from the root to the tip of the finger. At certain times, nail growth is accelerated, for instance in warm weather.

There are two areas of the nail in which growth occurs:
■ The germinal matrix – this is the area beneath the root of the nail. Here, epidermal cells divide, and become enriched with keratin, which thickens to become nail
■ The nail bed – this is the area underneath the nail plate; it provides a surface over which the growing nail divides.

### RATE OF GROWTH
On average, it takes around three to six months for a nail to grow from its base to the tip of the finger. The average fingernail grows at a rate of about 0.5 mm a week, with faster growth taking place in the summer. It is thought that blood circulates faster in the summer so that cell division is more rapid. Fingernails grow around four times faster than toenails; the reason for this is unknown.

Interestingly, if a person is right handed, the nail of the right thumb grows faster than that of the left thumb.

▶ *In most people, finger and toe nails are kept short due to abrasion or cutting. Without this, the nails are capable of growing to a great length.*

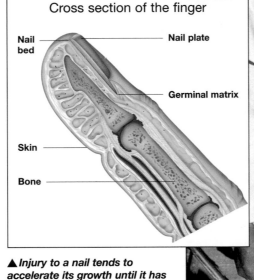
Cross section of the finger

Nail bed · Nail plate · Germinal matrix · Skin · Bone

▲ *Injury to a nail tends to accelerate its growth until it has recovered. However, if the root of the nail is destroyed, the nail will cease to grow.*

## Nail disorders and damage

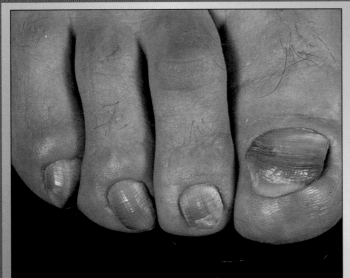

The nails can reveal much about the health of a person.

### Blood supply
Normally appearing pink in colour due to the rich blood supply in the skin beneath it, the nail acts as an indicator of oxygen supply to anaesthetists during surgery. This is the reason why women are always asked to remove any nail varnish before undergoing an

*In yellow nail syndrome, the nails become thickened and yellow. It is associated with swelling of the feet or may be due to thyroid disease.*

operation. If the nail were to become pale in colour or even to turn blue, this would alert the anaesthetist to the fact that the patient was not receiving enough oxygen.

### Nail disorders
The state of the nails can be useful in helping to diagnose a number of disorders.

Grooves running across all the nails may reveal that a person has suffered a serious illness several months before. This is because illness slows down the rate of nail growth, causing ridges to develop in the nail root. These ridges are then pushed outwards as the nail grows.

Similarly, misshapen nails which are bent backwards may indicate anaemia (iron deficiency).

The colour of the fingernails is also very revealing. For example, white opaque nails may indicate cirrhosis of the liver, while white bands on the nails may be a clue that mild arsenic poisoning has taken place.

### Nail damage
More severe changes in the nail such as the nail turning blue or falling off altogether are commonly due to the nail bed becoming damaged through injury. As long as the nail root is not destroyed, the nail will eventually replace itself and continue to grow.

*Brittle, spoon-shaped nails indicate that a person has koilonychia. This is a sign of anaemia and occurs because of a lack of iron in the cells.*

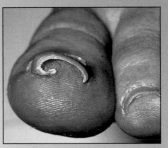
*Ingrowing toenails are caused by cutting nails too close at the edges. This causes the nail to grow into the flesh, resulting in inflammation and infection.*

# How skin protects the body

The skin is a remarkable organ, covering the entire surface area of the body. Skin plays a number of important roles in protecting the body and also helps to control body temperature.

The skin is the largest organ of the body. It can weigh from around 2.5 to 4.5 kg and covers an area of about two square metres.

### ANATOMY OF THE SKIN
The skin is composed of two distinct layers: the epidermis and the dermis.

The epidermis, or cuticle, is the outer protective layer of the skin. The outermost layer of the epidermis (the stratum corneum, or horny layer) accounts for up to three quarters of the epidermal thickness.

### KERATIN
Cells of the epidermis produce keratin (a fibrous protein also found in the hair and nails) and are progressively pushed outward by dividing cells beneath them.

As the cells move outwards they become enriched with keratin, flatten out and die. These dead cells are constantly shed, the epidermis thus being effectively replaced every few weeks. In fact, the average person sheds around 18 kg of skin (in the form of dandruff or dry skin flakes) in a lifetime.

### SKIN THICKNESS
The epidermis is thickest on the parts of the body that receive the greatest wear, for example the soles of the feet and the palms of the hands.

### DERMIS
The innermost layer of the skin is the dermis. This fibrous layer comprises a network of collagen and elastic fibres.

The dermis also contains blood vessels, nerves, fat lobules, hair roots, sebaceous glands and sweat glands.

*The skin is composed of two main layers: the epidermis and the dermis. The epidermis is nourished indirectly by the blood vessels in the dermis.*

### Anatomy of the skin

Hair

Epidermis

Dermis

Nerve fibre

Hair follicle

Blood vessel

Sweat gland

Fat

## Role of skin

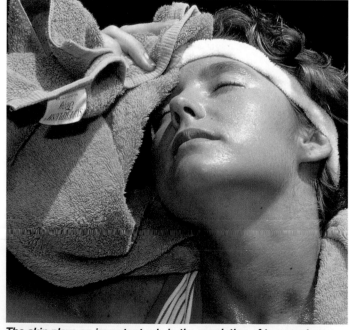

*The skin plays an important role in the regulation of temperature. Sweat glands produce a salty solution which cools the body as it evaporates.*

The skin plays a number of important roles. These include:

■ Protection – the collagen fibres of the dermis give the skin strength and resistance, preventing any object from penetrating the body.

■ Regulation of temperature – through vasoconstriction (narrowing) and vasodilation (widening) of blood vessels in the dermis. The production of sweat also helps to cool the body.

■ Barrier against bacterial infection – large numbers of micro-organisms are naturally present on the surface of the skin. These compete with harmful bacteria, preventing them from invading the body.

■ Sensitivity to touch and pain – the dermis contains a dense network of nerve endings sensitive to pain and pressure.

These nerves provide the brain with vital information about the body in relation to its environment, allowing it to act accordingly, for example retracting the hand when something hot is touched.

■ Prevention of unregulated water loss – the sebaceous glands of the dermis secrete an oily substance known as sebum. This coats the skin, making it effectively waterproof. Collagen fibres within the dermis also hold water.

■ Protection against ultraviolet (UV) radiation – the pigment melanin (produced by melanocytes in the epidermis) acts as a filter to the harmful ultraviolet radiation produced by the sun.

■ Manufacture of vitamin D – this is produced in response to sunlight and helps to regulate the metabolism of calcium.

# Skin colour

Skin colour largely depends on the presence of melanin. Production of this pigment protects the skin from harmful radiation produced by the sun.

The colour of the skin depends on a combination of factors, such as skin thickness, blood flow, and pigment concentration.

### PIGMENTS
In areas where the skin is very thin and blood flow is good, it will appear much darker (such as over the lips) due to the red colour of the pigment

haemoglobin in the blood.

In general, the production of melanin will determine how dark the skin is. This pigment is produced by melanocyte cells present in the epidermal layer.

Dark-skinned people have a high proportion of melanocytes, and hence greater concentrations of melanin in their skin.

### SUN EXPOSURE
Skin responds to ultraviolet rays in sunlight by producing greater amounts of melanin.

As levels of melanin increase, the skin darkens forming a filter against the harmful radiation produced by the sun.

Freckles are another example of the skin's reaction to the sun,

*Skin colour is mainly dependent upon the number of melanin-producing cells. People with albinism have no such cells, making them very pale skinned.*

representing concentrated areas of melanin-producing cells.

### SUN BURN
If sun exposure does not take place gradually however, the skin is unable to produce melanin fast enough to filter out the suns harmful rays.

As a result the skin burns, becoming inflamed and very tender. Prolonged exposure to UV radiation can permanently

*In response to sunlight, melanin-producing cells become more active. As levels of melanin increase the skin darkens, filtering out harmful radiation.*

damage the skin cells leading to premature ageing of the skin and, sometimes, skin cancer.

Skin cancer tends to be less common in dark-skinned people, which is testament to the protective role of melanin.

## Skin repair

When skin is cut, for example by surgical incision, the sides of the wound will automatically grow back together if they are held in place with stitches.

Where there is tissue loss however, a remarkable process

occurs whereby new skin is regenerated.

Skin cells adjacent to the wound break away from the cells below, migrate to the wounded area and enlarge.

Other cells surrounding the

wound multiply rapidly to replace the cells lost.

Eventually from all sides of the wound the migrating cells meet. Once the wound is entirely covered, cell migration stops.

The wound will continue to

heal as epithelial cells multiply, and normal thickness is restored.

*When skin is wounded, the surrounding cells move to the site of the wound, and multiply until the area is covered.*

## Skin grafts

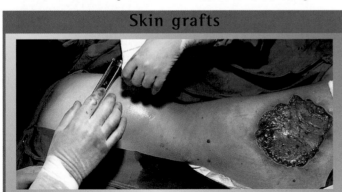

In cases where the skin is severely damaged, such as with third degree burns, medical intervention may be required. This is because the damaged area may be too large for the skin to regenerate itself before infection sets in.

### Transplantation of skin
A process known as skin grafting involves the removal of a fine sheet of skin from elsewhere on the body, usually a fleshy area such as the thigh or buttock.

*Sometimes damage to the skin is so bad that a skin graft is required. This procedure involves transplanting skin from elsewhere on the body.*

This skin is then transplanted on to the wound. With time these new skin cells proliferate, join together and heal the area.

New techniques are being developed, which involve the culturing of skin cells in a laboratory. Using this technique, skin can be grown specifically for transplantation.

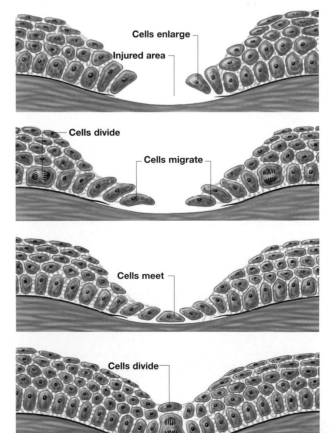

Cells enlarge

Injured area

Cells divide

Cells migrate

Cells meet

Cells divide

# How body temperature is controlled

Body temperature is regulated by a part of the brain called the hypothalamus. If the external temperature rises or falls, the body uses various mechanisms to ensure it maintains a comfortable equilibrium.

Endothermic (warm-blooded) animals, such as birds or mammals, maintain their bodies at a more or less constant temperature using internal control mechanisms. In comparison, ectothermic (cold-blooded) animals, such as fish and reptiles, have no such internal mechanisms and are dependent to a great extent on the surrounding temperature.

### CONTROLLING BODY HEAT
Humans, like all warm-blooded animals, produce heat as a result of metabolism. All of the body's tissues produce heat, but the most heat is produced by the tissues that are most active, such as the liver, heart, brain and endocrine glands.

Muscles also produce heat – about 25 per cent of body heat is produced by inactive muscles. Active muscles may produce up to 40 times more heat than the rest of the body, which is why the body warms during exercise.

### HOMEOSTASIS
Humans have a fairly constant body temperature that is, under normal conditions, maintained independently of their external surroundings. This maintenance of a constant internal environment, in spite of variations in the outside environment, is known as homeostasis.

One of the advantages of maintaining a constant body temperature is that the danger of overheating is greatly reduced. Extreme cases of overheating can result in convulsions and death, as nerve pathways are suppressed and the activities of vital proteins are affected.

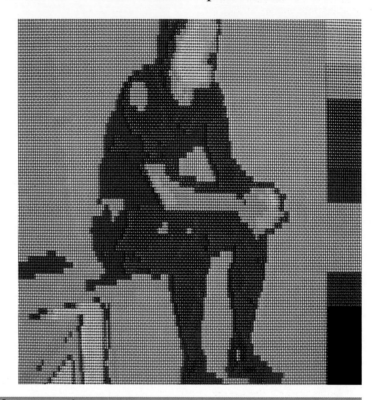

*A thermogram (heat image) shows the distribution of heat around the body after exercise. The hottest parts are white, followed by yellow and purple; the coldest parts are shown as red, blue and black.*

## Mechanisms for warming up

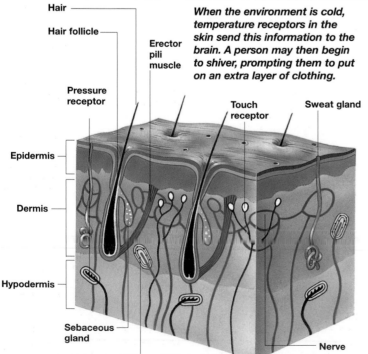

Hair
Hair follicle
Erector pili muscle
Pressure receptor
Touch receptor
Sweat gland
Epidermis
Dermis
Hypodermis
Sebaceous gland
Temperature receptor
Nerve

*When the environment is cold, temperature receptors in the skin send this information to the brain. A person may then begin to shiver, prompting them to put on an extra layer of clothing.*

The normal temperature of the human body varies between 35.6 °C and 37.8 °C. In order to maintain this degree of constancy, the temperature is monitored by a part of the brain called the hypothalamus. This operates using a feedback mechanism, similar to that used by the thermostat of a domestic central heating system.

When the external environment starts to cool the body down, temperature sensors in the skin send this information to the hypothalamus and the person starts to feel cold. This information is then passed to other parts of the brain, which initiate physiological responses designed to increase body heat and reduce heat loss.

Some reactions to feeling cold are conscious, such as jumping up and down, putting on extra clothing or moving to a warmer place. Other reactions occur spontaneously. Shivering occurs when body muscles contract and relax very rapidly, giving out four or five times as much heat as they do in their resting state. At the same time, adrenaline production is increased, which increases the body's metabolic rate – the rate at which energy, stored in the form of glucose, is used. As a result more heat is generated inside the whole body.

### REGULATING HEAT LOSS
To reduce heat loss from the body's surface, the capillaries near the surface of the skin become constricted, resulting in a reduced blood flow to the skin and a paler complexion. At the same time, the tiny muscles attached to the hair follicles contract, resulting in the hairs on the skin becoming erect. In most mammals, this has the effect of trapping a layer of warmer air near the skin, but because skin hair is sparse in humans, this pilo-erection has very little effect on heat loss, other than causing 'goose-pimples'.

# Temperature control mechanisms

Our skin is equipped with thousands of receptors that monitor the overall temperature of the body. These sensors detect changes in the external environment and alert the brain, which in turn stimulates shivering or sweating to maintain homeostasis.

## VASODILATION

Vasodilation is a key mechanism for conserving and losing heat. At high temperatures, the blood vessels dilate (widen), allowing heat to be lost and giving a flushed appearance. The degree of dilation of the blood vessels is controlled by nerves called vasomotor fibres, which are in turn controlled by the brain.

## VASOCONSTRICTION

At low temperatures, arterioles (branches of arteries) leading to capillaries in upper skin layers may constrict (vasoconstriction). This reduces blood flow to the skin, and reduces heat loss.

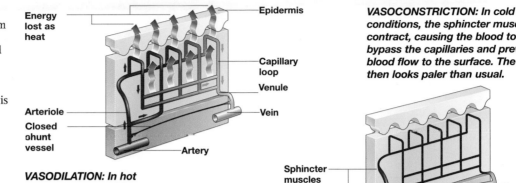

Labels: Energy lost as heat • Epidermis • Capillary loop • Venule • Arteriole • Vein • Closed shunt vessel • Artery

*VASODILATION: In hot conditions, tiny sphincter muscles in the walls of arterioles relax, allowing blood to flow to the surface. The dilated blood vessels cause the skin to redden.*

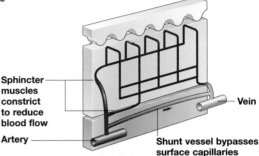

*VASOCONSTRICTION: In cold conditions, the sphincter muscles contract, causing the blood to bypass the capillaries and preventing blood flow to the surface. The skin then looks paler than usual.*

Labels: Sphincter muscles constrict to reduce blood flow • Vein • Artery • Shunt vessel bypasses surface capillaries

## Mechanisms for cooling down

The body's temperature is normally higher than that of the surrounding air. Therefore, heat is lost to the surrounding environment by radiation and convection, as currents of moving air pass over the surface of the skin.

If, however, the body starts to become too warm, due to either a high external temperature or an internal fever, heat sensors send nerve impulses to the hypothalamus, and the brain initiates cooling measures.

The blood capillaries near the surface of the skin become dilated so that blood flow increases and more heat is lost through the skin to the outside. Sweating also increases heat loss: as liquid produced by the sweat glands evaporates, it has a cooling effect on the skin.

In dry air, sweating works very effectively: a person can tolerate temperatures of up to 65 °C for several hours in dry conditions. However, if the air is moist, sweat cannot evaporate easily and the body becomes overheated more rapidly.

*A coloured electron micrograph shows droplets of sweat (blue) on human skin. Sweat, mostly in the form of dissolved salts, cools the body down.*

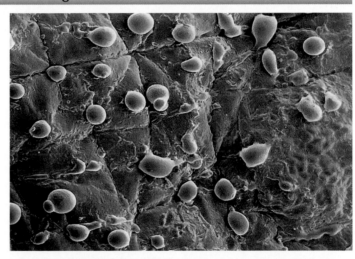

## Fever and hypothermia

A fever is a raised body temperature that may occur as a result of infection. Chemical substances called cytokines are released by white blood cells and damaged tissue cells. These

*Symptoms of hypothermia include lethargy, muscle stiffness and a confused mental state. If untreated, it results in unconsciousness, brain damage and ultimately death.*

chemicals cause the hypothalamus to produce prostaglandins (hormones that dilate blood vessels), which in turn 'reset' the thermostatic control mechanism of the hypothalamus to a higher temperature. The result is that heat-producing mechanisms are triggered; even though the body temperature may rise to 40 °C, the patient still feels a chill.

Body temperature remains high until the infection is cleared. At this point, the normal setting of the hypothalamus is restored and cooling mechanisms are initiated. The patient sweats and becomes flushed as the blood vessels in the skin dilate. Research has shown that fever both boosts the body's immune system and inhibits the growth of micro-organisms.

Hypothermia occurs when the core body temperature falls below 35 °C. It results from the body being exposed to cold conditions, rendering it unable to maintain normal body temperature. Newborn babies, the elderly and those suffering from illness are most susceptible. Hypothermia is usually the result of a combination of inadequate food, clothing and heating in cold conditions.

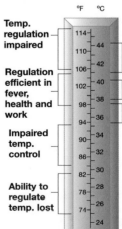

Labels: °F • °C • Upper limit of survival • Temp. regulation impaired — 114 • 110 — 44 — Heatstroke / Brain lesions / Fever therapy • 106 — 42 • Regulation efficient in fever, health and work — 102 — 40 — Fever disease / Hard exercise • 98 — 38 — Range of normal temp. • 94 — 36 • Impaired temp. control — 90 — 34 • 86 — 32 • 82 — 30 • Ability to regulate temp. lost — 78 — 28 • 74 — 26 — Lower limit of survival • 24

*Extremes of body temperature – whether too high or too low – have a devastating effect on mental and physical health.*

# How the body produces sweat

Sweat is secreted from the sweat glands during physical exercise, stress and in excessive heat. It is produced in two different types of glands, both of which are located in the dermis of the skin.

The body constantly produces sweat. This process is the body's main way of ridding itself of excess heat.

The amount of sweat the body produces depends upon the state of emotion and physical activity. Sweat can be produced in response to stress, high air temperature and exercise.

### SWEAT GLANDS

Sweat is manufactured in the sweat glands. These are located in the dermis of the skin, along with nerve endings and hair follicles. On average, each person has around 2.6 million sweat glands, which are distributed over the entire body, with the exception of the lips, nipples and genitals.

Sweat glands consist of long, coiled, hollow tubes of cells. The coiled portion in the dermis is where sweat is produced. The long portion is a duct that connects the gland to tiny openings (pores) located on the outer surface of the skin. Nerve cells from the sympathetic nervous system (a division of the autonomic nervous system) connect to the sweat glands.

### TYPES OF SWEAT GLAND

There are two types of gland:
■ Eccrine – these are the most numerous type of sweat gland, found all over the body, particularly on the palms of the hands, soles of the feet and forehead. Eccrine glands are active from birth
■ Apocrine – these sweat glands are mostly confined to the armpits and around the genital area. Typically, they end in hair follicles rather than pores. These are larger than eccrine glands, and only become active once puberty has begun.

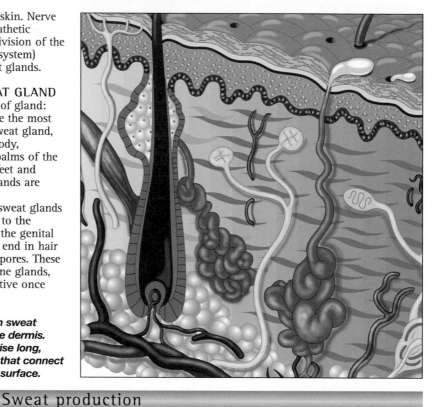

*Sweat is produced in sweat glands, located in the dermis. These glands comprise long, coiled tubes of cells that connect to pores on the skin surface.*

## Sweat production

Stimulation of an eccrine gland causes the cells lining the gland to secrete a fluid that is similar to plasma, but without the fatty acids and proteins. This is mostly water with high concentrations of sodium and chloride (salts) and a low concentration of potassium.

This fluid originates in the spaces between cells (interstitial spaces), which are provided with fluid by the blood vessels (capillaries) in the dermis.

The fluid passes from the coiled portion and up through the straight duct. What happens to this fluid when it reaches the straight portion of the sweat duct depends upon the rate of sweat production.

■ Low sweat flow – at rest and in a cool environment, the sweat glands are not stimulated to produce much sweat. The cells of the straight duct have time to reabsorb most of the water and salts, so not much fluid actually reaches the surface of the skin as sweat.

The composition of this sweat is different from that of its primary source: it contains less sodium and chloride, and more potassium.
■ High sweat flow – this occurs in higher temperatures or during exercise. Cells in the straight portion of the sweat duct do not have time to reabsorb all the water, sodium and chloride from the primary secretion. As a result, alot of sweat reaches the surface of the skin, and its composition is similar to that of the primary secretion.

### APOCRINE SWEAT

Sweat is produced in the apocrine glands in a similar way, but apocrine differs from eccrine sweat in that it contains fatty acids and proteins. For this reason, apocrine sweat is thicker and milky yellow in colour.

### ODOUR

Sweat itself has no odour, but when bacteria present on the hair and skin metabolize the proteins and fatty acids present in apocrine sweat, an unpleasant odour is produced. Deodorants are designed to eliminate this distinctive body odour.

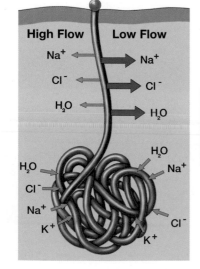

| High Flow | Low Flow |
|---|---|
| Na⁺ | Na⁺ |
| Cl⁻ | Cl⁻ |
| H₂O | H₂O |

| | |
|---|---|
| H₂O | Water |
| K⁺ | Potassium |
| Na⁺ | Sodium |
| Cl⁻ | Chloride |

*The constituents of sweat vary according to temperature and activity. If sweat production is minimal, then the sweat contains less salts.*

# The role of sweat

When sweat evaporates, it takes excess body heat with it. In a very hot climate, the sweat glands can produce up to three litres of sweat an hour.

The role of sweat is to cool the body. Sweat on the surface of the skin evaporates into the atmosphere, taking with it excess body heat.

### VAPORIZATION HEAT

Heat loss from sweating is governed by a basic rule of physics. Heat is required to convert water from a liquid to a vapour (gas); when sweat evaporates this heat is taken from the body.

However, not all of the sweat evaporates and much runs off the skin and is absorbed by items of clothing. Not all heat energy produced by the body is lost through sweat; some is directly radiated from the skin to the air, and some is lost through breathing.

### EVAPORATION RATE

Humidity affects the rate at which sweat evaporates. If the air is humid, for example, then it already has water vapour in it and might not be able to take more (near-saturation). If this is the case, then sweat does not evaporate and cool the body as it does when the air is dry.

When the water in sweat evaporates, it leaves the salts (sodium, chloride and potassium) behind on the skin, which is why the skin can taste salty.

### DEHYDRATION

A body that is not acclimatized to very hot temperatures can easily produce one litre of sweat per hour. In fact, the maximum amount that the body can produce appears to be around two to three litres per hour.

The loss of excessive water and salts from the body can lead to dehydration, causing circulatory problems, kidney failure and heat stroke. It is important therefore to drink plenty of fluids when exercising or in high temperatures.

Specialized drinks are also available for people taking part in sports – these contain vital salts to replace those lost through sweating.

*In areas of high humidity, such as tropical rain forests, the air is already saturated with water. Thus, reduced evaporation of sweat prevents body cooling.*

## Other causes of sweating

*People in stressful situations can sweat in the absence of a high temperature. This is due to an adrenaline surge that stimulates the sweat glands.*

Sweating can also occur as a result of nervous activity, or as the sign of a disorder.

**Nervous sweating**
Sweating responds to the emotional state. If a person is nervous, afraid or anxious, there is an increase in sympathetic nerve activity, and an increase in adrenaline secretion from the adrenal gland.

Adrenaline acts on the sweat glands, particularly those on the palms of the hands and armpits, causing them to produce sweat. This phenomenon is often referred to as a 'cold sweat' and is a factor exploited in the use of lie detector tests. This is because the increased sympathetic nerve activity in the skin changes its electrical resistance.

**Excessive sweating**
Diaphoresis or hyperhidrosis is a condition in which excessive sweating occurs. The exact cause of this embarrassing condition is not known, although it may be due to the following:
■ Overactive thyroid gland – the thyroid hormone increases body metabolism and heat production
■ Certain foods and medications
■ Overactivity of the sympathetic nervous system
■ Hormonal imbalances – for example the menopause.
If the problem of sweating becomes severe, surgery to remove the sympathetic nerve trunk may be performed – this procedure is know as a sympathectomy.

# How the lungs work

The lungs, which take up most of the upper chest cavity, have a surface area equivalent to a tennis court. They work tirelessly to sustain life, supplying the body with oxygen and filtering harmful carbon dioxide from the blood.

The lungs are a pair of large, cone-shaped, spongy organs that remove waste carbon dioxide from the body and exchange it for a fresh supply of oxygen. Air is drawn into the lungs by expanding the chest cavity and then expelled by allowing the cavity to collapse or by forcing the air out.

The lungs occupy most of the chest cavity. The upper part of the cavity is bounded by the ribs and the intercostal muscles. The base of the cavity is bounded by the diaphragm – a flat sheet of tissue that forms a wall between the chest and the abdomen.

### INSIDE THE LUNGS

Inside the lungs is a dense, branching latticework of tubes that get progressively smaller. The largest tubes are the two bronchi, which connect with the base of the trachea. Inside the lungs, the bronchi divide into smaller branches known as bronchioles, finally ending in clusters of tiny air sacs, or alveoli (singular: alveolus) In total, the lungs contain over 2,400 km of airway, and the surface area inside is about 260 m² – equivalent to an area the size of a tennis court.

*The right lung is divided into three lobes, and the left into two. The left lung is smaller than the right, as the heart takes up more room on the left.*

**Ribs**
Enclose and protect the cavity that houses the lungs

**Tertiary bronchus**
Branch off from the secondary bronchi and subdivide into terminal bronchi

**Secondary bronchus**
Five passages that branch off from the primary bronchus

**Larynx**

**Trachea**
Passage that takes air to the lungs; divides into the two primary bronchi

**Left primary bronchus**
Large air passage that branches off from the trachea, supplying each lung with oxygen

**Terminal bronchioles**
Divides into two or more respiratory bronchioles that lead to the alveoli

**Alveoli**
Balloon-like sacs that filters oxygen into the blood and removes carbon dioxide, ready for exhalation

**Diaphragm**
Flat fibromuscular sheet that separates the chest from the abdominal cavity; its contraction and relaxation moves air in and out of the lungs

## Breathing in and out

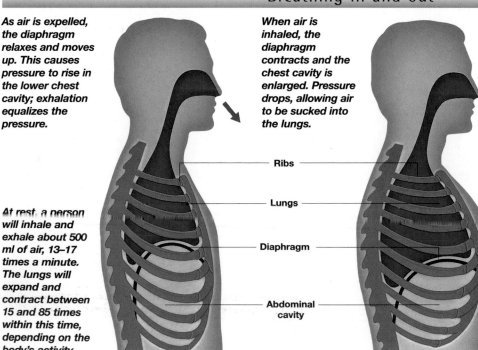

*As air is expelled, the diaphragm relaxes and moves up. This causes pressure to rise in the lower chest cavity; exhalation equalizes the pressure.*

*At rest, a person will inhale and exhale about 500 ml of air, 13–17 times a minute. The lungs will expand and contract between 15 and 85 times within this time, depending on the body's activity.*

*When air is inhaled, the diaphragm contracts and the chest cavity is enlarged. Pressure drops, allowing air to be sucked into the lungs.*

**Ribs**

**Lungs**

**Diaphragm**

**Abdominal cavity**

The lungs have a natural tendency to collapse. Inside the chest cavity, they are held open by surface tension created by a fluid produced by the inner pleural membrane. To draw air into the lungs, the chest cavity is expanded. The muscles of the diaphragm contract, causing it to become flatter. At the same time, the intercostal muscles of the ribs contract, lifting the ribs upwards and outwards. The pressure in the chest cavity is thus reduced and the lungs expand, drawing in air via the mouth or nose.

When the intercostal muscles relax, the ribs fall downwards and inwards and the lungs collapse, forcing the air out. At the same time, the diaphragm relaxes and is pulled up into the chest cavity. In order to force more air out of the chest cavity the abdominal muscles can be used to push the diaphragm further into the chest cavity.

# Controlling breathing

An adult's lung capacity is about 55 litres, but during normal breathing only 500 ml of air is exchanged. This movement is associated with inside and outside pressure.

Although breathing can be controlled voluntarily, respiratory movements are generally a series of reflex actions. There are controlled by the respiratory centre in the hindbrain (the part of the brain that regulates basic bodily systems). This has two regions: an inspiratory centre and an expiratory centre.

Nerve impulses from the inspiratory centre cause the contraction of the intercostal muscles (which move the ribs) and the diaphragm. This is the beginning of an intake of air into the lungs. As the lungs expand,

stretch receptors in the walls of the lungs send back signals that begin to inhibit the signals from the inspiratory centre.

At the same time, impulses from the inspiratory centre activate the expiratory centre, which sends back inhibitory signals. The result is the relaxation of the intercostal muscles and the diaphragm, which ceases the intake of air and begins exhalation. The whole process is now ready to start again.

Breathing is also controlled and regulated by the level of carbon dioxide ($CO_2$) in the blood. Excess $CO_2$ causes the blood to become more acid. This is detected by the brain, and the inspiratory centre starts to produce deeper breathing until the $CO_2$ level is reduced.

*This resin cast of the pulmonary arteries and bronchi clearly shows the network of vessels that supply blood and air to the lungs.*

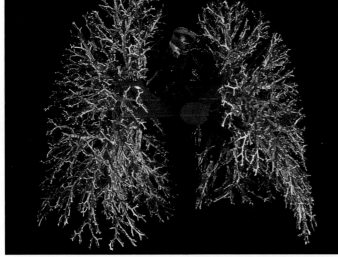

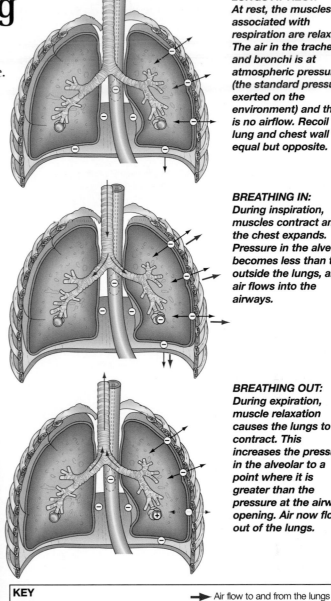

*LUNGS AT REST:*
*At rest, the muscles associated with respiration are relaxed. The air in the trachea and bronchi is at atmospheric pressure (the standard pressure exerted on the environment) and there is no airflow. Recoil of lung and chest wall are equal but opposite.*

*BREATHING IN:*
*During inspiration, muscles contract and the chest expands. Pressure in the alveolar becomes less than that outside the lungs, and air flows into the airways.*

*BREATHING OUT:*
*During expiration, muscle relaxation causes the lungs to contract. This increases the pressure in the alveolar to a point where it is greater than the pressure at the airway opening. Air now flows out of the lungs.*

**KEY**

(+) Pressure within the alveolar greater than external air pressure

(−) Pressure within the alveolar lesser than external air pressure

→ Air flow to and from the lungs

➤ Internal or external forces, resulting in an increase or decrease of pressure

➤ Muscular contraction or relaxation

## Gas exchange

The exchange of gases takes place in the alveoli, of which there are about 300 million. When fully expanded, the lungs can contain between 4 and 6 litres of air, but a much smaller amount is normally breathed in and out. When engaged in a quiet activity, a person breathes in and out about 15 times a minute, moving around 500 ml of air with each breath. During strenuous activity, however, the breathing rate may increase to up to 80 breaths a minute, and the volume of air moved may increase to between three and five litres.

Air that is breathed in contains about 21 per cent

oxygen. Inside the alveoli, some of this oxygen dissolves in the surface moisture and passes through the thin lining into the blood, where most of it is picked up by the haemoglobin of the red blood cells. At the same time, carbon dioxide, most of which is carried in the blood plasma, passes into the lungs, where it is released as a gas ready to be breathed out. Exhaled air contains about 16 per cent oxygen.

*The spaces seen in this meshwork of lung tissue are alveoli, which perform the lung's primary role of gas exchange.*

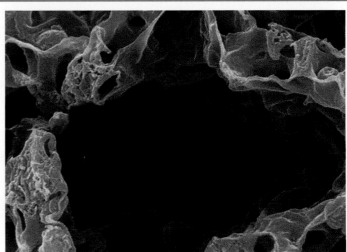

# How the heart pumps

The adult heart beats over 100,000 times and pumps about 8,000 litres of blood in a 24-hour period. Although the heart is a muscle, it does not tire like other muscles, and it never rests.

The heart is a powerful muscle that performs two vital tasks. It propels blood enriched with oxygen to all parts of the body, and it also pumps deoxygenated (used) blood to the lungs, where it will be re-oxygenated.

The heart is divided in two by a strong muscular wall called the septum. Each half is further divided into two chambers – the left and right upper chambers are known as the atria (singular: atrium), and the two lower chambers are the ventricles. Each of these four chambers plays a specific role in circulating blood around the heart and then back out into the body or to the lungs.

### THE CARDIAC MUSCLE

The wall of the heart is composed of three layers: the epicardium (outer layer), the myocardium (middle layer) and the endocardium (inner layer). The myocardial layer is responsible for the contraction of the heart. Muscle fibres are arranged to give a 'wringing' movement that effectively squeezes blood out of the heart.

The thickness of the myocardial layer varies according to the pressure generated within the various chambers in the heart. The right ventricular myocardial layer is moderately thick, as blood is only pumped through the pulmonary artery to the lungs. The myocardium of the left ventricle is much thicker because greater pressure is needed to pump blood into all parts of the body. The myocardial layer of the atria is relatively thin.

## Inner structure of the heart

*It takes about one minute for blood to circulate around the body, thanks to the powerful contractions of the heart. In an average lifetime, the heart contracts, usually without rest, over two-and-a-half billion times.*

**Aorta**
Carries oxygenated blood to the body. Branches off the aorta supply specific areas

**Pulmonary artery**
Carries deoxygenated blood from the right ventricle to the lungs

**Pulmonary valve**

**Left atrium**
Chamber into which fresh, oxygenated blood from the lungs enters, ready for redistribution around the body

**Superior vena cava**
Carries deoxygenated blood from the head and arms into the right atrium

**Aortic valve**

**Chordae tendineae**
Act as tension 'ropes' holding the valve cusps open

**Right atrium**
Chamber where deoxygenated blood enters the heart

**Left ventricle**
Chamber that receives blood from the left atrium and pumps it into the aorta

**Tricuspid valve**

**Ventricular septum**
Strong musculofibrous wall that divides the heart in two

**Endocardium**
Thin membrane that lines the internal structures of the heart

**Inferior vena cava**
Vein carrying deoxygenated blood from the lower body into the right atrium

**Myocardium**
Area of muscle fibres enabling the heart to contract, or beat

**Epicardium**
Thin membranous outer layer of the heart wall

**Right ventricle**
Chamber into which deoxygenated blood from the right atrium flows

**Descending aorta**
Supplies oxygenated blood to the lower trunk and limbs

**Pericardium**
Bag-like membrane that surrounds and protects the heart

## Controlling the flow of blood around the heart

Blood flow around the four chambers of the heart is controlled by four valves. The atrioventricular valves (the tricuspid valve and the mitral, or bicuspid, valve) lie between the atria and the ventricles. The two semilunar valves lie at the openings of the pulmonary artery and the aorta. The pulmonary artery takes deoxygenated blood to the lungs; the aorta carries blood to the body's organs and tissues.

The heart valves ensure that blood only flows in one direction. As pressure reaches a critical point, the valves open, allowing blood to pass through. When the heart is relaxed between contractions the aortic and pulmonary valves stay tightly sealed, but the atrioventricular valves stay open.

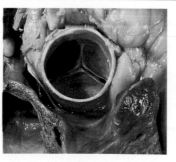

*Oxygenated blood enters the left atrium of the heart, is pushed into the left ventricle and is finally pumped to the arteries of the body via the aorta. The aortic valve (pictured) has three semilunar cusps. The purpose of the valve is to prevent the back-flow of blood into the left ventricle, maintaining the directional flow of blood through the heart.*

# The heartbeat cycle

There are three phases to every beat of our heart. As the cardiac muscle contracts, blood is moved around the internal chambers in strict rotation. At the same time, blood is pumped out to the body's organs and tissue, or transported back to the lungs, where it will be re-oxygenated, ready for re-use.

**1 DIASTOLE**     **2 ATRIAL SYSTOLE**     **3 VENTRICULAR SYSTOLE**

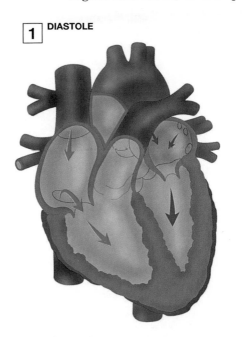

**KEY**
■ Deoxygenated blood ■ Oxygenated blood

*During the first phase (diastole), deoxygenated blood enters the right atrium and oxygenated blood enters the left atrium. As these chambers reach capacity, blood flows into the ventricles.*

*In the atrial systole phase, the heart muscles (myocardium) surrounding the atria contract, which in turn causes the two atrial chambers to empty and blood remaining in the atria is forced into the ventricles.*

*The ventricles contract during the third phase. Semilunar valves open, and blood is pumped out to the body via the aorta, or carried to the lungs by the pulmonary artery. The whole cycle can now start again.*

Deoxygenated blood enters the right side of the heart and is pumped out to the lungs to be re-oxygenated. This fresh blood then flows to the left side of the heart, from where it will be circulated throughout the body. This nutrient-rich blood flow is known as systemic circulation.

The atria and the ventricles hold blood as it is pumped into the heart. In the first phase of a heartbeat, deoxygenated blood flows into the right atrium and oxygenated blood enters the left atrium, causing both chambers to expand. As pressure builds up, the atria contract, forcing blood into the two ventricles. This is the second phase of the heartbeat cycle.

In the final phase, pressure begins to build in the ventricles as they fill with blood. At a critical point, blood is ejected from the heart via the aorta. The oxygenated blood is then distributed to the organs and tissue, and deoxygenated blood is pumped to the lungs.

## Cardiac muscle action

The rhythmic contractions of the heart are caused by the 'wringing' motion of the cardiac muscle. Heart muscle is unique in that it is inherently contractile – it undergoes rhythmical contractions even if the heart is removed from the body briefly.

The process that causes automatic contraction of the heart muscle is called self-excitation. Many cardiac muscle fibres display this capability, but it is especially true of fibres found in the heart's specialised conducting system, which controls the heartbeat cycle. The phases of the heartbeat cycle can be heard heart using a stethoscope. This technique is called auscultation of the heart.

In a normal person, the heart contracts about 72 times a minute and two heart sounds are distinguishable in each beat. These are described as 'lub dup'. The first sound, lub, is caused by closure of the mitral and tricuspid valves, and the second, dup, is caused by the closure of the aortic and pulmonary valves.

## Blood flow to and from the heart

Blood flows into the right atrium via the superior vena cava, the large vein that drains used blood from the head, neck, arms and parts of the chest. Blood also flows from the inferior vena cava – which drains blood from the rest of the body – and the coronary sinus, which drains blood from the heart itself.

Oxygenated blood leaves the heart via the aorta, which branches into the arterial system. It is the means by which nutrients and oxygen are carried to the cells. The arteries divide into arterioles and ultimately into capillaries. It is in these microscopic capillaries that fluid, nutrients and waste are exchanged between the tissue and the blood. The blood now containing waste products, drains into venules and veins, and ultimately into the great veins which drain into the heart.

For the heart to function, it must be constantly fed with a supply of oxygen and nutrients. These nutrients are carried to the heart by the blood via the coronary arterial system. Two coronary arteries (left and right) branch over the surface of the heart. Branches of these systems diffuse over the surface of the heart so the muscle fibre can receive oxygen and nutrients. The coronary veins carry used blood and waste products away from the heart's surface into the coronary sinus.

*To function effectively, the heart (seen here in cross-section) needs a substantial supply of blood. The brain is the only organ in the body that requires a larger supply.*

# How the heart beats

The heart contains specialized tissue that generates an intrinsic rhythmic beat. The brain controls the heart rate by sending nervous impulses that alter this inherent rhythm.

A remarkable feature of the heart is that as long as it is bathed with a solution containing vital nutrients, it will continue to beat for long periods when removed from the body. This is because the heartbeat originates from within the heart itself, rather than resulting from electrical impulses from the brain.

Specialized pacemaker tissue and an electrical conducting system are responsible for generating the electrical 'spark' underlying the heartbeat and transmitting it in an orderly sequence across the upper and lower heart chambers.

### SINOATRIAL NODE

The primary pacemaker of the heart is called the sinoatrial (SA) node, which is a small area of tissue located in the right atrium (upper chamber) of the heart. The SA node is about 20 mm long by 5 mm wide. Specialized electrical properties of the cells in the SA node allow it to generate regular 'sparks' of electricity that initiate each heartbeat.

Heart muscle cells are connected to one another in such a way that electrical events pass rapidly from cell to cell. Thus, when the cells of the SA node generate electrical impulses, the emerging wave of electrical excitation spreads very rapidly across both atria. This leads to a synchronized contraction of the atria, which pushes blood into the lower chambers of the heart – the ventricles.

*The heart can continue to contract long after it has been excised from the body. However, it must be bathed with the appropriate nutrients.*

## Spread of electrical activity across the heart

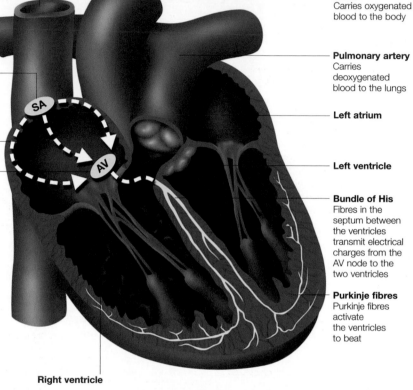

**Superior vena cava**
Carries deoxygenated blood from head and arms

**Sinoatrial node**
Site of pacemaker cells which generate electricity to initiate heartbeat

**Right atrium**

**Atrioventricular node**
Receives impulses from the SA node and passes them on to the bundle of His

*Pacemaker cells in the sinoatrial node beat spontaneously. They transmit an electrical wave of excitation to the atrioventricular node, which then spreads to the Purkinje fibres via the bundle of His.*

**Right ventricle**

**Aorta**
Carries oxygenated blood to the body

**Pulmonary artery**
Carries deoxygenated blood to the lungs

**Left atrium**

**Left ventricle**

**Bundle of His**
Fibres in the septum between the ventricles transmit electrical charges from the AV node to the two ventricles

**Purkinje fibres**
Purkinje fibres activate the ventricles to beat

## Atrioventricular node

In order for an impulse to reach the ventricles, it must pass through a specialized region called the atrioventricular (AV) node. The AV node functions as a kind of electrical junction box. Electrical conduction is normally slower through the AV node than through other areas. As a consequence, the impulse is delayed in its passage through the AV node for approximately 0.1 of a second, at resting heart rates. This allows time for the ventricles to receive the blood being pumped into them during contraction of the upper chambers.

From the AV node, the impulse enters a cluster of fibres between the ventricles called the bundle of His. This divides into

*When the heart stops beating, it can sometimes be started again by delivering a large electrical shock across the chest wall.*

two branches, spreading into a network of conducting fibres called Purkinje fibres that rapidly distribute electrical excitation throughout the ventricles. Once excited, the

ventricles contract, pumping blood into the circulation. Thus, a sequence of events starting with a spontaneous electrical impulse in the SA node ends with ventricular contraction.

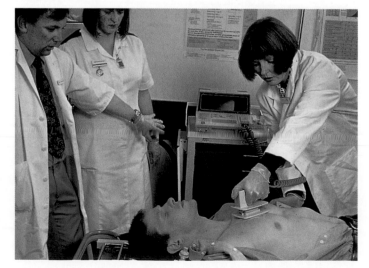

# How the heart rate is controlled

The brain is able to modulate the heart rate via parasympathetic and sympathetic nerve fibres. These adapt the strength and timing of the heartbeat during rest and exercise or intense emotion. The electrical activity of the heart can be studied using an ECG.

Although the heartbeat arises in the sinoatrial nodal tissue of the heart, it can be modulated by the brain via a series of nerve fibres. These nerve fibres are subdivided anatomically and functionally into two groups:
■ Parasympathetic nerves – these decrease heart rate.
■ Sympathetic nerves – these increase the rate and strength of the heart's beating.

## PARASYMPATHETIC CONTROL
In the absence of any influence from the nervous system, the inherent rate of SA node impulse generation is approximately 100 beats/minute in humans. This is somewhat higher than the normal resting heart rate which is near 70 beats/minute. The reason for this is that parasympathetic activity (via the vagus nerve) slows the rate of automatic sinoatrial impulse generation.

At rest, therefore, the heart is considered to be under 'vagal tone'; this allows the brain to increase the heart rate by reducing the activity of the vagus nerve.

## SYMPATHETIC CONTROL
During increased demands on the circulation, such as occurs during exercise, sympathetic fibres release noradrenaline, which speeds up the rate of sinoatrial nodal impulse generation. In addition, sympathetic activity increases the speed of electrical conduction through the AV node allowing the ventricles to be excited and therefore beat more frequently.

As well as exercise, intense emotional states (for example, fear) can increase the heart rate via increased sympathetic activity. This can be off-set by 'beta-blockers', drugs which block the excitatory effects of noradrenaline and circulating adrenaline.

*The brain is able to alter the heart's rate and strength of beating by sending nervous impulses along sympathetic and parasympathetic nerve fibres.*

## Nervous control of the heart

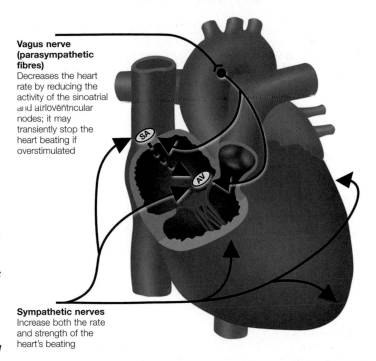

**Vagus nerve (parasympathetic fibres)**
Decreases the heart rate by reducing the activity of the sinoatrial and atrioventricular nodes; it may transiently stop the heart beating if overstimulated

**Sympathetic nerves**
Increase both the rate and strength of the heart's beating

## Recording the heart's electrical activity

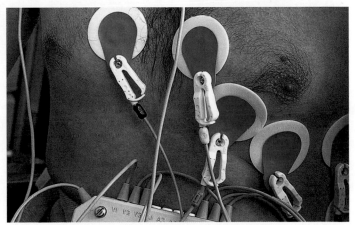

**Thousandths of a second**

(R — Ventricular excitation, Ventricular repolarization T, Atrial excitation P, Q, S)

The sequence of electrical events that occur during a single heartbeat can be detected on the body surface via an electrocardiogram (ECG).

### SEQUENCE OF EVENTS DURING AN ECG TRACE
During each heartbeat, the first perceptible event on the ECG is the combined electrical excitation of atrial tissue. This corresponds to the 'P wave' of the ECG. A period then follows during which atrial contraction occurs and excitation travels through the AV node.

The excitation of ventricular tissue which follows gives rise to the 'QRS' complex of the ECG. Ventricular tissue remains uniformly excited for 0.2–0.3 seconds, then recovers during electrical recovery

*This ECG shows a recording from a healthy person's heart. ECG equipment can detect the sequence of electrical events that occur during one heartbeat.*

(repolarization), which corresponds to the 'T wave' of the ECG.

For the cardiologist, ECG recordings provide valuable information in the diagnosis of a range of pathological conditions involving abnormal impulse generation and propagation, as these produce characteristic alterations to the ECG profile.

Abnormal heart rhythms are grouped together under the general terms 'arrhythmias' or 'dysrhythmias' and their treatment involves a range of pharmacological and non-pharmacological strategies aimed towards restoring the normal timing and rate of impulse generation and conduction.

*ECG recordings are made by attaching electrodes to the skin. The leads are connected to a monitor which displays voltage changes on the ECG.*

# How digestion begins

Digestion involves the movement of food through the body's alimentary canal so that nutrients can be absorbed. The first stage is the ingestion of food from the mouth into the alimentary canal.

Digestion is the process by which the complex chemicals in food are broken down into simpler chemicals that can be absorbed into the body. It takes place in the alimentary canal, which is made up of the mouth, oesophagus, stomach, small and large intestine, and rectum.

*The alimentary canal – also known as the gastrointestinal tract – contains the structures and associated organs concerned with digestion. It runs from the mouth to the anus, absorbing nutrients and expelling waste material.*

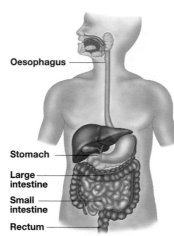

Oesophagus

Stomach

Large intestine

Small intestine

Rectum

## CHEWING

Digestion begins in the mouth, where chewing breaks down the food into smaller pieces and mixes it with saliva. The tongue, a muscular organ capable of a variety of movements, has two main functions in this process. Firstly, it moves the food around the mouth, acting with muscles in the neck and jaws, presenting it to the teeth for chewing.

It is also concerned with taste: its surface is covered with thousands of papillae (nipple-shaped protuberances) that increase the surface area coming into contact with food.

## SWALLOWING

The first stage of swallowing is under voluntary control. When chewing is complete, the tongue pushes up against the hard palate, and food is forced to the back of the mouth where it is formed into a soft mass (bolus).

The bolus is forced into the pharynx, where swallowing is a reflex action. The tongue prevents the food from re-entering the mouth, and the soft palate moves upwards to close off the nasal cavity. The epiglottis then closes the trachea, and pharynx muscles squeeze the bolus into the oesophagus.

## The action of swallowing

Hard palate

Bolus of food

Pharynx

Tongue

Nasal cavity

Soft palate

Bolus

Epiglottis

Trachea

Oesophageal sphincter

Nasal cavity

Soft palate

Tongue

Epiglottis

Bolus

**1** VOLUNTARY SWALLOW

*In the voluntary stage of swallowing, the tongue rises up towards the hard palate. This forces the bolus into the pharynx (throat).*

**2** THROUGH THE THROAT

*As the bolus passes through the pharynx, the nasal cavity and the trachea are both closed off. The upper oesophageal sphincter relaxes.*

**3** DOWN THE OESOPHAGUS

*Once the bolus has passed through, the sphincter contracts, forcing the bolus down the oesophagus towards the stomach.*

## What saliva does

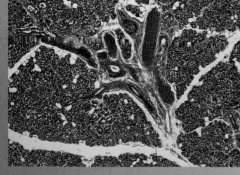

Saliva is a watery secretion produced by the salivary glands. There are three pairs of salivary glands situated in the face and neck, and many smaller ones in the tongue and lining of the mouth.

Saliva contains mucus, which surrounds the chewed pieces of food in the mouth. This lubricates them, assisting their passage down the oesophagus

*The structure of a salivary gland situated beneath the base of the tongue is shown in this light micrograph. The mauve regions contain the excretory ducts.*

when they are swallowed. It also contains a chemical called lysozyme, which acts as a disinfectant, and an enzyme called ptyalin that begins the process of digesting certain starches by splitting them into disaccharide sugars, such as dextrose and maltose.

Saliva is secreted constantly (about 1.7 litres each day), but the rate of flow can be altered by nervous stimulation. For example, more saliva is produced when we smell food and when food is in the mouth, while nervousness may cause a decrease – the 'dry mouth of fear'.

# Moving food down to the stomach

Swallowed food – in the form of a bolus – passes down the
oesophagus and into the stomach. Here, it is temporarily stored
while the process of chemical breakdown begins.

## Oesophagus

The oesophagus is an elastic, muscular tube about 25 cm long and lined with a mucous membrane that allows food to pass through easily. Its outer wall contains longitudinal and circular muscles that enable a process known as peristalsis to occur, in which waves of contractions pass down the tube.

*Successive muscular contractions (peristalsis) propel the bolus along the oesophagus and into the stomach.*

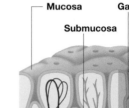

**Circular muscles**
Contract, propelling bolus down

**Bolus**

**Longitudinal muscles**
Contract, reducing space in front of bolus

**Gastro-oesophageal sphincter**

**Pyloric sphincter**

**Relaxed muscles**

**Gastro-oesophageal sphincter**
Opens to allow food into the stomach

### PERISTALSIS
The presence of a bolus of food automatically triggers peristalsis, and the bolus is carried progressively towards the stomach by the contractions.

The contents of the stomach are normally prevented from returning upwards by the muscular walls of the oesophagus. This effectively forms a sphincter at the lower end, although its structure is not noticeably different from the rest of the oesophageal wall.

## Stomach

The stomach is a muscular bag situated in the upper part of the abdomen. It consists of four regions: the cardia is the part that immediately adjoins the oesophagus; the fundus is the upper, dome-shaped part; the corpus, or body, is the main central part; and the antrum is the lower third. At its lower end, the stomach is separated from the small intestine by the pyloric sphincter. This opens at intervals to allow some of the contents through to the intestine.

### MUSCULAR WALL
The function of the stomach is to act as a reservoir for food and to begin the process of digesting proteins and fats. The walls are made up of muscles that run up and down, transversely and

diagonally across. Rhythmical contractions of these muscles mix the food with gastric juices to form a thick, creamy, acid fluid known as chyme. On average, the stomach contains 1–1.5 litres of chyme, but it can expand to hold much more.

When full, the stomach is shaped like a boxing glove, about 25–30 cm long and with a diameter of 10–12 cm at its widest point. When empty, its walls contract, developing internal folds, or rugae, of the lining mucosa. In this state, it is shaped more like a letter 'J'.

*The wall of the stomach is made up of a muscular layer, a layer of connective submucosa and a lining of mucosa containing millions of gastric pits.*

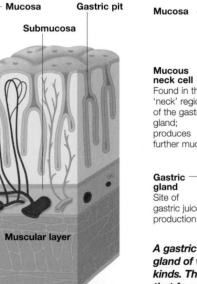

**Mucosa**

**Gastric pit**

**Submucosa**

**Muscular layer**

**Mucosa**

**Mucous neck cell**
Found in the 'neck' region of the gastric gland; produces further mucus

**Gastric gland**
Site of gastric juice production

*A gastric pit leads into a gastric gland of which there are three kinds. These secrete chemicals that form the gastric juices.*

## Digestive juices

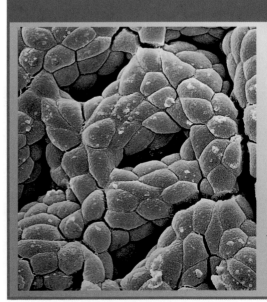

*A false-colour micrograph reveals the complex structure of the stomach lining. The cells on the surface (green) secrete mucus; between them are the deeper 'pits' containing the gastric glands.*

Embedded in the wall of the stomach are glands which contain a variety of secretory cells that together produce the gastric juices. Hydrochloric acid is produced by parietal cells, which are found mostly in the body and fundus of the stomach. Hydrochloric acid enables the gastric enzyme pepsin to work, and helps to sterilize the food by killing most types of bacteria and other micro-organisms.

Production of hydrochloric acid is stimulated by the hormone gastrin, which is secreted by glands in the antrum, the lower part of the stomach. Gastrin is then absorbed into the body of the stomach and

carried to parietal cells in the blood.
Gastric juices contain three enzymes:
- Renin: coagulates milk and is more important in infants than in adults
- Pepsin: begins the digestion of proteins by splitting them into short chain molecules known as peptides
- Gastric lipase: starts to convert fats to fatty acids and glycerol.

Another secretion, known as 'intrinsic factor', enables the body to absorb vitamin $B_{12}$, a substance vital for the healthy function of most body tissue.

The contents of the stomach are acidic enough to dissolve a razor blade. To prevent the stomach wall from being digested, it is protected by a layer of alkaline mucus. In addition, the cells of the stomach lining are replaced continuously at the rate of half a million each minute, so that the stomach effectively has a new lining every three days.

# How food is absorbed

Digestion begins in the mouth and stomach, but it is in the small intestine that most of the digestive processes take place. This part of the digestive tract is divided into three sections: the duodenum, jejunum and ileum.

The total length of the small intestine is 6.5 m. The duodenum is about 25 cm long, and it is here that material from the stomach is mixed with digestive juices. The jejunum is about 2.5 m long and merges with the ileum, which makes up the rest of the small intestine. The division between them is gradual, but the jejunum has a thicker wall and a larger diameter (about 3.8 cm).

Food moves along the bowel by peristalsis (muscular contraction) and the process of digestion continues throughout the small intestine. The main function of the jejunum and ileum is to absorb the products of digestion into the body.

### DIGESTIVE JUICES
The digestive juices of the duodenum contain the alkali sodium bicarbonate, which neutralizes the acid produced in the stomach and provides an alkaline environment that allows the intestinal enzymes to work.

The digestive juices of the duodenum have two sources. Firstly, the glands in the duodenal wall produce the enzymes maltase, sucrase, enterokinase and erepsin.

The second source is the pancreas, which in addition to its endocrine function, produces three digestive enzymes: lipase, amylase and trypsinogen. Together, these enzymes continue the digestion of proteins, sugars and fats.

### DIGESTION OF PROTEINS, FATS AND CARBOHYDRATES
Some proteins are broken down into peptides (small chains of amino acids, the building blocks of protein) in the stomach. In the small intestine, enterokinase activates pancreatic trypsin. This continues the process of protein digestion by breaking down both proteins and peptides into amino acids. Duodenal erepsin converts peptides into amino acids.

The digestion of fats is aided by salts present in the greenish mixture called bile, produced by the liver and stored in the gall bladder. Bile enters the duodenum via the bile duct. Bile salts emulsify the fats, producing small globules that present a greater surface area to the enzyme lipase, which converts fats into fatty acids and glycerol.

Any starch not already acted on by the ptyalin in saliva is now converted into the sugar maltose by the pancreatic enzyme amylase. Maltase continues the process, breaking down maltose into glucose. Sucrase converts sucrose into glucose and fructose.

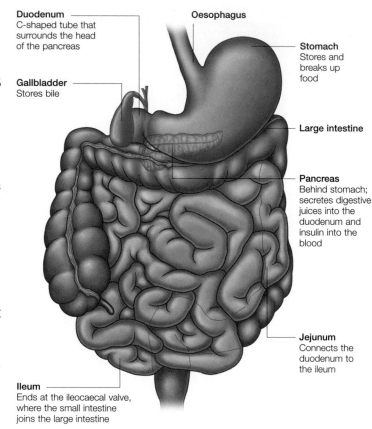

**Duodenum**
C-shaped tube that surrounds the head of the pancreas

**Oesophagus**

**Gallbladder**
Stores bile

**Stomach**
Stores and breaks up food

**Large intestine**

**Pancreas**
Behind stomach; secretes digestive juices into the duodenum and insulin into the blood

**Jejunum**
Connects the duodenum to the ileum

**Ileum**
Ends at the ileocaecal valve, where the small intestine joins the large intestine

*The small intestine starts with the duodenum, which receives bile from the gall bladder and secretions from the pancreas. The intestine then continues through the jejunum and on to the ileum.*

## How nutrients are absorbed

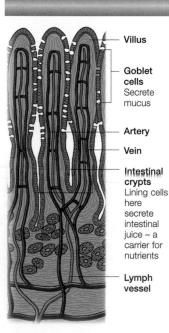

**Villus**

**Goblet cells**
Secrete mucus

**Artery**

**Vein**

**Intestinal crypts**
Lining cells here secrete intestinal juice – a carrier for nutrients

**Lymph vessel**

The lining of the jejunum and ileum is the main absorptive surface for the products of digestion. The total volume of fluid that is absorbed by the intestines every day amounts to about 9 litres. About 7.5 litres of this is absorbed by the small intestine.

The inner surfaces of the jejunum and ileum are covered with small finger-like projections called villi, which protrude about 1 mm into the centre of the intestinal tube. The purpose of these specially adapted structures is to greatly increase the surface area over which

*A section through the mucosa that lines the wall of the small intestine reveals the structure of the villi.*

absorption can take place.

The walls of each villus are formed by long epithelial cells. Inside each villus is a network of small capillaries and a single lacteal – a blind-ending tube connected to the body's lymphatic system.

The epithelial cells absorb the products of digestion together with litres of water and pass the sugars and amino acids into the blood stream. Fatty acids and glycerol are converted by the epithelial cells back into fats, which form a fine whitish emulsion that passes directly into the lacteals.

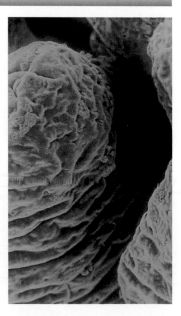

*The surface area of the small intestine is increased by villi. In this micrograph, food particles are coloured green.*

# The liver's role in digestion

Although not actually a part of the digestive tract, the liver is vital for the digestion of food, along with the pancreas and gall bladder. The liver is the body's chemical unit for the processing of the products of digestion.

The products of digestion are processed by the liver. Chemical processing takes place in the liver cells, or hepatocytes, which line blood-filled spaces, or sinusoids, inside the liver.

These cells carry out the liver's several important functions, including a regulatory role in the maintenance of glucose (sugar) in the blood.

After eating, the blood contains a large amount of glucose. Blood pumped from the intestine arrives in the liver through the hepatic portal vein, and cells within the liver remove excess glucose from the blood and store it in the form of glycogen. As glucose is used elsewhere in the body, and the blood sugar level falls, the liver gradually reconverts glycogen back into glucose.

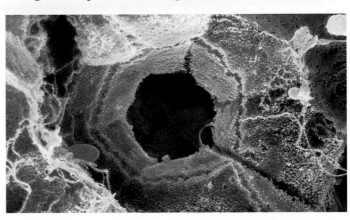

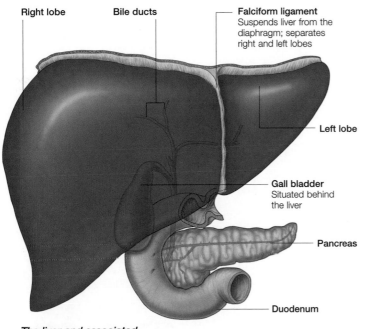

The liver and associated structures are situated in the right of the abdominal cavity.

Right lobe

Bile ducts

Falciform ligament
Suspends liver from the diaphragm; separates right and left lobes

Left lobe

Gall bladder
Situated behind the liver

Pancreas

Duodenum

*This false-colour electron micrograph shows one of the functional units within the liver. Hepatic cells (brown) surround sinusoid channels through which blood cells (red, at centre) flow to a central vein.*

## AMINO ACIDS

The amino acids produced during digestion cannot be stored in the body. Some are converted immediately into proteins, a process that occurs in most body cells, but those that are not required are broken down in the liver by a process called deamination. The nitrogen they contain is used to make ammonia. This is immediately converted into urea and transported in the blood to the kidneys to be excreted.

## LIVER FUNCTION

The liver also manufactures blood proteins, such as fibrinogen, and stores iron for use in the manufacture of the red blood cell pigment haemoglobin. It also breaks down the haemoglobin of worn-out red blood cells, producing a substance called bile. This is removed via the bile canaliculi and the bile duct and then stored in the gall bladder.

The liver is very versatile: if certain types of food material are in short supply, the liver can convert certain kinds of food into others. Carbohydrates can be converted into fats, such as cholesterol, for storage, and some amino acids may be converted into carbohydrates or fats.

The liver also deals with toxins ingested by the body (such as alcohol), breaking them down to render them less harmful.

## How gallstones form

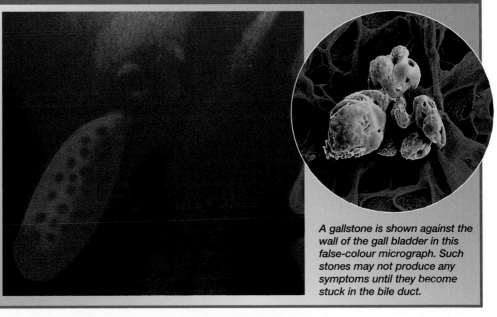

Gallstones are solid masses that form in the gall bladder and bile duct. Single stones may be very small or they can grow to the size of a hen's egg.

Fifteen per cent of gallstones are formed by the crystallization of bile pigment salts. This is often associated with the excessive destruction of red blood cells.

Eighty per cent of gallstones are composed of cholesterol. An excess of cholesterol in the blood compared to the amount of bile available to suspend it leads to the excess cholesterol crystallizing in the gall bladder.

Gallstones are found in about 30 per cent of the adult population in Europe, and they are more common in females.

*A gallstone is visible as the elongated, pitted mass on this coloured X-ray. It has developed because of an upset in the chemical composition of bile.*

*A gallstone is shown against the wall of the gall bladder in this false-colour micrograph. Such stones may not produce any symptoms until they become stuck in the bile duct.*

# How the body uses carbohydrates

Carbohydrates, also known as saccharides, are used in the body as a fuel source, an energy store and as building blocks for more complex molecules.

Carbohydrates are made entirely from carbon, hydrogen and oxygen atoms. They are classified, according to their size, into three main groups: monosaccharides, disaccharides and polysaccharides.

### MONOSACCHARIDES

The most common monosaccharides are fructose, galactose and glucose. Of these, glucose is the most important because the body's cells are unable to metabolize directly any other saccharides; they must first be converted into glucose before they can be broken down to release energy. Thus the level of free glucose in the blood is very important.

## Monosaccharides

### Glucose

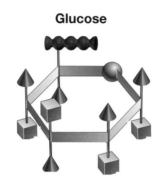

*Glucose is the most important carbohydrate in the body. Free glucose is not found in many foods; it is obtained by breaking down complex saccharides.*

### Galactose

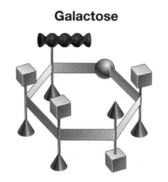

*Although galactose has a similar chemical structure to glucose, cells cannot metabolize galactose, so it is converted into glucose in the liver.*

### Fructose

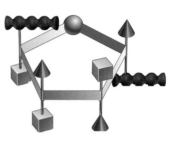

*Fructose is found in sweet fruits and fruit juices. When fructose is chemically joined to glucose, the disaccharide sucrose (or 'table sugar') is produced.*

## Disaccharides – ingestible sugars

Disaccharides consist of two monosaccharide molecules joined together. For example, lactose, a disaccharide found in milk, consists of a glucose and a galactose molecule joined together. Lactose is the only disaccharide made by the body. The other two common disaccharides are sucrose ('table sugar') and maltose ('malt sugar').

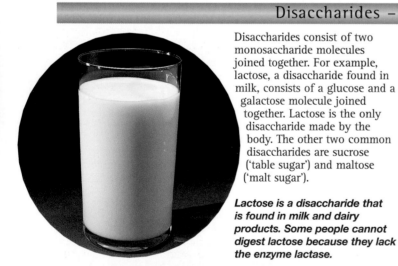

*Lactose is a disaccharide that is found in milk and dairy products. Some people cannot digest lactose because they lack the enzyme lactase.*

### Lactose

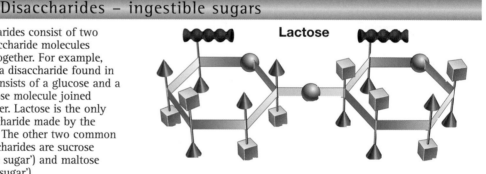

Saccharides are also important components of many complex molecules including cartilage and bone. They are also present in small quantities within cell membranes.

*Disaccharides are made up of two monosaccharides joined together. For example, lactose is made by the joining of a molecule of glucose to a molecule of galactose.*

## Polysaccharides – energy stores

Polysaccharides are long branched chains of monosaccharides joined together. Their large size makes them relatively insoluble in water and also means that they remain trapped inside the cell. This makes them ideal energy stores.

Two polysaccharides, starch and glycogen, are especially important. Both are made of long chains of glucose molecules:

■ Starch is the major long-term store of carbohydrates for plants and so is an important part of the human diet

■ Glycogen, in contrast, is synthesized and used as a carbohydrate store by animals. It is mainly found in skeletal muscle and liver cells. When blood glucose levels fall, glycogen is rapidly converted into glucose.

*Potatoes contain a large quantity of starch, a polysaccharide made by a number of glucose molecules joining together.*

# How the body uses lipids

Lipids are a large group of organic molecules (i.e. they contain carbon) that are insoluble in water, but are soluble in alcohol. There are three main groups of lipids: triglycerides, phospholipids and steroids.

## Triglycerides – long-term energy stores

Triglycerides are made up of one glycerol molecule (an alcohol) attached to three long chains of fatty acids. The glycerol backbone is the same in all triglycerides, but the composition of the fatty acid chains varies, creating a large number of different triglycerides.

Fatty acids yield a large amount of energy when they are metabolized inside the cell. This, together with the fact that they are insoluble in water, makes them an excellent energy store. Indeed, a large proportion of the body's long-term energy requirements are catered for by fatty acids.

### SATURATED AND UNSATURATED FATS

The carbon atoms of saturated fats have a full complement of hydrogen atoms attached (hence they are said to be 'saturated') and are common in animal fats. In contrast, the carbon atoms in unsaturated fats can bind to additional hydrogen atoms. Exactly how many hydrogen atoms they can bind to determines whether they are mono- or polyunsaturated fats.

*Olive oil is rich in monounsaturated fats. In contrast, sunflower oil contains mainly polyunsaturated fats.*

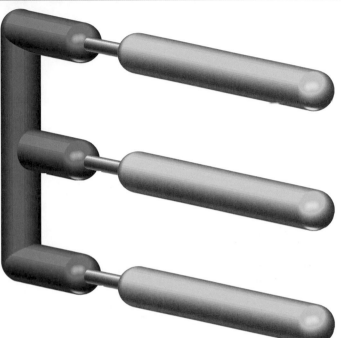

*Triglycerides are made from a glycerol molecule (green) attached to three fatty acid chains (yellow).*

## Phospholipids – building blocks of cell membranes

**Phospholipid** — **Cell membrane** —

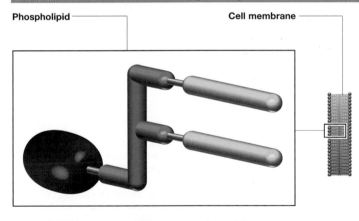

*Phospholipids are made up of a phosphorus-containing head (red), a glycerol backbone (green) and two fatty acid chains (yellow).*

Phospholipids are similar to triglycerides, in that they have a glycerol backbone. However, unlike triglycerides, phospholipids have only two fatty acid chains; instead of a third chain, they have a phosphorus-containing head.

The 'tail' of a phospholipid (made up of the two fatty acid chains) has no electrical charge and so does not mix with water (water is electrically charged), whereas the phosphorus-containing 'head' attracts water because it is electrically charged.

It is this property that makes phospholipids ideal building blocks for the cell membrane. Cell membranes are made of two layers of phospholipid molecules; the 'water-hating' (hydrophobic) tails point towards each other, whereas the 'water-loving' (hydrophilic) heads point towards water – which is present both inside and outside the cell.

## Steroids

Steroids have a very different structure from both triglycerides and phospholipids, though they are classified as lipids since they are fat soluble. Probably the most important steroid in the human body is cholesterol as it is the precursor for many of the steroid hormones which are essential for human development and long-term health. Other steroids, for example the sex hormones, are present in very small amounts, but are still essential.

*Anabolic steroids are derivatives of the sex hormone testosterone. One of their physiological effects is to increase muscle mass.*

## Other lipid-based molecules

Lipids are also major components of three other important groups of molecules.

### Fat-soluble vitamins

Fat-soluble vitamins include vitamins A, D, E and K. Since these vitamins can only be absorbed after they have bound to ingested lipids, anything which interferes with fat absorption (such as cystic fibrosis) also prevents fat-soluble vitamins from being absorbed.

### Eicosanoids

These include prostaglandins and leukotrienes, which are both involved in inflammation, and thromboxanes, which cause blood vessels to constrict.

### Lipoproteins

These chemicals transport fatty acids and cholesterol in the bloodstream. The two main groups are high-density lipoproteins (HDL) and low-density lipoproteins (LDL).

# How proteins work

Proteins are vital to the structure, growth and metabolism of humans and all living organisms. Their large molecules are built up from smaller units – amino acids – and often have very complex structures.

Proteins of various kinds play important roles in the human body. Structural proteins include collagen in connective tissue; keratin in skin; actin and myosin in muscles; and tubulin in cells. Proteins in cell membranes act as carriers, transporting chemicals in to and out of cells.

Other proteins include enzymes, which promote chemical reactions within cells, essential hormones and antibodies which play an important role in defence against disease. Blood proteins include haemoglobin, albumin and a series of proteins needed to ensure that the blood clots properly when injury occurs.

## AMINO ACID BUILDING BLOCKS

Like all organic chemicals, protein molecules are made up largely of carbon, hydrogen and oxygen atoms. However, proteins also contain nitrogen, and, in many cases, sulphur as well.

The basic units of protein molecules are amino acids. There are only 20 types of amino acids, but they can be joined together in an enormous number of different combinations. Some amino acids can be synthesized in the body; others have to be obtained from proteins in food. In order to maintain health, a human must eat at least 30 grams of protein each day.

An amino acid molecule consists of a core chain of

*This model of collagen shows individual molecules as spheres. Collagen is found in connective tissues such as bone and skin.*

carbon atoms. There are two different chemical groups at the ends of the molecule: at one end an amino group; at the other end a carboxylic acid group. The amino group of one amino acid can bond chemically with the carboxylic acid group of an adjacent amino acid, releasing a molecule of water in the process – this facilitates the formation of long chains of amino acids.

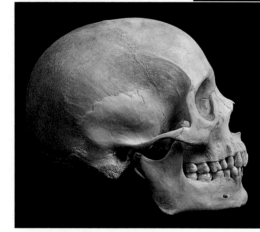

The structure of an amino acid makes it soluble in water and renders it amphoteric (it can act as either an acid or an alkali in solution). This allows it to resist changes in acidity and alkalinity, and to act as a buffer (a

*The skull – like all bones – derives its strength from a combination of calcium and collagen (protein).*

regulator of pH), playing an important role in homeostasis – the maintenance of a constant internal environment.

The template for the manufacture of proteins is DNA. The cell synthesizes amino acid

chains (the basis of proteins) on ribosomes (structures in the cell) using a DNA related molecule – this is called RNA.

## PRIMARY STRUCTURE

The sequence of amino acids assembled on the ribosome gives the protein its primary structure, like the pattern of beads on a string. This sequence is dictated by the DNA sequence, and forms the 'backbone' of the protein molecule.

## Protein denaturation

Under normal circumstances, proteins are relatively stable. Their activity is dependent on their 3-D structure and the bonds holding the molecule together. However, these bonds are sensitive to factors such as acidity and heat.

When proteins lose their 3-D shape, they are said to be denatured. Often this can be reversed and proteins will regain their normal shape when conditions are restored. However, if the change in pH or temperature is extreme, they become irreversibly denatured.

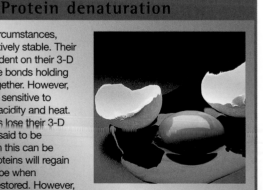

*The white of an egg is made primarily from albumin. When cooked, it changes from clear to opaque white because the protein has denatured.*

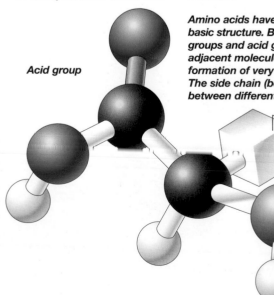

*Amino acids have a common basic structure. Binding of amino groups and acid groups between adjacent molecules allows the formation of very long chains. The side chain (box) varies between different amino acids.*

Acid group

Variable region

Amino group

# How proteins fold

The sequence of amino acids in a protein determines its final three-dimensional shape. The resulting shapes and folds will confer a protein's particular properties.

**α-helix**  **β-helix**

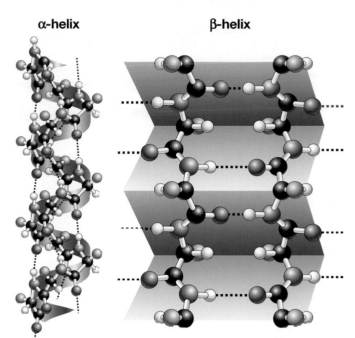

## SECONDARY STRUCTURE

When a long polypeptide chain (string of amino acids) is formed, it rarely exists as a simple long chain, but tends to arrange itself in a complex shape or pattern. This is a result of a type of chemical bond called a hydrogen bond, which is relatively weak but strong enough to pull the chain into a particular shape. Hydrogen atoms form these bonds with certain other atoms in the structure and two distinct shapes tend to be created.

The most common pattern is an α-helix, a right-handed spiral. This shape is the result of

*Depending on their sequence of amino acids, proteins can form either long helical shapes (α-helix,) or pleated sheets (β-sheet).*

hydrogen bonds between approximately every fourth amino acid. The other is the ß-pleated sheet, a flat structure in which hydrogen bonds form between two polypeptide chains running parallel to each other, similar to an accordion. In some proteins both kinds of secondary structure can be seen in different places along the length of the chain.

## Tertiary and quaternary structures

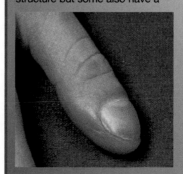

**Iron atom**

A protein with a very long polypeptide chain tends to have an additional tertiary structure superimposed on the secondary structure. This occurs when spirals, sheets and other bends in the molecule fold in on each other, producing a ball-like or globular shape. The structure is maintained by attractive forces resulting from the proximity of chemical groups to each other, especially those in amino acids that contain sulphur atoms.

Finally, the protein may acquire a quaternary structure

*Haemoglobin, pictured, forms a complicated globular shape. This shape allows the binding of iron atoms, which confer its oxygen-binding properties.*

in which two or more polypeptide chains that already have a complex tertiary structure become bonded to one another to form an even more complicated molecule. This may be further enhanced by the binding of non-protein groups, for example an iron atom, in the blood protein haemoglobin. This has a quaternary structure formed from four globular polypeptide chains, each of which incorporates an iron-containing 'haem' group.

The overall configuration of a protein with a tertiary or quaternary structure is very specific to the protein and is determined by its primary structure; that is, the sequence of amino acids.

## Fibrous and globular proteins

Proteins are classified in two groups according to their general shape. Fibrous or structural proteins resemble the strands of a rope. They are stable and provide the body's tissue with strength and support. Most fibrous proteins have a secondary structure but some also have a

quaternary structure. Collagen, found in all connective tissues, is a triple helix of three polypeptide chains. Other fibrous proteins include keratin, elastin and actin.

Globular, or functional, proteins are more chemically active and play roles in the body's chemical processes. They are soluble in water and have spherical shapes with at least a tertiary structure. Enzymes are globular proteins.

*Fingernails and animal horn consist of keratin. This protein provides strength and stability.*

*Globular proteins (X-shaped structure, right) are found in the outer membranes of cells. They control cellular entry and exit of chemicals.*

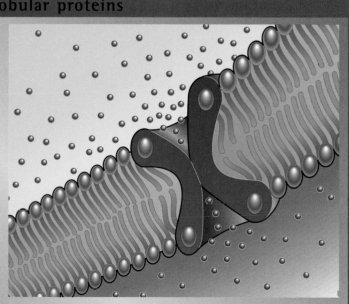

# The role of fat

Fat has a number of important roles in the body,
including the provision of energy. However, an excess of fat can
lead to problems such as obesity and heart disease.

Fat is a necessary component of a healthy diet and constitutes the body's greatest source of stored energy. Fat also protects the organs, strengthens the joints, aids hormone production, and helps absorption of fat-soluble vitamins.

## STORING FAT

Fat (usually in the form of triglycerides) is derived from food and stored in adipose tissue

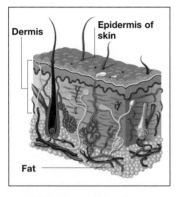

*Dermis* · *Epidermis of skin*

*Fat*

throughout the body. Some fat is stored just above the kidneys, but most is located just beneath the dermis of the skin, in the subcutaneous layer, which has a rich supply of blood vessels.

The distribution of this fat is influenced by gender:
■ Men tend to store fat around the chest, abdomen and buttocks (producing an apple-like shape)
■ Women tend to carry fat on the breasts, hips, waist and buttocks (creating a pear-like appearance).

The difference in distribution is due to the sex hormones oestrogen and testosterone.

## TYPES OF FAT

There are two types of body fat:
■ White fat – important for

*Most of the body's fat is stored in adipose tissue beneath the dermis of the skin. When no carbohydrates are available, this fat is broken down for energy.*

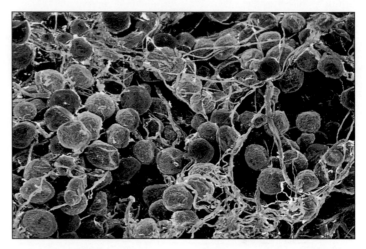

energy metabolism, insulation and also forms a protective layer for the skeleton and organs
■ Brown fat – mostly found in newborns, this is important in the production of heat.

Fat tissue is made up of fat cells known as adipocytes:
■ White fat cells are large cells

*Fat that is not used up by metabolic processes is stored in fat cells (shown in brown and yellow). These rounded cells are supported by connective tissue.*

with one large fat droplet
■ Brown fat cells are smaller, with many small fat droplets.

## The digestion and storage of fat

In order for any food component to be used by the body, it must first be absorbed into the body cells. Fat molecules are too large to pass directly across cell membranes, so fats must first be broken down into their component parts.

## ABSORBING FAT

Fats are absorbed as follows:
■ Food containing fat (mostly in the form of triglycerides) passes into the stomach and intestines
■ Bile salts produced by the liver mix with the large fat droplets in a process called emulsification. The bile breaks up the large fat droplets into several smaller droplets known as micelles. This increases the surface area of the fat droplets and speeds up their digestion
■ Meanwhile, the pancreas secretes enzymes known as lipases that attack the surface of each micelle, breaking down the fats into their component parts: glycerol and fatty acids. These can then be absorbed into the cells lining the intestine
■ Once absorbed into the intestinal cells, the fat components are reassembled into microparticles known as

chylomicrons. These have a protein coating to make the fat dissolve more easily in water
■ As the chylomicrons are too large to pass directly through capillary walls into the bloodstream, they pass first into the lymphatic system
■ The lymphatic system eventually drains into the veins

and the chylomicrons pass into the bloodstream.

## STORING FAT

Once in the bloodstream, chylomicrons last only a few minutes before they are broken down again. Enzymes known as lipoprotein lipases (found in the walls of blood vessels that

supply fat tissue, muscle tissue and heart muscle) break the fats down into fatty acids.

The activity of these enzymes depends upon the body's levels of insulin (a hormone produced by the pancreas):
■ If insulin is high, the lipases will be highly active and fat will be broken down quite rapidly
■ If levels of insulin are low, the lipases will be inactive.

The resulting fatty acids can then be absorbed from the blood into fat cells, muscle cells and liver cells, where they are made into fat molecules once more and stored as fat droplets. As the body stores more fat, the number of fat cells remains the same, but the size of each fat cell gets bigger.

## ABSORBING MOLECULES

It is also possible for fat cells to absorb other food molecules, such as glucose and amino acids, (derived from protein) and to convert them into fat for storage.

*Fat from food must be absorbed into the body's cells to release energy. It moves through the intestine and lymphatic system before reaching the blood.*

# Converting fat into energy

The body is able to produce energy from fats by a process called lipolysis. This involves the break-down of fats by enzymes into glycerol and fatty acids.

The body's prime source of energy is glucose, which is usually obtained by the breakdown of carbohydrates in the diet.

However, during stamina-building exercise such as walking or cycling, the body relies on fat as a rich reserve of stored energy. Fatty acids are also used by the body for energy whenever glucose (in the form of carbohydrates) is not available.

### ENERGY FROM FAT
Energy is derived from fat by the process of lipolysis (the breakdown of fats into glycerol and fatty acids). This process is activated by enzymes (lipases) in the fat cell, which are in turn controlled by various hormones, such as glucagon and adrenaline.

The resulting fatty acids are then released into the blood and are carried in the bloodstream to the liver. Once in the liver, the glycerol and fatty acids can be broken down further or converted into glucose by a multi-step process known as gluconeogenesis.

*Long-distance swimming and other forms of endurance training utilize the body's fat stores as the most efficient form of muscle fuel.*

## Excess body fat

Most nutritionists recommend a diet that includes around 35 per cent fat. This should be unsaturated, such as olive oil, rather than saturated, such as fats derived from meat.

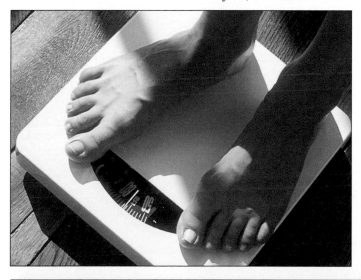

If a person consumes more fat than they metabolize, it is stored in fat reserves, causing the person to gain weight.

Obesity is defined by the level of body fat; men are classified as obese at more than 25 per cent body fat and women 32 per cent. Although fat plays a vital role, excess fat is linked to a number of health problems.

### HIGH BLOOD PRESSURE
Obese people tend to have high cholesterol levels, making them more prone to atherosclerosis (in which fatty plaque deposits cause a narrowing of the arteries). This becomes life-threatening when blood vessels become so narrow that vital organs are deprived of blood.

In addition, the narrowing of blood vessels forces the heart to work harder, causing blood pressure to rise. High blood pressure carries many serious

*People become obese if their body fat approaches one-third of their total weight. This can cause severe health problems, such as diabetes and heart attacks.*

health risks including heart attack, kidney failure and stroke.

### DIABETES
Obesity increases the risk of diabetes by disrupting the delicate balance between blood sugar, body fat and insulin.

This is because excess blood sugar is stored in the liver and other vital organs. When these organs are 'full', the excess blood sugar is converted to fat. As the fat cells themselves become full, they take in less blood sugar.

In some people the pancreas produces more and more insulin to regulate this excess sugar, which the body cannot use, and as a result the whole system becomes overwhelmed.

This poor regulation of blood sugar results in diabetes, a disease associated with long-term consequences including heart disease, kidney failure and blindness.

## Heat production

When babies are first born, their bodies do not contain much fat to help insulate them and retain body heat. While they do have white fat cells, there is hardly any fat stored in them.

Newborn babies produce heat by breaking down fat molecules into fatty acids within brown cells (heat-producing cells found mainly around the central organs):
■ Instead of the fatty acids leaving the brown fat cells (as is the case with white fat cells), they remain within them
■ They are broken down further

in the mitochondria (the part of the cell that produces energy)
■ This releases energy in the form of heat. (The same process occurs in hibernating animals that have more brown fat reserves than humans).

Once the baby starts to eat more, layers of white fat develop and the brown fat disappears.

*Newborn babies do not have enough stored fat to retain body heat effectively. Instead they have special heat-producing brown fat cells.*

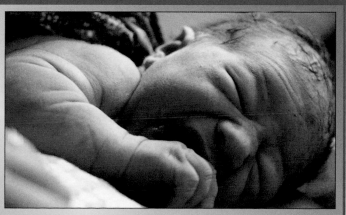

# How the body uses vitamins

The body requires all of the thirteen vitamins for growth, maintenance and repair. Long-term deficiencies, often caused by intestinal disorders or alcoholism, can lead to serious disease.

Vitamins are organic (carbon-containing) compounds that are found only in living organisms (plant or animal). They are required in tiny amounts by the body for it to function effectively.

Vitamins act as catalysts: they combine with proteins to create enzymes, which in turn give rise to important chemical reactions throughout the body. Without vitamins, many of these reactions would slow down or stop altogether.

### VITAMIN SOURCES
The term 'vitamin' was first used by the chemist Casimir Funk in 1912, who noted that certain diseases appeared to be linked to a lack of specific substances in the diet.

Vitamins were defined as substances absolutely necessary for life which cannot be produced by the body. Later research showed that the exception to this is vitamin D, which can be synthesized by the skin when exposed to sunlight and niacin ($B_3$), which can be synthesized in tiny amounts by the liver.

The two main sources of vitamins are food and drink.

### VITAMIN SUPPLEMENTS
A well-balanced diet should provide all the vitamins that the body requires. However, certain people, such as those on restricted diets, pregnant or breast-feeding women or those with intestinal disorders, may require vitamin supplements to bolster their metabolism.

Vitamin supplements should not be seen as a substitute for a healthy diet; nutritionists believe the naturally occurring balance of micronutrients within food may be of great importance.

The 13 vitamins can be

divided into two main groups:
- Fat-soluble – vitamins A, D, E and K
- Water-soluble – Vitamins C and B complex.

*A balanced diet provides a perfect mix of water and fat-soluble vitamins in a form the body can easily use. All 13 vitamins are essential for life.*

## Fat-soluble vitamins

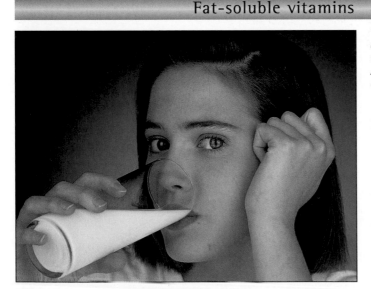

The four fat-soluble vitamins are mainly ingested in meat and dairy products. They can be stored in the body, so do not have to be consumed every day.

### VITAMIN A
Vitamin A is stored mainly in the liver. It is vital for the formation and health of the skin, mucous membranes, bones and teeth, and for vision and reproduction. Vitamin A can be obtained from liver, eggs, cream or butter, or derived from beta-carotene (a pigment that occurs in leafy green vegetables and in orange fruits and vegetables).

### VITAMIN D
Vitamin D is necessary for the formation of healthy bone and

*The calcium found in milk can only be retained by the body in the presence of vitamin D. A deficiency of this vitamin can cause rickets.*

for retention of calcium and phosphorus in the body. It is found in eggs, liver and fish oil, and is also made by the body during interaction with sunlight.

### VITAMIN E
Vitamin E is found in vegetable oils, wheat germ, liver and green, leafy vegetables, and it is stored mainly in body fat. It is an antioxidant (a substance that is able to neutralize certain harmful molecules) and plays a role in the formation of red blood cells and muscle.

### VITAMIN K
Vitamin K is mainly necessary for blood coagulation, by helping to form prothrombin (an enzyme required during blood clotting). Alfalfa and liver are both rich sources of vitamin K, as are leafy green vegetables, eggs and soybean oil.

## Vitamin C

Vitamin C, otherwise known as ascorbate, is a water-soluble vitamin that is important in the formation and maintenance of collagen. This is a connective tissue used in the formation of bones, cartilage, muscle and blood vessels. Vitamin C also enhances the absorption of iron from vegetables and plays a role in metabolizing food.

Sources of vitamin C include most fruits (particularly citrus), green peppers, tomatoes, broccoli, potatoes and cabbage. Interestingly, all other meat-eating mammals are able to synthesize vitamin C within their bodies; humans are the only ones to rely entirely on outside sources for vitamin C.

Research has shown that vitamin C acts as an antioxidant and protects the body's cells and tissues against the harmful effects of free radicals (damaging molecules produced in metabolic reactions and by certain factors, such as disease and UV radiation).

# Water-soluble vitamins

The body is largely unable to store water-soluble vitamins and consequently they should be consumed every day.

### THE B VITAMINS

The large group of B vitamins includes:

■ Thiamine ($B_1$) – this is essential for the metabolism of carbohydrates and the proper functioning of the nervous system. Whole grain cereals, bread, red meat, eggs and brown rice are all good sources

■ Riboflavin ($B_2$) – this is required to complete certain metabolic reactions. It is also vital for healthy skin, mucous membranes, cornea and nerve sheaths. Riboflavin is found in

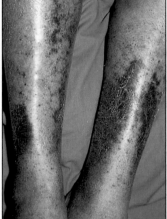

*Pregnant women are advised to take folic acid supplements. This B vitamin is essential for the healthy brain and nerve development of the fetus.*

meat, dairy products, whole grain products and peas

■ Niacin ($B_3$) – essential for the metabolism of food and maintaining healthy skin, nerves and gastrointestinal tract. It is found in protein-rich foods such as meat, fish, brewer's yeast, milk, eggs, legumes (pod vegetables), potatoes and peanuts

■ Pyridoxine ($B_6$) – this is vital to the metabolism of amino acids, glucose and fatty acids and for the production of red blood cells. Pyridoxine is found in many foods, so a deficiency is rare, except in alcoholics. It is present in many foods, including liver, brown rice, fish, and whole grain cereals

■ Cyanocobalamin ($B_{12}$) – this is a compound that functions in all cells, most significantly in the intestines, nervous system and bone marrow. It is used in the manufacture of healthy blood cells and is essential for

*A severe vitamin C deficiency can result in scurvy. This disease causes subcutaneous bleeding, swollen and bleeding gums and if untreated, ultimately death.*

maintaining nerve sheaths and synthesizing nucleic acids (the building blocks of DNA). Rich sources include liver, meat, eggs, and milk

■ Folic acid – this interacts with $B_{12}$ to allow the synthesis of nucleic acids and is used in the formation of red blood cells. It is essential for brain and nerve development in the fetus. Folic acid is found in many foods,

notably yeast, liver and green vegetables

■ Pantothenic acid and biotin – these B vitamins are produced by bacteria in the intestines and are important in a number of metabolic reactions. Pantothenic acid is found in abundance in meats, legumes and whole grain cereals, and biotin is found in beef liver, eggs, brewer's yeast, peanuts and mushrooms.

## Vitamin deficiencies

| Vitamin | Result of deficiency | People at risk |
|---|---|---|
| Vitamin A | Dry skin, reduced mucus secretion, poor night vision | Those with cystic fibrosis or liver disease; alcoholics |
| Vitamin $B_1$ (thiamine) | Beriberi disease, Wernicke-Korsakoff's syndrome | Alcoholics |
| Vitamin $B_2$ (riboflavin) | Skin disorders, anaemia, light sensitivity, cracked lips, sore tongue | Those on poor diets |
| Vitamin $B_3$ (niacin) | Pellagra (sore mouth and skin, diarrhoea, dementia) | Alcoholics and transients |
| Vitamin $B_6$ (pyridoxine) | Skin disorders, depression, poor co-ordination, insomnia | Alcoholics; women on birth control pills |
| Vitamin $B_{12}$ (cyanocobalamin) | Pernicious anaemia, brain disorders, mouth irritation | Strict vegetarians; elderly people (absorption decreases with age) |
| Vitamin $B_9$ (folic acid) | Folate-deficient anaemia (gastro-intestinal problems, ulcers) | Alcoholics; pregnant women |
| Vitamin C | Scurvy (skin and tissue haemorrhages, stiff limbs) | Elderly people on restricted diets; babies drinking only cows' milk |
| Vitamin D | Rickets (due to the body's subsequent inability to absorb calcium) | Babies; elderly people with low sunlight exposure |
| Vitamin E | None known | None known |
| Vitamin K | Blood clotting disorders; can affect baby during pregnancy | People with jaundice, liver cirrhosis; those on long-term antibiotics |

## Alcoholism

Three types of malnutrition affect alcoholics:

■ Primary malnutrition due to a decreased nutrient intake

■ Secondary malnutrition caused by digestion impairment and malabsorption of nutrients

■ Tertiary malnutrition due to an inability to convert nutrients.

In addition, alcohol itself inhibits fat absorption and with it, all fat-soluble vitamins.

**Resulting deficiencies**

Alcoholics typically become severely deficient in:

■ Vitamin A – even moderate alcoholic disease can cause a severe vitamin A deficiency

■ Vitamin B – alcoholics become deficient in all of the B vitamins, but particularly $B_1$ (thiamine), leading to Wernicke-Korsakoff's syndrome (causing disorientation, lack of memory and a tendency to invent material to fill memory blanks)

■ Vitamin $B_9$ (folic acid) – the most common deficiency, this causes anaemia and adversely alters the small intestine.

# How the body uses minerals

Minerals are inorganic elements from the earth and make up five per cent of the total body weight. Minerals are essential to the body's function, and are required in small amounts only.

Although vitamins are essential to the functioning of the body, they cannot be assimilated without minerals. Minerals are inorganic elements, which make up 4-5 per cent of the total body weight. They are vital to mental and physical wellbeing and are essential constituents of the bones, teeth, soft tissue, blood, muscle and nerve cells.

Like vitamins, minerals act as catalysts or co-enzymes for a number of biological reactions within the body, including muscle control, the transmission of nerve impulses, hormone production, digestion and the assimilation of nutrients. The body utilizes over 80 minerals for optimum performance.

### MINERAL SOURCES

Minerals originate in the earth and, as they are inorganic, they cannot be made by living systems. Plants obtain minerals from the soil, and most of the minerals in our diet come directly from plants or indirectly from animal sources.

Foods with a high mineral content include vegetables, legumes (vegetables containing pods) and milk and milk products, whereas refined foods such as cereals, bread, fats and sugary foods contain hardly any minerals.

### TWO GROUPS

As long as a person eats a well-balanced diet, their body will receive all the minerals it needs to function adequately. Minerals can be categorized into two main groups: macrominerals and trace minerals.

*Vegetables, legumes and fruits have a high mineral content. Eaten as part of a balanced diet, they enable the body to acquire all the minerals required.*

## Macrominerals

Macrominerals (from the Greek word 'macro', meaning 'large') are required by the body in larger amounts than other minerals and include:
■ Calcium – required for the development and maintenance of bones and teeth. It also contributes to the formation of cell membranes, and regulates nerve transmission and muscular contraction. About 90 per cent of calcium in the body is stored in the bones, forming a reservoir which can be reabsorbed by blood and tissue. A deficiency of calcium can lead to bone disorders such as osteoporosis
■ Phosphorus – combines with calcium in the bones and teeth and plays a role in cell metabolism of carbohydrates, lipids and proteins
■ Potassium – the third most abundant mineral in the body. It works with sodium and chloride to maintain fluid distribution and pH balance, and plays a role

*Nerve cells (shown here magnified) require magnesium in order to function well. Magnesium can be found in vegetables such as broccoli.*

in transmitting nerve impulses, muscle contraction and regulation of heartbeat and blood pressure. Potassium participates in the process by which the blood vessel constricting effects of adrenaline are moderated, thus reducing the rise in blood pressure that occurs during stress. Potassium is also required for protein synthesis, metabolism of carbohydrates and insulin secretion by the pancreas
■ Sodium – helps to maintain fluid balance in the body. Together with potassium, sodium also helps to control muscle contraction and nerve function. Most of the sodium in the diet

*Sodium is found in the earth's crust. The mineral – seen here in block form in a petri dish – is essential for the body's fluid and electrolyte balance.*

comes from salt. Increased levels of sodium can cause the body to lose potassium and retain water, elevating blood pressure
■ Magnesium – plays a role in nerve and muscle function and is required for healthy bones. It helps the body to absorb calcium and protects the atrial lining of the heart from the stress of sudden blood pressure changes. Magnesium deficiency may be related to angina and an increased risk of heart attack. A lack of it has also been linked to pre-menstrual syndrome (PMS).

## Trace minerals

Trace or microminerals are minerals that the body requires in only tiny amounts. Even in very small quantities, trace minerals can have a powerful effect on health. Trace minerals include the following:

■ Zinc – important in growth, appetite, development of the testicles, skin integrity, mental activity, wound healing and proper functioning of the immune system.

Zinc is a cofactor for many enzymes, and is a necessary component in a number of biological reactions, including the metabolism of carbohydrates, lipids and proteins. Zinc also plays an important role in the regulation of bone calcification

■ Copper – this mineral is indispensable to health and plays a number of important roles including: the formation of haemoglobin, absorption and

*Iodine (seen in crystal form under the microscope) is an essential trace element. Its benefits have been recognized for centuries.*

assimilation of iron, regulation of heart rate and blood pressure, strengthening of blood vessels, bones, tendons and nerves, and the promotion of fertility

■ Fluoride – this mineral is required for healthy teeth and bones. It helps form tooth enamel (which prevents teeth from decay) and also increases bone strength. Fluoride may be added to water supplies as well as toothpaste in order to promote healthy teeth

■ Manganese – this is essential to the formation and maintenance of bone, cartilage and connective tissue. Manganese contributes to the synthesis of proteins and genetic material and helps produce energy from food. Manganese is necessary for normal skeletal development and maintains sex hormone production

■ Chromium – works with insulin to help regulate the body's use of sugar and is essential to the metabolism of fatty acids. Supplemental chromium may be used to treat some cases of adult-onset diabetes, to reduce insulin requirements of some diabetic children, and to relieve the symptoms of hypoglycaemia

■ Selenium – this mineral is thought to stimulate metabolism and, in combination with vitamin E, acts as an antioxidant to protect cells and tissues from damage due to free radicals. Selenium also promotes immune function

■ Iodine – one of the first minerals recognized to be

essential to human health, iodine has been used for hundreds of years to treat goitres (swellings caused by enlargement of the thyroid gland).

Iodine is a constituent of several thyroid hormones and plays a role in metabolism, nerve and muscle function, nail, hair, skin and teeth condition, as well as physical and mental development. Seafoods such as shellfish and saltwater fish are rich sources of iodine. It also occurs in bread and dairy foods

*Shellfish and saltwater fish are good sources of iodine. The thyroid gland needs iodine for thyroid hormones, which are essential for growth in children.*

■ Iron – this mineral is essential to the formation of haemoglobin, a blood protein that transports oxygen. Iron is also an important component of myoglobin, a protein that provides oxygen to muscles during exertion. Iron deficiency may lead to anaemia.

## Mineral supplements

Despite a well-balanced diet, some people may require mineral supplements. Women who suffer from excessive menstrual bleeding, for example, may benefit from taking iron supplements.

However, it is important that any such supplements are discussed with a doctor first. Because minerals are stored in bone and muscle tissue, stores of minerals can build up to toxic

*Even if people are getting a balanced diet, mineral supplements may be needed. Amounts taken should be discussed with a doctor first.*

levels. Toxicity risks increase when one isolated mineral is ingested without any supportive cofactor nutrients, which help the body to assimilate the mineral.

### Toxic levels
Toxic levels only accumulate if massive overdoses persist for a prolonged period of time. Mildly elevated levels of any minerals, such as may occur in the consumption of contaminated water or excessive mineral supplements, can give rise to the development of adverse symptoms such as nausea, diarrhoea, dizziness, headaches and abdominal pain.

# How enzymes work

Enzymes are vital for the body's chemistry. Without them, many of the chemical reactions on which life depends would not occur – such as those in which glucose is broken down to produce energy.

The life of every cell in the human body depends on the production of energy. Yet the chemical reactions that release this energy normally require a temperature in excess of 90 °C. It is enzymes that allow these reactions to occur – and so life to exist – at normal body temperatures.

The vast majority of enzymes are complex proteins – that is, strings of amino acids, which in turn, are made up of carbon, hydrogen, oxygen and nitrogen

*Enzymes are utilized in a number of products, such as this pregnancy testing kit. Enzymes embedded in the test stick react with chemicals in urine, causing a colour change.*

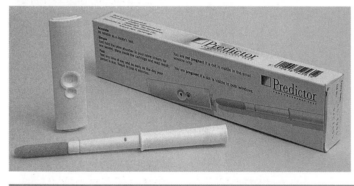

atoms, and in many cases sulphur atoms as well. Like all proteins, they are produced by the cell using DNA as a template. A few of them, however, are made up of RNA (ribonucleic acid, which along with DNA is part of the genetic code), in which case they are known as ribozymes.

## WHAT ENZYMES DO

Enzymes act as catalysts to chemical reactions, speeding them up and reducing the amount of energy that they require. They may be either 'catabolic' – involved in breaking complex substances down to their simpler components – or 'anabolic', when they help reactions that build up materials by putting their components together. Other enzymes are involved in helping chemicals cross the membrane that encloses each cell.

An enzyme called sucrase, for example, is catabolic: it helps break sucrose (sugar) down into glucose and fructose, forms in which it can be more easily digested. An enzyme called carbonic anhydrase is anabolic: it helps water to combine with carbon dioxide ($CO_2$), a by-product of the energy-producing process within the cells, to make

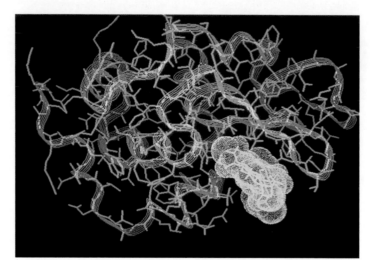

*This image is a representation of the enzyme lysozyme, which is present in tears. It is able to break up chains of sugar molecules (yellow), which make up bacterial cell walls.*

carbonic acid. In this form, it is transported in the blood to the lungs, to be expelled from the body as $CO_2$. An enzyme called glucose permease (the names of most enzymes end in '-ase') helps transport glucose across cell membranes so that it can be used to produce energy.

## The 'lock and key' model

Every enzyme in the body has a specific task, and various theories have been put forward to explain how each enzyme fulfils this one task and no other. The first such theory is known as the 'lock and key' hypothesis. This theory works on the principle that there is an area or 'active site' on the surface of the enzyme molecule into which a molecule of a chemical, known as 'the substrate', fits and is then held in place by electrical attraction. As the reaction proceeds, the substrate is turned into another chemical (the 'product') that has different electrical properties, so the electrical attraction disappears and the product molecule abandons the site. The whole process repeats itself with new substrate molecules many thousands of times in a fraction of a second.

Unfortunately, the lock and key theory does not completely fit the facts. For one thing, enzyme activity can be inhibited by factors such as a change in temperature or pH, which would not be the case if the fit was a purely physical matter. Also, molecules other than the substrate can lock on to the site.

Another concept, known as the 'induced fit' theory, satisfies these objections. It holds that the active site has elastic properties and expands and contracts as necessary to accommodate the substrate – rather as a glove changes shape to accommodate the hand.

*In the 'lock and key' model, a region of the enzyme (purple) is complementary to the substrate (orange). Here the enzyme breaks up the substrate without being chemically involved.*

# Enzymes and energy

Enzymes reduce the amount of energy required for a chemical reaction. However, being proteins, they are sensitive to changes in their surroundings.

Whenever a chemical reaction takes place, energy is used. For a reaction to take place, bonds between atoms must be broken for new ones to form – the energy required to break these bonds is called 'activation energy.' For instance, many substances will burn, but only after energy has been supplied (such as the heat from a lighted match). Enzymes work by lowering this activation energy, allowing reactions to proceed at lower temperatures, without chemically becoming involved in the reaction.

*For a chemical reaction to take place, activation energy must be supplied. Enzymes reduce the amount of activation energy, speeding up the reaction.*

## WHAT AFFECTS ENZYME ACTIVITY?

The three main factors that affect enzyme activity are temperature, pH and the presence of other chemicals that either occupy the active site or distort its shape. Depending on their action, such chemicals are known as competitive and non-competitive inhibitors.

For each enzyme in the body, there is a temperature range within which it works at maximum efficiency. Outside this range, the bonds that hold together the complex protein structures of which most enzymes are made, start to break down. As a result, the shape of the enzyme's active site changes, making it impossible for the substrate to lock on to the

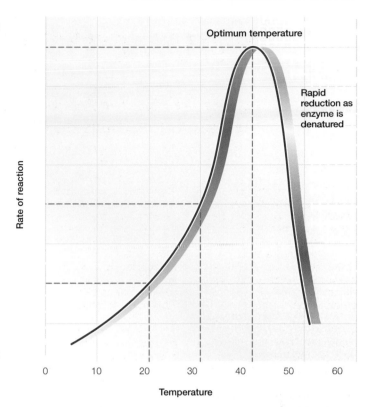

Optimum temperature

Rapid reduction as enzyme is denatured

Rate of reaction

Temperature

enzyme. This is why body systems start to shut down when the temperature is too high (hyperthermia), or too low (hypothermia).

As with temperature, enzymes have an optimum range of pH values within which they work most effectively. Outside this range, the action of an enzyme is inhibited, and at extremes it does not work at all. (pH is a value that indicates the concentration of hydrogen ions in a solution and so how acid or alkaline a solution is; distilled water, for example, has a pH of 7, while bleach has a pH of 12 and orange juice has a pH of 2.)

The optimum pH range varies

*The activity of most enzymes rises with temperature until about 40 °C, where it peaks. Beyond that, the protein begins to denature and the enzyme rapidly loses its activity.*

from enzyme to enzyme, but this is not normally a problem because it is matched to the enzyme's environment, and a buffering system (which compensates for small changes in pH) helps keep pH in different areas of the body relatively constant. Stomach enzymes, such as pepsin and chymotrypsin, work best at a low, acidic pH, which is brought about by the acidic conditions in the stomach.

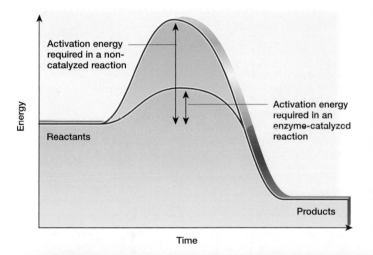

Activation energy required in a non-catalyzed reaction

Activation energy required in an enzyme-catalyzed reaction

Reactants

Products

Energy

Time

## Competitive and non-competitive inhibition

Enzyme activity can be inhibited by other chemicals. In competitive inhibition, the active site is taken up by a competing molecule. Competitive inhibition accounts for the ability of various chemicals – including cyanide – to shut down enzyme activity and cause death. Other poisons, such as lead and mercury, have the same effect, but are 'non-competitive inhibitors', since they do not 'compete' for occupation of the active site, but fix themselves onto the enzyme, thereby distorting its shape.

*In competitive inhibition (top), two molecules with similar shapes compete for the active site of the enzyme. In non-competitive inhibition (bottom), the inhibitor binds to another site on the enzyme, changing the shape of the active site and preventing the reaction.*

*This woman and child are receiving oxygen for carbon monoxide (CO) poisoning. CO is a competitive inhibitor for oxygen, reducing the amount available to the body.*

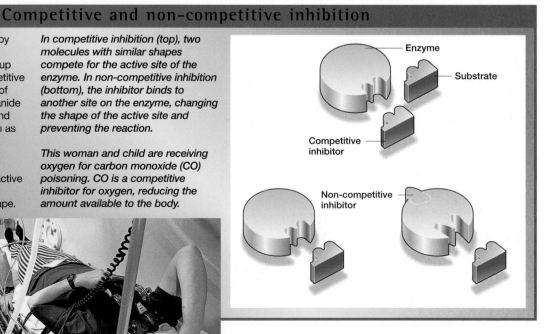

Enzyme

Substrate

Competitive inhibitor

Non-competitive inhibitor

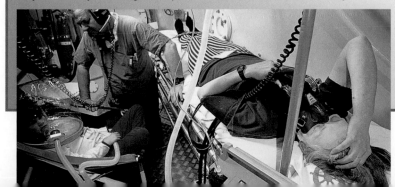

# How blood sugar is controlled

Sugar is an important source of energy for the body, and it exists naturally in the blood in the form of glucose. The correct balance of blood-sugar levels is vital to life, and this is regulated by hormones secreted from the pancreas.

Glucose is a simple sugar that is vital for brain function, and an important source of energy for the rest of the body. Glucose is stored in the body in the form of glycogen – which is simply long chains of sugar molecules found in the liver and muscles – and transferred around the body in the blood.

There is a natural level of glucose in the blood, but when we eat, or do not eat enough, this level changes. The size of this change is regulated in the pancreas by hormones (which means 'to spur on').

### THE PANCREAS

The pancreas is a long, whitish gland, about 20–25 cm in length, that lies just behind the lower part of the stomach and is connected to the duodenum. It produces enzymes that flow along a duct into the duodenum and assist in the digestion of food. But this is not its only job.

The digestive portion of the pancreas makes up 90 per cent of its total cell mass. About five per cent is made of cells that produce the hormones that regulate the blood sugar level: insulin and glucagon.

These 'endocrine' cells, known as islets, are clustered in groups throughout the pancreas. Unlike most pancreatic products, the hormones do not enter the duct leading to the duodenum; instead, they are delivered directly into the bloodstream.

## Blood sugar

The ideal level of blood glucose is between 70 and 110 mg per 100 ml. After a meal, it is normal for the sugar level to rise for a few hours, but it should not go beyond 180 mg. Anyone with a higher glucose level is described as suffering from *hyperglycaemia*. Anyone with a blood glucose level of 70 or lower is described as having *hypoglycaemia*, or being *hypoglycaemic*.

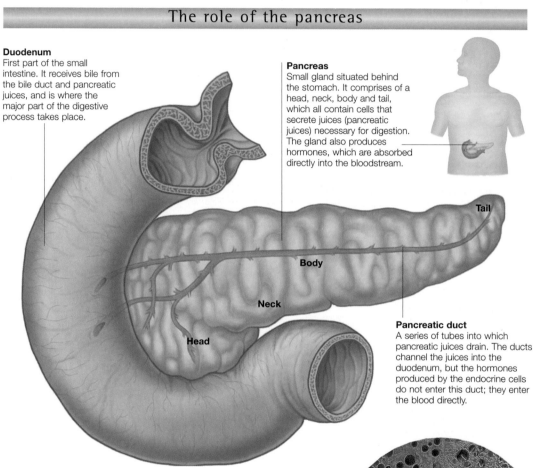

## The role of the pancreas

**Duodenum**
First part of the small intestine. It receives bile from the bile duct and pancreatic juices, and is where the major part of the digestive process takes place.

**Pancreas**
Small gland situated behind the stomach. It comprises of a head, neck, body and tail, which all contain cells that secrete juices (pancreatic juices) necessary for digestion. The gland also produces hormones, which are absorbed directly into the bloodstream.

**Tail**

**Body**

**Neck**

**Head**

**Pancreatic duct**
A series of tubes into which pancreatic juices drain. The ducts channel the juices into the duodenum, but the hormones produced by the endocrine cells do not enter this duct; they enter the blood directly.

### INSULIN

There are different types of pancreatic cell, each responsible for producing a different hormone. Insulin is normally secreted by the beta cells of the pancreatic islets. A low level of the hormone is secreted continuously, but if the amount of glucose in the blood increases, the cells are stimulated into producing more insulin. If the blood glucose level falls, insulin production decreases.

Insulin has an effect on a number of body cells, including muscle cells, red blood cells and fat cells.

When insulin levels increase, these cells are forced to absorb more glucose from the blood and use it to produce energy. Insulin production is also

controlled by another hormone, called somatostatin. This is secreted in response to high levels of other hormones, and its action is to slow down, among other things, the production of insulin.

### GLUCAGON

Glucagon is secreted by the alpha cells of the pancreatic islets. These cells are stimulated into action when the level of glucose in the blood becomes too low. The hormone causes glycogen, particularly in the liver, to be converted into glucose and released into the blood. It also induces the liver, muscle and other body cells to make glucose from other chemicals in the body, such as protein.

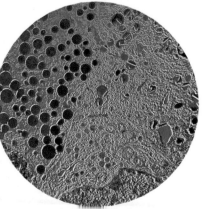

*Under the microscope, endocrine cells resemble islands, hence their name 'pancreatic islets'. They are also known as 'islets of Langerhans', after the German physician Paul Langerhans. These cells produce the hormones insulin and glucagon.*

# Abnormal blood-sugar levels

A fine balance in blood-sugar levels is vital for good health. A fall in glucose levels can result in profuse sweating, confusion and even coma. A rise can lead to the disorder diabetes.

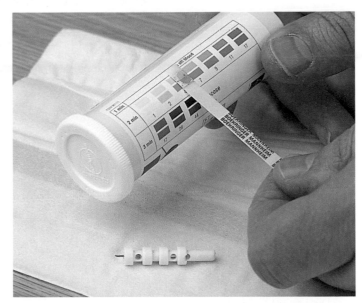

## Diabetes

The inability of the pancreas to produce enough insulin leads to the disorder known as diabetes mellitus. Lack of insulin means that the body's cells are unable to take up glucose, which then accumulates in the blood. Because the muscles cannot absorb enough sugar, they become weak and start to waste away.

The exact cause of pancreas failure is not known, but diabetes often runs in families. Diabetes usually appears quite slowly in middle-aged people, and those who are overweight are particularly at risk. However, it can also appear in children, when the onset tends to be sudden.

Diabetes may be triggered in susceptible people by a range of factors, such as exposure to cold and wet, overwork and depression, but the most common cause is infection, particularly by viruses.

Symptoms include weakness, loss of weight, increased thirst and increased production of urine. Constipation and dryness of the mouth and skin also occur. Most patients do not develop any complications, but the disorder can affect the heart, blood vessels and nerves, and diabetics are more prone to cataracts of the eyes.

In extreme cases, patients can suffer pulmonary tuberculosis or a diabetic coma.

*Blood glucose levels can be tested using a simple diagnostic kit. A lancet is used to prick the finger, and blood is placed on a test strip. At the tip of the strip are two reactive patches, which* *change colour from yellow to black and white to dark blue depending on the level of sugar in the blood. In this case, the reading is normal. Raised levels can lead to diabetes.*

## Controlling diabetes

Diabetes cannot be anticipated, prevented or cured. However, it can be controlled with proper treatment. In older patients, this may involve simply eating regularly and keeping to a reduced-sugar diet prescribed by a doctor. The doctor may also prescribe tablets that increase the effect of the insulin that is present in the blood.

In severe cases, it is necessary to take insulin. This has to be administered in the form of injections once or twice a day, as insulin is destroyed if taken by mouth.

Care must be taken with injections, as excess insulin induces hypoglycaemia, which brings on sweating, unsteadiness and disturbed behaviour. In extreme cases, the patient appears drunk, at which point medical help must be sought, as there is a risk of coma.

*Diabetics give themselves an intramuscular insulin injection, which regulates blood-sugar levels. If there is a natural deficiency in insulin, regular replacement therapy is needed to prevent coma and death.*

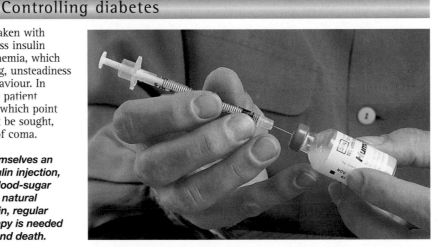

## Natural balance of glucose levels

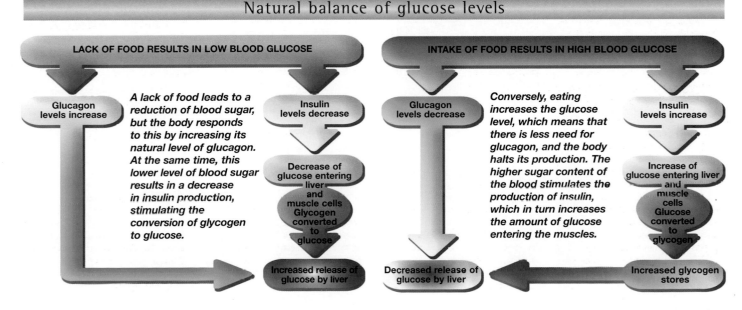

| LACK OF FOOD RESULTS IN LOW BLOOD GLUCOSE | | INTAKE OF FOOD RESULTS IN HIGH BLOOD GLUCOSE | |

Glucagon levels increase

*A lack of food leads to a reduction of blood sugar, but the body responds to this by increasing its natural level of glucagon. At the same time, this lower level of blood sugar results in a decrease in insulin production, stimulating the conversion of glycogen to glucose.*

Insulin levels decrease

Decrease of glucose entering liver and muscle cells Glycogen converted to glucose

Increased release of glucose by liver

Glucagon levels decrease

*Conversely, eating increases the glucose level, which means that there is less need for glucagon, and the body halts its production. The higher sugar content of the blood stimulates the production of insulin, which in turn increases the amount of glucose entering the muscles.*

Insulin levels increase

Increase of glucose entering liver and muscle cells Glucose converted to glycogen

Decreased release of glucose by liver

Increased glycogen stores

# How waste is excreted

Almost all of the useful nutrients in food are absorbed into the body by the small intestine. The function of the large intestine is to excrete the unwanted waste material while retaining any useful chemicals that remain.

The large intestine is about 1.5 m in length and forms an arch that surrounds the folds and twists of the small intestine. It consists of four sections: the caecum, colon, rectum and anal canal. Food passes from the ileum of the small intestine into the upper end of the caecum via the ileocaecal valve. This valve prevents material in the large intestine from returning to the small intestine, even when the large intestine is distended. The caecum is a downward-pointing pouch that ends in the worm-like appendage called the vermiform appendix.

### THE COLON

The caecum leads into the ascending colon, a straight section of the colon that travels up to the liver. There it bends and becomes the transverse colon, which crosses the abdomen and bends to become the descending colon and then the sigmoid colon. Altogether the colon measures about 1.3 m in length and is the longest section of the large intestine.

The primary function of the colon is the propulsion of faeces towards the anal canal. This process can be achieved by a relatively short length of intestine, which is why some or even all of the colon can, if necessary, be surgically removed. The colon is long to provide the maximum possible area for the reabsorption of water, dissolved salts and water-soluble vitamins.

## The large intestine

**Right colic flexure**
Point at which ascending colon becomes transverse colon, beneath the liver

**Ascending colon**
Rises from caecum

**Ileum**
Final length of small intestine

**Ileocaecal valve**
Prevents contents of large intestine from flowing back into the small intestine

**Caecum**
Pouch situated below the ileocaecal valve; joins the small and large intestines

**Vermiform appendix**
Attached to the caecum

**Transverse colon**
Runs from right to left along the lower abdomen

**Left colic flexure**
Point at which transverse colon becomes descending colon, at the level of the spleen

**Descending colon**

**Epiploic appendage**
Attachment between the colon and the epiploon (omentum) that covers the intestines

**Small intestine**

**Sigmoid colon**
Final, s-shaped, part of descending colon

**Rectum**

**Anal canal**

*The colon, rectum and anus make up the large intestine, which is the final part of the digestive tract. The sac-like caecum links the large intestine to the small intestine.*

## Passage of faeces

Movement of the faeces along the colon is achieved by muscular movements in the colon wall. Three types of muscular movement occur and these serve not only to propel faeces along, but also to keep mixing the material, allowing water to be taken up by the colon wall more easily.

Faecal material passes through the colon far more slowly than through the small intestine. Each day, the large intestine will absorb approximately 1.4 litres of water, and smaller amounts of sodium and chloride.

*Segmentation is a series of ring-like contractions that churn the faecal material without moving it forwards. Water is thus more easily absorbed.*

*Peristaltic contractions, like those in the small intestine, mix and move the faeces. Muscles behind each segment contract, while those in front relax.*

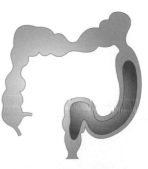

*Mass movements, which are stronger than the peristaltic contractions, propel large quantities of faeces. They occur two or three times a day.*

# Defecation

The process of digestion ends when the waste products are removed from the body. Although an involuntary impulse, defecation can be consciously delayed.

The colon leads to the rectum, which is about 12 cm long and is equipped with muscular walls. These are capable of stretching, allowing the rectum to act as a reservoir for faeces, and are used to expel the faeces into the anal canal. Faeces arriving in the rectum are relatively dry, but the rectum has a glandular lining that secretes mucus, helping to lubricate the faeces and ease their passage through the rectum and anal canal.

The faeces that arrive in the rectum contain undigested food residues, mucus, epithelial cells (from the lining of the digestive tract), bacteria and enough water to enable smooth passage.

### LACK OF BULK

If the faeces in the colon lack bulk, due to a lack of fibrous, indigestible material in the diet, the colon may become narrowed and its contractions, with nothing to work against, can become too powerful. This causes an increased pressure on the walls of the colon and can result in the formation of sac-like herniations (pouches) known as diverticula.

Diverticulosis usually occurs in the region of the sigmoid colon. It is associated with left-sided pelvic pain and may have serious consequences. The diverticula may rupture, releasing faecal matter into the abdominal cavity, and this can lead to severe infection.

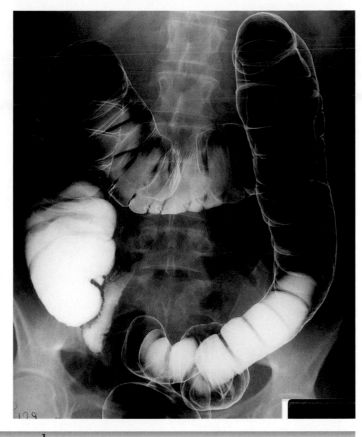

*A barium X-ray shows the twists and turns of the colon.*
*Of the 500 ml of food residue that usually enters the caecum daily, approximately only 150 ml becomes faeces.*

## Anal canal

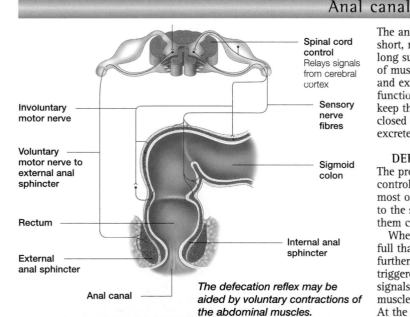

Spinal cord control
Relays signals from cerebral cortex

Sensory nerve fibres

Involuntary motor nerve

Voluntary motor nerve to external anal sphincter

Sigmoid colon

Rectum

Internal anal sphincter

External anal sphincter

Anal canal

*The defecation reflex may be aided by voluntary contractions of the abdominal muscles.*

The anal canal, or anus, is a short, narrow tube, about 4 cm long surrounded by two rings of muscle, known as the internal and external anal sphincters. The function of the anal canal is to keep the opening to the exterior closed until a person is ready to excrete the faeces.

### DEFECATION CONTROL

The process of defecation is controlled by the brain, which most of the time sends signals to the sphincter muscles to keep them contracted.

When the rectum becomes so full that it cannot stretch any further, a defecation reflex is triggered in the spinal cord, and signals are sent to the rectal muscles to start contracting. At the same time, signals are sent to the brain, giving warning that defecation is necessary, but the brain remains in conscious control of the sphincter muscles until such time as it becomes convenient to defecate. When the decision to defecate is made, the brain allows the sphincter muscles to relax and the muscular wall of the rectum propels the faeces through the anal canal.

Involuntary defecation occurs in infants because they have not yet gained control of their external and anal sphincter. It also occurs in those who have damage to the spinal cord. Watery stools (diarrhoea) result when the food residue is rushed through the large intestine. Dehydration can result from inadequate water absorption.

## The appendix

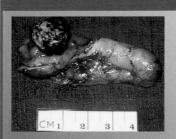

*When the appendix becomes inflamed, the result is appendicitis. This condition can be life-threatening.*

Neither the caecum nor the appendix has any obvious function in humans and both are probably relics of our ancestry. The appendix, for example, is a narrow, blind-ending piece of gut, up to 10 cm long and 1 cm in diameter, which extends downwards from the caecum. It is found only in humans, certain species of ape and, curiously, in the wombat, an Australian marsupial. Its origin is probably connected with the fact that a number of herbivorous animals have an organ in the same position that acts as an extra stomach in which the cellulose in their plant food is digested by bacteria. If so, the human appendix is clearly in this respect a vestigial organ, as humans cannot digest cellulose.

It does, however, appear to have developed a secondary function; that of acting as an early warning of infection: like the adenoids and tonsils, the appendix contains a large number of lymph glands whose purpose is to counter infection.

However, the appendix can itself become inflamed and if this happens appendicitis results. This can be fatal and the appendix usually has to be removed surgically. It can be removed at any age, but is more likely to be necessary in early life, as by the time a person has reached the age of 40 their appendix has almost completely shrivelled up.

# How the liver works

The liver is one of the most complex organs in the body.
It controls more than 500 chemical reactions, and manufactures
and stores substances that are vital to sustaining life.

The liver is the largest of the body's internal organs, weighing about 1.8 kg in a man and 1.3 kg in a woman. It forms a right-angled triangle whose bulk is on the right side of the abdomen although it continues across the midline of the body to lie below the apex of the heart and behind the stomach on the left side. Its top lies beneath the fifth rib, and it reaches down on the right side to just below the 10th rib – this is why doctors push their fingers underneath the ribs on the patient's right side to check whether the liver is enlarged.

### LIVER STRUCTURE

Reddish-brown in colour, the liver is not only the largest internal organ but also the most complex. It consists of eight lobes, each one made up of hexagonally shaped areas called lobules, which consist of a central vein surrounded by liver cells.

The whole structure is permeated by a network of veins, arteries and ducts. The ducts are channels that collect bile, which is produced by liver cells, and direct it to the gall bladder, where it is stored. This is a pear-shaped sac, about 8 cm long, that lies underneath and extends just below the ninth rib. When the gall bladder is swollen, it can sometimes be felt just below the ninth rib and a few centimetres to the left of its point.

## Cross-section through the liver

**Hepatic vein**
From the central veins, blood enters the hepatic veins, which drain the liver and empty into the inferior vena cava

**Sinusoids**
Receive oxygenated blood from the hepatic artery and nutrients from the intestines via the portal vein. Oxygen and nutrients diffuse through the capillary walls into the liver cells

**Portal triad**
Found at each of the six corners of a lobule; consists of a branch of the hepatic artery, a branch of the hepatic portal vein and a bile duct

**Common hepatic duct**
Duct collects bile and channels it to the gall bladder

**Hepatic artery**
Supplies oxygenated blood to the liver

**Hepatic portal vein**
Collects blood from digestive tract and delivers it to the liver cells

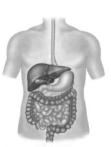

*The liver is one of the body's most important organs. It can be seen here as the reddish-brown triangular organ lying in the upper abdominal cavity.*

## Processes in the liver

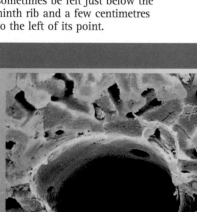

The functions of the liver involve the control of more than 500 chemical reactions, making the liver the most important organ of metabolism – that is, the process whereby chemicals are changed in the body. These include:
■ Storing carbohydrates. The liver breaks down glucose, the form in which carbohydrates are carried in the blood, and stores it as glycogen. The process is reversed when blood glucose levels fall or there is a sudden demand for extra energy
■ Disposal of amino acids. The liver breaks down surplus amino acids, which make up proteins, and turn the ammonia that is produced into urea, a constituent of urine

*Blood is detoxified as it flows along the sinusoids towards the centre of the lobule. All the lobules of the liver have a central vein (pictured).*

■ Using fat to provide energy. When there is insufficient carbohydrate in the diet to fulfil energy needs, the liver breaks down stored fat into chemicals (ketones), which are used to produce energy and heat
■ Manufacturing cholesterol. Naturally produced cholesterol is essential for the production of bile and hormones such as cortisol and progesterone
■ Storing minerals and vitamins. The liver stores sufficient minerals, such as iron and copper (needed for red blood cells), and vitamins A (which it synthesizes as well as stores), $B_{12}$ and D to meet the body's requirements for a year
■ Processing blood. The liver breaks down old red blood cells, using some of their constituents to make bile pigments. It also manufactures prothrombin and heparin – proteins that affect blood clotting.

# Circulation within the liver

The liver has its own circulation system made up of an intricate network of veins and arteries.

The veins and arteries form the liver's own circulation system, known as the 'hepatic portal system' (the Latin word for the liver is *hepaticus*). The purpose of this system is to remove harmful substances from the digestive organs and deal with them before they reach the heart. It also takes some constituents of food out of the digestive tract so that they can be stored for future use.

The portal vein collects blood from the digestive tract and delivers it to the liver cells for processing, while the hepatic artery branches off the aorta to supply nutrients to the liver cells. After it has circulated through the liver's capillaries, the blood is collected by the hepatic veins at the centre of each lobule and passed through the main hepatic vein to the inferior vena cava, to be transported back to the heart.

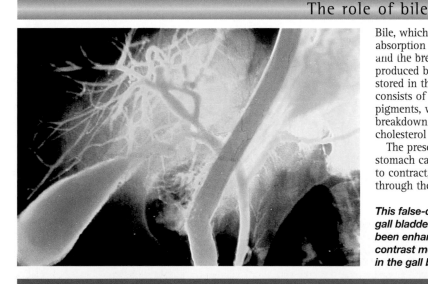

**Central vein**

**Kupffer cells**
Star-shaped cells inside the sinusoids remove bacteria and old blood cells from the blood as it flows past

**Portal triad**
The portal arteriole, vein and bile duct combine to make the portal triad

**Bile duct**

**Portal vein**

**Portal arteriole**

**Plates of hepatocytes**

**Sinusoids**
Blood from the hepatic portal vein and the hepatic artery runs from the portal triads through the sinusoids and empties into the central vein

## The role of bile

Bile, which is essential for the absorption of vitamins D and E and the breakdown of fats, is produced by liver cells and stored in the gall bladder; it consists of bile salts and bile pigments, which come from the breakdown of red blood cells, cholesterol and lecithin.

The presence of fats in the stomach causes the gall bladder to contract, which squeezes bile through the common bile duct and into the duodenum. Here, it emulsifies fats, making them easier to digest.

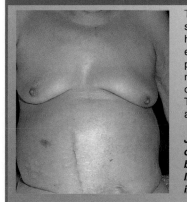

*This false-colour X-ray of the gall bladder and bile ducts has been enhanced by injecting a contrast medium. Bile is stored in the gall bladder.*

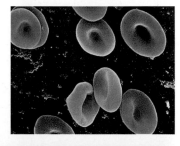

*Electron micrograph of red blood cells. Each minute, between 1.2 and 1.7 litres of blood pass through the liver.*

## Liver problems

The liver breaks down toxic substances, such as alcohol, into harmless constituents that can be excreted from the body. It also processes chemicals produced naturally in the body, although their constituents are usually recycled. This is the reason why substance abuse can cause serious damage by overloading the liver.

In extreme cases, cirrhosis can result. This is a serious disorder in which healthy liver tissue is damaged and replaced by fibrous scar tissue, eventually hardening the whole organ. The long-term effect is that the liver's regenerative capability is greatly reduced.

*Jaundice – yellowing of the skin due to excessive bilirubin in the blood – is a possible symptom of liver damage caused by the intake of high levels of alcohol.*

*Cirrhosis is a liver disease that can be caused by alcohol. In this condition, fibrous tissue breaks up the internal structure of the liver (shown here).*

# How kidneys produce urine

The kidneys are responsible for maintaining the volume and chemical composition of bodily fluids. They do this by filtering impurities from the blood and excreting excess water and metabolic by-products as urine.

The kidneys are the major excretory organs of the body, and are situated towards the back of the abdomen, below the diaphragm. They are responsible for maintaining the constancy of body fluids by filtering toxins, metabolic waste products and excess ions from the blood. The end result of this process is the excretory fluid urine.

At the same time, the kidneys also maintain blood volume (the correct balance of water and salts) and the correct acidity of body fluids. This complex process is called homeostasis.

### INSIDE THE KIDNEY

There are three distinct zones within the kidney: the renal cortex (outermost zone), the renal pelvis (inner zone) and the renal medulla (middle zone). The cortex is granular and pale in appearance, and contains a network of arteries, veins and capillaries. The medulla is a darker, striped area divided into conical structures known as renal pyramids. At the apex of each pyramid are papillae, nipple-shaped projections that extend into the renal pelvis via cavities known as calyces.

There are over one million blood processing units within the kidney that are called nephrons. Urine produced by the nephrons drains into the pelvis via calyces. In turn, the pelvis is linked to the ureter, the tubes that channel the urine to the bladder.

## Internal structure of the kidney

**Renal cortex**
The outermost region of the kidney; contains the capillary bundles of the nephrons

**Renal medulla**
Middle region of the kidneys, composed of renal pyramids and urine-collecting units

**Renal pelvis**
Innermost region of the kidneys; divides into two or three branches known as calyces

**Renal artery**
Supplies blood to the kidney via artery directly connected to the aorta

**Renal vein**
Drains blood from the kidney directly into the vena cava (one of the main veins to the heart)

**Ureter**
30 cm-long tubes that channel urine from the renal pelvis to the bladder

**Renal pyramid**
Formed of parallel bundles of urine-collecting tubules

**Papilla**
The tip of the renal pyramid; drains urine into the pelvis via the calyces

**Calyx**
Major and minor cavities that cup the apexes of the renal pyramids; urine is collected here before being drained into the pelvis

**Adipose tissue**
A soft, fatty tissue that cushions the calyces

**Arcuate veins**
Channels blood leaving the kidney into the renal vein

**Renal capsule**
Fibrous tissue that surrounds each kidney

**Arcuate arteries**
Delivers blood to kidneys; about 90 per cent is channelled to the cortex

*The kidneys process about 180 litres of blood every day, but less than one per cent (1.5 litres) is excreted from the body as urine. This waste is carried directly to the bladder, via the ureter, where it is stored until excreted from the body.*

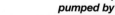

Vein

Kidney

Artery

Ureter

Bladder

*The kidneys are paired organs situated on either side of the spine at the back of the abdomen. They only weigh about one per cent of the overall body weight, but receive 20 per cent of the blood pumped by the heart.*

## Urinary drainage

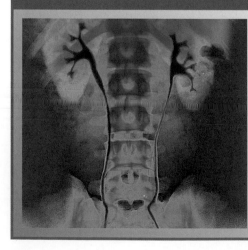

The production of urine is a three-step process: filtration, reabsorption and secretion. Once the required water and essential nutrients have been reabsorbed, the fluid remaining in the tubule is urine, which empties into the collecting ducts and then to the ureters to be excreted from the body via the bladder.

The walls of the ureter are muscular. Regular waves of contraction (peristalsis) move the urine from the renal pelvis towards

*This contrast medium X-ray clearly shows the kidneys (green) and the ureters (red – the vessels connecting the ureters to the kidneys). The bladder is the dark red circular mass at the bottom of the X-ray.*

the bladder every 10–60 seconds. The ureters pass obliquely through the bladder wall, tending to close the uretic opening except during a peristaltic contraction. This prevents the backflow of urine.

The bladder muscle is controlled by involuntary nerve action. The bladder fills without increasing internal pressure until it is near capacity. When the bladder is full, the pressure within rises dramatically, triggering a spinal nerve reflex which acts to cause the bladder muscle to contract and empty its contents via the urethra. This is the process of micturition (urination). The first urge to micturate is felt when the bladder volume is about 150 ml. This increases to a sense of urgency at 400 ml.

# Urine production

Approximately one litre of blood flows into an adult kidney every minute.
There are over one million urine-producing units within the kidney, and from all
of these, one millilitre of urine is produced every minute.

The nephron is the functional, structural unit of the kidney which filters blood and is responsible for urine production. There are over a million nephrons in each kidney, as well as thousands of collecting ducts into which the urine drains.

The nephron is formed from two main units: a glomerulus and its associated renal tubule. The glomerulus is a tight ball of capillaries situated in the renal cortex, and its tubules, through which water and chemicals absorb into the blood, extend down into the medulla.

### BOWMAN'S CAPSULE

At one end of the renal tubule, completely encasing the glomerulus, is a closed unit called the Bowman's capsule. Together, the Bowman's capsule and its glomerulus are called a renal corpuscle, and are responsible for filtering waste products into the renal tubule.

The other end of the renal tubule connects to a urine-collecting tubule. The specific nature and function of the cells within the renal tubule are essential to the excretory and homeostatic function of the nephron as a whole.

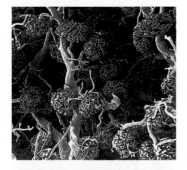

*Glomeruli are tight knots of blood capillaries (seen here in blue) in the kidneys. Each glomerulus forms part of a tiny filtration unit that removes toxic waste from the blood.*

## The nephron and its blood supply

**Glomerulus**
Tight knot of capillary blood vessels located in the renal cortex; blood is fed into this capillary network and drained out via two arterioles

**Bowman's capsule**
Cup-shaped end of a nephron which encloses the glomerulus; it is the site of blood filtration into the kidney tubule

**Afferent arteriole**
Arteriole (blood vessel linking capillaries to arteries) that feeds blood into the glomerulus from the interlobular artery

**Interlobular artery**
Branch of the renal artery, which delivers blood to the kidney

**Arcuate vein**
Branch of the renal vein, which empties blood into the heart

**Loop of Henle**
Hairpin bend in the renal tubule; nutrient reabsorption can also take place here

**Efferent arteriole**
Drains blood from the glomerulus into the renal tubules.

**Proximal convoluted tubule**
Location of the first stage of the reabsorption process, in which water and useful chemicals begin to re-enter the blood

**Distal convoluted tubule**
Another section of the renal tubule concerned with reabsorption; also largely responsible for water regulation and the balance of chemically active solutions

**Urine collecting tubule**
Drains urine into the ureter, for removal to the bladder

*The nephron is the active unit of filtration within the kidneys. It is composed of two main elements: the glomerulus, which filters blood, and the renal tubule, which re-absorbs the useful substances back into the blood and extracts the waste material. The tubule is divided into distinct segments: the proximal tubule, the loop of Henle and the distal tubule.*

### EXCRETION OF METABOLIC WASTE PRODUCTS

The waste products of metabolism are eliminated by the kidneys via the nephrons. They also excrete toxins ingested or produced by the body. The principle waste products in urine are urea (from protein metabolism), creatinine (from muscle), uric acid (from metabolism of nucleic acids), bilirubin (from haemoglobin metabolism) and the broken down products of hormones.

The nephron works by a process of secretion followed by reabsorption. Nutrients and waste products flow freely out of the blood in the glomerulus into the Bowman's capsule. These chemicals are accompanied by water and many essential nutrients, which must be reclaimed by the body.

This reabsorption occurs in the remaining parts of the nephron and renal tubules. The waste eventually drains into the collecting ducts to be eliminated from the body.

Most of this reabsorption takes place in a section of the renal tubules called the distal convoluted tubule (see diagram above). The reabsorption and some secretion that takes place here, and in another section known as the loop of Henle, is dependent upon the body's requirements at the time.

Closely associated with the capillary bed of the glomerulus and the renal tubules are the peritubular capillaries. These are another vital element to the reabsorption process. The pressure in these capillaries is much lower than that of the glomerulus and allows water and nutrients to flow freely into them, re-absorbing them back into the blood.

## Capillary networks

On entering the kidney, the renal artery divides into several branches, each radiating towards the cortex. In the cortex, the branches subdivide repeatedly into smaller and smaller vessels. The final sub-branch is called an arteriole. Each arteriole supplies blood to one nephron.

The anatomy of the arterial blood supply to the kidney nephrons is unique, in that each nephron is supplied by two, rather than one, capillary beds. The arteriole supplying the nephron is known as the efferent arteriole. It is the tight knotting of the resulting capillaries that forms the glomerulus.

On leaving the capillary tuft, the microvessels join together to form the outgoing arteriole, known as the afferent arteriole. This arteriole then redivides into the peritubular capillaries – a second network of microvessels surrounding the urine collecting tubule further down its length. These capillaries empty into the vessels of the venous system, eventually draining into the renal vein.

The pressure in the glomerulus is high, forcing fluid, nutrients and waste products out of the blood into the nephron capsule. The pressure in the peritubular capillaries is low, allowing fluid reabsorption. Adjustments to the pressure differences between the two capillary beds control the excretion and reabsorption of water and chemicals within the blood.

*A cast of a normal kidney shows the complex capillary networks within the organ. There are approximately one million arterioles in each kidney.*

# How the kidneys control blood pressure

The kidneys play a fundamental role in the long-term regulation of blood pressure. The blood pressure must be kept stable so that organs receive an adequate supply of blood and oxygen.

The kidneys are two bean-shaped organs located on either side of the pelvis. They have two main roles:
■ Regulating the salt and water balance in the body
■ Excreting waste substances such as urea, excess salt and other minerals, in the form of urine.

### FILTRATION SYSTEM

The kidneys contain millions of microscopic filtering units, called nephrons, which are the working components of the kidneys. Certain substances in the blood (such as glucose) are filtered but reabsorbed back into the bloodstream, while harmful wastes and excess water are excreted in the form of urine.

### BLOOD PRESSURE

The kidneys play an extremely important role in the long-term regulation of blood pressure. Blood pressure is defined as the pressure of blood against the walls of the main arteries and is an indication of the efficiency of a person's circulation.

### REGULATION

Blood pressure must be regulated in order to provide an adequate supply of blood and oxygen to the organs.
■ Hypotension (low blood pressure) may indicate that there is insufficient blood in the circulation. This can result in vital organs being deprived of oxygen rich blood and result in shock
■ Hypertension (abnormally high blood pressure) means that the heart has to work harder to pump blood against a greater resistance within the arterial circulation, putting great strain on the heart.

*Blood is filtered through the kidneys. Some substances are reabsorbed into the blood, while others, such as excess water and waste, are excreted as urine.*

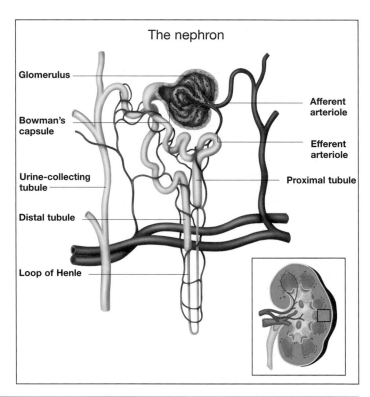

The nephron

Glomerulus

Bowman's capsule

Urine-collecting tubule

Distal tubule

Loop of Henle

Afferent arteriole

Efferent arteriole

Proximal tubule

## Blood volume

A number of mechanisms within the body act to ensure that blood pressure is kept within normal limits, on both a short- and long-term basis. The kidneys play an important part in this long-term regulation of blood pressure.

### BLOOD VOLUME

The kidneys help to maintain homeostasis (equilibrium) in the circulation by regulating blood volume. Although the volume of blood varies with age and gender, the kidneys usually maintain total circulating volume at around five litres.

Any significant alteration in this level will affect blood pressure:
■ An increase in blood volume

*Drinking water is an important way of maintaining blood volume. The kidneys use water levels and salt concentration to control blood pressure.*

leads to an increase in blood pressure. For example, an excessive intake of salt with resulting water retention can lead to a higher blood pressure
■ A decrease in blood volume causes a decrease in blood pressure. Severe blood loss or dehydration are common causes. A sudden drop in blood pressure may indicate internal bleeding.

### FEEDBACK SYSTEM

The role of the kidneys is to detect any changes in blood volume or pressure via a feedback system and to react accordingly
■ When blood volume increases, the kidneys remove more water from the blood, reducing the blood volume and restoring normal blood pressure
■ When blood volume decreases, due to dehydration for example, the kidneys absorb less water, thus restoring blood pressure.

# Renal hormones

Blood volume is a direct indicator of blood pressure. The kidneys continually monitor blood absorption and sodium levels to maintain an even pressure.

The kidneys regulate blood pressure by altering the amount of urine passed, thereby regulating blood volume. When blood pressure is low, the kidneys conserve water in the circulation and when it is raised, they ensure that greater volumes of water are passed as urine.

### FILTRATION RATE

Within each nephron (functional unit of the kidney) is a bundle of arterioles (blood vessels) called the glomerulus. Water and solutes are 'pushed' out of the blood into the collecting tubules by the higher blood pressure in the glomerulus. An average person filters about 125 mls of filtrate per minute. If the blood pressure is too low, water will remain in the circulation to help boost the blood pressure. If the blood pressure is high, more water is forced into the tubules and passed as urine.

### FEED-BACK MECHANISM

The walls of the blood vessels supplying the nephrons contain specialized cells that are able to detect blood pressure. It is these cells that set into motion additional processes needed to rectify abnormal pressure.
■ The blood pressure falls below normal limits and the specialized cells detect this change
■ A hormone called renin is secreted into the blood stream
■ Renin converts a substance called angiotensin into angiotensin I, which then becomes angiotensin II as it passes through the lungs in the blood
■ Angiotensin II stimulates the adrenal glands (located on the top of the kidneys) to produce aldosterone
■ Aldosterone acts directly on the nephrons in the kidneys so that more salt and water are reabsorbed back into the blood circulation. This results in an increase in blood pressure
In addition to this mechanism, angiotensin II constricts blood vessels, thus increasing the pressure within them.

### ANTI-DIURETIC HORMONE

The hypothalamus in the brain also has a role to play. When the water concentration in the blood is low, potentially leading to a drop in blood pressure, the hypothalamus secretes anti-diuretic hormone (ADH). This acts on the tubules in the nephrons, making them more permeable so that more water is reabsorbed into the blood.

*The kidneys help to control blood pressure using a feedback mechanism. This diagram shows the sequence of events following a change in pressure.*

## Control of blood pressure

**Adrenal glands**
Stimulated by angiotensin II to produce aldosterone

**Hypothalamus**
Produces anti-diuretic hormone that is secreted when blood pressure falls

**Kidney**
Secretes an enzyme called renin into the blood stream when blood pressure falls

**Aldosterone**
Produced by adrenal glands. Aldosterone acts directly on kidneys to conserve water

**Renin**
This enzyme activates angiotensin, which is a vasoconstrictor

## The causes of high and low blood pressure

The normal blood pressure of a resting adult is usually about 120/80 mmHg, but this can be influenced by a wide range of factors:
■ Age. Blood pressure naturally increases throughout life. This is because the arteries lose the elasticity that, in younger people, absorbs the force of heart contractions
■ Gender. Men generally experience higher blood pressure than women or children
■ Lifestyle choices. Being overweight, consuming high levels of alcohol or enduring a long period of stress can all contribute to high blood pressure.

*Blood pressure is influenced by a number of factors, such as age and stress. Regular monitoring and life-style advice are vital in those at risk.*

### Hypertension

Abnormally high blood pressure (hypertension) may be caused by a number of factors, but is commonly caused by atherosclerosis, a disease that causes narrowing of the blood vessels.

When the disease affects the arteries of the kidney (renal arteries), it may cause long-term problems with blood pressure regulation.

### Hypotension

Abnormally low blood pressure (hypotension) is usually due to reduced blood volume or increased blood-vessel capacity. This can happen in the case of severe burns or dehydration, which both lower blood volume, or through an infection such as septicaemia which causes a widening of the blood vessels.

# How we vomit

Vomiting (emesis) is a protective reflex that serves to remove toxins from the stomach and small intestine. The unpleasant sensation that often precedes vomiting (nausea) is also a component of this reflex.

Feeling nauseated usually occurs prior to vomiting and serves as an 'early warning signal'. Nausea prevents further ingestion of a toxin and induces a powerful aversive response to stop future toxin ingestion.

However, nausea and vomiting can occur inappropriately due to pregnancy, motion, radiation, cytotoxic chemotherapeutic agents (for example, cisplatin) and anaesthetics (post-operative sickness). Under these conditions, there is no toxin in the stomach, so ejecting its contents from the body is clearly not going to be beneficial to the subject.

## NERVOUS INPUT

Mucosal enterochromaffin cells located in the stomach and small intestine respond to the presence of toxins by releasing the neurotransmitter serotonin.

The serotonin molecules in turn activate nearby nerve fibre endings in the vagus nerve. This nerve carries electrical impulses through the abdominal and thoracic cavities, eventually terminating in a region of the brainstem (situated just above the spinal cord) called the nucleus of the tractus solitarius (NTS).

The vomiting reflex is co-ordinated by groups of neurones that are located in the brainstem; the precise location(s) of these neurones, which are often termed 'the vomiting centre', is currently unknown. However, the inputs capable of

### The vomiting reflex

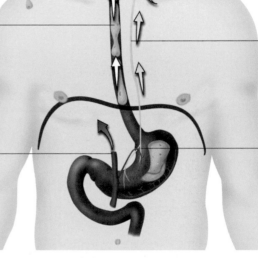

*The brain is informed of the presence of toxins in the stomach and small intestine via signals carried along nerves and in the blood.*

**Brainstem**
This region of the brain is thought to control the vomiting reflex

**Carotid artery**
Carries toxins contained in the blood to a region of the brainstem called area postrema

**Oesophagus**
Waves of contraction propel the stomach's contents upwards against the force of gravity

**Vagus nerve**
Carries electrical nerve impulses from the stomach and small intestine to the brainstem

**Portal vein**
Carries toxins contained in the blood to the liver and then into the general circulation

**Vagal nerve fibre endings**
A chemical called serotonin, released from enterochromaffin cells in the presence of toxins, activates these nerve endings

activating the vomiting reflex all converge on the NTS, suggesting that NTS neurones either form part of the vomiting centre itself, or are able to modulate its activity in some way.

## BLOODSTREAM

Alternatively, toxins absorbed into the bloodstream from the stomach or small intestine may activate a brainstem region adjacent to the NTS, called the

area postrema. These neurones are thought to be able to detect the presence of toxins in the blood. The NTS and area postrema communicate with each other via a series of nerves.

### Motion sickness

Scientists believe that motion sickness occurs when information about the body's position supplied by the eyes does not match information supplied by the vestibular (balance) system, which is located in the inner ear.

This is supported by the fact that when the region of the brain that receives input from the balance organs is damaged – following a stroke, for example – the patient no longer suffers from motion sickness.

*A rollercoaster ride can often induce nausea owing to the disorientating effects of conflicting sensory inputs.*

*The vestibular apparatus located in the inner ear controls our sense of balance, carrying information about the body's movements in space.*

# Ejecting stomach contents

The preliminaries to vomiting are a relaxation of the
stomach muscles, followed by retching – a repeated contraction
of the abdominal muscles and diaphragm.

Approximately 2 to 10 minutes prior to vomiting the stomach relaxes. Next, a giant migrating contraction starts in the mid portion of the small intestine and spreads rapidly (5–10 cm per second) towards the stomach. This contraction forces the contents of the small

*Nausea and vomiting are often evoked inappropriately during pregnancy. One cause of this is the regurgitation of stomach acid into the oesophagus.*

intestine back into the stomach, confining the ingested toxin to the stomach and preventing it from being absorbed further.

## MUSCLE CONTRACTIONS

The abdominal muscles and diaphragm repeatedly contract and relax in a synchronous manner, squeezing the stomach and forcing its contents into and out of the oesophagus (retching). Retching gives the contents of the stomach momentum.

A characteristic body posture is often assumed to assist in the movement of the vomit – bent over with the head forward and a straight back. Then, the abdominal and diaphragm muscles produce a strong, maintained contraction, which produces an intra-abdominal pressure of 200 mm Hg.

Meanwhile, the glottis closes (preventing the stomach contents entering the lungs), the oesophagus shortens, the mouth involuntarily opens and internal pressure propels the stomach contents out of the body.

*This illustration demonstrates how various muscular actions combine to expel the stomach contents from the body. This is commonly known as retching.*

## The mechanics of vomiting

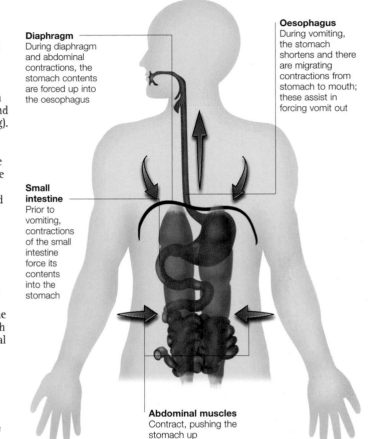

**Diaphragm**
During diaphragm and abdominal contractions, the stomach contents are forced up into the oesophagus

**Oesophagus**
During vomiting, the stomach shortens and there are migrating contractions from stomach to mouth; these assist in forcing vomit out

**Small intestine**
Prior to vomiting, contractions of the small intestine force its contents into the stomach

**Abdominal muscles**
Contract, pushing the stomach up

## Anti-emetic therapy

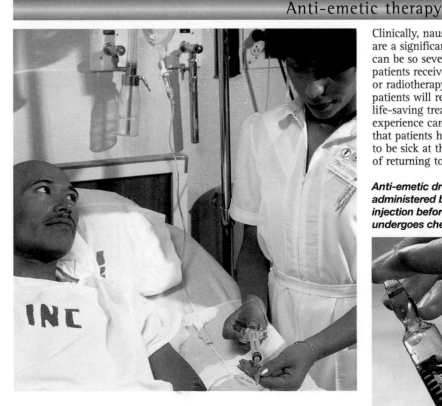

Clinically, nausea and vomiting are a significant problem. They can be so severe in cancer patients receiving chemotherapy or radiotherapy that some patients will refuse to take their life-saving treatment. Indeed, the experience can be so unpleasant that patients have been known to be sick at the mere thought of returning to the hospital.

*Anti-emetic drugs are usually administered by intravenous injection before a cancer patient undergoes chemotherapy.*

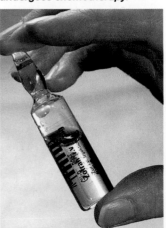

### SEROTONIN ANTAGONISTS

Consequently, drugs such as ondansetron, which block serotonin receptors, have been widely used for the prevention of vomiting caused by chemotherapeutic agents.

These drugs work by binding to the serotonin receptors located on the abdominal vagal fibres, preventing the serotonin released from enterochromaffin cells from activating them.

Serotonin receptor antagonists are not a universal anti-emetic, however. Their clinical efficacy is limited to vomiting induced by radiation and cytotoxic drugs. They are ineffective against nausea and vomiting caused by motion, anaesthetics and other pharmacological agents, such as L-dopa (used to treat Parkinson's disease).

*This ampoule contains a single dose of an emetic drug used to control the nausea and vomiting associated with chemotherapy.*

# How puberty occurs

During puberty, both boys and girls undergo enormous physical and emotional change. This is due to the production of sex hormones, triggering development essential to fertility.

Puberty is the period of physical change that occurs during adolescence and results in sexual maturity. In girls it tends to occur between the ages of 10 and 14, while in boys it is likely to start between 10 and 14 and continue until about 17.

### SECONDARY SEXUAL CHARACTERISTICS

The physical changes that take place during puberty are manifested in the appearance of secondary sexual characteristics, such as a deepening of the voice in boys and the growth of the breasts in girls.

### ACCELERATED GROWTH

During puberty a striking growth spurt occurs, at around the age of 10 in girls and 12 in boys. A rate of growth of around 8–10 cm per year is attained. Since boys do not reach full maturity until later than girls, their growth period is extended, with the result that they tend to be significantly taller.

This accelerated growth spurt affects different parts of the body at any one time, so the body may appear to be out of proportion during this period.

Growth acceleration tends to affect the feet first, followed by the legs and the torso. Finally, the face, particularly the lower jaw, undergoes development.

Body weight may almost double during this time. In girls this is largely due to increased fat deposition in response to changing hormone levels, while in boys it is due to an increase in muscle bulk.

### TRENDS

Studies have shown that the menarche (the onset of menstruation) appears to be occurring at an increasingly early age in girls, at a rate of four to six months earlier every decade. This is thought to be due to improved nutrition. It is likely that boys are also maturing at an earlier age.

*Girls tend to start puberty at different ages. However, most girls will have reached the same level of sexual maturity by the time they are 16.*

## Hormonal triggers

*In addition to undergoing major physical changes, teenagers also suffer the emotional consequences of hormonal fluctuations.*

Puberty is triggered by the production of a gonadotrophin-releasing hormone from a region of the brain known as the hypothalamus.

It is not clear what triggers the release of this hormone. There is speculation that it may be controlled by the interaction between the pineal gland and the hypothalamus, acting as a biological clock.

### SEX GLAND STIMULATION

Gonadotrophin-releasing hormone stimulates a small gland in the brain known as the pituitary. This triggers the release of a group of hormones known as gonadotrophins (sex gland stimulators), at around the age of 10–14 years.

Gonadotrophins stimulate the ovaries to secrete oestrogens, and the testes to produce testosterone. It is these hormones that are responsible for the development of the secondary sexual characteristics during puberty.

### EMOTIONAL CHANGES

The many physical changes that take place during puberty are accompanied by a number of emotional changes.

The main reasons for this are as follows:

■ The individual may have difficulties in coming to terms with the many physical changes taking place in the body. The onset of menstrual periods in girls and the deepening of the voice in boys, for example, can be extremely distressing and cause great self-consciousness

■ The fluctuating levels of hormones during puberty can seriously affect mood, with the result that pubescent individuals are prone to mood swings, aggression, tearfulness and loss of confidence.

# Physical changes during puberty

Testosterone is a key hormone during the period of puberty, causing both complex and profound change in both boys and girls.

Boys start to go through puberty between the ages of 10 and 14. The physical changes that occur during this time are brought about by the male sex hormone, testosterone. This is a growth-promoting hormone that is produced by cells within the testes.

### SPERM PRODUCTION
Before puberty, the testes contain numerous solid cords of cells. With the onset of puberty, the cells at the centre of the cords die, so that the cords become the hollow tubes called seminiferous tubules, in which sperm cells develop.

The production of testosterone within the testes in turn triggers:
■ The onset of sperm production. Large numbers of sperm cells are produced – around 300-600 per gram of testicle every second
■ Growth of the testes, scrotum and penis
■ Spontaneous erections; present since birth, these can now be psychologically induced
■ Maturation of the sperm-carrying ducts and enlargement of the seminal vesicles (sperm-storing sacs)
■ Enlargement of the prostate gland, which starts to secrete fluid that makes up part of the seminal fluid
■ Ejaculation – first occurs around a year after the penis undergoes accelerated growth.

### OTHER CHANGES IN BOYS
Changes continue until the age of around 17. The voice box enlarges, the vocal cords lengthen, and the voice deepens and becomes more resonant. Body hair begins to grow in the pubic region, in the armpits and on the face, chest and abdomen.

Testosterone also accelerates muscular development.

*The release of testosterone triggers puberty in boys. It leads to growth of sexual organs and body hair, and an increase in muscle mass.*

## Male physical changes

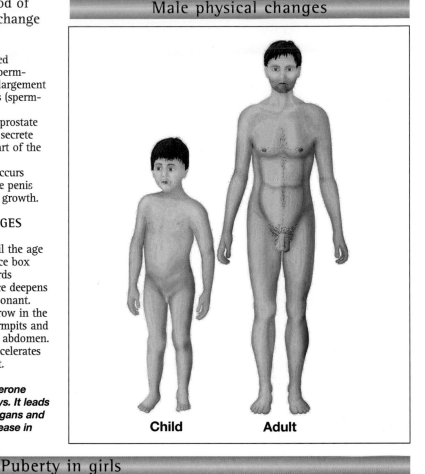

**Child**　　　**Adult**

## Puberty in girls

Puberty in girls tends to start between the ages of 10 and 14, but varies from person to person, and so some girls reach sexual maturity before others.

By the age of 16, however, most girls will have reached the same level of sexual maturity. This period of puberty is characterized by considerable body growth, alterations in body proportions and major changes in the the sexual and reproductive organs.

### BREAST BUDDING
The first sign of puberty in girls is usually breast budding. Hormones trigger the nipples to enlarge and the breast tissue to grow, as milk glands and ducts develop. After this time, breast growth is very rapid.

### ADRENAL GLANDS
During puberty the adrenal glands start producing male sex hormones, such as testosterone. These key hormones:
■ Cause a sudden surge of physical growth
■ Alter the development of hair, causing pubic and underarm hair to develop for the first time.

Menstruation usually begins around a year after these hormones are released.

### HIP DEVELOPMENT
Changes take place in the bones of the pelvis, making it wider in relation to the rest of the skeleton. These changes occur in conjunction with increased deposits of fat around the breasts, hips and buttocks, and create a more curvaceous and womanly appearance.

Puberty is deemed complete when menstruation assumes a regular pattern. This means that ovulation is taking place on a monthly basis and that conception is possible.

## Female physical changes

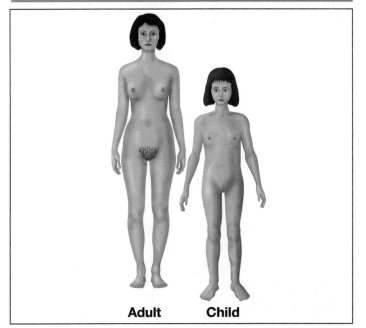

**Adult**　　　**Child**

*Girls undergo huge physical change in puberty. This includes the menarche, breast budding, pelvic bone widening, selective fat deposits and hair growth.*

### Abnormal puberty

Abnormal changes in the hypothalamus or adrenal glands, such as a tumour, can cause the process of puberty to occur at a much earlier age. This rare phenomenon is known as precocious puberty, and can result in full sexual development in young children.

Puberty in both sexes can be delayed by malnutrition or constant physical exertion. Many athletes and gymnasts do not develop sexual characteristics until they have more relaxed training regimes.

A number of genetic disorders (such as cystic fibrosis) can also affect puberty.

# Male reproductive system

The male reproductive system includes the penis, scrotum and the two testes (contained within the scrotum). The internal structures of the reproductive system are contained within the pelvis.

The structures constituting the male reproductive tract are responsible for the production of sperm and seminal fluid and their carriage out of the body. Unlike other organs it is not until puberty that they develop and become fully functional.

## CONSTITUENT PARTS

The male reproductive system consists of a number of interrelated parts:
- Testis – the paired testes lie suspended in the scrotum. Sperm are carried away from the testes through tubes or ducts, the first of which is the epididymis
- Epididymis – on ejaculation sperm leave the epididymis and enter the vas deferens
- Vas deferens – sperm are carried along this muscular tube en route to the prostate gland
- Seminal vesicle – on leaving the vas deferens sperm mix with fluid from the seminal vesicle gland in a combined 'ejaculatory' duct
- Prostate – the ejaculatory duct empties into the urethra within the prostate gland
- Penis – on leaving the prostate gland, the urethra then becomes the central core of the penis.

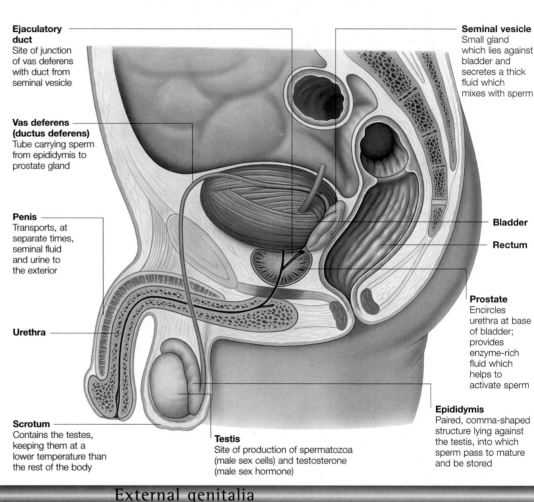

**Ejaculatory duct**
Site of junction of vas deferens with duct from seminal vesicle

**Vas deferens (ductus deferens)**
Tube carrying sperm from epididymis to prostate gland

**Penis**
Transports, at separate times, seminal fluid and urine to the exterior

**Urethra**

**Scrotum**
Contains the testes, keeping them at a lower temperature than the rest of the body

**Testis**
Site of production of spermatozoa (male sex cells) and testosterone (male sex hormone)

**Seminal vesicle**
Small gland which lies against bladder and secretes a thick fluid which mixes with sperm

**Bladder**

**Rectum**

**Prostate**
Encircles urethra at base of bladder; provides enzyme-rich fluid which helps to activate sperm

**Epididymis**
Paired, comma-shaped structure lying against the testis, into which sperm pass to mature and be stored

## External genitalia

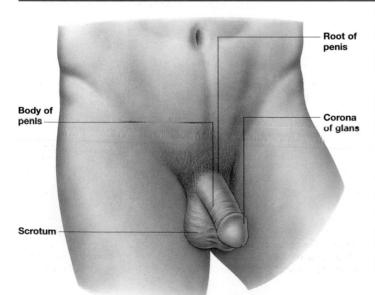

**Root of penis**

**Body of penis**

**Corona of glans**

**Scrotum**

The external genitalia are those parts of the reproductive tract which lie visible in the pubic region, while other parts remain hidden within the pelvic cavity.
   Male external genitalia consists of:
- The scrotum
- The penis.
In adults, these are surrounded by coarse pubic hair

### SCROTUM
The scrotum is a loose bag of skin and connective tissue which

*The external male genitalia consist of the scrotum and the penis, which are situated in the pubic area. In adults, pubic hair surrounds the root of the penis*

holds the testes suspended within it. There is a midline septum, or partition, which separates each testis from its fellow.
   Although it would seem unusual for the testes to be held in such a vulnerable position outside the protection of the body cavity, it is necessary for sperm production for them to be kept cool.

### PENIS
Most of the penis consists of erectile tissue, which becomes engorged with blood during sexual arousal, causing the penis to become erect. The urethra, through which urine and semen pass, runs through the penis.

# Prostate gland

The prostate gland forms a vital part of the male reproductive system, providing enzyme-rich fluid, and produces up to a third of the total volume of the seminal fluid.

About 3 cm (1.2 in) in length, the prostate gland lies just under the bladder and encircles the first part of the urethra. Its base lies closely attached to the base of the bladder, its rounded anterior (front) surface lying just behind the pubic bone.

### CAPSULE
The prostate is covered by a tough capsule made up of dense fibrous connective tissue. Outside this true capsule is a further layer of fibrous connective tissue, which is known as the prostatic sheath.

### INTERNAL STRUCTURE
The urethra, the outflow tract from the bladder, runs vertically through the centre of the prostate gland, where it is known as the prostatic urethra. The ejaculatory ducts open into the prostatic urethra on a raised ridge, the seminal colliculus.
  The prostate is said to be divided into lobes, although they are not as distinct as they may be in other organs:
■ Anterior lobe – this lies in front of the urethra and contains mainly fibromuscular tissue
■ Posterior lobe – this lies behind the urethra and beneath the ejaculatory ducts
■ Lateral lobes – these two lobes, lying on either side of the urethra, form the main part of the gland
■ Median lobe – this lies between the urethra and the ejaculatory ducts.

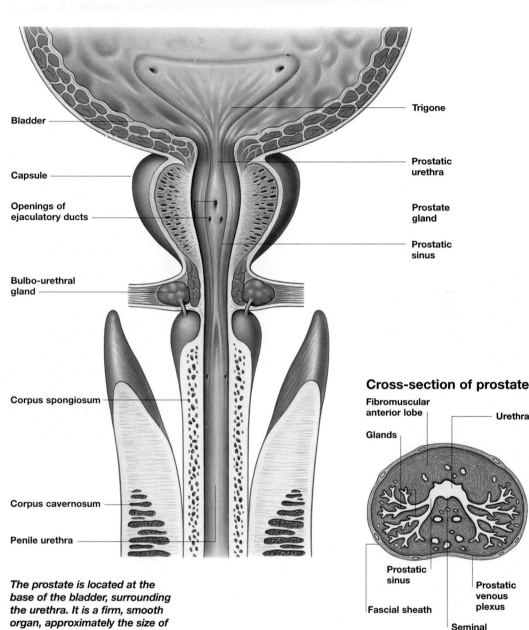

**Location of the prostate gland**

Bladder
Capsule
Openings of ejaculatory ducts
Bulbo-urethral gland
Corpus spongiosum
Corpus cavernosum
Penile urethra

Trigone
Prostatic urethra
Prostate gland
Prostatic sinus

*The prostate is located at the base of the bladder, surrounding the urethra. It is a firm, smooth organ, approximately the size of a walnut.*

### Cross-section of prostate

Fibromuscular anterior lobe
Glands
Urethra
Prostatic sinus
Fascial sheath
Prostatic venous plexus
Seminal colliculus

## Seminal vesicles

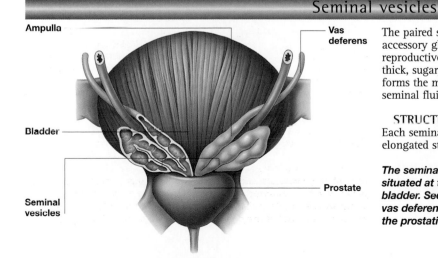

Ampulla
Vas deferens
Bladder
Seminal vesicles
Prostate

The paired seminal vesicles are accessory glands of the male reproductive tract and produce a thick, sugary, alkaline fluid that forms the main part of the seminal fluid.

### STRUCTURE AND SHAPE
Each seminal vesicle is an elongated structure about the

*The seminal vesicles are situated at the back of the bladder. Secretions pass into the vas deferentia, which empty into the prostatic urethra.*

size and shape of a little finger and lies behind the bladder and in front of the rectum, the two forming a V-shape.

### PROSTATE VOLUME
The prostate gland is sac-like, with a volume of approximately 10–15 millilitres. It consists internally of coiled secretory tubules with muscular walls.
  The secretions leave the gland in the duct of the seminal vesicle, which joins with the vas deferens just inside the prostate to form the ejaculatory duct.

69

# Testes, scrotum and epididymis

The testes, which lie suspended within the scrotum, are the sites of sperm production. The scrotum also contains the two epididymides – long, coiled tubes, which connect to the vas deferens.

The paired testes are firm, mobile, oval-shaped structures about 4 cm in length and 2.5 cm in width. The testes lie within the scrotum, a bag formed as an outpouching of the anterior abdominal wall, and are attached above to the spermatic cord, from which they hang.

### TEMPERATURE CONTROL
Normal sperm can only be produced if the temperature of the testes is about three degrees lower than the internal body temperature. Muscle fibres within the spermatic cord and walls of the scrotum help to regulate the scrotal temperature by lifting the testes up towards the body when it is cold, and relaxing when the ambient temperature is higher.

### EPIDIDYMIS
Each epididymis is a firm, comma-shaped structure which lies closely attached to the upper pole of the testis, running down its posterior surface. The epididymis receives the sperm made in the testis and is composed of a highly coiled tube which, if extended, would be six metres in length.

From the tail of the epididymis emerges the vas deferens. This tube will carry the sperm back up the spermatic cord and into the pelvic cavity on the next stage of the journey.

## Sagittal section of the contents of the scrotum

**Spermatic cord**

**Vas deferens**

**Head of epididymis**
Joined to the testis by the efferent ducts

**Efferent ducts**
Carry sperm from testis into the epididymis

**Rete testis**
Tubular network situated on the posterior side of the testis

**Body of epididymis**
Sperm is stored in the epididymis as it matures

**Tail of epididymis**

**Skin of the scrotum**
The scrotal skin is thin wrinkled and pigmented

**Testis**

**Lobule**
Contains one to four tightly coiled seminiferous tubules, the sites of sperm production; in the connective tissue around the tubules are the Leydig cells, which produce male sex hormones

**Tunica albuginea**
Each testis is enclosed within this tough protective capsule

*The paired testes are the male sex organs that produce sperm. The testis and the epididymis on each side lie within the soft scrotal sac.*

## Walls of the scrotum

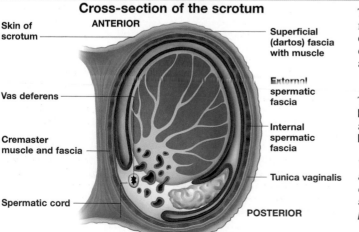

### Cross-section of the scrotum

**Skin of scrotum**

**ANTERIOR**

**Vas deferens**

**Cremaster muscle and fascia**

**Spermatic cord**

**Superficial (dartos) fascia with muscle**

**External spermatic fascia**

**Internal spermatic fascia**

**Tunica vaginalis**

**POSTERIOR**

*The scrotum contains the testes and hangs outside the body. It consists of an outer covering of skin, which surrounds several protective layers.*

The walls of the scrotum have a number of layers, as would be expected from its origin as an outpouching of the multi-layered anterior abdominal wall.

### LAYERS OF THE SCROTUM
The scrotum consists of:
■ Skin, which is thin, wrinkled and pigmented
■ Dartos fascia, a layer of connective tissue with smooth muscle fibres
■ Three layers of fascia derived from the three muscular layers of the abdominal wall, with further cremasteric muscle fibres
■ Tunica vaginalis, a closed sac of thin, slippery, serous membrane, like the peritoneum in the abdomen, which contains a small amount of fluid to lubricate movement of the testes against surrounding structures.

Unlike the abdominal wall, there is no fat in the coverings around the testes, which is believed to help keep them cool.

# Blood supply of the testes

The arterial blood supply of the testes arises from the abdominal aorta, and descends to the scrotum. Venous drainage follows the same route in reverse.

During embryonic life, the testes develop within the abdomen; it is only at birth that they descend into their final position within the scrotum. Because of this the blood supply of the testes arises from the abdominal aorta, and travels down with the descending testis to the scrotum.

### TESTICULAR ARTERIES

The paired testicular arteries are long and narrow and arise from the abdominal aorta. They then pass down on the posterior abdominal wall, crossing the ureters as they go, until they reach the deep inguinal rings and enter the inguinal canal.

As part of the spermatic cord they leave the inguinal canal and enter the scrotum where they supply the testis, also forming interconnections with the artery to the vas deferens.

### TESTICULAR VEINS

Testicular veins arise from the testis and epididymis on each side. Their course differs from that of the testicular arteries within the spermatic cord where, instead of a single vein, there is a network of veins, known as the pampiniform plexus.

Further up in the abdomen, the right testicular vein drains into the large inferior vena cava, while the left normally drains into the left renal vein.

*The blood supply to the testes originates from high up in the abdominal blood vessels. These resulting long vessels allow for the testes' descent in early life.*

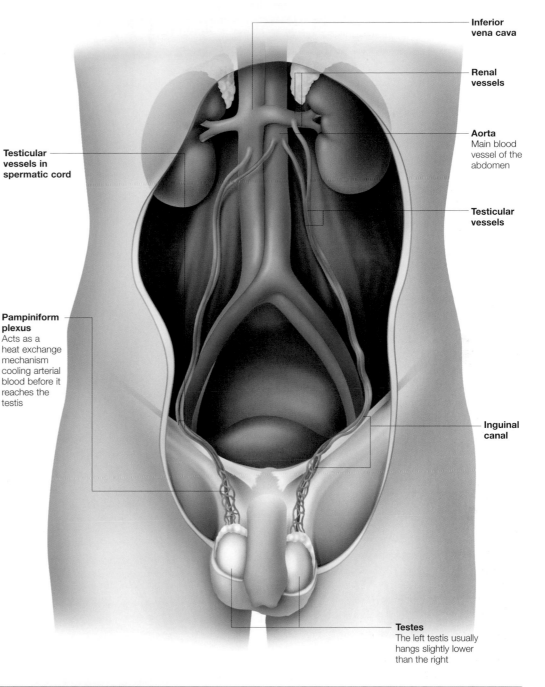

**Inferior vena cava**

**Renal vessels**

**Aorta**
Main blood vessel of the abdomen

**Testicular vessels in spermatic cord**

**Testicular vessels**

**Pampiniform plexus**
Acts as a heat exchange mechanism cooling arterial blood before it reaches the testis

**Inguinal canal**

**Testes**
The left testis usually hangs slightly lower than the right

## Internal structure of the testis

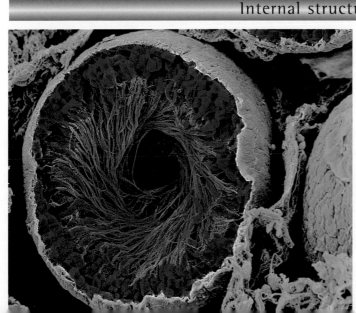

Each testis is enclosed within a tough, protective capsule, the tunica albuginea, from which numerous septa, or partitions, pass down to divide the testis into about 250 tiny lobules.

Each wedge-shaped lobule contains one to four tightly coiled seminiferous tubules, which are the actual sites of production of sperm.

*This micrograph shows a sectioned seminiferous tubule. Developing sperm (red) are inside the tubule, which is surrounded by Leydig cells (green).*

It has been estimated that there is a total of 350 metres of sperm-producing tubules in each testis.

### TUBULES

Sperm are collected from the coiled seminiferous tubules into the straight tubules of the rete testis and from there into the epididymis.

Between the seminiferous tubules lie groups of specialized cells, the interstitial or Leydig cells, which are the site of production of hormones such as testosterone.

# How sperm are produced

Sperm are the male sex cells, produced and stored in the testes.
Owing to the process of meiosis, a specialized division of the
cell nucleus, each cell contains a unique set of genes.

Sperm are mature male sex cells, vital to fertilization. They are produced in the testes, two walnut-sized organs located in the scrotum. The scrotum is the pouch that hangs below the penis, and is around two degrees cooler than the core temperature of the body, so providing the optimum temperature for the production of sperm.

In order to maintain this temperature, the scrotum can pull up closer to the body when the surrounding temperature is low, and can drop farther away as the temperature rises.

### SEXUAL ORGANS

The testes are the primary producers of testosterone (the male sex hormone).

These specialized organs each contain around 1,000 seminiferous tubules, which are responsible for the manufacture and storage of sperm. The tubules are lined by small cells known as spermatogonia.

From puberty onwards spermatogonia cells start to divide to produce cells which

eventually develop into sperm.

Alternating with the spermatogonia are much larger cells, the Sertoli cells, which secrete nutrient fluid into the tubules.

### SPERMATOGENESIS

Spermatogenesis (the formation of sperm) is a complex process, involving the constant proliferation of spermatogonia cells, to form primary spermatocytes. These cells have a full set of genes, identical to those in other body cells.

### MEIOSIS

The primary spermatocytes then undergo a specialized division known as meiosis, in which they split twice to produce cells with a random half (haploid) set of genes. These cells, known as spermatids, develop and grow to produce mature, motile sperm.

*The seminiferous tubules of the testes are lined with small cells, called spermatogonia. These cells divide to produce primary spermatocytes.*

## Formation of sperm

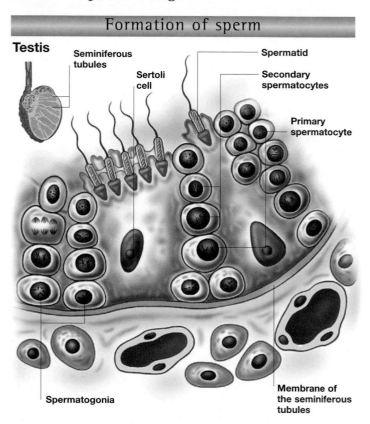

**Testis**

Seminiferous tubules

Sertoli cell

Spermatid

Secondary spermatocytes

Primary spermatocyte

Spermatogonia

Membrane of the seminiferous tubules

## Division of genetic information

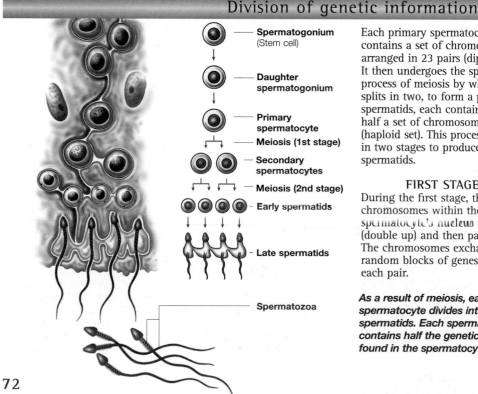

- Spermatogonium (Stem cell)
- Daughter spermatogonium
- Primary spermatocyte
- Meiosis (1st stage)
- Secondary spermatocytes
- Meiosis (2nd stage)
- Early spermatids
- Late spermatids
- Spermatozoa

Each primary spermatocyte contains a set of chromosomes, arranged in 23 pairs (diploid set). It then undergoes the specialized process of meiosis by which it splits in two, to form a pair of spermatids, each containing only half a set of chromosomes (haploid set). This process occurs in two stages to produce four spermatids.

### FIRST STAGE

During the first stage, the chromosomes within the spermatocyte's nucleus replicate (double up) and then pair off. The chromosomes exchange random blocks of genes within each pair.

*As a result of meiosis, each spermatocyte divides into four spermatids. Each spermatid contains half the genetic material found in the spermatocyte.*

This exchange is nature's way of 'shuffling' the gene pool and introducing variation within the offspring. The paired chromosomes separate as the cell divides, each cell receiving two copies of one member of each chromosome pair. The spermatocytes then divide again.

### SECOND STAGE

During the second stage of meiosis, the 23 replicated chromosomes within each nucleus split up and the spermatocytes divide again.

The end result of meiosis is the production of spermatids that contain half the number of chromosomes of a spermatocyte. The genetic make-up of each resulting spermatid is unique, due to the mixing process and the chances of any two being identical are virtually zero.

# Structure of sperm

Mature sperm cells are specially designed to facilitate the swimming movement used to propel them towards the female's egg.

The spermatids move towards the nearest Sertoli cell, where they receive nourishment in the form of glycogen, proteins, sugars and other nutrients. This provides them with energy and helps them to mature into spermatozoa.

Spermatozoa are among the most specialized cells in the body. Each sperm (spermatozoon) measures 0.05 mm in length and consists of a head, neck and tail.

### SPERMATOZOA

The head of the sperm is shaped like a flattened teardrop, and contains a sac of enzymes known as the acrosome. These enzymes are vitally important to the sperm's ability to break down and penetrate the protective outer layer of the female's egg during fertilization.

Behind the acrosome is the cell nucleus, which contains a random half set of male genetic material (DNA) tightly coiled within 23 chromosomes. Thanks to the process of meiosis, each sperm possesses a unique set of genetic information.

The neck is a fibrous area where the middle part of the sperm joins the head. It is a flexible structure and allows the head to swing from side to side, facilitating the swimming movement.

### TAIL STRUCTURE

The sperm tail consists of a pair of a long filaments surrounded by two rings each containing nine fibrils. At the front end of the tail are a further ring of outer dense fibres and also a protective tail sheath. The tail is divided into three sections:

■ The middle piece – the fattest part of the tail, due to an additional spiral layer full of energy-producing units known as mitochondria. These produce energy which fuels the sperm, allowing it to swim.

■ The principal piece – consists of the 20 filaments, along with the outer dense fibres and tail sheath.

■ The end piece – here the dense fibres and tail sheath thin out, with the result that this part of the tail is enclosed only by a thin cell membrane. This gradual tapering is what produces the sperm's characteristic whiplash-like swimming motion, driving the sperm towards the egg.

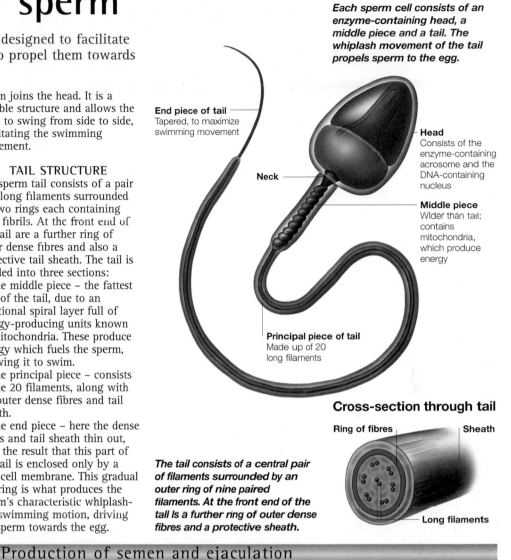

*Each sperm cell consists of an enzyme-containing head, a middle piece and a tail. The whiplash movement of the tail propels sperm to the egg.*

**End piece of tail**
Tapered, to maximize swimming movement

**Neck**

**Head**
Consists of the enzyme-containing acrosome and the DNA-containing nucleus

**Middle piece**
Wider than tail; contains mitochondria, which produce energy

**Principal piece of tail**
Made up of 20 long filaments

### Cross-section through tail

**Ring of fibres**   **Sheath**

**Long filaments**

*The tail consists of a central pair of filaments surrounded by an outer ring of nine paired filaments. At the front end of the tail is a further ring of outer dense fibres and a protective sheath.*

## Production of semen and ejaculation

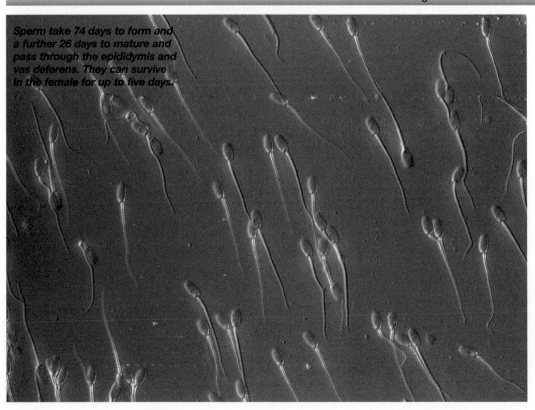

*Sperm take 74 days to form and a further 26 days to mature and pass through the epididymis and vas deferens. They can survive in the female for up to five days.*

Once their tails are fully developed the sperm are released by the Sertoli cell into the seminiferous tubule. As fluid is secreted into the tubule by the Sertoli cells, a current is produced which washes the sperm cells towards the epididymis. This is a long tube coiled against the testes in which the mature sperm are stored.

### EJACULATION

The sperm are propelled from the epididymis during sexual stimulation and up the vas deferens via a wave of muscular contractions within the ducting system. They travel to the ejaculatory duct, through the prostate, and into the urethra. Here they are bathed in secretions from the prostate gland and seminal vesicles (small sacs that hold constituents of semen). The result is a thick, yellowish-white fluid, known as semen.

The average discharge of semen (ejaculate) contains approximately 300 million sperm.

# Female reproductive system

The role of the female reproductive tract is twofold.
The ovaries produce eggs for fertilization, and the uterus nurtures
and protects any resulting fetus for its nine-month gestation.

The female reproductive tract is composed of the internal genitalia – the ovaries, uterine (Fallopian) tubes, uterus and vagina – and the external genitalia (the vulva).

## INTERNAL GENITALIA

The almond-shaped ovaries lie on either side of the uterus, suspended by ligaments. Above the ovaries are the paired uterine tubes, each of which provides a site for fertilization of the oocyte (egg), which then travels down the tube to the uterus.

The uterus lies within the pelvic cavity and rises into the lower abdominal cavity as a pregnancy progresses. The vagina, which connects the cervix to the vulva, can be distended greatly, as occurs during childbirth when it forms much of the birth canal.

## EXTERNAL GENITALIA

The female external genitalia, or vulva, is where the reproductive tract opens to the exterior. The vaginal opening lies behind the opening of the urethra in an area known as the vestibule. This is covered by two folds of skin on each side, the labia minora and labia majora, in front of which lies the raised clitoris.

*The female reproductive system is composed of internal and external organs. The internal genitalia are T-shaped and lie within the pelvic cavity.*

**Fimbriae**
Finger-like projections at end of uterine tube which curve around ovary

**Uterus**
Hollow organ, also known as the womb, which contains, nurtures and protects the growing fetus

**Uterine (Fallopian) tube**
Extends from ovary to uterus; receives egg released from ovary

**Ovary**
Site of production of eggs; produces the female sex hormones, the oestrogens

**Ligament of ovary**

**Broad ligament**
Double layer of serous membrane; contains blood vessels

**Ovary (coronal section)**
Eggs develop within follicles inside the ovary during the menstrual cycle; normally, only one egg is released in each cycle

**Cervix**
Thickened lower portion of the muscular uterus which connects the vagina to the uterine cavity

**Vagina**
Thin-walled tube that runs from the cervix to open to the exterior at the vulva

## Position of the female reproductive tract

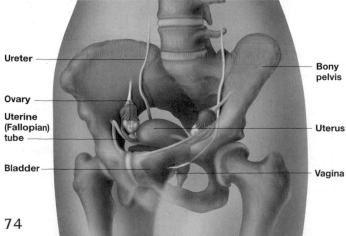

Ureter
Ovary
Uterine (Fallopian) tube
Bladder
Bony pelvis
Uterus
Vagina

In adult women the internal genitalia (which, apart from the ovaries, are basically tubular in structure) are located deep within the pelvic cavity They are thus protected by the presence of the circle of bone which makes up the pelvis.

This is in contrast to the

*The internal reproductive organs in adult women are positioned deep within the pelvic cavity. They are therefore protected by the bony pelvis.*

pelvic cavity of young children, which is relatively shallow. A child's uterus, therefore, like the bladder behind which it sits, is located within the lower abdomen.

### BROAD LIGAMENTS

The upper surface of the uterus and ovaries is draped in a 'tent' of peritoneum, the thin lining of the abdominal and pelvic cavities, forming the broad ligament which helps to keep the uterus in its position.

# Blood supply of the internal genitalia

The female reproductive tract receives a rich blood supply via an interconnecting network of arteries. Venous blood is drained by a network of veins.

The four principal arteries of the female genitalia are:

■ **Ovarian artery** – this runs from the abdominal aorta to the ovary.
    Branches from the ovarian artery on each side pass through the mesovarium, the fold of peritoneum in which the ovary lies, to supply the ovary and uterine (Fallopian) tubes. The ovarian artery in the tissue of the mesovarium connects with the uterine artery
■ **Uterine artery** – this is a branch of the large internal iliac artery of the pelvis. The uterine artery approaches the uterus at the level of the cervix, which is anchored in place by cervical ligaments.
    The uterine artery connects with the ovarian artery above, while a branch connects with the arteries below to supply the cervix and vagina
■ **Vaginal artery** – this is also a branch of the internal iliac artery. Together with blood from the uterine artery, its branches supply blood to the vaginal walls
■ **Internal pudendal artery** – this contributes to the blood supply of the lower third of the vagina and anus.

## VEINS

A plexus, or network, of small veins lies within the walls of the uterus and vagina. Blood received into these vessels drains into the internal iliac veins via the uterine vein.

**Uterine vein**
Receives blood from small vessels in walls of uterus and vagina and drains into internal iliac vein

**Uterine artery**
A branch of the internal iliac artery, this connects with the ovarian artery, and supplies the body of the uterus

**Ovarian artery**
Runs from the aorta in the abdomen down to the pelvis to reach the ovary through its suspensory ligament

**Ovarian vein**
Vein through which venous drainage of the ovaries occurs; ascends along the posterior abdominal wall to empty into the inferior vena cava or left renal vein in the abdomen

**Vaginal artery**
Supplies blood to vaginal walls

**Internal pudendal artery**
Supplies the lower third of the vagina; it is a branch of the internal iliac artery

*In this illustration, the surface layer of the female pelvic organs has been removed. This reveals the vasculature beneath.*

## Visualizing the female reproductive tract

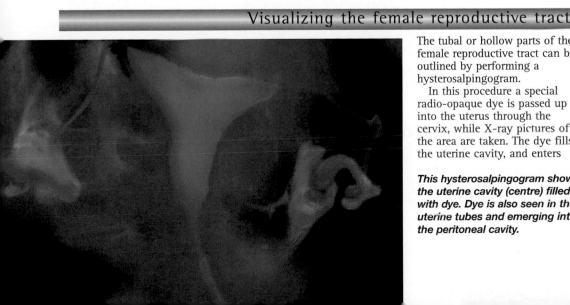

The tubal or hollow parts of the female reproductive tract can be outlined by performing a hysterosalpingogram.
    In this procedure a special radio-opaque dye is passed up into the uterus through the cervix, while X-ray pictures of the area are taken. The dye fills the uterine cavity, and enters

*This hysterosalpingogram shows the uterine cavity (centre) filled with dye. Dye is also seen in the uterine tubes and emerging into the peritoneal cavity.*

the uterine tubes. It then runs along their length until it flows into the peritoneal cavity at their far end.

### ASSESSING TUBES

A hysterosalpingogram is sometimes carried out in the investigation of infertility to determine whether the uterine tubes are still patent (unobstructed). If the tubes have been blocked, as may happen after an infection, the dye will not be able to travel along their full length.

# The uterus

The uterus, or womb, is the part of the female reproductive tract that nurtures and protects the fetus during pregnancy. It lies within the pelvic cavity and is a hollow, muscular organ.

During a woman's reproductive years, in the non-pregnant state, the uterus is about 7.5 cm (3 in) long and 5 cm (2 in) across at its widest point. However, it can expand hugely to accommodate the fetus during pregnancy.

## STRUCTURE

The uterus is said to be made up of two parts:

■ The body, forming the upper part of the uterus – this is fairly mobile as it must expand during pregnancy. The central triangular space, or cavity, of the body receives the openings of the paired uterine (Fallopian) tubes

■ The cervix, the lower part of the uterus – this is a thick, muscular canal, which is anchored to the surrounding pelvic structures for stability.

## UTERINE WALLS

The main part of the uterus, the body, has a thick wall which is composed of three layers:

■ Perimetrium – the thin outer coat which is continuous with the pelvic peritoneum

■ Myometrium – forming the great bulk of the uterine wall

■ Endometrium – the delicate lining, which is specialized to allow implantation of an embryo should fertilization occur.

*The uterus resembles an inverted pear in shape. It is suspended in the pelvic cavity by peritoneal folds or ligaments.*

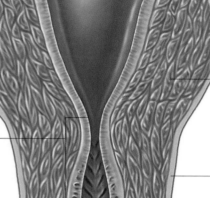

**Uterine (Fallopian) tubes**
Extend to the ovaries, which they envelop; open ends are fringed with finger-like processes called fimbriae

**Body of the uterus**
Upper part is connected to the two uterine tubes; lower part joins the cervix and vagina

**Cervix of the uterus**
Protrudes slightly into the vagina, where the cervical canal opens at the external os

**Fornix**
Shallow gutter formed by the cervix pushing into the vagina

**External os**

**Fundus of uterus**
Part of the body of the uterus that lies above the level of the uterine tubes

**Endometrium**
Lining that becomes thicker during the menstrual cycle in preparation for implantation of the embryo

**Myometrium**
A thick muscle layer, containing the majority of the blood vessels and nerves supplying the uterus

**Perimetrium**
Continuous with the pelvic peritoneum, this is the slippery layer of connective tissue lining the pelvic cavity

**Vagina**

## Position of the uterus

**Normal position of the uterus**

**Bladder**

**Vagina**

**Uterus in extreme retroverted position**

**Rectum**

The uterus lies in the pelvis between the bladder and the rectum. However, its position changes with the stage of filling of these two structures and with different postures.

### NORMAL POSITION

Normally the long axis of the uterus forms an angle of 90 degrees with the long axis of the vagina, with the uterus lying forward on top of the bladder. This usual position is known as anteversion.

*In most women the uterus lies on the bladder, moving backwards as the bladder fills. However, it may lie in any position between the two extremes shown.*

### ANTEFLEXION

In some women, the uterus lies in the normal position, but may curve forwards slightly between the cervix and fundus, This is termed anteflexion.

### RETROFLEXION

In some cases, however, the uterus bends not forwards but backwards, the fundus coming to lie next to the rectum. This is known as a retroverted uterus.

Regardless of the uterine position it will normally bend forwards as it expands in pregnancy. A pregnant retroverted uterus, however, may take longer to reach the pelvic brim, at which point it becomes palpable abdominally.

# The uterus in pregnancy

In pregnancy the uterus must enlarge to hold the growing fetus. From being a small pelvic organ, it increases in size to take up much of the space of the abdominal cavity.

Pressure of the enlarged uterus on the abdominal organs pushes them up against the diaphragm, encroaching on the thoracic cavity and causing the ribs to flare out to compensate. Organs such as the stomach and bladder are compressed to such an extent in late pregnancy that their capacity is greatly diminished and they become full sooner.

After pregnancy, the uterus will rapidly decrease in size again although it will always remain slightly larger than one which has never been pregnant.

### HEIGHT OF FUNDUS

During pregnancy the enlarging uterus can be accommodated within the pelvis for the first 12 weeks, at which time the uppermost part, the fundus, can just be palpated in the lower abdomen. By 20 weeks, the fundus will have reached the region of the umbilicus, and by late pregnancy it may have reached the xiphisternum, the lowest part of the breastbone.

### WEIGHT OF UTERUS

In the final stages of pregnancy the uterus will have increased in weight from a pre-pregnant 45 g to around 900 g. The myometrium (muscle layer) grows as the individual fibres increase in size (hypertrophy). In addition, the fibres increase in number (hyperplasia).

**Stretched abdominal wall**

**Pregnant uterus**
Increases greatly in size, taking up most of the abdominal cavity and compressing other organs

**Sacrum**
Curved, triangular element of the backbone

**Umbilicus**
Uterus reaches this level at 20 weeks' pregnancy

**Bladder**
Has less capacity due to being compressed by the enlarged uterus, so pregnant women tend to pass urine frequently

**Coccyx**
Rudimentary 'tail' bone

**Rectum (cut)**

**Levator ani muscle**
The 'pelvic diaphragm'; holds the pelvic organs in place

*During pregnancy, the uterus expands to hold the fetus. The abdominal contents become compressed between uterus and diaphragm.*

## Lining of the uterus

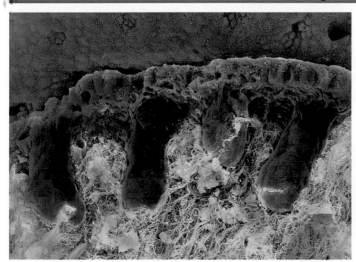

The endometrium is the name given to the lining of the uterus. It consists of a simple surface layer, or epithelium, overlying a thicker layer of highly cellular connective tissue, the lamina propria. Numerous tubular glands are also present within the endometrium.

### MENSTRUAL CYCLE

Under the influence of sex hormones the endometrium undergoes changes during the

*This enlarged section through the endometrium of the uterus shows the layer of epithelial cells (blue). Three tubular glands are also clearly visible.*

monthly menstrual cycle which prepare it for the possible implantation of an embryo. It may vary in thickness from 1 mm to 5 mm before being shed at menstruation.

### BLOOD SUPPLY

Arteries within the myometrium, the underlying muscle layer, send numerous small branches into the endometrium. There are two types: straight arteries, which supply the lower, permanent layer; and tortuous (twisted) spiral arteries, which supply the upper layer shed during menstruation. The tortuosity of the spiral arteries prevents excess bleeding during menstruation.

# Menstrual cycle

The menstrual cycle is the regular process by which an egg is released from an ovary in preparation for pregnancy. This occurs approximately every four weeks from the time of a woman's first period right up to the menopause.

The menstrual cycle is characterized by the periodic maturation of oocytes (cells that develop into eggs) in the ovaries and associated physical changes in the uterus. Reproductive maturity occurs after a sudden increase in the secretion of hormones during puberty, usually between the ages of 11 and 15.

## CYCLE ONSET

The time of the first period, which occurs at about the age of 12, is called the menarche. After this, a reproductive cycle begins, averaging 28 days. This length of time may be longer, shorter or variable, depending on the individual. The cycle is continuous, apart from during pregnancy. However, women suffering from anorexia nervosa or athletes who train intensively may cease to menstruate.

## MENSTRUATION

Each month, if conception does not occur, oestrogen and progesterone levels fall and the blood-rich lining of the uterus is shed at menstruation (menses). This takes place every 28 days or so, but the time can range from 19 to 36 days.

Menstruation lasts for about five days. Around 50 ml (about an eggcup) of blood, uterine tissues and fluid is lost during this time, but again this volume varies from woman to woman. Some women lose only 10 ml of blood, while others lose 110 ml.

Excessive menstrual bleeding is known as menorrhagia; temporary cessation of menstruation – such as during pregnancy – is called amenorrhoea. The menopause is the complete cessation of the menstrual cycle, and usually occurs between 45 and 55.

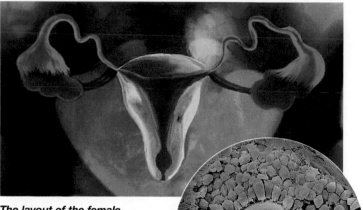

*The layout of the female reproductive system is shown here as a computer-enhanced image of the major structures over a false-colour X-ray.*

*A developing egg in the centre of its follicle. The number of eggs is finite, and they are usually used up by the age of 50.*

## Monthly physiological changes

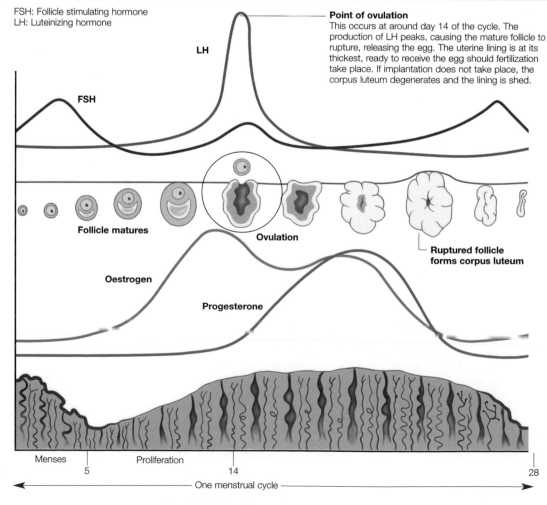

*This diagram illustrates the ongoing changes during the cycle. Between days one and five, the lining is discharged, while another follicle is developing. The uterine lining thickens, and around day 14, the egg is released, at the point called ovulation.*

**Gonadotrophic hormones**
Released by the pituitary gland to promote the production of the egg and of sex hormones in the gonads (ovaries)

**Ovarian activity**
Each month, one follicle develops to maturity, then releases an egg at ovulation; the surviving tissue in the ovary forms the corpus luteum, a temporary hormone-producing gland

**Ovarian hormones**
Secreted by the ovary to encourage the lining to grow; extra progesterone is produced by the corpus luteum after ovulation to prepare the uterus for pregnancy

**Lining of uterus**
Progressively thickens to receive the fertilized egg; if the egg does not implant, the lining is shed (menses) during the first five days of the cycle

FSH: Follicle stimulating hormone
LH: Luteinizing hormone

**Point of ovulation**
This occurs at around day 14 of the cycle. The production of LH peaks, causing the mature follicle to rupture, releasing the egg. The uterine lining is at its thickest, ready to receive the egg should fertilization take place. If implantation does not take place, the corpus luteum degenerates and the lining is shed.

LH

FSH

Follicle matures

Ovulation

Ruptured follicle forms corpus luteum

Oestrogen

Progesterone

Menses  Proliferation

**Days**  5  14  28

One menstrual cycle

# Egg development

The process of developing a healthy egg for release at ovulation takes around six months. It occurs throughout life until the stock of oocytes is exhausted.

Two million eggs (oogonia) are present at birth, distributed between the two ovaries, and 400,000 are left by the time of the first period. During each menstrual cycle, only one egg – from a pool of around 20 potential eggs – develops and is released. By the time menopause is reached, the process of atresia (cell degeneration) in the ovaries is complete and no eggs remain.

Eggs develop within cavity-forming secretory structures called follicles. The first stage of follicle development occurs when an oogonium becomes surrounded by a single layer of granulosa cells and is called a primordial (primary) follicle. The genetic material within the egg at this stage remains undisturbed – but susceptible to alteration –

until ovulation of that egg occurs, up to 45 years after it first developed. This helps to explain the increase in abnormal chromosomes in eggs and offspring of women who conceive later in life.

Primordial follicles develop into secondary follicles by meiotic (reductive) division and then into tertiary (or antral, meaning 'with a cavity') follicles. As many as 20 primary follicles will begin to mature, although 19 will eventually regress. If more than one follicle develops to maturity, twins or triplets may be conceived.

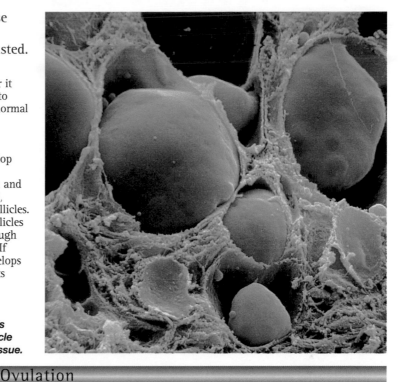

*The follicles are located in the cortex of the ovary. This micrograph shows the follicle separated by connective tissue.*

## Ovulation

The final 14 day period of follicular development takes place during the first half of the menstrual cycle and depends on the precise hormonal interplay between the ovary, pituitary gland and the hypothalamus.

The trigger for selecting a

healthy egg for development at the start of each cycle is a rise in the secretion of follicle stimulating hormone (FSH) by the pituitary gland. This occurs in response to a fall in the hormones oestrogen and progesterone during the luteal

phase (second 14 days) of the previous cycle if conception has not occurred.

### EGG SELECTION
At the time of the FSH signal, there are about 20 secondary follicles, 2–5 mm (0.1–0.2 in) in diameter, distributed between the two ovaries. A single follicle is selected from this pool, while the others undergo atresia. Once a follicle is selected, the development of further follicles is prevented. A typical 5 mm (0.2 in) secondary follicle will then require 10–12 days of sustained stimulation by FSH to grow to a diameter of 20 mm (0.8 in) before rupturing, releasing the

*Under a light microscope, a secondary oocyte (mature egg) can be seen surrounded by the cells of the corona radiata that support it during development.*

egg into the uterine (Fallopian) tube. As the follicle enlarges, there is a steady rise in oestrogen production, triggering a mid-cycle rise in luteinizing hormone (LH) by the pituitary, which in causes release and maturation of the egg. The interval between the LH peak and ovulation is relatively constant (about 36 hours). The ruptured follicle (corpus luteum) that remains after ovulation becomes a very important endocrine gland, secreting oestrogen and progesterone.

### HORMONE REGULATION
Progesterone levels rise to a peak about seven days after ovulation. If fertilization takes place, the corpus luteum maintains the pregnancy until the placenta takes over at about three months' gestation. If no conception takes place, the gland has a lifespan of 14 days, and oestrogen and progesterone levels decline in anticipation of the next cycle.

In the first half of the cycle, oestrogen secreted by the developing follicle (stage before corpus luteum) enables the lining of the uterus (endometrium) to proliferate and increase in thickness ready to nourish the egg should it become fertilized. Once the corpus luteum is formed, progesterone converts the endometrium to a more compact layer in anticipation of an embryo implanting.

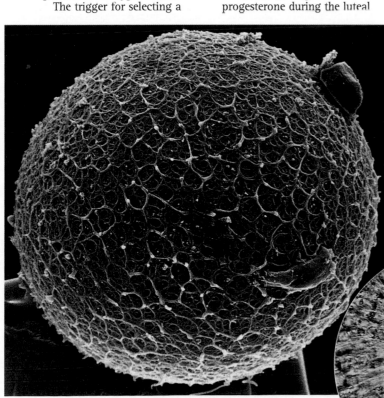

*The fully developed egg is surrounded by a protein coating called the zona pellucida. This serves to trap and bind a single sperm during the process of fertilization.*

# How ovulation occurs

### The total supply of eggs for a woman's reproductive years is determined before she is born. The immature eggs are stored in the ovary until puberty, after which one is released every month.

An ovum (egg) is the female gamete, or sex cell, which unites with a sperm to form a new individual. Eggs are produced and stored in the ovaries, two walnut-sized organs connected to the uterus via the uterine (Fallopian) tubes.

## THE OVARY
Each ovary is covered by a protective layer of peritoneum (abdominal lining). Immediately below this layer is a dense fibrous capsule, the tunica albuginea. The ovary itself consists of a dense outer region, called the cortex, and a less dense inner region, the medulla.

## GAMETE PRODUCTION
In females, the total supply of eggs is determined at birth. Egg-forming cells degenerate from birth to puberty and the timespan during which a woman can release mature eggs is limited from puberty until menopause. The process by which ova are produced is known as oogenesis, which literally means 'the beginning of an egg'. Germ cells in the fetus produce many oogonia cells. These divide to form primary oocytes which are enclosed in groups of follicle cells (support cells).

## GENETIC DIVISION
The primary oocytes begin to divide by meiosis (a specialized nuclear division) but this process is interrupted in its first phase and is not completed until after puberty. At birth, a lifetime's supply of primary oocytes, numbering between 700,000 and two million, will have been formed. These specialized cells will lie dormant in the cortical region of the immature ovary and slowly degenerate, so that by puberty only 40,000 remain.

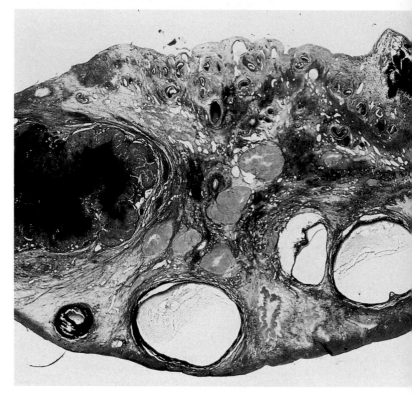

*This micrograph shows an ovary with several large follicles (white). During ovulation, up to 20 follicles begin to develop, but only one matures to release an egg.*

---

## Egg development

### How an egg develops

**BEFORE BIRTH** — Primordial follicle

**CHILDHOOD**

Zona pellucida — Follicular development arrested

**AT PUBERTY** — Primary follicle

Granulosa cells — Developing secondary follicle

Cumulus mass — **Graafian follicle**
Although several primary follicles develop with each menstrual cycle, only one Graafian follicle is formed; the other follicles regress

*Follicular development begins in the fetus, stops during childhood and is stimulated to continue each month by the onset of the ovarian cycle at puberty.*

— Ruptured follicle

— Released egg

Before puberty the primary oocyte is surrounded by a layer of cells (the granulosa cells), forming a primary follicle.

### PUBERTY
With the onset of puberty, some of the primary follicles are stimulated each month by hormones to continue development and become secondary follicles:
■ A layer of clear viscous fluid, the zona pellucida, is deposited on the surface of the oocyte.
■ The granulosa cells multiply and form an increasing number of layers around the oocyte.
■ The centre of the follicle becomes a chamber (the antrum) that fills with fluid secreted by the granulosa cells.
■ The oocyte is pushed to one side of the follicle, and lies in a mass of follicular cells called the cumulus mass.
  A mature secondary follicle is called a Graafian follicle.

## Meiosis

The first meiotic division produces two cells of unequal size – the secondary oocyte and the first polar body. The secondary oocyte contains nearly all the cytoplasm of the primary oocyte. Both cells begin a second division; however, this process is halted, and is not completed until the oocyte is fertilized by a sperm.

*Meiosis, a specialized nuclear division, occurs in the ovaries, giving rise to a female sex cell and three polar bodies.*

# Egg release

Ovulation occurs when a follicle ruptures, releasing a mature oocyte into the uterine tube. It is at this stage in the menstrual cycle that fertilization may occur.

As the Graafian follicle continues to swell, it can be seen on the surface of the ovary as a blister-like structure.

### HORMONAL CHANGES

In response to hormonal changes, the follicular cells surrounding the oocyte begin to secrete a thinner fluid at an increased rate, so that the follicle rapidly swells. As a result, the follicular wall becomes very thin over the area exposed to the ovarian surface, and the follicle eventually ruptures.

### OVULATION

A small amount of blood and follicular fluid is forced out of the vesicle, and the secondary oocyte, surrounded by the cumulus mass and zona pellucida, is expelled from the follicle into the peritoneal cavity – the process of ovulation.

Women are generally unaware of this phenomenon, although some experience a twinge of pain in the lower abdomen. This is caused by the intense stretching of the ovarian wall.

### FERTILE PERIOD

Ovulation occurs around the 14th day of a woman's menstrual cycle, and it is at this time that a woman is at her most fertile. As sperm can survive in the uterus for up to five days, there is a period of about a week when fertilization can occur.

In the event that the secondary oocyte is penetrated by a sperm cell and pregnancy ensues, the final stages of meiotic division will be triggered. If, however, the egg is not fertilized, the second stage of meiosis will not be completed and the secondary oocyte will simply degenerate.

The ruptured follicle forms a gland called the corpus luteum that secretes progesterone. This hormone prepares the uterine lining to receive an embryo.

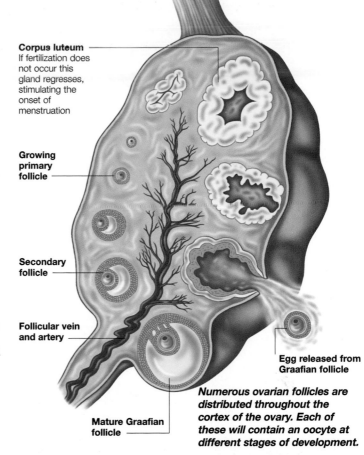

**Corpus luteum**
If fertilization does not occur this gland regresses, stimulating the onset of menstruation

**Growing primary follicle**

**Secondary follicle**

**Follicular vein and artery**

**Mature Graafian follicle**

**Egg released from Graafian follicle**

*Numerous ovarian follicles are distributed throughout the cortex of the ovary. Each of these will contain an oocyte at different stages of development.*

---

## The menstrual cycle

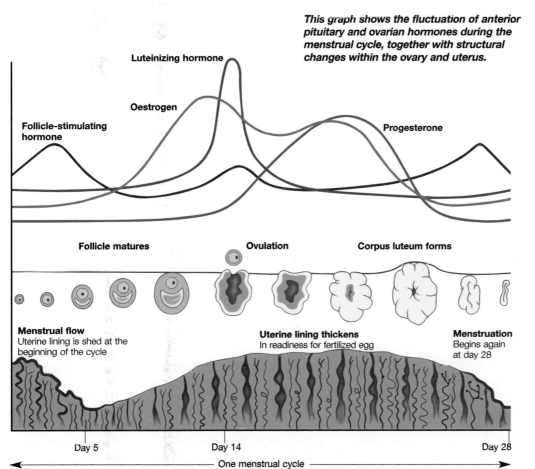

*This graph shows the fluctuation of anterior pituitary and ovarian hormones during the menstrual cycle, together with structural changes within the ovary and uterus.*

**Luteinizing hormone**

**Oestrogen**

**Follicle-stimulating hormone**

**Progesterone**

**Follicle matures**

**Ovulation**

**Corpus luteum forms**

**Menstrual flow**
Uterine lining is shed at the beginning of the cycle

**Uterine lining thickens**
In readiness for fertilized egg

**Menstruation**
Begins again at day 28

Day 5      Day 14      Day 28

← One menstrual cycle →

The oestrus, or menstrual cycle, refers to the cyclical changes which take place in the female reproductive system during the production of eggs.

These changes are controlled by hormones released by the pituitary gland and ovaries: oestrogen, progesterone, luteinizing hormone and follicle-stimulating hormone.

### UTERINE CHANGES

Following menstruation the endometrium thickens and becomes more vascular under the influence of oestrogen and follicle-stimulating hormone.

During the first 14 days of the menstrual cycle a Graafian follicle matures. Ovulation occurs around day 14 when the secondary oocyte is expelled and swept into the uterine tube.

The ruptured follicle becomes a hormone-secreting body called the corpus luteum. This secretes progesterone, stimulating further thickening of the uterine lining (endometrium) in which the fertilized ovum will implant.

If fertilization does not occur, the levels of progesterone and oestrogen decrease. This causes the endometrium to break down and be excreted into the menstrual flow.

# How orgasm occurs

Men and women undergo many physiological changes during orgasm
– the climax of sexual intercourse. Male orgasm involves ejaculation,
and female orgasm increases the likelihood of successful fertilization.

Sexual intercourse is the means by which the male sex cells (sperm) are transferred to the female reproductive tract.

During sexual intercourse, the man inserts his erect penis into the woman's vagina. Sexual stimulation causes semen to be pumped from the testicles out through the penis, causing ejaculation to occur.

## STAGES OF AROUSAL

Sexual arousal occurs in a series of definite stages. During each of these phases, the body experiences different physical changes as it reaches different levels of arousal. After an initial period of desire, both men and women go through four phases:
- Excitement
- Plateau
- Orgasm
- Resolution.

Men and women exhibit different sexual responses, and these differ significantly from person to person. For both sexes, however, orgasm is the climax of sexual intercourse.

## PHYSIOLOGICAL REASONS

The ejaculation of semen that accompanies male orgasm is a prerequisite for fertilization occurring, and it is believed that the female orgasm increases the chance of an egg being fertilized.

Orgasm also creates the urge for sexual intercourse in the first place; for many, it is the pursuit of this pleasurable sensation that is the driving force to copulate.

*For orgasm to occur, men and women must be aroused both physically and mentally. The exact extent of the orgasm will differ from person to person.*

## Male sexual response

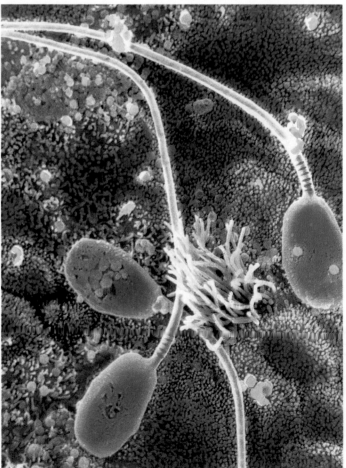

*The contractions during male orgasm are strong enough to propel semen into the woman's reproductive tract. A man usually has three to five main contractions during orgasm.*

### EXCITEMENT

When a man becomes aroused, there is a sudden increase in blood flow to his genitals that causes the penis to become erect. In addition, his heart rate, blood pressure and breathing rate will rise.

### PLATEAU

As the penis continues to stiffen, it deepens in colour, and the tip may become lubricated by secretions from the bulbourethral glands (situated at the base of the penis). The testicles swell and contract towards the man's body.

Sperm is moved by a series of muscular contractions from the epididymides to the end of the vas deferens. Here, the sperm is mixed with the prostate and fluids from the seminal vesicles to produce semen. It is at this stage that a man experiences a sensation known as 'ejaculatory inevitability' so that even if stimulation to the penis is ceased, ejaculation will still occur.

### ORGASM

An orgasm is the climax of sexual excitement. The intense release of sexual tension built up during sexual stimulation and arousal is generally focused on the genitals, but it may also affect the rest of the body.

Orgasm in men is generally accompanied by simultaneous ejaculation. This occurs when intense contractions of the muscles in the urethra and around the base of the penis force semen out of the body. There are usually three to five main contractions at intervals of 0.8 seconds. The sensation of orgasm can be overwhelming, and many men may involuntarily thrust their pelvis forward, forcing their penis deeper into the woman's vagina.

Male orgasms tend to be shorter than the majority of female orgasms, generally lasting around seven or eight seconds. During orgasm, breathing, heart rate and blood pressure all reach a peak.

### RESOLUTION

After orgasm, the penis and testicles return to their normal size. The man's breathing and heart rate slow down, and his blood pressure drops.

# Female sexual response

The female orgasm is believed to aid the passage of sperm into the uterus during sexual intercourse, thereby maximizing the chance of fertilization. However, some women never experience an orgasm during intercourse, and are still able to conceive.

## EXCITEMENT

During the female excitement phase the clitoris and vagina swell as a result of increased blood supply. The labia majora darken in colour, and the labia minora flatten and part.

One of the first signs of sexual arousal in women is wetness around the opening to the vagina. This is caused by stimulation of the secretory cells lining the vagina. This fluid lubricates the vagina, preparing it for penetration, which may or may not occur at a later stage.

The breasts become slightly enlarged, and the nipples become erect. The areolae (around the nipple) swell and darken. Blood pressure, heart rate, breathing rate and muscle tension all increase.

This stage of excitement can last a variable length of time. It may lead to the plateau phase or gently subside.

## PLATEAU

If sexual excitement and stimulation continue, a woman will enter the plateau phase. This is characterized by increased blood flow to the entire genital area. The lower part of the vagina narrows to help grip the penis during intercourse. The upper vagina becomes enlarged and the uterus rises from the pelvic cavity, causing an expansion of the vaginal cavity and creating an area where semen can pool.

During this phase the labia minora deepen in colour, and the clitoris shortens and withdraws under the labial hood. A few drops of fluid may be secreted by

## Physical arousal in women

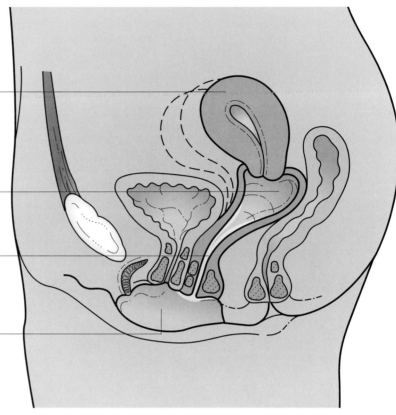

*The contractions during orgasm may help to move sperm into the uterus and uterine (Fallopian) tubes.*

**Uterus**
Rises from the pelvic cavity during the plateau phase; begins to contract rhythmically during orgasm

**Upper vagina**
Enlarges in the plateau phase, creating a space for semen to pool, maximizing chances of fertilization

**Vaginal secretion**
Lubricates the vagina, aiding entry of the penis

**Genital area**
The clitoris and labia engorge with blood as a result of increased blood flow in the excitement phase

the vestibular glands, which are situated at the junction between the vagina and vulva. With continued stimulation this phase may lead to orgasm – the third and shortest of the four phases.

## ORGASM

Female orgasms can be intense, but rarely last for longer than 15 seconds. An orgasm begins with a wave of rhythmic contractions in the lower part of the vagina. The first contractions occur every 0.8 seconds – the same frequency with which the penis expels semen. After the initial contractions the interval becomes progressively longer. It is possible that a woman's contractions help to move sperm into the uterus and uterine (Fallopian) tubes.

Orgasmic contractions spread along the length of the vagina up to the uterus. The muscles of the pelvis and perineum (the part of the body between the anus and the vagina) and around the opening of the bladder and rectum also contract. Women usually experience 5 to 15 orgasmic contractions, depending on the intensity of the orgasm.

Muscles in the back and feet may also undergo involuntary spasms during orgasm, causing the back to arch and the toes to curl. The heart rate can rise to as much as 180 beats per minute and the breathing rate to as much as 40 breaths per minute. Blood pressure rises and the pupils and nostrils dilate. A woman may breathe rapidly or hold her breath for the duration of the orgasm.

## RESOLUTION

Once the orgasm phase is complete, the resolution phase begins. During this time the woman's breasts return to their normal size, the body muscles relax, and her normal heart and breathing rates are restored.

## Refractory period

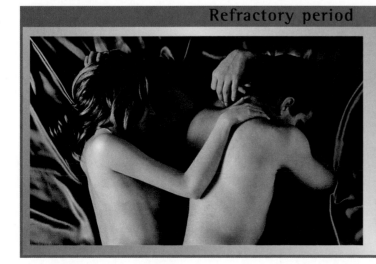

After ejaculation, men experience a refractory period, during which time they are unable to achieve another orgasm. This latent period can last from about two minutes to several hours.

Women do not experience a refractory period, and some may experience multiple orgasms.

*Men and women react differently after an orgasm. However, it is common for both men and women to feel relaxed and sleepy.*

# How conception occurs

Millions of sperm cells travel up the female reproductive tract in search of the oocyte (egg). It takes hundreds of sperm to break down the outer coating of the oocyte, but only one will fertilize it.

Fertilization occurs when a single male gamete (sperm cell) and a female gamete (egg or oocyte) are united following sexual intercourse. Fusion of the two cells occurs and a new life is conceived.

### SPERM
Following sexual intercourse, the sperm contained in the man's semen travel up through the uterus. Along the way they are nourished by the alkaline mucus of the cervical canal. From the uterus the sperm continue their journey into the uterine (Fallopian) tube.

Although the distance involved is only around 20 cm, the journey can take up to two hours, since in relation to the size of the sperm the distance is considerable.

### SURVIVAL
Although an average ejaculation contains around 300 million sperm cells, only a fraction of these (around 10,000) will manage to reach the uterine tube where the oocyte is located. Even fewer will actually reach the oocyte. This is because many sperm will be destroyed by the hostile vaginal environment, or become lost in other areas of the reproductive tract.

Sperm do not become capable of fertilizing an oocyte until they have spent some time in the woman's body. Fluids in the reproductive tract activate the sperm, so that the whiplash motion of their tails becomes more powerful.

The sperm are also helped on their way by contractions of the uterus, which force them upwards into the body. The contractions are stimulated by prostaglandins contained in the semen, and which are also produced during female orgasm.

### THE OOCYTE
Once it has been ejected from the follicle (during ovulation) the oocyte is pushed towards the uterus by the wave-like motion of the cells lining the uterine tube. The oocyte is usually united with the sperm about two hours after sexual intercourse in the outer part of the uterine tube.

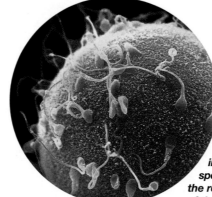

*Following sexual intercourse, millions of sperm cells make their way up the reproductive tract in search of the oocyte.*

## The path to fertilization

**Union of sperm and egg**
Fertilization generally occurs in the outer part of the uterine (Fallopian) tube

**Lost sperm**
Many sperm swim in the wrong direction

**Release of egg**
Each month a follicle ruptures during ovulation, releasing an egg

**Uterine cavity**

**Cervix**

**Hostile environment**
Many sperm will be destroyed by the acids present in the vagina

*Although many sperm begin the journey towards the oocyte, only a fraction reach the uterine tube. The majority are destroyed or become lost on the way.*

## Reaching the oocyte

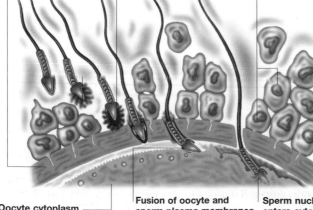

**Zona pellucida**

**Acrosomal reaction**

**Granulosa cells of corona radiata**

**Oocyte cytoplasm**

**Fusion of oocyte and sperm plasma membranes**

**Sperm nucleus enters cytoplasm**

On the journey towards the oocyte, secretions present in the female reproductive tract deplete the sperm cells' cholesterol, thus weakening their acrosomal membranes. This process is known as capacitation, and without it fertilization could not occur.

Once in the vicinity of the oocyte, the sperm are chemically attracted to it. When the sperm cells finally come in to contact with the oocyte, their acrosomal membranes are completely

*When sperm cells reach the oocyte they release enzymes. These enzymes break down the protective outer layers of the ovum, allowing a sperm to enter.*

stripped away, so that the contents of each acrosome (the enzyme-containing compartment of the sperm) are released.

### PENETRATION
The enzymes released by the sperm cells cause the break-down of the cumulus mass cells and the zona pellucida, the protective outer layers of the oocyte. It takes at least 100 acrosomes to rupture in order for a path to be digested through these layers for a single sperm to enter.

In this way the sperm cells that reach the oocyte first sacrifice themselves, to allow penetration of the cytoplasm of the oocyte by another sperm.

# Fertilization

When a single sperm has entered the oocyte, the genetic material from each cell fuses. A zygote is formed, which divides to form an embryo.

Once a sperm has penetrated the oocyte, a chemical reaction takes place within the oocyte, making it impossible for another sperm to enter.

### MEIOSIS II
Entry of the sperm nucleus into the oocyte triggers the completion of nuclear division (meiosis II) begun during ovulation. A haploid oocyte and the second polar body (which degenerates) are formed.

Almost immediately, the nuclei of the sperm and oocyte fuse to produce a diploid zygote, containing genetic material from both the mother and father.

### DETERMINATION OF SEX
It is at the point of fertilization that sex is determined. It is the sperm, and therefore the father, that dictates what sex the offspring will be.

Sex is determined by a combination of the two sex chromosomes, the X and the Y. The female will contribute an X chromosome, while a male may contribute either an X or a Y. Fertilization of the oocyte (X), will either be by a sperm containing an X or a Y to give a female (XX) or a male (XY).

### CELL DIVISION
Several hours after fertilization the zygote undergoes a series of mitotic divisions to produce a cluster of cells known as a morula. The morula cells divide every 12 to 15 hours, producing a blastocyst comprised of around 100 cells.

The blastocyst secretes the hormone human chorionic gonadotrophin. This prevents the corpus luteum from being broken down, thus maintaining progesterone secretion.

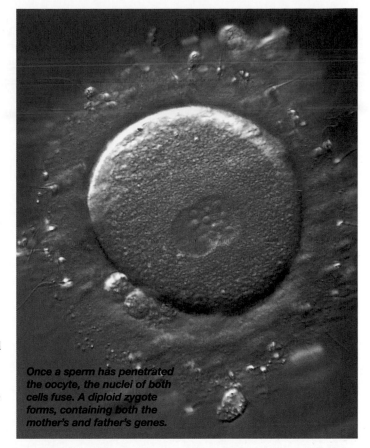

*Once a sperm has penetrated the oocyte, the nuclei of both cells fuse. A diploid zygote forms, containing both the mother's and father's genes.*

## Implantation and development

*As it travels down the uterine tube, the zygote divides. A blastocyst is formed, which implants itself in the lining of the uterine wall.*

**Fertilization**
The ovum and a single sperm fuse to form a zygote.

**Early cleavage**
The zygote begins to divide as it travels down the uterine (Fallopian) tube

**Morula**
The zygote continues to divide forming a cluster of cells known as the morula

**Ovulation**
The oocyte is released from a follicle during ovulation

**Endometrium**
Blood enriched lining of the uterus into which the embryo implants

**Blastocyst**
Continued division leads to the formation of the blastocyst, a fluid-filled hollow sphere

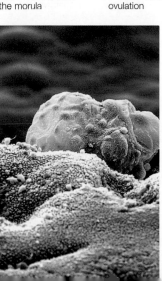

Around three days after fertilization, the blastocyst will begin its journey from the uterine (Fallopian) tube to the uterus.

Normally the blastocyst would be unable to pass through the sphincter muscle in the uterine tube. However, the increasing levels of progesterone triggered by fertilization cause the muscle to relax, allowing the blastocyst to continue its journey to the uterus.

A damaged or blocked uterine tube preventing the blastocyst from passing at this stage would result in an ectopic pregnancy in which the embryo starts to develop in the uterine tube.

### MULTIPLE BIRTHS
In most cases a woman will release one oocyte every month from alternate ovaries.

Occasionally however, a woman may produce an oocyte from each ovary both of which are fertilized by separate sperm, resulting in the development of non-identical twins. In this case, each fetus will be nourished by its own placenta.

*When the zygote reaches the uterus it will adhere to the endometrium. Nourished by the rich blood supply, it begins to develop.*

Very occasionally a fertilized oocyte may split spontaneously in two to produce two embryos. This will result in identical twins that share exactly the same genes, and even the same placenta.

Siamese twins occur when there is an incomplete split of the oocyte several hours after fertilization.

### IMPLANTATION
Once it has reached the uterus, the blastocyst will implant itself in the thickened lining of the uterine wall.

Hormones released from the blastocyst mean that it is not identified as a foreign body and expelled. Once the blastocyst is safely implanted, gestation will begin.

### IMPERFECTIONS
About one third of fertilized oocytes fail to implant in the uterus and are lost.

Of those that do implant, many embryos contain imperfections in their genetic material, such as an extra chromosome.

Many of these imperfections will cause the embryo to be lost soon after implantation. This can occur even before the first missed period, so that a woman will not even have known that she was pregnant.

# How childbirth occurs

Towards the end of pregnancy physiological changes occur in both mother and fetus. Hormonal triggers cause the muscles in the uterine wall to contract, expelling the baby and placenta.

Parturition – meaning 'bringing forth the young' – is the final stage of pregnancy. It usually occurs 280 days (40 weeks) from the last menstrual period.

The series of physiological events that lead to the baby being delivered from the mother's body are referred to collectively as labour.

### INITIATION OF LABOUR

The precise signal that triggers labour is not known, but many factors which play a role in its initiation have been identified.

Before parturition, levels of progesterone secreted by the placenta into the mother's circulation reach a peak. Progesterone is the hormone responsible for maintaining the uterine lining during pregnancy and has an inhibitory effect on the smooth muscle of the uterus.

### HORMONAL TRIGGERS

Towards the end of the pregnancy, there is increasingly limited space in the uterus and the fetus' limited oxygen supply becomes increasingly restricted (resulting from a more rapid increase in the size of the fetus than in the size of the placenta). This causes an increased level of adrenocorticotropic hormone (ACTH) to be secreted from the anterior lobe of the fetus' pituitary.

Consequently, the fetus' adrenal cortex is triggered to produce chemical messengers (glucocorticoids) which inhibit

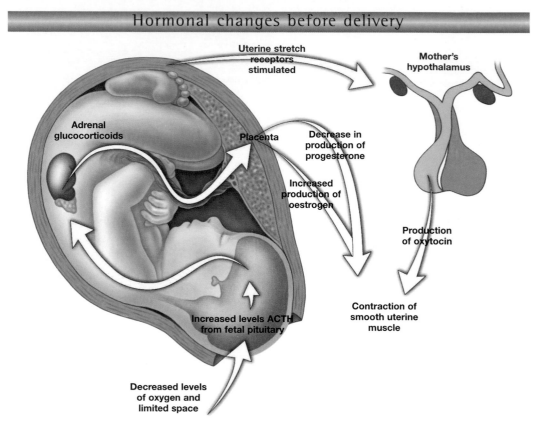

**Hormonal changes before delivery**

Uterine stretch receptors stimulated

Mother's hypothalamus

Adrenal glucocorticoids

Placenta

Decrease in production of progesterone

Increased production of oestrogen

Production of oxytocin

Increased levels ACTH from fetal pituitary

Contraction of smooth uterine muscle

Decreased levels of oxygen and limited space

progesterone secretion from the placenta.

Meanwhile the levels of the hormone oestrogen released by the placenta into the mother's circulation reach a peak. This causes the myometrial cells of the uterus to form an increased number of oxytocin receptors (making the uterus more sensitive to oxytocin).

### CONTRACTIONS

Eventually the inhibitory influence of progesterone on the smooth muscle cells of the uterus is overcome by the stimulatory effect of oestrogen.

The inner lining of the uterus (myometrium) weakens, and the uterus begins to contract irregularly. These contractions, known as Braxton Hicks

*As the pregnancy reaches full term a number of hormonal changes occur. These cause the lining of the uterus to weaken and contractions to commence.*

contractions, help to soften the cervix in preparation for the birth and are often mistaken by pregnant mothers for the onset of labour.

## Onset of labour

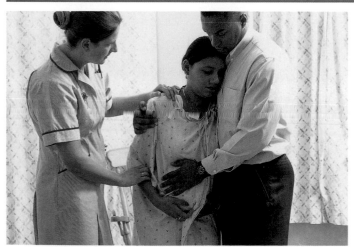

As the pregnancy reaches full term, stretch receptors in the uterine cervix activate the mother's hypothalamus (a region of the brain) to stimulate her posterior pituitary gland in order to release the hormone oxytocin. Certain cells of the fetus also begin to release this hormone

Elevated levels of oxytocin trigger the placenta to release prostaglandins and together they stimulate the uterus to contract.

*Oxytocin triggers uterine contractions that push the fetus against the cervix. Further stretch of the cervix stimulates more oxytocin to be released.*

### INTENSIFICATION OF CONTRACTIONS

As the uterus is weakened due to suppressed levels of progesterone and is more sensitive to oxytocin, the contractions become stronger and more frequent, and the rhythmic contractions of labour begin.

A 'positive feedback' mechanism is activated whereby the greater the intensity of the contractions the more oxytocin is released, which in turn causes the contractions to become more intense. The chain is broken when the cervix is no longer stretched after delivery and oxytocin levels drop.

# Stages of labour

The birth can be divided in to three distinct stages: dilatation of the cervix, expulsion of the fetus and delivery of the placenta.

### DILATATION
In order for the baby's head to pass through the birth canal, the cervix and vagina must dilate to around 10 cm in diameter. As labour commences, weak but regular contractions begin in the upper part of the uterus.

These initial contractions are 15–30 minutes apart and last around 10–30 seconds. As the labour progresses, the contractions become faster and more intense, and the lower part of the uterus begins to contract as well.

The baby's head is forced against the cervix with each contraction, causing the cervix to soften, and gradually dilate.

Eventually the amniotic sac, which has protected the baby for the duration of the pregnancy, ruptures, and the amniotic fluid is released.

### ENGAGEMENT
The dilatation stage is the longest part of labour and can last from 8 to 24 hours.

During this phase the baby begins to descend through the birth canal, rotating as it does so, until the head engages, entering the pelvis.

*Dilatation is the longest stage of labour. It can take up to 24 hours for the cervix to dilate sufficiently to allow delivery.*

**Head engaged**
As contractions continue the baby's head is forced against the cervix

**Cervix**
Continues to dilate as contractions progress

## Expulsion

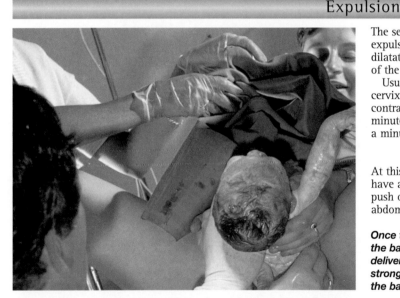

The second stage of labour, expulsion, lasts from full dilatation to the actual delivery of the child.

Usually by the time the cervix is fully dilated, strong contractions occur every 2–3 minutes and each lasts around a minute.

### URGE TO PUSH
At this point the mother will have an overwhelming urge to push or bear down with the abdominal muscles.

*Once the cervix is fully dilated the baby is ready to be delivered. The mother will feel a strong urge to push, expelling the baby through the cervix.*

This phase can take as long as two hours, but is generally much quicker in subsequent births.

### DELIVERY
Crowning takes place when the largest part of the baby's head reaches the vagina. In many cases the vagina will distend to such an extent that it tears.

Once the baby's head has exited, the rest of the body is delivered much more easily.

When the baby emerges head first, the skull (at its widest diameter) acts as a wedge to dilate the cervix. This head-first presentation allows the baby to breathe even before it is completely delivered from the mother.

## Delivery of the placenta

The final stage of labour, when the placenta is delivered, can take place up to 30 minutes after the birth.

After the baby has been delivered the rhythmical uterine contractions continue. These act to compress the uterine blood vessels thus limiting bleeding. The contractions also cause the placenta to break away from the wall of the uterus.

### AFTERBIRTH
The placenta and attached fetal membranes (the afterbirth) are then easily removed by pulling gently on the umbilical cord. All placental fragments must be removed to prevent continued uterine bleeding and infection after birth.

The number of vessels in the severed umbilical cord will be counted, as the absence of an umbilical artery is often associated with cardiovascular disorders in the baby.

### HORMONE LEVELS
Blood levels of oestrogen and progesterone fall dramatically once their source, the placenta, has been delivered. During the four or five weeks after parturition the uterus becomes much smaller but remains larger than it was before pregnancy.

*Contractions continue after the birth. This causes the placenta to detach from the uterine wall, and it can be removed with a gentle tug of the umbilical cord.*

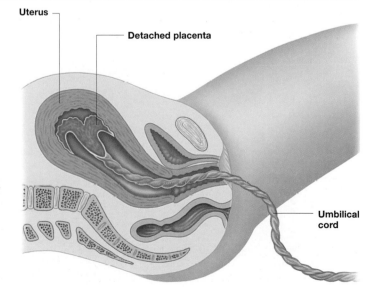

**Uterus**

**Detached placenta**

**Umbilical cord**

# The function of blood

Blood transports life-giving oxygen and all the vital nutrients
which the cells of our bodies need in order to function. It also
carries away the waste products which are produced by our tissues.

Blood makes up about eight per cent of the weight of the human body. The average adult man has around 5 litres (8.8 pints) of it, although the volume varies a great deal, depending mainly on the size of the person.

The blood volume of the average adult woman is about 4 litres (7 pints); a six-year-old child will have around 1.6 litres and a newborn baby will have only about 0.35 litres.

### BLOOD CIRCULATION

Blood circulates inside a closed system of blood vessels, made up of arteries, capillaries and veins. This complex network transports blood to and from all tissues and organs of the body.

At any one time in the average man, the amount of blood in the various parts of the circulation is approximately as follows:

- Arteries      1,200 ml
- Capillaries    350 ml
- Veins        3,400 ml

Therefore, most of the blood in circulation is actually in our veins, and very little is in the capillaries.

The blood in the veins (venous blood, returning to the heart) is much darker in colour than arterial blood because it contains relatively little oxygen. Oxygenated blood from the heart, which is found in the arteries, is strikingly scarlet. Capillary blood – which we see when we cut ourselves – has a slightly less bright red colour than arterial blood.

## Inside an artery

**Arterial wall**
Composed of different connective and elastic layers that protect the artery

**Red blood cells**
Also known as erythrocytes; contain haemoglobin, a red pigment which transports oxygen

**Plasma**
Straw-coloured liquid in which blood cells are suspended

**White blood cells**
Also known as leucocytes; these blood cells have nuclei and protect against infection; there are three major types

**Platelets**
Disc-shaped cells whose function is to cause clotting, thereby reducing bleeding

*Blood is made up of a fluid (plasma) in which the blood cells are suspended. It also transports the body's vital chemicals. The average adult body contains about 5 litres of blood.*

## How blood is made

Blood cells are mostly manufactured in the bone marrow – the soft tissue found in the centre of bones – and this process is called erythropoiesis. Some blood cells are also made in the spleen, a large organ located in the top left-hand corner of the abdomen.

In children, blood cells are mainly manufactured in the marrow of the long bones – the bones of the arms and legs. In adults they are mostly produced in the flatter bones of the body, such as those of the pelvis.

Blood production goes on at an astonishing rate. Literally billions of new red cells are turned out by bone marrow every 24 hours. The reason for this massive rate of manufacture is simply the fact that the cells of the blood are very rapidly worn out; the average red blood cell only lasts between 80 and 120 days, and approximately two million die every second.

*This false-coloured micrograph shows immature red and white blood cells in bone marrow. All the cells derive from a single ancestral cell type by a process called haemopoiesis.*

# Components of blood

The blood that circulates around our bodies is not a single substance, but consists of several important ingredients. Suspended in plasma are red and white blood cells and platelets; each type of cell has a specific purpose.

Blood is made up of various cells suspended in a pale yellow liquid called plasma. Plasma is a sticky fluid containing various chemicals which are in transit from one part of the body to another. Its constituents include:
- Proteins    7 per cent
- Salt    0.9 per cent
- Glucose    0.1 per cent

The main proteins in blood plasma are called albumin,

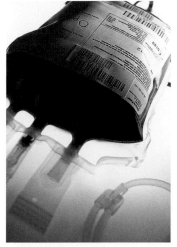

globulin and fibrinogen. They help to supply nutrition to tissues of the body, and are also important in protecting against infectious diseases. Fibrinogen plays a vital role in blood clotting – it turns into fibrin, a mesh-like material, which helps to stop bleeding after an injury.

Glucose – a form of sugar is the body's principal fuel, and salt is the body's most important mineral. Its presence is the reason why blood tastes salty.

### RED BLOOD CELLS
There are three types of cells in blood: red cells, white cells and platelets. Red cells (also known as red corpuscles or erythrocytes) are by far the commonest cells in the blood. Red cells contain the pigment haemoglobin. This is the iron-containing chemical which takes up oxygen in the lungs.

*Donated blood can be used whole for transfusions during surgery or after trauma. Sometimes the red cells can be separated out and concentrated.*

## Major blood elements

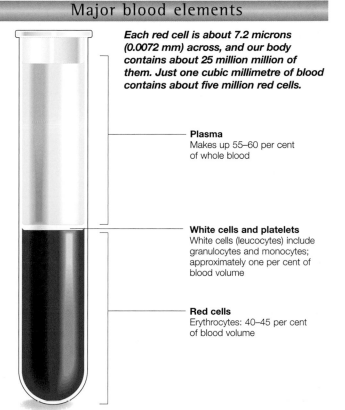

*Each red cell is about 7.2 microns (0.0072 mm) across, and our body contains about 25 million million of them. Just one cubic millimetre of blood contains about five million red cells.*

**Plasma**
Makes up 55–60 per cent of whole blood

**White cells and platelets**
White cells (leucocytes) include granulocytes and monocytes; approximately one per cent of blood volume

**Red cells**
Erythrocytes: 40–45 per cent of blood volume

## White cells and platelets

White cells (also known as white corpuscles or leucocytes) are far fewer in number than red cells. Children have about 10,000 of them in a cubic millimetre of blood, but adults have much less than this.

White cells are vital in protecting against disease. They are divided into various types:
- Neutrophils: combat bacterial and fungal infection
- Eosinophils: help defend the body against parasites, and also

in allergic reactions
- Lymphocytes: involved in creating immunity to infection
- Monocytes: capable of engulfing invading particles in the bloodstream
- Basophils: can also engulf invaders, but little is known about them.

Platelets (also known as thrombocytes) are very small cells involved in the process of blood clotting. In a cubic millimetre of blood, there are

about a quarter of a million of them. When a blood vessel is cut or damaged, platelets – which are very sticky – immediately adhere to the injured spot, and to each other, and so (along with fibrin) help to plug the gap and stop the bleeding.

*This white blood cell is a T-lymphocyte, or T-cell, covered by characteristic microvilli (hair-like structures). These cells are important for immunity.*

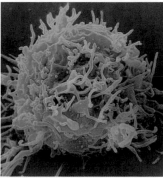

## What happens when we bleed

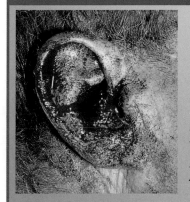

If our skin is cut, we immediately start bleeding. Most cuts are small, and only involve slight loss from the capillaries. The blood flow soon stops, particularly if firm pressure is applied to the wound.

The main reason why the bleeding ceases is the blood's

*Bleeding from the ear may be serious, as it can indicate brain trauma; alternatively, it may be a superficial cut to the ear tissue. A doctor would have to assess the wound and treat accordingly.*

natural ability to clot. Threads of a substance called fibrin form a mesh-like plug at the bleeding point, and this helps stop the blood loss.

If a wound involves a vein or an artery, however, it is rather more serious. Veins are quite large tubes – as can be seen just under the skin – and if they are sliced through, they tend to ooze quite large quantities of blood over a long period. Pressure on the spot may stop this, but surgical stitching may be needed.

Even more serious is a cut through an artery, because very large amounts of blood can pump forcibly out of it in a very short time. If firm pressure is not applied promptly, the person can bleed to death in a few minutes.

The reason why heavy blood loss can rapidly cause death is that the body – and particularly the brain – needs a constant supply of blood to function. If there is insufficient blood, then there is insufficient oxygen, and as a result our cells soon die.

# How the blood circulates

The circulation transports blood to and from every tissue in the body, maintaining an optimal environment for cell survival and function. It also allows the transport of hormones around the body.

The function of the circulation is to supply blood to every bodily tissue, carrying fuel, nutrition and oxygen to the cells. It also carries waste products away from the tissues, transporting them to the kidneys or lungs for excretion.

Circulation is achieved by the heart pumping blood forcefully, in a series of 'jets', through the arterial system. The arteries divide into increasingly smaller branches, and the smallest arteries (arterioles) deliver blood into microscopic capillaries. The capillaries pass through the tissues and anastomose (join) with the smallest veins (venules).

The venules join up to form veins, which take blood back to the heart again. The blood on returning to the heart is then pumped to the lungs to be re-oxygenated.

*The arteries and veins are linked by a meshwork of capillaries. Over 150,000 km long, this network allows the exchange of oxygen and nutrients between the arterial and venous systems.*

## Circulatory system

### DE-OXYGENATED BLOOD

**Internal and external jugular veins**
Paired veins running down the neck; drain blood from brain, scalp, head, face and neck

**Subclavian vein**
Drains blood directly into the heart from the neck and arms

**Aortic arch**
Bend in aorta after it rises from the left ventricle of the heart

**Superior vena cava**
Conveys blood from the head, neck, arms and thorax to the heart

**Inferior vena cava**
Drains blood from the lower body

**Femoral vein**
Drains blood from the thigh; becomes the external iliac vein

**Great saphenous vein**
Longest vein in the body; empties from feet, calves and knees into femoral vein

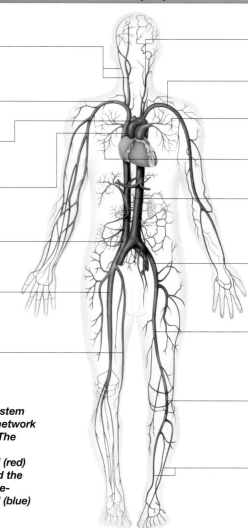

*The circulatory system is the branching network of blood vessels. The arteries carry oxygenated blood (red) to the tissues, and the veins return the de-oxygenated blood (blue) to the heart.*

### OXYGENATED BLOOD

**Common carotid artery**
One of two arteries that supply blood to the head and brain

**Axillary artery**
Paired arteries supplying blood to the head and brain

**Pulmonary arteries**
Carry deoxygenated blood from heart to lungs

**Pulmonary veins**
Carry oxygenated blood from lungs back to the heart

**Aorta**
Largest artery in the body; rises from heart and branches to the head, limbs arms, trunk and abdomen

**Common iliac artery**
Supplies blood to the pelvis and lower limbs; branches into the external and smaller internal arteries

**Femoral artery**
Rises from the external iliac, and passes through the thigh to become the popliteal artery

**Popliteal artery**
Rises from femoral; continues down back of the lower leg

**Anterior and posterior tibial arteries**
Branches of popliteal artery serving the lower leg; divides into metatarsal (feet) and digital (toes) arteries

## Blood pressure

Blood pressure is force per unit area exerted by the blood in the arterial system. It is measured in millimetres of mercury (mm Hg – UK and USA), or kilopascals (other European countries).

Blood pressure is expressed as two figures, for instance 150/110. The first, or upper figure represents the pressure in the arteries when the heart is contracting (systole) – the systolic pressure. The second, or lower figure represents the

pressure in the arteries while the heart is relaxing (diastole) – the diastolic pressure.

The diastolic pressure is often considered to be more clinically important, especially when assessing high blood pressure – because the systolic pressure is so readily affected by factors such an anxiety. Blood pressure is generally measured by placing an inflatable cuff, connected to a measuring device, around the upper part of the arm.

Hypertension (high blood pressure) affects millions of people; in most cases, its cause is unknown. But it is important to detect and to treat, because its presence increases the risk of heart attack or stroke.

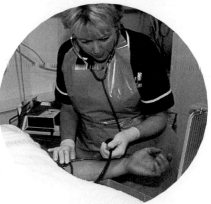

*A doctor takes a blood pressure reading in his patient's upper arm. Ideally, pressure in this part of the body should be below 140/90 mm Hg.*

# Blood flow through the body

Blood flow is the volume of blood flowing through the circulation, an organ of the body or an individual blood vessel in a given period of time.

The flow of blood through a blood vessel is determined by a combination of the pressure difference between the two ends of the vessel and the resistance to blood flow through the vessel.

Blood pressure is greatest in the vessels nearest the pump, that is, in the aorta and pulmonary artery. As the blood flows away from the heart, the pressure falls. However, of the two parameters – pressure and resistance – it is resistance that has the greater influence on

blood flow. The total blood flow in the the circulation of an adult at rest is about five litres per minute; this is referred to as the cardiac output.

The blood flow to individual tissues is almost precisely controlled in relation to the tissue's needs. When tissues are active, they may require up to 20 or 30 times more blood flow than when they are at rest. However, cardiac output cannot increase more than about four to seven times.

Since the body cannot simply increase total blood flow, local blood flow to specific tissues is control by internal monitoring mechanisms. Blood is distributed according to the specific tissues' needs, and redirected away from tissues that do not require nutrients or oxygen at that time.

### VENOUS BLOOD FLOW
The 'drive' produced by the heartbeat is not carried on through the tiny capillaries. Therefore, there is no pulse in the veins. However, blood flows back through veins towards the heart by a combination of mechanisms: the contraction of the leg and arm muscles; the presence of efficient valves in the veins; and the simple process of breathing, which helps to 'suck' the blood through the veins, towards the chest.

*When an artery is cut, blood spurts out of the wound because aterial blood is pumped under pressure. Venous blood, however, is not pressurized and so flows out more slowly.*

## Distribution of blood

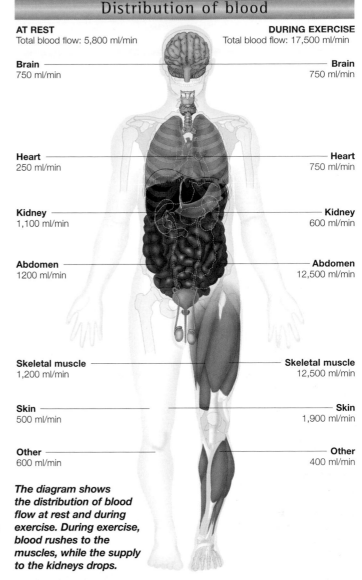

| AT REST | DURING EXERCISE |
|---|---|
| Total blood flow: 5,800 ml/min | Total blood flow: 17,500 ml/min |
| **Brain** 750 ml/min | **Brain** 750 ml/min |
| **Heart** 250 ml/min | **Heart** 750 ml/min |
| **Kidney** 1,100 ml/min | **Kidney** 600 ml/min |
| **Abdomen** 1200 ml/min | **Abdomen** 12,500 ml/min |
| **Skeletal muscle** 1,200 ml/min | **Skeletal muscle** 12,500 ml/min |
| **Skin** 500 ml/min | **Skin** 1,900 ml/min |
| **Other** 600 ml/min | **Other** 400 ml/min |

*The diagram shows the distribution of blood flow at rest and during exercise. During exercise, blood rushes to the muscles, while the supply to the kidneys drops.*

## Distribution of blood volume

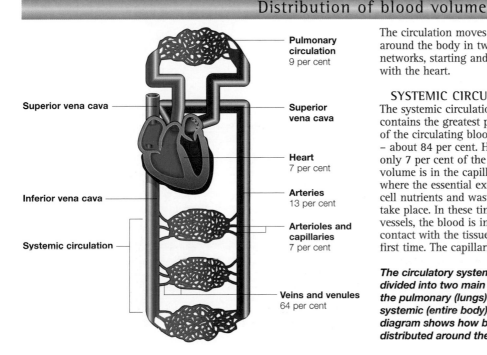

**Pulmonary circulation**
9 per cent

Superior vena cava

**Superior vena cava**

**Heart**
7 per cent

Inferior vena cava

**Arteries**
13 per cent

**Arterioles and capillaries**
7 per cent

Systemic circulation

**Veins and venules**
64 per cent

The circulation moves blood around the body in two networks, starting and finishing with the heart.

### SYSTEMIC CIRCULATION
The systemic circulation contains the greatest proportion of the circulating blood volume – about 84 per cent. However, only 7 per cent of the blood volume is in the capillary beds, where the essential exchange of cell nutrients and waste products take place. In these tiny blood vessels, the blood is in intimate contact with the tissues for the first time. The capillaries have

*The circulatory system can be divided into two main portions: the pulmonary (lungs) and systemic (entire body). The diagram shows how blood is distributed around these areas.*

permeable walls, allowing chemical molecules to pass out of the blood into the tissues. Similarly, chemicals that have been formed in the tissues can diffuse through the capillary walls into the blood so that they can be carried away.

### PULMONARY CIRCULATION
The pulmonary circulation allows the discharge of waste products from the blood into the lungs, and the uptake of oxygen from the air. Blood returning from the major veins of the body to the right side of the heart is pumped out again via the pulmonary artery to the lungs. Here, the artery divides into tiny arterioles and then capillaries, which traverse the tissues of the lung. The pulmonary veins then take the oxygen-rich blood back to the heart.

# How blood is transported

Blood vessels are the tubes that carry blood around the body.
Arteries carry blood from the heart to the body's tissues. From there
veins carry the deoxygenated blood back to the heart.

## TYPES OF BLOOD VESSEL

Blood vessels vary in size according to the amount of blood they carry; thus the largest vessels are found nearest the heart. Blood destined for body tissues leaves the heart via the aorta, which arches over and behind the heart and carries blood down the trunk. From the aorta, smaller arteries lead to the main organs of the body, where they branch into smaller vessels.

The smallest arteries, or arterioles, deliver blood to the capillaries, from which oxygen and nutrients are absorbed into the tissues, and into which carbon dioxide and waste materials are taken up. Blood leaving the tissues collects into veins, which feed blood into larger and larger vessels, the largest of which, the two vena cavae, deliver blood back to the heart. From the heart, the blood is pumped to the lungs where it is reoxygenated for circulation.

## Structure of a typical artery

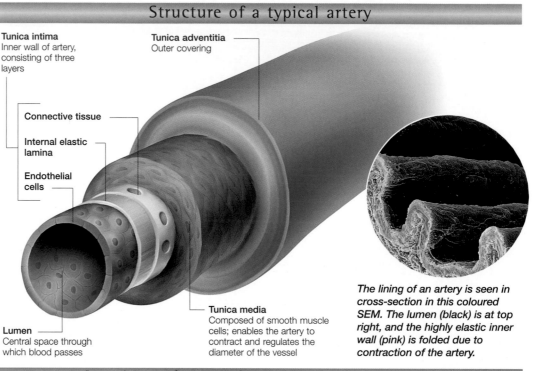

**Tunica intima**
Inner wall of artery, consisting of three layers

**Tunica adventitia**
Outer covering

**Connective tissue**

**Internal elastic lamina**

**Endothelial cells**

**Lumen**
Central space through which blood passes

**Tunica media**
Composed of smooth muscle cells; enables the artery to contract and regulates the diameter of the vessel

*The lining of an artery is seen in cross-section in this coloured SEM. The lumen (black) is at top right, and the highly elastic inner wall (pink) is folded due to contraction of the artery.*

## Arteries and arterioles

Blood leaves the heart under pressure, so arteries have thick, muscular walls made up of several layers (tunicae). Surrounding the central canal (lumen) is the tunica intima which consists of a lining of endothelial cells, a layer of connective tissue and a layer of tissue called the internal elastic lamina. The middle layer (tunica media) is made up of smooth muscle cells and sheets of elastic tissue known as elastin. The outer layer (tunica adventitia) is a tough outer coat of fibrous connective tissue.

The largest arteries lead directly from the heart. They are known as elastic, or conducting, arteries because they contain a relatively high proportion of elastic tissue. This allows them to expand as they fill with blood and then contract again, forcing the blood onwards towards the smaller arteries.

### ARTERIOLES

Arteries with a diameter of between 0.3 mm and 0.01 mm are called arterioles. The largest of these possess all three tunicae, but the tunica media contains only scattered elastic fibres. The smallest have no outer coat and consist only of an endothelial lining surrounded by a single layer of spiralling muscle cells. The flow of blood from arterioles into capillaries is controlled by sympathetic nerves, which cause the muscle cells to contract, thus constricting or dilating the lumen of the arterioles.

## Pulse

When the heart beats, the impact of the blood being forced into the aorta from the left ventricle causes a pressure wave to travel down all the arteries of the body. Where an artery lies close to the skin, this pressure wave can be felt as a pulse. The easiest points at which a pulse can be felt are at the radial artery in the wrist and the common carotid artery in the neck.

*Doctors usually feel for a pulse at the patient's wrist. The pulse corresponds to the heart rate, and the average for a healthy adult at rest is 60–80 beats per minute.*

*Red blood cells are visible travelling through the lumen (centre) of this arteriole. The vessel is surrounded by connective tissue (yellow).*

# Veins and capillaries

Veins are the vessels that move deoxygenated blood from around the body to the heart. The capillaries make up the network between veins and arteries in all the tissues.

## Veins

The structure of veins is very similar to that of arteries, but veins are generally larger and have thinner walls, and contain less muscle and less elastic and collagenous tissue, so they can be compressed or distended. Venules – the smallest veins collect blood from the capillaries, and it is then collected into increasingly larger veins. Blood from the lower body arrives at the inferior vena cava and drains into the right atrium of the heart. Blood from the upper body is collected by the superior vena cava and also drains into the right atrium.

Most veins have a system of one-way valves that allow blood to flow in one direction only. The valves are semi-lunar, formed of two half-circles of tissue, and are prevalent in veins of the lower limbs.

The blood pressure in veins is low. Movement of the blood is helped by the skeletal muscle pump, in which the contraction of surrounding skeletal muscles squeezes the vein and forces the blood along. In veins of less than one mm diameter and in regions where muscular activity is more or less continuous, such as the chest and abdominal cavities, there are no valves, as the blood flow is maintained by muscle pressure alone.

*Erythrocytes (red blood cells) can be seen in the lumen of this vein. They contain haemoglobin, which transports oxygen.*

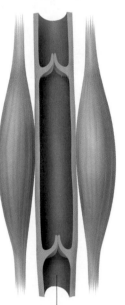

**Muscles relaxed**

**Muscles contracted**

**One-way valve**
Blood is forced through in the direction of the arrow

**Skeletal muscles**
As the muscles contract, they squeeze the vein and keep the blood moving from valve to valve

**Vein**
Each vein is divided into segments by non-return valves to prevent the blood flowing backwards

*The skeletal muscle pump moves blood through the veins back to the heart. Muscles contract against the flexible vein, forcing the valves to open.*

## Types of capillary

There are at least three different kinds of capillary:
■ Continuous capillaries are made up of a single long endothelial cell curved round to form a tube
■ Fenestrated capillaries are made up of two or more endothelial cells that have a number of pores (fenestrations), especially near the junctions of the cells
■ Discontinuous capillaries, also called sinusoids or vascular sinuses, are made up of a number of cells with large fenestrations.

Continuous capillaries are the least permeable, and liquids are transferred to and from the surrounding tissues by exocytosis and endocytosis, processes by which vesicles containing the liquids are moved across the endothelial cells.

In fenestrated capillaries and sinusoids, chemicals pass more easily through the thin membranes that cover the pores. Fenestrated capillaries are common in the endocrine glands and kidneys; sinusoids are found in the liver and spleen.

### Structure of a fenestrated capillary

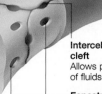

**Endothelial cell**
Inner wall of capillary is just one cell thick

**Lumen**
Wide enough to allow red blood cells to pass singly

**Nucleus of endothelial cell**

**Intercellular cleft**
Allows passage of fluids

**Fenestrations**
Pores in the cells which allow rapid transfer of materials into the tissues

**Basement membrane**
Surrounds endothelial layer

## Fainting

Fainting (syncope) is a temporary loss of consciousness due to a decrease in the supply of blood to the brain. This can be caused by a stuffy atmosphere, standing up suddenly, standing for a long time in one position, an obstruction to the neck arteries on moving the head suddenly or by an emotional reaction to shock. It can also be caused by poor output from the heart, due to a heart attack, arrhythmia (disturbance of the heartbeat) or disease of the heart valves.

Fainting can affect anyone at any age, irrespective of health or fitness, but it is more common in the elderly. Before losing consciousness, the victim may complain of light-headedness and nausea, and their skin may be pale and clammy to the touch.

*Faintness from standing for long periods is due to blood collecting in the legs. Blood flow can be restored by flexing the leg muscles.*

# How blood clots

Blood makes a complete circuit of the body every minute, and injury to the vascular bed must therefore be plugged quickly in order to prevent excessive blood loss. This process is called haemostasis.

Blood flows freely in intact blood vessels due partly to an excess of naturally occurring anticoagulants. However, if the blood vessel wall breaks, a series of chemical reactions are initiated to stop the bleeding (haemostasis). Without these haemostatic processes, even the smallest cut could cause a person to bleed to death.

Haemostasis involves many blood coagulation factors, which are present in the plasma, as well as chemicals released from platelets and injured cells.

## THE STAGES OF HAEMOSTASIS

Haemostasis can be broken down into three main stages, which occur in rapid succession after an injury:

■ Vasoconstriction – the first stage involves the constriction of the damaged blood vessel; this can significantly reduce blood loss in the short term

■ Platelet plug formation – damage to the blood vessel causes platelets, which are present within the plasma, to become sticky and adhere to each other and to the damaged vessel wall

■ Coagulation (blood clotting) – next, the platelet plug is reinforced with a meshwork of fibrin fibres. This fibrin net traps red and white blood cells to form a secondary haemostatic plug, or blood clot.

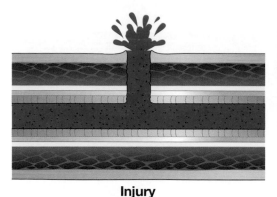

**Injury**

*When a blood vessel is damaged, blood escapes the circulation, reducing blood volume. Excessive blood loss is prevented by haemostasis.*

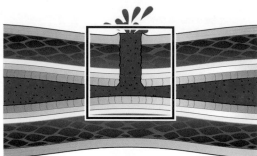

**Stage 1**

*The first stage of haemostasis is vasoconstriction; the damaged blood vessel constricts to reduce the amount of blood flowing through it.*

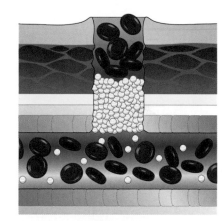

**Stage 2**

*The second stage is the formation of a platelet plug. Platelets (white) stick to one another to temporarily seal the hole in the vessel wall.*

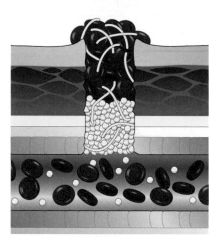

**Stage 3**

*Finally, a blood clot is formed; blood cells are trapped in a fibrin mesh (yellow strands) which seals the hole until it can be permanently repaired.*

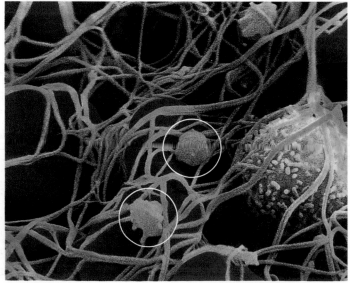

*A web of fibrin strands can be seen trapping red blood cells during clot formation. This micrograph also reveals a white blood cell (yellow) and platelets (circled) within the clot.*

## How blood clots form

The formation of a blood clot is a very complicated process involving over 30 different chemicals. Some of these chemicals, called coagulation factors, enhance clot formation, whereas others, called anticoagulants, inhibit clotting.

Clotting is initiated by a complex cascade of biochemical reactions involving 13 coagulation factors. The end result is the formation of a complex chemical called prothrombin activator. This compound catalyses the conversion of a plasma protein called prothrombin into a smaller protein called thrombin. Thrombin, in turn, catalyses the joining together of fibrinogen molecules present in the plasma to produce a fibrin mesh. It is this mesh that traps blood cells in the hole in the blood vessel wall.

The large number of chemical steps involved in the clotting process means that coagulation must be tightly controlled. This is important because unnecessary clotting can be very dangerous, especially if it blocks a blood vessel supplying a major organ.

## Clot contraction and repair

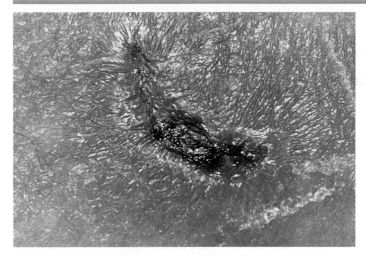

About 30–60 minutes after a blood clot has formed, the platelets within the clot contract – like muscle, platelets contain two contractile proteins called actin and myosin. This contraction pulls on the fibrin strands, bringing the edges of the injured tissue closer together and helping the wound to close.

The blood clot is temporary; at the same time as the clot is contracting, surrounding tissues divide to repair the vessel wall.

*A healing dog bite on the shin can be seen here. Scar tissue is forming at either end of the laceration.*

### FIBRINOLYSIS

Once the tissue has healed (after about two days), the fibrin mesh which holds the clot together is dissolved. This process, called fibrinolysis, is catalysed by the enzyme plasmin, which is produced from the plasma protein plasminogen.

Plasminogen molecules are incorporated into the blood clot during its formation, where they lie dormant until activated by the healing process. As a result, most of the plasmin is restricted to the clot.

Normally, a balance between coagulation and fibrinolysis is maintained in the body.

## Platelets

Platelets are cytoplasmic fragments that are able to survive in the circulation for up to 10 days. They are formed in bone marrow by extremely large cells called megakaryocytes. Strictly speaking, they are not cells as they do not have a nucleus and so cannot divide.

Electron microscopy reveals three platelet zones:

**1** The outer membrane consists of a glycoprotein surface coat which causes it to adhere only to injured tissues. The membrane also contains large numbers of phospholipids which play a number of roles in the blood clotting process.

**2** The cytosol (solution inside the cellular membrane) contains contractile proteins (including actin and myosin), microfilaments and microtubules. These are important for clot contraction.

**3** Platelet granules contain a variety of haemostatically active compounds which are released when platelets are activated. These compounds are potent aggregating agents that attract more platelets to the wound site. Thus, the formation of the platelet plug is a self-perpetuating process.

*This electron micrograph shows activated blood platelets grouping on the surface of a damaged blood vessel wall.*

*A single activated blood platelet is seen in this micrograph. In this activated state, platelets develop extensions (pseudopodia) from the cell wall, which are also visible in this image.*

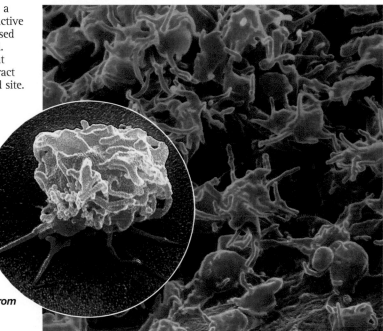

## Anticoagulant drugs

The main clinical use of anti-coagulants is to prevent the formation of a blood clot (thrombus) in an undamaged blood vessel. A large clot could potentially block a blood vessel, leading to the death of the tissues that it supplies.

### CLINICAL USES

Anticoagulants, such as heparin, are given by intravenous injection (parenterally), while others drugs, such as warfarin, are administered orally. The two types of drugs have different modes of action; whereas

warfarin takes 48 to 72 hours to take effect, the effect of heparin is immediate.

Heparin is the anticoagulant most often used clinically, particularly for cardiac operations and for patients receiving blood transfusions. Warfarin is predominantly used in patients at risk of suffering arrhythmia (irregular heart rate).

Aspirin blocks platelet aggregation and platelet plug formation. A dose of 75-150 mg per day is used in the secondary prevention of thrombotic cerebrovascular (stroke) or cardiovascular disease.

*Warfarin has been widely used as a rat poison. Rats who eat food laced with warfarin die from blood loss because their blood is unable to coagulate.*

### Haemophilia

Haemophilia is a group of inherited bleeding disorders caused by a lack of one of the clotting factors. The most common (85 per cent of cases) is haemophilia A, which is caused by a deficiency of clotting factor VIII. The disease is characterized by painful spontaneous bleeding into joints and muscles. The most famous case of haemophilia A is Queen Victoria's family, where many of the males fell victim to the disease.

The condition is treated by replacing the missing factor obtained from human plasma. Genetically engineered versions are also available for patients who cannot produce factors VIII or IX (which results in Christmas disease).

# How blood protects us from disease

As well as carrying nutrients to and waste products from all tissues of the body, blood contains components that are a vital part of the human immune response to infection.

The blood is the great defensive fluid of our bodies. It is constantly present in the circulatory (cardiovascular) system, ready to respond to any microbial threat which may present.

### BONE MARROW

All blood cells begin life in the bone marrow – the jelly-like substance contained within the cavities of bones. All types of blood cells are derived from a single type of cell called a stem cell, which may go on to form red blood cells, platelets or the white blood cells of the immune system.

Cells may migrate to other regions, such as the spleen or thymus (in the neck) where they mature in to other cell types.

### THE LYMPHATIC SYSTEM

The functioning of the immune system is facilitated by the lymphatic system. The lymphatic system circulates a liquid mixture called lymph around the whole of the body, but is different to the circulatory system, which carries blood. Importantly, the lymphatic system carries white blood cells around the body.

In capillaries – the smallest of the blood vessels – pressure causes fluid and small molecules to be forced into the spaces between cells. This is called interstitial fluid, which bathes and feeds surrounding tissues. This is subsequently drained into the lymphatic system, where it circulates and eventually drains back into the bloodstream. It is not actively pumped, but relies on the vessels being squeezed by surrounding muscles.

*When the body is infected by bacteria, chemical signals are released. These cause white blood cells, called leucocytes, to leave the capillaries and attack the invading bacteria.*

## Defending against infection

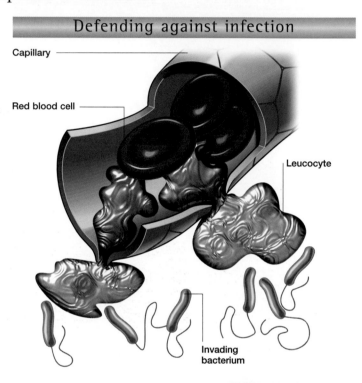

Capillary

Red blood cell

Leucocyte

Invading bacterium

## Viruses

Because viruses are so small (only 0.00001 mm in diameter), they are very efficient at entering the respiratory and gastro-intestinal tracts. Blood is able to fight viruses by delivering antibodies to the affected area.

*The rhinovirus, shown here, is one of the causes of the common cold. Blood defends against such viruses by carrying antibodies.*

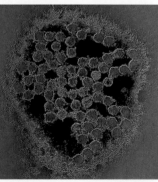

## Single-cell invaders

Bacteria and protozoans are sought out, ingested (engulfed by phagocytosis) and killed by white blood-cell phagocytes.

Invading microbes cause the production of factors that attract phagocytes to the infected area; they are then coated with antibodies and ingested.

*E. coli bacteria are associated with food poisoning. Phagocytes in the blood are capable of ingesting such microbes.*

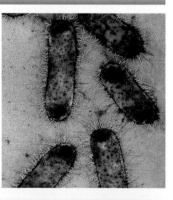

## Multi-cellular invaders

Helminths are parasitic worms, commoner in warmer countries. The blood attacks them with specialized white cells called eosinophils – so named because they stain red when exposed to eosin laboratory dye.

*Parasites, such as this hookworm, are often found in the intestines. Eosinophils in the bloodstream are capable of attacking some of these invaders.*

## Fungi

Fungal organisms are very effective at invading moist, warm areas of the human body, such as between the toes. The body tries to fight back against these invasions by bringing antibodies to the site, via the blood, as part of the immune response.

*The body responds to many fungal infections by producing antibodies. These are carried in the blood to the relevant area.*

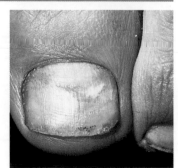

# Defensive components of blood

Although some infections can overcome our defences, the various components of the blood successfully fight back against most invaders.

The components of the blood which combat infections are:

■ Phagocytes. If a microbe enters the body it will almost certainly encounter specialized white blood cells: neutrophil polymorphs and monocytes. Their function is to engulf (phagocytose) invading particles and break them up through a process of intracellular digestion.

Phagocytes do not live exclusively in the blood. Instead, they spread out from the blood vessels and into the tissues where they are best placed to attack invading microbes.

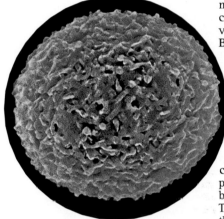

*Neutrophil polymorphs – the commonest type of white blood cell – attack invading organisms by phagocytosis.*

Of the two types of phagocyte, polymorphs are relatively short-lived, while monocytes are longer-lasting and turn into another group of cells, termed macrophages. Macrophages create a zone of inflammation around microbes, helping to limit their spread. Where possible, they engulf them.

■ Lymphoid cells. These white cells come in three forms:

**T-lymphocytes.** These are very effective at attacking viruses. Virologists classify them into various groups (helper T cells; suppressor T-cells; cytotoxic T-cells; and hypersensitivity-mediating T-cells), which all combine to attempt to destroy viruses.

B-lymphocytes. These are involved in the production of antibodies against microbes.

**Killer cells and natural killer (NK) cells.** These are often able to recognize human cells that have been taken over by viruses as intracellular 'factories' and destroy them.

■ **Interferons.** These are chemical agents which are produced by cells which have been infected by viruses and T-lymphocytes. Interferons flow through the bloodstream, activating NK cells and providing defence against viruses.

■ Complement. This blood

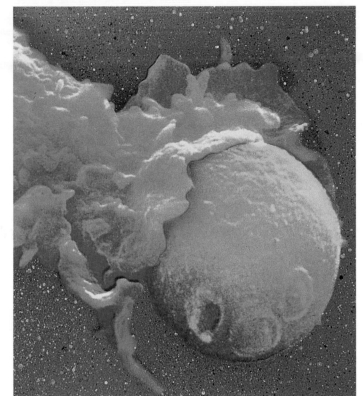

component consists of about 20 proteins. When infection occurs, they work together to attack bacteria and organize inflammation around the infected area.

■ Acute phase proteins. These are blood proteins with the ability to attach to certain bacteria and disable them in the early stages of an infection.

■ Eosinophils. These are specialized white blood cells

*A lymphocyte (blue) engulfs a yeast spore (yellow) by phagocytosis. Lymphocytes normally attack invaders with enzymes, rather than by phagocytosis.*

which play a role in fighting off infection by helminths. They are capable of inactivating some of these parasites by binding to them and releasing a toxic protein.

## Blood antibodies

Antibodies are vital components of the blood. They are complex molecules called immunoglobulins, which are formed in response to infection. There are various types of immunoglobulin:

■ IgG makes up about three-quarters of the immunoglobulin in normal blood.

It is very effective in neutralizing the toxins (poisons) produced by certain microbes.

■ IgM makes up about one-fourteenth of the serum immunoglobulins. It activates complement so that it can attack foreign cells.

■ IgA makes up about a fifth of the blood's immunoglobulin load,

and it is mainly delivered to areas such as the mouth, air passages and intestine, where germs are likely to attack. It acts as an antiseptic secretion, helping to keep microbes from penetrating the mucous surfaces of the body.

■ IgE is thought to play a part in defending the body against helminths, by creating defensive inflammations. Unfortunately, it is often produced in vastly excessive amounts in people who have allergies. In these individuals, it causes inappropriate inflammation, and this is associated with the symptoms of asthma, hay fever and allergic skin reactions.

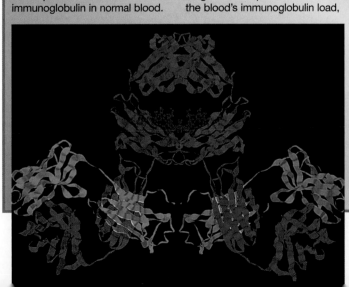

*The structure of an antibody is shown on this computer-generated image. Antibodies are able to bind to foreign cells or toxins and neutralize them.*

*In some cases, excessive amounts of an antibody called IgE are produced. This can result in the symptoms of an allergic reaction.*

# What is blood pressure?

The heart must pump out blood at sufficient pressure to supply the body's tissues with both oxygen and nutrients. Blood pressure is closely monitored by the body and maintained at its optimal level.

Blood leaves the heart in a pulsatile fashion: each time the heart contracts, about 70 millilitres of blood are ejected from it. However, despite this discontinuous and choppy flow of blood through the root of the aorta, the blood flow through the capillaries is smooth and continuous.

### ELASTIC ARTERIES

Continuous flow happens because arteries are not rigid cylinders. Rather, they have elastic walls that can expand or recoil like an elastic band. Thus during systole (when the heart contracts), blood enters the arteries quicker than it leaves the capillary beds; the increased volume of blood present in the arteries forces the arterial walls to expand.

In contrast, during diastole (when the heart is relaxed and

**Heart contracting**

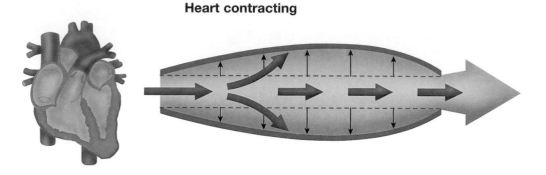

**Heart relaxing**

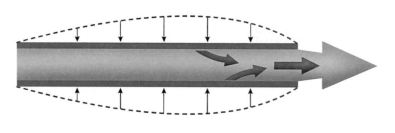

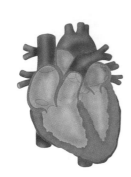

*Arterial pressure changes during each heart beat from about 80 (diastolic) to 120 (systolic) millimetres of mercury (mm Hg). The difference (40 mm Hg) is called the pulse pressure.*

no blood is ejected from it) the blood stored in the arteries is propelled towards the capillaries by the recoil of the expanded arterial walls.

### SMOOTH BLOOD FLOW

This elasticity causes the blood to flow more smoothly as it travels down the vascular tree; while the arterial pressure fluctuates with each heartbeat, it would be much more pulsatile if the arteries were rigid, inflexible tubes (an analogy to this would be the flow of water from a garden hose if the tap were to be intermittently turned on and

*During systole (top) blood is forced into elastic arteries, which expand. During diastole (bottom), they recoil, propelling the blood smoothly onwards.*

off). The smooth flow of blood through the capillaries is advantageous because large changes in pressure would damage the capillaries, whose walls are only one cell thick.

## How blood pressure is measured

Doctors measure blood pressure using a sphyngmomanometer:
1. A cuff is wrapped around the patient's upper arm and inflated to block the flow of blood through the brachial artery.
2. Air is gradually let out of the cuff while the doctor listens with a stethoscope placed 'downstream' from the cuff. The pressure at which the blood can be heard running through the artery is noted (the systolic pressure).
3. As more air is let out of the cuff, blood flows smoothly through the artery again and the sound of blood rushing through the artery disappears. This pressure is called the diastolic pressure.

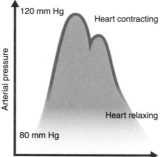

*The brachial artery is blocked using an inflatable cuff. When the cuff is deflated, the sound of blood flowing back through the vessel can be heard.*

**1** No sound heard through stethoscope

**2** Pulse heard as 'banging' sound

**3** Sound of pulse disappears

## What determines blood pressure?

At its simplest level, blood pressure is the product of two factors: cardiac output and total peripheral resistance.

■ Cardiac output is the amount of blood that the heart pumps around the body each minute. For example, in a healthy adult man, the heart beats around 70 times per minute, with each ventricular contraction pumping out around 70 millilitres (ml) of blood (called the stroke volume). Thus the cardiac output would be 4,900 millilitres (70 ml multiplied by 70 ml equals 4,900 ml) per minute.

■ Total peripheral resistance (TPR) is the resistance that the blood encounters as it flows around the body. Resistance is very sensitive to the diameter of the vessel that the blood is flowing through; halving the diameter of a vessel increases its resistance by 16 times.

### IMPORTANCE OF BLOOD VOLUME

However, the circulation is a closed system – blood is returned to the heart by the veins and does not drain out of the body after each contraction. Thus the volume of circulating blood also determines blood pressure. This can be important in severe haemorrhage (blood loss), for example.

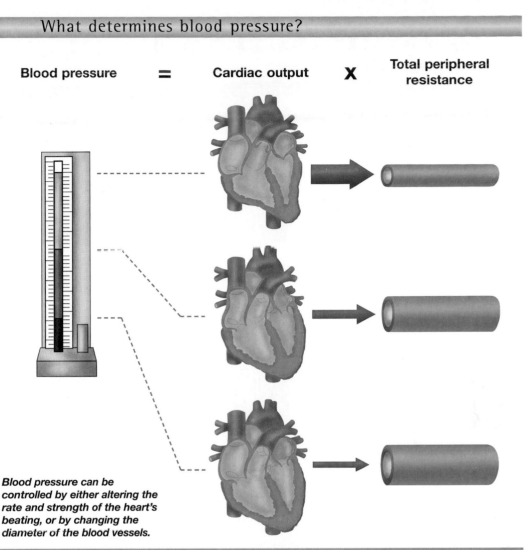

**Blood pressure** = **Cardiac output** X **Total peripheral resistance**

*Blood pressure can be controlled by either altering the rate and strength of the heart's beating, or by changing the diameter of the blood vessels.*

## How is blood pressure controlled?

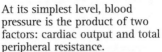

**Hypothalamus and pituitary gland**
These control the secretion of hormones involved in blood pressure regulation

**Carotid sinus**
Pressure sensors in the carotid sinus keep the brain informed of any changes in blood pressure

**Kidney**
The kidneys control how much urine is produced and so also regulate blood volume

**Medulla**
A region of the brain that is responsible for the short-term control of blood pressure

**Aortic arch**
Pressure sensors in the aortic arch keep the brain informed of any changes in blood pressure

*A large number of structures are involved in the regulation of blood pressure, both in the short and the long term.*

The body has three ways of regulating blood pressure: it can alter the cardiac output by changing the force or rate of the heart's contraction; it can alter the diameter and elasticity of the blood vessels to regulate TPR; or it can change the circulating volume of blood.

### SHORT-TERM CONTROL

There are two mechanisms that control blood pressure in the short term:

■ Nervous control
Blood pressure sensors in the arteries send information, via nerves, to a region of the brain called the medulla, which calculates whether blood pressure needs to be corrected. If so, the medulla in turn sends nerve signals to the heart, to modify its rate and strength of beating, and to the blood vessels to modify their diameter.

■ Chemical control
A large number of blood-borne chemicals can either constrict or dilate blood vessels.

### LONG-TERM CONTROL

In the long term, blood volume is controlled by chemicals that act on the kidneys. If blood pressure falls, the kidneys conserve water by producing a more concentrated amount of urine, thus increasing blood volume.

*Excessive stress may contribute to the development of high blood pressure by causing a region of the brain called the medulla to malfunction.*

# How the brain controls blood pressure

The medulla, a region of the brain situated just above the spinal cord, constantly monitors arterial pressure. It corrects changes in pressure by sending nervous signals to the heart and blood vessels.

The pressure of blood in the arteries is constantly measured by specialized pressure sensors called baroreceptors (baro- is a prefix for pressure). Baroreceptors are nerve endings contained within the walls of an artery which are able to detect even the smallest distension of the arterial wall. These pressure sensors are mainly found in the aortic arch and the carotid sinuses.

### BARORECEPTOR NERVES
The baroreceptor endings are part of nerve fibres which travel up to a region of the brain called the medulla.

The afferent (from the Latin 'afferere' – to carry towards) fibres of the aortic baroreceptors form the aortic nerve, which joins the vagus (10th cranial) nerve before entering the medulla, where they terminate in a region called the nucleus tractus solitarii (NTS).

The afferent fibres of the carotid baroreceptors form the carotid sinus nerve, which joins the glossopharyngeal nerve (ninth cranial nerve) before also terminating in the NTS.

## Anatomy of the baroreceptor reflex

*Baroreceptors are found in two locations – the aortic arch and carotid sinus. They send nerve fibres (axons) to a region of the brain called the medulla.*

**Medulla**
The medulla receives nervous input from a large number of sources, including baroreceptors

**Vagus nerve**
An extremely important nerve that carries a wide variety of information to and from the brain

**Aortic nerve**
Connects the aortic baroreceptors to the medulla

**Aortic arch**
Contains the aortic baroreceptors

**Carotid sinus nerve**
Carries information from the carotid baroreceptors to the medulla

**Carotid sinus**
Contains the carotid baroreceptors

**Internal carotid artery**
A major artery that carries oxygenated blood from the heart to the brain

## Response of baroreceptors

**The response of baroreceptor nerves to increasing pressures**

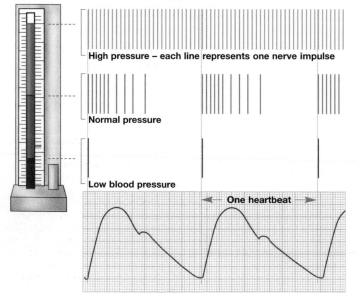

High pressure – each line represents one nerve impulse

Normal pressure

Low blood pressure

One heartbeat

Since blood moves through the arteries via pulsatile, rather than constant flow, the baroreceptor nerves do not 'fire' at a uniform rate.

This is because during systole (when the heart contracts and the pressure is highest) the arterial walls are distended causing the baroreceptor nerves to fire a volley of nervous impulses which travel up to the medulla. However, during diastole (when the heart is relaxed and the pressure is lowest) the arterial walls are not stretched, and this causes the baroreceptors to fall silent.

*Arterial wall stretching is transformed into electrical activity in the baroreceptor nerve fibres. When pressure rises, nerve activity increases.*

Importantly, many baroreceptors will be active at normal pressures; this allows them to inform the medulla when the pressure falls (by slowing the rate of nervous impulses), which would be impossible if the nerves were silent at rest.

### BARORECEPTOR PROPERTIES
Not all baroreceptors have the same properties:
■ Some are responsive at low pressures, whereas others fire only when the arterial pressure has reached very high levels
■ The range of pressure over which they are sensitive also varies considerably
■ Baroreceptors vary in their sensitivity to the rate of change of arterial pressure – this parameter is thought to be very important, as it allows the brain to pre-empt changes in pressure.

## Role of medulla

The baroreceptor nerves project to, and terminate in, a region of the medulla called the nucleus tractus solitarii (NTS). The NTS plays an important role in the control of autonomic (unconscious) functions, including, but not restricted to, the control of blood pressure. If it is damaged, for example following a stroke, the consequences can be fatal.

### ROLE OF THE NTS
The NTS receives information not just from baroreceptors, but also from a large number of other sources including receptors found in the heart, gastro-intestinal tract, lungs, oesophagus and tongue. The NTS neurones do not act as a simple relay station for this diverse afferent input. Rather, they calculate what the correct blood pressure should be after taking into account information obtained from all the other sources.

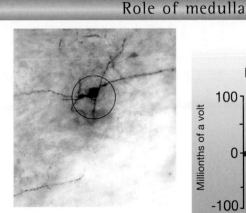

*A micrograph of a neurone located in the NTS, which receives input from baroreceptors. The cell body, which contains the nucleus, is the dark oval (circled).*

*The top trace shows the electrical activity of a neurone located in the NTS. The neurone's rate of firing increases when arterial pressure is raised (bottom).*

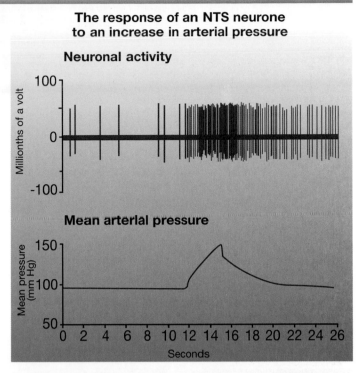

**The response of an NTS neurone to an increase in arterial pressure**

**Neuronal activity**

**Mean arterial pressure**

## The baroreceptor reflex pathway

### The baroreceptor reflex pathway

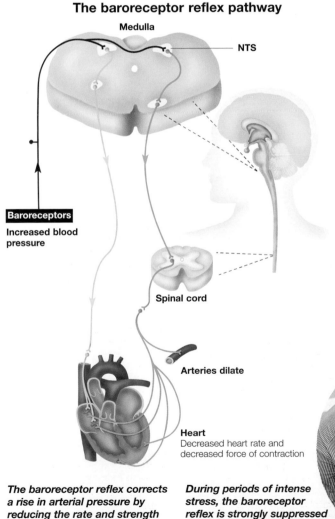

Medulla

NTS

Baroreceptors

Increased blood pressure

Spinal cord

Arteries dilate

**Heart**
Decreased heart rate and decreased force of contraction

*The baroreceptor reflex corrects a rise in arterial pressure by reducing the rate and strength of the heartbeat, as well as causing the arteries to relax, so lowering blood pressure.*

*During periods of intense stress, the baroreceptor reflex is strongly suppressed by nerves originating from the hypothalamus. This may be one of the causes of hypertension.*

If arterial pressure rises, baroreceptors respond to the distension of the arterial wall by sending a volley of nervous impulses to the NTS.

Under normal conditions, the NTS will try to correct this increase in pressure by sending nervous impulses to the heart, telling it to reduce its rate and strength of contraction; and to the arteries, telling them to become more elastic. This will have the effect of reducing both the cardiac output (the amount of blood that the heart pumps out each minute) and the resistance to blood flow in the arteries. These combined effects will act to lower blood pressure.

### RESETTING THE BARORECEPTOR REFLEX
The baroreceptor reflex acts to maintain blood pressure at what physiologists call the 'set-point'.

An analogy to the set-point is the temperature setting of a central heating thermostat; the set-point of the baroreceptor reflex can be altered in the same way as a thermostat. The body does this either by affecting the threshold pressure at which the baroreceptors fire (peripheral resetting), or by altering the sensitivity of the neurones within the medulla (central resetting).

### PERIPHERAL RESETTING
If pressure is maintained at a raised level for many minutes, the baroceptors become accustomed to the new pressure and 'think' that it is the correct level. Thus baroreceptors cannot accurately inform the brain about blood pressure levels over the long-term.

### CENTRAL RESETTING
When we are exposed to a stressful situation, the neurones within the NTS which mediate the baroreceptor reflex are strongly suppressed, allowing blood pressure to rise. This was advantageous to our ancestors because it prepared them either to fight or to run away from their aggressors. However, this neural mechanism could be responsible for the high incidence of hypertension seen in modern Western society. The stress that we experience in our day-to-day lives, could, in some people at least, raise the set-point and so cause hypertension.

# Lymphoid cells and lymph drainage vessels

Lymphoid cells are divided into B-lymphocytes, which produce antibodies, and T-lymphocytes, which kill infected cells. The whole lymph network eventually drains into the venous system.

Scattered throughout the body are discrete groups of lymphoid tissue, which have an important role in the immune system:

■ The spleen – provides a site for the cells of the immune system to proliferate and monitor the blood for foreign or damaged cells

■ The thymus – a small gland which lies in the chest just behind the upper part of the sternum (breastbone). It receives newly formed lymphocytes from the bone marrow, which mature into T-lymphocytes, an important group of lymphoid cells

■ Lymphoid tissue of the gastro-intestinal tract – lymphoid tissue lying beneath the lining of the gut generally, the ring of lymphoid tissue at the back of the mouth and some discrete clumps of lymphoid nodules known as 'Peyer's patches', found in the walls of the last part of the small intestine. These are thought to be the site of maturation of B-lymphocytes, another important set of lymphocytes.

The large amount of lymphoid tissue in the gut wall helps to protect against infection by organisms entering through the mouth.

## Lymphoid tissues and organs

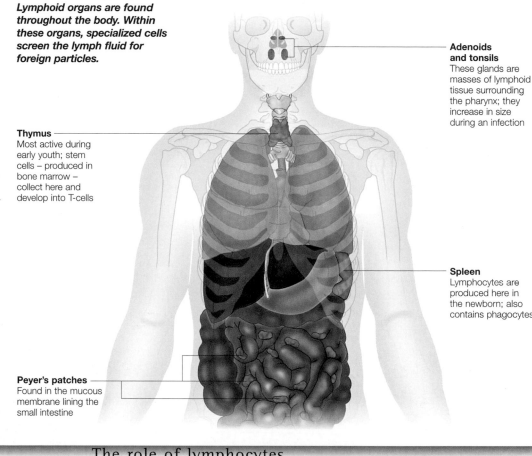

*Lymphoid organs are found throughout the body. Within these organs, specialized cells screen the lymph fluid for foreign particles.*

**Adenoids and tonsils**
These glands are masses of lymphoid tissue surrounding the pharynx; they increase in size during an infection

**Thymus**
Most active during early youth; stem cells – produced in bone marrow – collect here and develop into T-cells

**Spleen**
Lymphocytes are produced here in the newborn; also contains phagocytes

**Peyer's patches**
Found in the mucous membrane lining the small intestine

## The role of lymphocytes

*'Natural killer cells' are a type of lymphocyte. They are able to destroy cancer cells and cells infected with viruses.*

The cells of the immune system, lymphocytes, can recognize foreign proteins, such as those found on the surface of invading micro-organisms or on the cells of transplanted organs.

In response, the lymphocyte cells multiply and mount an immune response, some (T-cells) by directly attacking the foreign cells and some (B-cells) by manufacturing antibodies which attach to the foreign proteins, allowing them to be found and destroyed.

Lymphocytes are made in the bone marrow and circulate freely in the bloodstream. As they circulate, they can quickly mount a response to infections.

# Lymph drainage vessels

The lymphatic vessels form a network that runs through the tissues. These vessels converge and empty into the veins.

### DRAINAGE OF THE CHEST

Of the lymph nodes that lie in the chest, the most important clinically are the internal mammary nodes on either side of the sternum. They receive 25 per cent of the lymph from the breast and may be a site for spread of breast cancer. Within the chest, the largest group of lymph nodes lie around the base of the trachea (windpipe) and the bronchi. Other lymph node groups within the chest lie alongside the major blood vessels.

### UPPER AND LOWER LIMBS

In the limbs, there are superficial and deep lymph vessels; the superficial vessels tend to lie alongside the veins while the deep vessels accompany the arteries. The axillary (armpit) group of nodes receives lymph from the whole of the upper limb, the trunk above the umbilicus and the breast. The inguinal (groin) lymph nodes receive lymph from the superficial vessels and the deep lymph vessels that run alongside the arteries. Lymph travels up from the inguinal nodes to the nodes alongside the aorta and eventually join the lumbar lymph trunks.

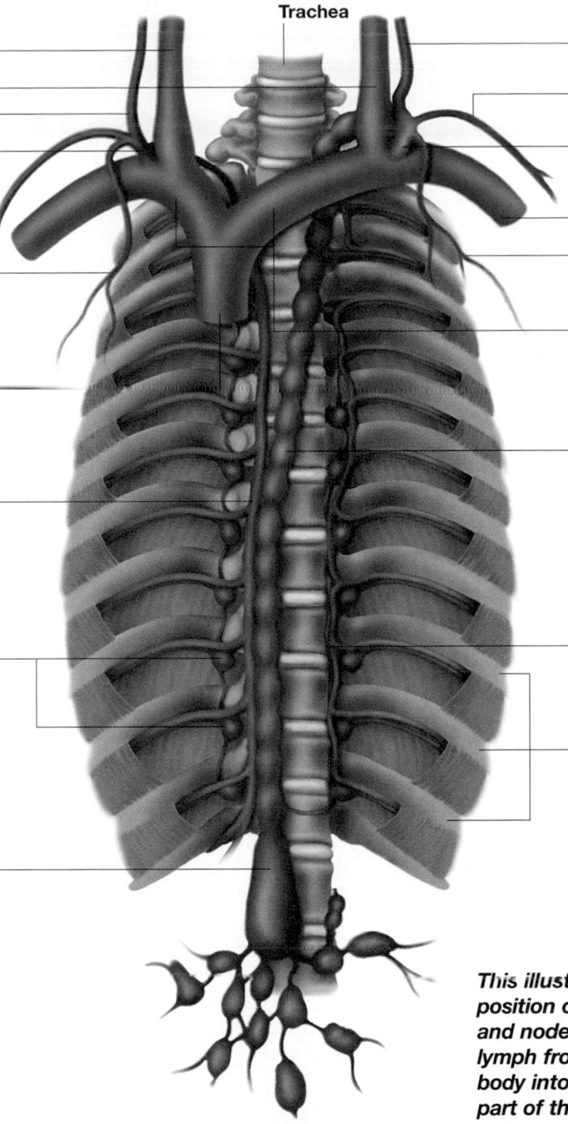

**Trachea**

**Internal jugular veins**

**Right jugular trunk**

**Right lymphatic duct**
Receives lymph from the right half of the head, the right arm and the upper chest

**Right broncho-mediastinal trunk**
Drains lymph from the right side of the lungs

**Superior vena cava**
Drains blood from the neck, head, chest and arms

**Azygos vein**
Receives blood from the chest and abdominal cavity and drains into the superior vena cava

**Lymph nodes**
Situated in front of the thoracic vertebral column in the chest

**Cysterna chyli**
Collects lymph that drains from the lower limbs and intestinal trunk; runs into the thoracic duct

**Left jugular trunk**

**Left subclavian trunk**

**Entrance of thoracic duct into left subclavian vein**

**Left subclavian vein**

**Left broncho-mediastinal trunk**

**Brachiocephalic veins**
Drain into the superior vena cava

**Thoracic duct**
Runs up from the cysterna chyli to the left subclavian vein, receiving all the lymph in the body except from the right arm, right half of the head and upper chest

**Hemiazygos vein**
A partially paired vein draining the lower thorax

**Ribs**

*This illustration shows the position of the lymphatic ducts and nodes in the chest draining lymph from the lower half of the body into the veins in the upper part of the thorax.*

## Disorders of the lymphatic system

As lymph is carried from the tissues back to the bloodstream in the lymphatic vessels, it passes through a series of lymph nodes. These act as filters, removing cells and micro-organisms. Lymph from each area of the body drains through a particular set of lymph nodes and this pattern of drainage is of great clinical importance in the diagnosis and treatment of cancer and infection.

In cancer, the lymph nodes draining the affected area may enlarge and become firmer or even hard and may be felt by a doctor. Finding such enlarged lymph nodes may allow the doctor to suspect a secondary tumour and will give an indication of the site of the primary tumour. Knowledge of lymphatic drainage also allows a surgeon to remove the associated lymph nodes when he is removing a tumour to check for, or help prevent, secondary spread.

Bacterial infection of the skin can lead to a condition known as lymphangitis where the lymphatic vessels themselves become infected and inflamed. Where the pathway of these affected lymphatic vessels lies just under the skin, it can be seen as a series of red lines which are painful and tender to the touch. Lymphangitis, along with painful enlargement of the associated lymph nodes, is a feature of infection with *Streptococcus* bacteria.

*The red line along the inside of this man's arm is caused by lymphangitis – an infection of the lymphatic vessels.*

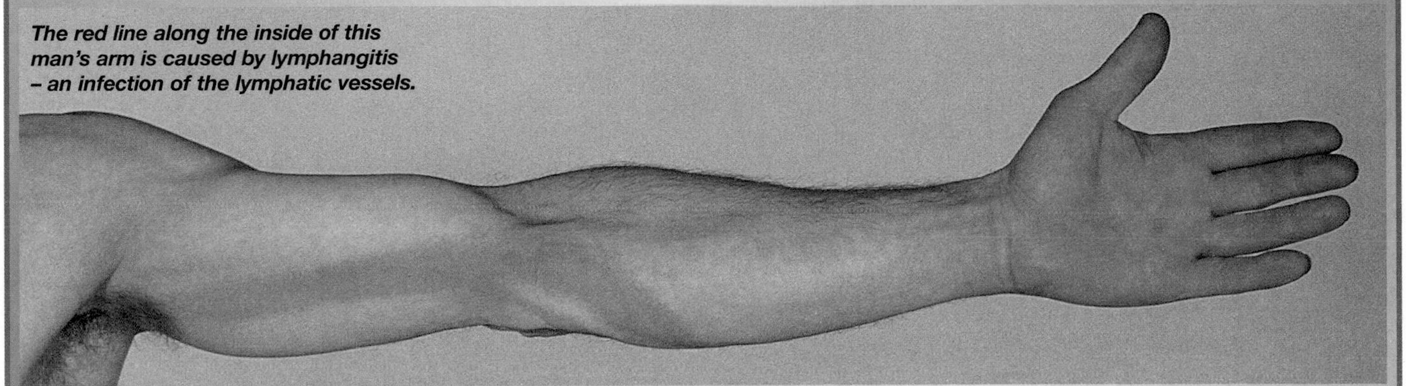

# Regional lymphatic drainage

Lymph from every part of the body returns to the bloodstream via a series of lymph nodes. An understanding of the lymph drainage pattern is vital in monitoring the spread of cancers or infection.

Lymph is the fluid present within the vessels of the lymphatic system. The main function of the lymphatic vessels is to collect excess tissue fluid and return it to the blood circulation.

Lymph from each part of the body follows a specific path on its way back to rejoin the blood circulation, passing through lymph node groups – which have a filtering role – on the way.

## HEAD AND NECK NODES

The lymph node groups of the structures of the head and neck are named according to their positions. The important lymph node groups include the:
■ Occipital
■ Mastoid, or retroauricular (behind the ear)
■ Parotid
■ Buccal
■ Submandibular (under the jaw)
■ Submental (under the chin)
■ Anterior cervical
■ Superficial cervical
■ Deep within the neck lie other groups of nodes which surround and drain the pharynx, larynx and trachea.

## DEEP CERVICAL NODES

These lymph nodes all drain ultimately into the deep cervical group of nodes which lie in a chain alongside the major blood vessels of the neck.

**Mastoid (retroauricular) nodes**
Drain a strip of scalp above the ear

**Occipital lobes**
Receive lymph from the back of the scalp

**Superficial cervical nodes**
Drain the skin of the angle of the jaw and the earlobe

**Angle of the jaw**

**Parotid nodes**
Drain part of the ear, the outer parts of the eyelid and an area of scalp

**Buccal node**
Some lymph passes through the buccal nodes on its way to the submandibular nodes

**Submental node**
Drains the tip of the tongue, the centre of the lower lip and the chin

**Submandibular nodes**
Lying under the jaw, these nodes receive lymph from a wide area including the front of the scalp, much of the face, the sinuses and most of the teeth

*Lymph from the head and neck is transported through groups of lymph nodes. All the nodes drain into the deep cervical nodes around the major blood vessels.*

## Lymphatic drainage of the tongue

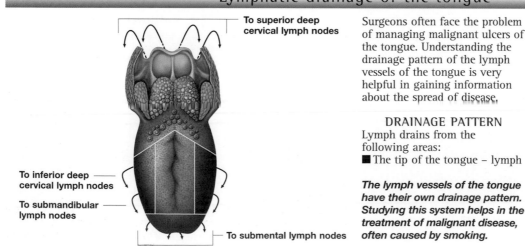

**To superior deep cervical lymph nodes**

**To inferior deep cervical lymph nodes**

**To submandibular lymph nodes**

**To submental lymph nodes**

Surgeons often face the problem of managing malignant ulcers of the tongue. Understanding the drainage pattern of the lymph vessels of the tongue is very helpful in gaining information about the spread of disease.

### DRAINAGE PATTERN

Lymph drains from the following areas:
■ The tip of the tongue – lymph

from both sides of this area of the tongue drains into the submental group of lymph nodes, under the chin
■ The sides of the tongue – lymph drains from each side to the submandibular group of nodes
■ The central part of the tongue – this area drains to the inferior (lower) deep cervical nodes which lie alongside the internal jugular vein, deep within the neck
■ The back of the tongue – lymph from both sides of this area drains into the superior (upper) deep cervical lymph nodes.

*The lymph vessels of the tongue have their own drainage pattern. Studying this system helps in the treatment of malignant disease, often caused by smoking.*

# Lymph drainage of the intestines

The lymph vessels and nodes that make up the lymphatic drainage of the gastrointestinal system follow the general pattern of the arteries which supply the gut with blood. Lymph from the small intestine transports fats absorbed from food into the bloodstream.

Much of the gut is enclosed and suspended within a fold of connective tissue, known as a mesentery. The blood vessels that supply the gut lie within this mesentery, forming arcades that connect with each other to reach all parts of this lengthy structure.

### SITE OF NODES
The lymph nodes which initially receive lymph from the intestine are found within the mesentery in a number of places:
■ By the wall of the intestine
■ Among the arterial arcades
■ Alongside the large superior and inferior mesenteric arteries.

These mesenteric groups of nodes are, in some cases, named according to their positions in relation to the intestine or to the artery they accompany. From the intestinal wall, lymph drains through these nodes in turn to eventually reach the pre-aortic nodes, which lie next to the large central artery, the aorta.

### ABSORPTION OF FAT
In addition to its normal function, the lymph which leaves the small intestine has a further role – that of transporting the fats absorbed from food.

The lining of the small

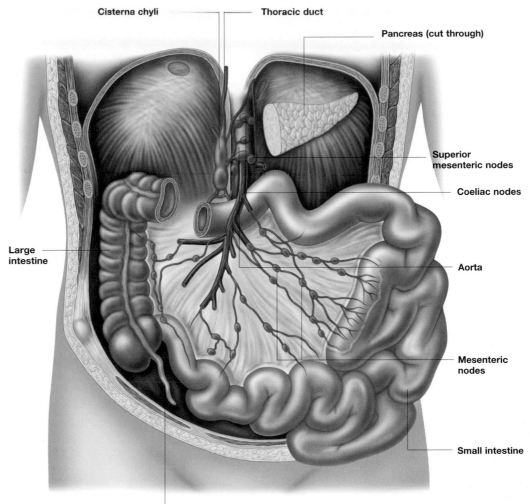

Cisterna chyli · Thoracic duct · Pancreas (cut through) · Superior mesenteric nodes · Coeliac nodes · Large intestine · Aorta · Mesenteric nodes · Small intestine · Appendix
This has its own lymph node

*The lymph nodes of the gastrointestinal system are located in the mesentery. This is a fold of membrane that encloses a large part of the gut.*

intestine bears numerous microvilli. These tiny projections of the mucous membrane greatly increase the surface area of the intestine to help absorption.

### CENTRAL VESSELS
Within each microvillus lies a central lymph vessel, called a lacteal. The function of the lacteals is to carry away fat particles absorbed from food

which are too big to enter the blood capillaries.

These fats travel through the lymphatic system to be delivered into the bloodstream with the rest of the lymph.

## Lymphatic drainage of the stomach

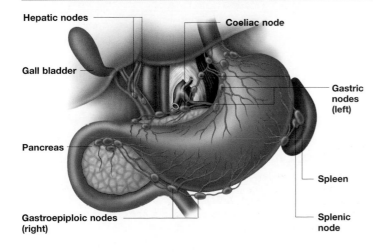

Hepatic nodes · Coeliac node · Gall bladder · Gastric nodes (left) · Pancreas · Spleen · Gastroepiploic nodes (right) · Splenic node

*There are four main groups of lymph nodes within the stomach. These comprise the gastric, splenic, gastroepiploic and coeliac nodes.*

Like the intestine, the lymphatic drainage of the stomach tends to follow the pattern of the arterial blood supply.

### FOUR GROUPS
The nodes which receive lymph from the stomach comprise four main groups:
■ The left and right gastric nodes receive lymph from the area supplied by the left and

right gastric arteries, respectively. They lie along the lesser curve of the stomach
■ The splenic nodes lie at the hilum (hollow) of the spleen on the left side of the stomach. These nodes receive lymph from the area of the stomach supplied by the short gastric arteries
■ The left and right gastroepiploic nodes lie along the greater curve of the stomach and receive lymph from areas supplied by the corresponding gastroepiploic arteries.

All the lymph received from the stomach by these groups travels on to drain into the coeliac nodes.

105

# How cells work

All the living tissue in the body is made up of cells – microscopic membrane-bounded compartments filled with a concentrated solution of chemicals. Cells are the smallest living unit in the body.

Every tissue in the body is made up of groups of cells performing specialized functions, linked by intricate systems of communication. There are over 200 different types of cells in the body. Although enormously complex, the final structure of the human body is generated by a limited repertoire of cell activities. Most cells grow, divide and die while performing functions particular to their tissue type, such as the contraction of muscle cells.

Typically, cells contain structural elements called organelles, which are involved in the cell's metabolism and life cycle. This includes the uptake of nutrients, cell division and synthesis of proteins – the molecules responsible for most of the cell's enzymatic, metabolic and structural functions.

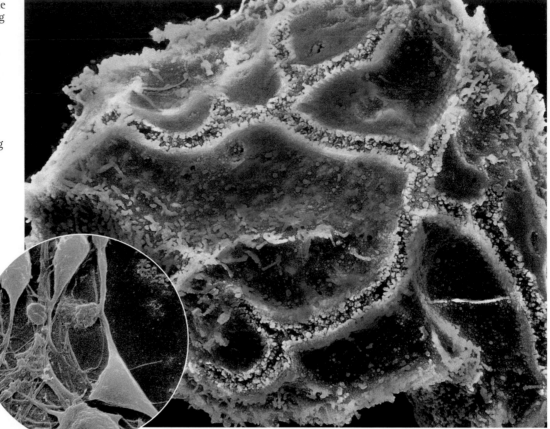

*A hepatocyte is seen on a micrograph (far right). This is a specialized liver cell that performs several functions. Neurones – nerve cells – of the cerebral cortex are shown in the inset (green).*

## Immortal cells

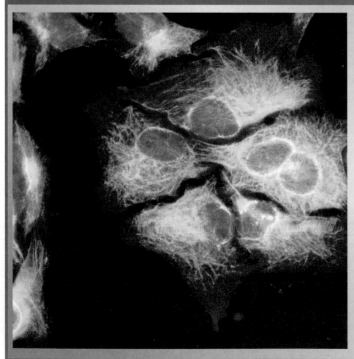

Most cells, when grown in a laboratory, can divide only about 50 times before they die. Immortal cells are cells that can be grown in Petri dishes indefinitely, and such cells are extremely useful in research.

In 1951, Henrietta Lacks, a 31-year-old American woman, was found to have a small lesion on her cervix, and a biopsy was taken to determine if the cells were malignant (cancerous). The sample of cells sent to the laboratory were indeed malignant, and despite treatment, she died eight months later from cervical cancer.

The sample of cells ended up in the laboratory of George Gey, a pioneer of tissue culture, and after working with the cells for several

*HeLa cells, unlike normal cells, continue to divide indefinitely. They have been used in research worldwide because they are so easily cultured.*

weeks, he concluded that they divided faster than any cells he had ever seen before.

The cells, now called HeLa cells, proved to be robust and immortal, and because they grow so rapidly and reliably, they were eventually made available to other researchers and have been used extensively in biological research ever since. The polio vaccine was developed in under a year thanks to their use.

Unfortunately, HeLa cells have the ability to contaminate and subvert other cells growing in the same laboratory, and there were instances of experiments performed on one particular type of cell, unknowingly being performed on HeLa cells instead.

HeLa cells are still maintained in laboratory cultures. Such colonies have been maintained for the 40 years since the tumour they were cultured from was removed from Henrietta Lacks' cervix.

# Structure of a cell

The cell structure can be divided into the outer membrane, the DNA-containing nucleus and the structures called organelles within the cell. Each component of a cell has a specific function, such as energy production, storage or the synthesis of proteins.

## THE PLASMA MEMBRANE

The plasma membrane surrounds each cell and separates it from its external environment, which includes other cells. Contained inside the membrane is a solution of proteins, electrolytes and carbohydrates called the cytosol, as well as membrane-bound subcellular structures called organelles. Spanning across the membrane are proteins responsible for communication with the external environment and for transport of nutrients and waste.

## THE NUCLEUS

The nucleus is in the centre of the cell, and contains the cell's DNA arranged into chromosomes, as well as structural proteins for coiling and protecting the DNA. The nucleus is surrounded by a membrane with large pores in it, allowing for movement of molecules between the nucleus and the cytosol, while retaining the chromosomes inside the nucleus.

***The shape of each type of cell varies according to function. Many organelles found in most cells are seen in this cut-away.***

**Cytosol**
Fluid within the cell, made up of electrolytes, proteins and carbohydrates

**Plasma membrane**
Encloses the cell and regulates the passage of substances into and out of the cell

**Nucleolus**
contains ribonucleic acid for the synthesis of ribosomes

**Golgi apparatus**
Modifies and re-packages proteins before they are released from the cell

**Cytoskeleton**
Protein filaments which form a meshwork to maintain the cell's shape and anchors the internal structures

**Endoplasmic reticulum**
Network of sacs and tubes which transport and store materials in the cell

**Vesicles**
Sacs containing substances that are released at the cell membrane

**Vacuole**
Storage regions bounded by a membrane

**Nucleus**
Contains the cell's genetic material, the DNA

**Ribosomes**
Small structures, either free floating or situated on the rough endoplasmic reticulum; site of protein production

**Mitochondrion**
Site of energy production; breakdown of sugars and fats is carried out to make ATP

---

## Inside the cell – the cytoplasm

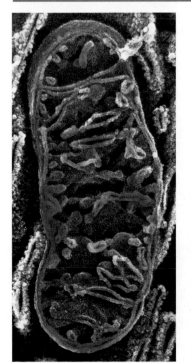

The cytoplasm is the inner contents of the cell, not including the nucleus, which is made up of fluid (the cytosol) and large numbers of organelles. The organelles include:

■ **Mitochondria**
Responsible for energy production. Nutrients in the form of sugars and fats are broken down in the presence of oxygen to make ATP (adenosine triphosphate), a source of energy used by a cell.

■ **Ribosomes**
Ribosomes carry out the production of proteins, using the blueprint recorded in the genetic material of the cell.

■ **Endoplasmic reticulum**
This is a vast network of tubes, sacs and sheets of membrane

*A single mitochondrion is seen coloured pink in this high-powered micrograph. These are the 'powerhouses' of the cell, where respiration occurs.*

that runs throughout the cell. It allows for the transport and storage of molecules.

■ **Golgi apparatus**
The Golgi apparatus is a stack of flattened sacs, critical in the modification, packaging and sorting of large molecules in the cell.

■ **Vesicles and vacuoles**
Vesicles are membrane-bounded areas within a cell for specialized processes or storage. Vacuoles appear as 'holes' under the microscope, and are typically

regions of storage or digestion surrounded by a membrane.

■ **Cytoskeleton**
The cytoskeleton is the fine meshwork of protein filaments used to maintain the cell's shape, to anchor components in place and to provide a basis for the cell's movements.

*This electron micrograph shows a section through the rough endoplasmic reticulum of an animal cell (red lines). Attached to the surface are ribosomes.*

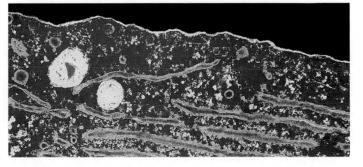

# How cells divide

The vast majority of cells that make up the human body divide
on a regular basis. This occurs not only during periods of growth,
but also when worn out cells need to be replaced.

All tissues are made up of cells, microscopic membrane-bounded compartments. New cells are made by cell division, during which a cell replicates its genetic material and then separates its contents into two daughter cells. The process of cell division occurs continuously throughout the body, both during the development of the fetus and throughout adulthood.

### WHY DO CELLS DIVIDE?

Cells divide when body tissue is growing, or when the cells in that tissue wear out and need to be replaced. Division is carefully regulated and must occur in accordance with the needs of the surrounding tissue, as well as in time with the internal cell growth cycle.

Cells that divide out of control can become cancers. Most chemotherapy is based around regimens that kill dividing cells, but which have less of an effect on non-dividing cells.

### EMBRYONIC CELLS

The most prolific cell division occurs during early embryonic development; in nine months, a fertilized egg (one cell) develops into an embryo and, subsequently, a fetus of over 10 thousand million cells.

As development proceeds, many cells switch from dividing to performing a specialized function (such as becoming pacemaker cells in the heart), a process called differentiation.

In almost all tissues there are stem cells, which are cells that are not fully differentiated, but which can divide and differentiate in response to stimuli or wounding.

*Once an egg cell is fertilized, it divides progressively; this human embryo is at the four cell stage.*

*During the process of cell division, the chromosomes, which contain genetic material, separate into each of the two new (daughter) cells.*

## The life cycle of a cell

The cell division cycle is the process by which one cell doubles its genetic material and then divides into two identical daughter cells. The cycle is divided into two main stages: interphase, when the cell's components are replicated, and mitosis, when the cell divides into two.

Interphase is divided into two gap phases ($G_1$ and $G_2$) and a synthesis (S) phase.

During the first gap phase ($G_1$), the cell produces carbohydrates, lipids and proteins. Slow-growing cells, such as liver cells, may remain in this phase for years, whereas fast-growing cells, such as those in bone marrow, spend only 16–24 hours in the $G_1$ phase.

If a cell is not actively dividing, it exits the cell cycle during $G_1$ and enters a state called $G_0$. For example, in adults many highly specialized cells, such as neurones (nerve cells) and heart muscle cells, do not divide and remain in phase $G_0$. This makes healing and regeneration in these tissues slow and sometimes impossible.

### REPLICATING CHROMOSOMES

The next period of interphase – which is known as the S phase – sees the replication of the chromosomes so that the cell temporarily has 92 chromosomes instead of the normal 46. Proteins are also synthesized during the S phase, including those that form the spindle structures that pull the chromosomes apart. In most human cells, the S phase lasts between 8 and 10 hours.

Additional proteins are synthesized in the second gap phase, $G_2$.

The cell divides into two daughter cells during a process called mitosis. Mitosis is subdivided into four phases: prophase, metaphase, anaphase and telophase.

The duration of a complete cell cycle varies from a day to a year, depending on the type of cell concerned. Examples of the rates of replacement for different cell types are:

■ Liver cells: 12 months
■ Red blood cells: 80–120 days
■ Skin cells: 14–28 days
■ Intestinal mucosa: 3–5 days.

*Cell division is divided into two stages: interphase (purple), when the cell contents are replicated, and mitosis (orange), when the cell divides. Interphase is subdivided into $G_1$, S and $G_2$ phases. Mitosis is subdivided into prophase, metaphase, anaphase and telophase.*

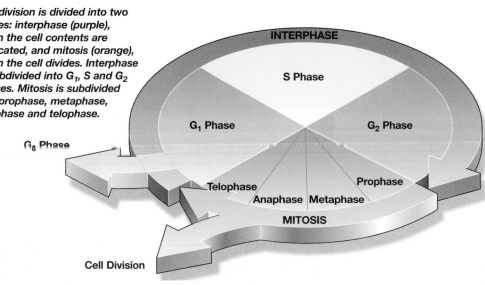

INTERPHASE

S Phase

$G_1$ Phase

$G_2$ Phase

$G_0$ Phase

Telophase

Prophase

Anaphase   Metaphase

MITOSIS

Cell Division

# The four stages of mitosis

**1 Prophase**
During prophase, the DNA condenses into recognizable chromosomes, the nucleus disbands and the nuclear contents enter the cytoplasm.

*This scanning electron micrograph (SEM) shows the condensed chromosomes (red), nuclear membrane (orange) and cytoplasm (green).*

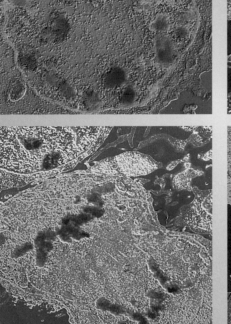

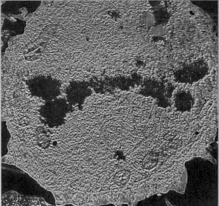

**2 Metaphase**
During metaphase the chromosomes attach to the mitotic apparatus, a series of specially synthesized protein filaments anchored to opposite sides of the cell.

*Here, the cell is in late metaphase: the nuclear membrane has disappeared and the chromosomes (red) are aligned along the centre of the cell.*

**3 Anaphase**
During anaphase, the chromosomes are pulled away from each other by the mitotic apparatus in the cell. Half of the chromosomes go to each side of the cell.

*This SEM shows the first stages of anaphase, when the chromosomes separate and the cell membrane becomes indented.*

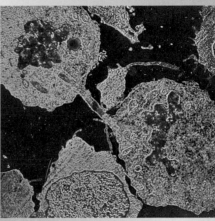

**4 Telophase**
During telophase, the nuclear membranes re-form, the cell's contents are redistributed and the membrane 'pinches off' to form two cells.

*The cell is in late telophase in this SEM: the two newly-formed cells are still joined by a narrow bridge containing elements of the mitotic apparatus.*

# Cell death and cell suicide

There are two ways that cells can die: they can be killed by injurious agents, a process called necrosis; or they can be induced to 'commit suicide', a mechanism that scientists call apoptosis.

## NECROSIS

When the body is exposed to mechanical or chemical damage, cells may die simply because they are no longer able to function properly. This process, called necrosis, happens when the cell's integrity is violated, or when molecules or structures essential to the cell's survival are no longer available or functional. For example, after a person dies, nutrients and oxygen are unavailable to all of the cells of the body, which then undergo necrosis and die. Gangrene is another example of necrosis – the dead tissue turns black due to the action of certain bacteria on haemoglobin, which is broken down to produce dark iron sulphide deposits.

## APOPTOSIS

The majority of cells have an in-built programme which makes them commit suicide. Scientists believe that this programme is as intrinsic to the cell as mitosis.

There are two main reasons why a cell would commit suicide. First, programmed cell death is often needed for the proper development of the human body. For example, the formation of the fingers and toes of the fetus requires the removal of the tissue between them by apoptosis. Second, cell suicide may be needed to destroy cells that represent a threat to the organism. For example, defensive T-lymphocyte cells kill virus-infected cells by inducing apoptosis in them.

*In the early stages of fetal development, fingers are connected, giving them a webbed appearance. This webbing disappears as the fetus develops, due to apoptosis.*

# Meiosis

Meiosis is a special form of cell division that only occurs during the formation of sperm and eggs. During meiosis, there are two cycles of division, but only one duplication of chromosomes, so that sperm and eggs end up with only 23 chromosomes. Meiosis is unique, since 'crossing-over' occurs between paired chromosomes. As a result, the chromosomes that are in the sperm and eggs are not identical to the chromosomes from the parent.

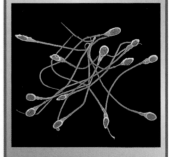

*Meiosis is the process that creates both sperm and eggs. Unlike all the other cells in the body, these gametes (sex cells) contain only 23 – rather than 46 – chromosomes*

# How cells communicate

## For the body to act in a co-ordinated manner, it is essential that cells communicate with each other. They do this either by releasing chemical messengers or by electrically exciting neighbouring cells.

The human body contains a total of around 10,000,000,000,000 (10 trillion) cells, made from just over 200 different cell types. However, the benefits of having specialized cells can only be realized if this multicellular organization acts in a co-ordinated manner.

■ **Internal stimuli**
The body must be able to respond to changes in its internal environment. For example, cells in the pancreas detect the rise in blood glucose concentration after a meal; they release a hormone – insulin – which makes the cells of other tissues absorb glucose from the blood to provide energy.

■ **External stimuli**
Similarly, the body must also be able to detect and respond to external stimuli. For example, it would be no good having eyes with which to see a predator if this visual information could not be relayed to the rest of the body to prepare it to fight with, or run away from, an aggressor.

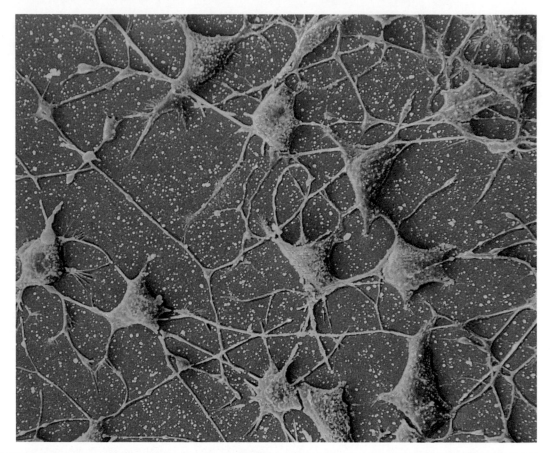

*Nerve cells communicate by releasing chemical messengers which affect the electrical excitability of neighbouring cells.*

## Electrical and chemical communication between cells

### Heart cells communicate electrically

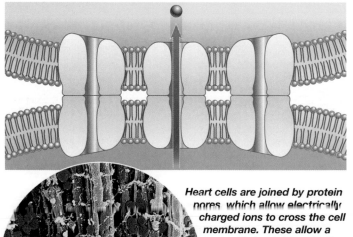

*Heart cells are joined by protein pores, which allow electrically charged ions to cross the cell membrane. These allow a wave of electrical excitation to travel through the heart.*

*Heart cells (green) communicate with each other electrically. Chemicals (for example, adrenaline) released by distant tissues can affect their behaviour, however.*

Both internal and external stimuli are detected by specialized chemicals (normally proteins) called 'receptors', which transduce (convert) information into a form that can be relayed to other cells within the body. Broadly speaking, communication between the body's cells is accomplished using either chemical messengers or electrical currents.

### ELECTRICAL COMMUNICATION
Most electrical messages are carried by nerve cells (though heart cells also communicate electrically) which are specially adapted for carrying nerve impulses from one region of the body to another. For example, some nerve fibres can be up to a metre in length.

The main advantage of electrical communication is the speed at which information can be transmitted; some nerves are able to propagate nerve impulses at rates of 120 metres per second. Furthermore, because the 'wiring' of neurones is very precise, information can be delivered to very specific locations.

### CHEMICAL COMMUNICATION
In contrast, by virtue of the fact that many chemical messengers, such as hormones, are released into the bloodstream, these molecules can affect a wide number of cells, but can do so only relatively slowly. For example, when a person is exposed to a stressful situation, the adrenaline rush does not 'kick in' for 15–30 seconds. This is because the adrenaline molecules have to diffuse from the adrenal gland (located just above the kidneys) into the bloodstream, which then carries them around the body to the target organs (such as the heart, increasing both its rate and strength of beating).

# Types of chemical communication

Chemical messengers can be classified into three groups based on the type of cell that releases the chemical and how the chemical messenger reaches its site of action. These groups include hormones, paracrine and autocrine factors and neurohormones.

## Hormones

Hormones are chemicals that are released by a gland into the bloodstream, which then carries them to distant sites throughout the body. They may have a specific site of action or may affect a wide variety of different cells, simultaneously regulating a large number of different bodily processes.

For example, adrenaline is released into the blood from the adrenal medulla, the central region of each of the adrenal glands, which lie above the kidneys. Adrenaline has a wide number of actions, which include constriction of the blood vessels, increased cardiac activity, dilatation of the pupils in the eye and inhibition of the gastro-intestinal tract.

### HORMONE SPECIFICITY
Since all the body's cells are in close proximity to passing blood vessels, one might expect a hormone to be able to affect every cell in the body. However, this is not the case. For a hormone to affect the internal biochemistry of a cell (a cell's 'behaviour'), the cell must have an appropriate protein receptor embedded within its cell membrane; by way of an analogy, a front door must contain a letterbox to allow the postman to deliver a letter.

*Hormones are chemical messengers that are released by a gland into the bloodstream which then carries the hormone to distant tissues.*

**Glandular tissue**
The cells within a gland release certain hormones into the bloodstream

**Blood vessel**
The hormone travels through the bloodstream to reach the target cells

**Target cells**
Only the target cells are affected by the hormone

## Paracrine and autocrine factors

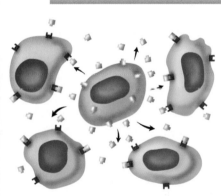

*Paracrine factors are released into the water-filled space between the cells. They affect cells of a different type to the one that released them.*

The second group of chemical messengers differ from hormones in that they are not transported by the bloodstream to their target cells.

Rather, these chemicals are released into the watery space that lies between the cells to affect either the same type of cell that released them (autocrine factors – 'auto' meaning 'self') or different, though nearby, cells (paracrine factors). It should be noted, however, that a chemical can be both an autocrine and paracrine factor.

### PARACRINE FACTORS
One of the most common paracrine factors is the chemical histamine. Histamine is released

from specialized cells called mast cells that are present in most tissues. It is involved in allergic reactions and in some of the inflammatory chemical pathways that are initiated when a tissue is damaged. Anti-histamines work by preventing mast cells from releasing this paracrine factor.

### AUTOCRINE FACTORS
Autocrine factors affect the same type of tissue that released them. For example, most cells release autocrine factors which inhibit their own cell division and that of similar nearby cells. Cancerous cells are thought to either not release, or not respond to, these inhibitors resulting in cell division proceeding unabated.

*Autocrine factors are chemical messengers which only affect the same type of cell that originally released them.*

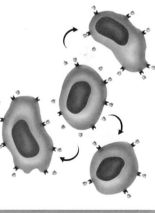

## Neurohormones

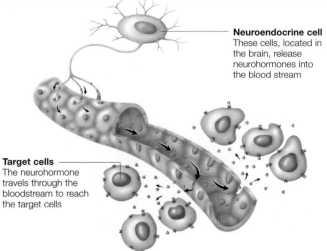

**Neuroendocrine cell**
These cells, located in the brain, release neurohormones into the blood stream

**Target cells**
The neurohormone travels through the bloodstream to reach the target cells

Most neurones communicate with each other by releasing a chemical messenger which diffuses between the gap (called a synapse) that separates them.

However, some neurones do not synapse with another nerve cell. Rather, their synaptic terminals are located near blood vessels; when these neurones are stimulated they release a neurohormone into the

*Neurohormones are released by specialized nerve cells called neuroendocrine cells. These chemicals are carried in the bloodstream to the target cells.*

bloodstream, which is then carried to distant target organs in much the same way that a hormone is released from a gland.

### OXYTOCIN
Oxytocin is a neurohormone which is released into the bloodstream by neuroendocrine cells located in the hypothalamus. This occurs in response to the stimulation of sensory nerves in the mother's nipple by a suckling infant. The blood carries the neurohormone to the mammary gland where it causes milk to be ejected from the nipple.

# Structure of the cell membrane

The cell membrane separates the inside from the outside of the cell. Since it is only permeable to certain molecules, the internal environment of the cell can be tightly controlled.

Every cell is covered in a membrane, made mainly of phospholipids (phosphate-containing fat molecules) and proteins, which acts as a barrier between the inside and outside of the cell. Some molecules can pass freely through it, while others have either restricted or no access.

A membrane surrounds the cell as a whole (also called the plasma membrane), as well as the organelles (the sub-cellular components) which are contained within the membrane.

The cell membrane is much more than a simple protective covering; by determining which chemicals are allowed to pass into and out of the cell, the cell is able to tightly control its internal environment, as well as communicate with other cells.

## CHEMICAL CONSTRUCTION
The cell membrane is composed of four groups of chemicals: phospholipids (25 per cent), proteins (55 per cent), cholesterol (15 per cent) and carbohydrates and other lipids (5 per cent).
■ Phospholipid molecules are arranged in two layers (known as a 'bilayer'). They act as a very thin yet impenetrable barrier to water, and to water-soluble molecules such as glucose.

## How the cell membrane is made up

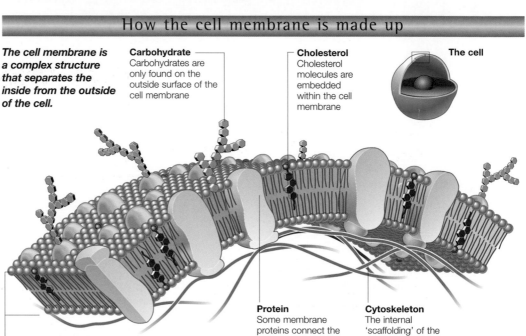

**The cell membrane is a complex structure that separates the inside from the outside of the cell.**

**Carbohydrate**
Carbohydrates are only found on the outside surface of the cell membrane

**Cholesterol**
Cholesterol molecules are embedded within the cell membrane

**The cell**

**Phospholipid bilayer**

**Protein**
Some membrane proteins connect the inside to the outside of the cell

**Cytoskeleton**
The internal 'scaffolding' of the cell is called the cytoskeleton

However, fat-soluble molecules, such as oxygen, carbon dioxide and steroids, can pass through it freely.

The phospholipid portion of the membrane is extremely thin – if a human were shrunk to the height of the membrane, a passing red blood cell would appear to be about a mile wide

■ Proteins provide a means by which water-soluble molecules can enter and leave a cell. They also allow cells to communicate with, recognize and adhere to each other
■ Cholesterol molecules are, in a sense, 'dissolved' within the phospholipid bilayer. Cholesterol reduces the fluidity of the

membrane by interfering with the lateral movement of the phospholipid tails
■ Carbohydrates are attached to proteins (glycoproteins) and to lipids (glycolipids). They invariably protrude on the outside surface of the membrane and are important for cell adhesion and communication.

## Specializations of the membrane

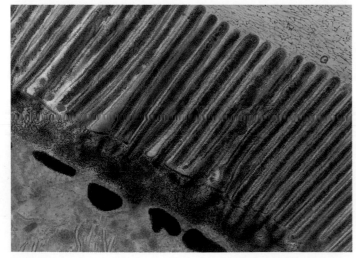

*Microvilli (purple) increase the surface area available for absorption of nutrients from the gut lumen (yellow).*

Cell membranes are not the same in all cells. This is because of the huge variety of functions that cells perform in different parts of the body.

### MICROVILLI
Microvilli are specialized infoldings of the cell membrane which greatly increase its total surface area. This is especially useful in cells whose main role is to absorb chemicals from the outside to the inside of the cell. For example, around 1,000

microvilli are found in each intestinal epithelial cell, which act to absorb nutrients from the gastro-intestinal tract. Each of these microvilli is about one-thousandth of a millimetre in length, and so increases the surface area available for uptake of nutrients by up to 20 times.

### ADHESION BETWEEN CELLS
While some cells, such as blood cells and sperm, are independent entities with some degree of movement, the majority of the body's cells are knitted together to form tissues; the body's cells are joined together by specialized membrane junctions.

# The role of membrane proteins

Proteins embedded in the cell membrane play an important role in many cellular functions. Some span the cell membrane, connecting the inside to the outside of the cell, and this allows cells to communicate with each other chemically.

Membrane proteins are responsible for most of the specialized functions of the cell membrane. They can be broken down into two main groups:

■ Integral proteins – while some integral proteins protrude through the cell membrane on one side only, the vast majority cross the membrane and so are exposed to both the inside and outside of the cell.

These 'trans-membrane' proteins often allow substances to be exchanged between the internal and external environments, either by providing a pore through the membrane, or by physically ferrying the molecules across.

Integral proteins also provide binding sites for chemicals released by other cells; this allows cells, including neurones (nerve cells), to communicate with each other.

■ Peripheral proteins – these are not imbedded in the phospholipid bilayer. Rather, they are usually attached to the internal side of integral proteins. They may act as enzymes, which speed up chemical reactions inside the cell, or may be involved in changing the cell's shape; for example, during cell division.

## Functions of membrane proteins

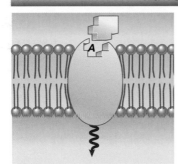

The external surface of some proteins provides a 'binding site' (A) for chemical messengers released from other cells.

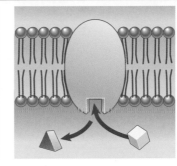

The internal surface of some proteins acts as an enzyme, speeding up chemical reactions that occur inside the cell.

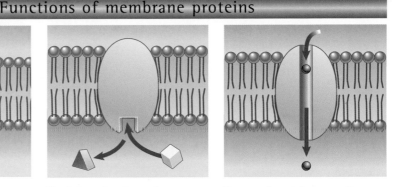

Transport proteins span the membrane, providing a pore for chemicals to travel either into, or out of, the cell.

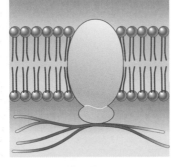

The internal scaffolding of the cell (cytoskeleton – red strands) attaches to the internal surface of membrane proteins.

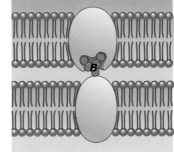

Some glycoproteins (molecules made of proteins joined to carbohydrates) act as 'identification tags' (B).

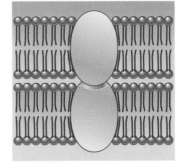

Membrane proteins of adjacent cells may join together, providing various kinds of junctions between the two cells.

## Why are phospholipids so important?

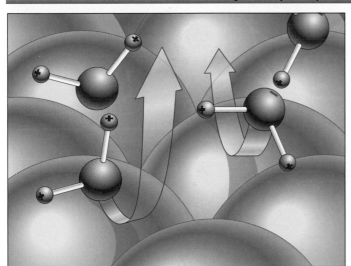

Water molecules are made of a slightly negative oxygen atom (red), attached to two slightly positive hydrogen atoms (blue). Since the phospholipid 'tails' are non-polar, the cell membrane is impermeable to water.

Cell membrane

### WATER MOLECULES

Water molecules are composed of two hydrogen atoms attached to one oxygen atom (hence the chemical formula $H_2O$). Although they have no net electrical charge (a water molecule as a whole is electrically neutral), the oxygen at one end of the molecule tends to be slightly negative and the two hydrogens at the other tend to be slightly positive.

As a result of this chemical property, water is said to be a 'polar' molecule since, like a magnet, it has two electrical 'poles'.

This results in water molecules interacting with each other electrically: the negative oxygen in one water molecule is attracted to the positive hydrogens of neighbouring water molecules. The degree of this attraction, which is dependent on the surrounding temperature, determines whether the molecules form ice, water or steam.

### PHOSPHOLIPIDS AND WATER

Water also interacts with other polar molecules, such as glucose (hence glucose is 'water soluble'). However, non-polar molecules, which include fats, are insoluble in water.

Phospholipids are ideal building blocks for the cell membrane, which is designed to separate the internal contents of the cell from the outside environment, by virtue of its special chemical structure: a phospholipid molecule is composed of a phosphorus-containing, 'water-loving' head attached to a lipid-containing, 'water-hating' tail. This means that when phospholipids are mixed with water, the 'water-loving' heads mix with, while the 'water-hating' tails avoid, the surrounding water molecules. Thus water molecules can only pass through the cell membrane by travelling through pores in proteins which are embedded within it.

# How chemicals cross the cell membrane

Cells in the body need to control their internal environment carefully in order to function properly. The cell membrane provides a barrier that regulates which chemicals can pass into and out of the cell.

Each cell in the body is surrounded by a membrane. This is an important barrier which separates the cells' internal contents from their external environment. This is vital because the contents within cells need to be tightly regulated in order for cells to function properly.

### SEMI-PERMEABLE MEMBRANES

The cell membrane is not an impenetrable barrier. Rather, it allows some substances to pass freely across it, while restricting, or totally preventing, the passage of other chemicals; hence the term 'semi-permeable membrane'.

For example, glucose, an essential molecule which provides the body with energy, is able to move easily through the cell membrane. However, in order to prevent unused glucose leaking back out of the cell, glucose is converted into a

chemical called glucose-6-phosphate, which is unable to travel back across the cell membrane.

Other molecules that can pass through the cell membrane easily include oxygen, which is used in the metabolism of glucose; and carbon dioxide, a waste-product which diffuses out of the cell.

### PROTEIN PORES

Other particles, such as sodium ions or amino acids, can only pass through the membrane via 'pores' provided by specific membrane proteins; many of these act like gates – opening or closing only in response to a predetermined chemical signal.

For example, some protein pores only open when a chemical released from another cell (for example a hormone) binds to its external surface. Other protein pores open in response to a change in electrical voltage.

## Passive transport

### Simple diffusion

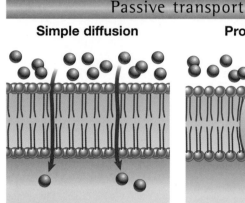

*Some molecules, such as steroids, can travel freely across the cell membrane (green) into the cell.*

### Protein pores

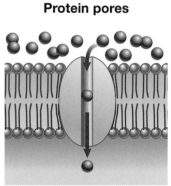

*Some proteins provide 'pores' which allow small chemicals, such as sodium atoms, to cross the cell membrane.*

### Facilitated transport

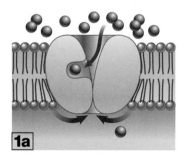

**1a** *Larger molecules, such as glucose, are 'ferried' across the membrane. These differ from pores as they are not permanently open.*

**1b** *The protein channel alters its shape slightly after the chemical has 'docked' with it, allowing the chemical to be released on the inside of the cell membrane.*

## Osmosis

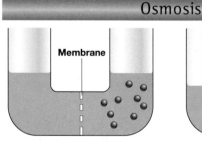

*A U-shaped tube is separated into two compartments, one containing pure water, the other a concentrated sugar solution.*

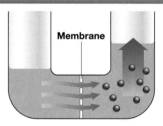

*The membrane is permeable to water, but not sugar molecules; therefore water travels across the membrane to the sugar solution.*

Osmosis is the movement of water molecules across a membrane from where they are at high concentration to where they are at low concentration.

This process can be illustrated by filling one half of a two compartment vessel with pure water and the other half with a concentrated sugar solution. Separating the compartments is a semi-permeable membrane whose small pores allow the passage of water but not sugar molecules.

Water molecules will travel across the membrane from the side containing the pure water into the sugar solution.

### IMPORTANCE OF OSMOSIS

Osmosis plays a very important role in the human body. For example, blood volume can be controlled by altering the concentration of sodium in the urine; water flows into the urinary tract as a result of osmosis and is then excreted, thus lowering the blood volume.

### Receptor-mediated opening of protein pore

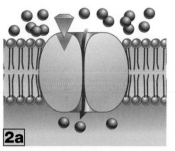

**2a** *Some protein channels only open when a messenger molecule (often released by another cell) binds to the outer surface of the protein, like a key.*

**2b** *These 'receptor proteins' are especially important in neurones (nerve cells), as they allow one neurone to influence the internal environment of another.*

# Active transport

Some molecules are unable to cross the cell membrane unaided. This may be because they are insoluble in the cell membrane or too large to pass through the protein pores.

Like the osmotic action of water, other molecules have a natural tendency to move from a high to a low concentration (like a ball rolling downhill) until they are evenly dispersed in the space available. This is termed 'diffusing down the concentration gradient'.

If a molecule has to travel against its concentration gradient ('uphill') to pass into or out of a cell, it is carried by a process called active transport. However, active transport requires the cell to use energy.

There are two main types of active transport: membrane pumps and vesicular transport. Membrane pumps are proteins that run through the membrane which are able to propel a small number of molecules across the membrane. Vesicular transport, in contrast, involves the transport of many molecules.

## Membrane pumps

### Simple active transport

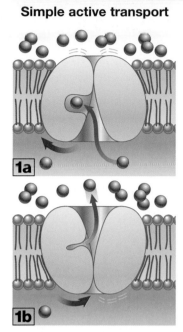

**1a**

**1b**

*One way of carrying a chemical against its concentration gradient (in this case from inside to outside a cell) is for a protein to ferry it; this process requires energy.*

### Co-transport

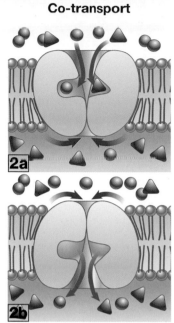

**2a**

**2b**

*If one molecule is diffusing down its concentration gradient (red spheres), another molecule (purple triangles) can 'hitch a ride' and so travel against its concentration gradient.*

### Counter-transport

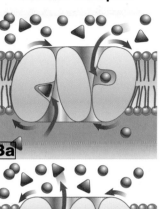

**3a**

**3b**

*Counter-transport is very similar to co-transport in that the 'downhill' movement of one chemical provides the energy for another chemical to be transported 'uphill'.*

## Vesicular transport – exocytosis

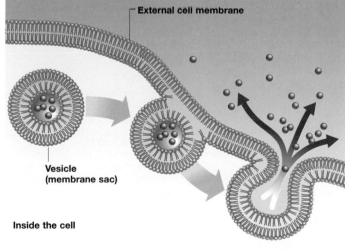

┌ **External cell membrane**

**Vesicle (membrane sac)**

**Inside the cell**

Exocytosis is a process by which large quantities of a substance are transported from the inside to the outside of the cell.

Like membrane pumps, exocytosis requires energy. This mode of transport is responsible for the secretion of hormones from endocrine glands and for the release of neurotransmitters from nerve cells. As a result, exocytosis plays a major role in allowing communication between cells.

*The chemical to be released from the cell is packaged in a membrane sac (vesicle). This sac fuses with the cell membrane, releasing its contents.*

### THE PROCESS OF EXOCYTOSIS

The substance to be released from the cell is first packaged within a sac, called a 'vesicle', composed of phospholipids and proteins, just like those found in the plasma membrane. The vesicle then moves to the cell membrane. Proteins on the vesicle recognize, and bind with, proteins on the membrane causing the two membranes to fuse and finally rupture, spilling the contents of the vesicle outside of the cell. The cell membrane does not increase in size as more of these vesicles dock with it, instead these vesicles are constantly recycled.

## Vesicular transport – endocytosis

Endocytosis is in many ways the complete opposite of exocytosis; it is a process which allows substances to be taken into the cell from the external environment. There are three main types of endocytosis:
■ Phagocytosis (literally 'cell eating'): large, solid material (for example a bacterium) is engulfed by the cell's membrane and taken into the cell where it is digested

■ Pinocytosis (literally 'cell drinking'): droplets of fluid from outside the cell, containing dissolved molecules, are engulfed
■ Receptor-mediated endocytosis: when only very specific molecules are engulfed.

*A cell (brown) is seen eating a Clostridium bacterium (blue). The cell's membrane engulfs the bacterium by a process called phagocytosis.*

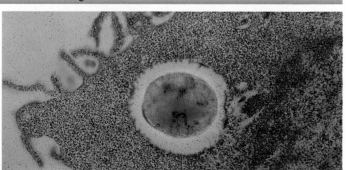

# Neurones

A neurone is a specialized cell of the nervous system.
The main function of neurones is to carry information in the form
of electrical impulses from one part of the body to the other.

The tissues of the nervous system are made up of two types of cells: neurones, or nerve cells, which transmit information in the form of electrical signals; and the smaller supporting cells (glial cells) which surround them.

### COMMON FEATURES
Neurones are the large, highly specialized cells of the nervous system, whose function is to receive information and transmit it throughout the body. Although variable in structure, neurones have some features in common:
■ Cell body – the neurone possesses a single cell body from which a variable number of branching processes emerge
■ Dendrites – these are thin, branching processes of the neurone, which are in fact extensions of the cell body
■ Axon – each neurone has an axon carrying electrical impulses away from the cell body.

### CHARACTERISTICS
Neurones have several other special characteristics:
■ Neurones cannot divide and so cannot replace themselves if damaged or lost
■ Neurones live for a very long time; as they cannot replace themselves they need to last for a lifetime
■ Neurones have very high energy requirements and so cannot survive for more than a few minutes without oxygen or glucose from the blood.

## Structure of a motor neurone

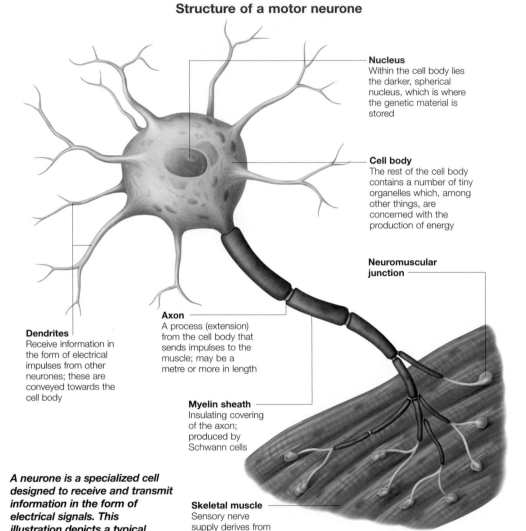

**Nucleus**
Within the cell body lies the darker, spherical nucleus, which is where the genetic material is stored

**Cell body**
The rest of the cell body contains a number of tiny organelles which, among other things, are concerned with the production of energy

**Neuromuscular junction**

**Dendrites**
Receive information in the form of electrical impulses from other neurones; these are conveyed towards the cell body

**Axon**
A process (extension) from the cell body that sends impulses to the muscle; may be a metre or more in length

**Myelin sheath**
Insulating covering of the axon; produced by Schwann cells

**Skeletal muscle**
Sensory nerve supply derives from the neurone

*A neurone is a specialized cell designed to receive and transmit information in the form of electrical signals. This illustration depicts a typical motor neurone.*

## Structural types of neurone

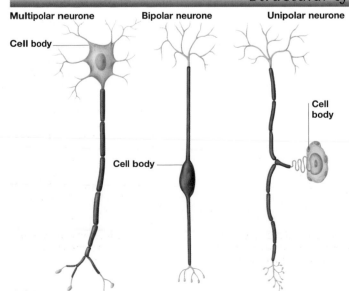

**Multipolar neurone**

**Cell body**

**Bipolar neurone**

**Cell body**

**Unipolar neurone**

**Cell body**

*The arrangement of cell processes from the cell body of a neurone fall into three categories. The structural type of the cell is related to function.*

There are three major groups of neurones, based on the number of processes extending from their cell bodies:
■ Multipolar neurones – have many processes extending from the cell body, all except one of which (the axon) are dendrites. This is the most common form of neurone, especially within the central nervous system (CNS). Sometimes the axon is absent
■ Bipolar neurones – have only two processes: a single dendrite

and an axon. This type of neurone is unusual within the body, and they are found in special sense organs, such as the retina of the eye
■ Unipolar neurones – have a single process, which is divided into a peripheral process that receives information, often from a sense receptor, and a central process which enters the CNS.

### NEURONE FUNCTION
Neurones may also be classified according to their functions into sensory (or afferent) neurones and motor (or efferent) neurones. Most sensory neurones are unipolar while motor neurones are multipolar.

# The myelin sheath

The speed of an electrical signal along a neurone's axon is increased by the presence of a myelin sheath – a layer of fatty insulation.

The myelin sheath is formed differently according to where it is located:
■ In the peripheral nervous system (those nerves lying outside the brain and spinal cord), the myelin sheath is produced by specialized Schwann cells. These wrap themselves around the axon of a nerve cell to form a sheath of concentric circles of their cell membranes
■ In the central nervous system, neurones are given their myelin sheath by cells known as oligodendrocytes, which can myelinate more than one nerve axon at a time.

### APPEARANCE
Nerve fibres with myelin sheaths tend to look whiter than unmyelinated ones, which have a grey tinge. The 'white matter' of the brain is composed of dense collections of myelinated nerve fibres, whereas the 'grey matter' is made up of nerve cell bodies and unmyelinated fibres.

### FUNCTION
Each Schwann cell lies adjacent to, but not touching, the next. The gap between the cells, where there is no myelin, is known as the node of Ranvier. As an electrical signal passes down the nerve it must 'hop' from one node to the other, which makes it travel faster overall than if no myelin sheath were present.

## Insulation of a peripheral nerve

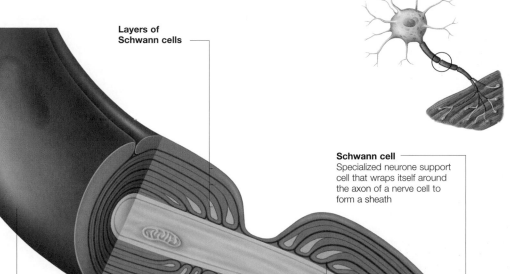

**Layers of Schwann cells**

**Schwann cell**
Specialized neurone support cell that wraps itself around the axon of a nerve cell to form a sheath

**Myelin sheath**
Insulates the axon, speeding up the transmission of nerve impulses; myelinated nerve fibres can transmit information at up to 150 times the speed of unmyelinated ones

**Node of Ranvier**
The gap between Schwann cells, where no myelin is found

**Cell membrane of Schwann cell**
The cell membrane has a particularly high content of fatty substances, which are good electrical insulators

**Axon**
Carries nerve impulses away from the cell body to the receiving cell

*Insulation of a neurone's axon by a myelin sheath increases the speed of impulse transmission along it. A typical peripheral nerve arrangement is shown in this illustration.*

## Supporting cells of the central nervous system

Neurones are surrounded by neuroglia, a collective name given to the group of small support cells which make up about half the bulk of the central nervous system.

Neuroglial cells outnumber neurones by about 10 to 1 and have a variety of functions:
■ Astrocytes – the most abundant neuroglial cells; they are star-shaped. They anchor the neurones to their blood supply and determine what substances can pass between the blood and the brain (the so-called blood–brain barrier)
■ Microglia – like similar cells in other parts of the body, these small oval cells are specialized to ingest, or phagocytose, any invading micro-organisms or dead tissue
■ Oligodendrocytes – these cells provide the myelin sheath for neurones of the CNS
■ Ependymal cells – lining the fluid-filled ventricles of the CNS, these cells may be of a variety of shapes, from flat to columnar. They have tiny brush-like cilia on their surfaces which beat to maintain circulation of the cerebrospinal fluid.

*Astrocytes are star-shaped cells in the central nervous system. Their numerous branches of connective tissue provide support and nutrition for neurones.*

117

# How nerve cells work

Nerve cells generate nerve impulses, electrical messages which travel
from one end of a nerve cell to the other. This ability is essential for
us to interact successfully with the world around us.

The human central nervous
system contains at least two
hundred billion neurones (nerve
cells); on average, each neurone
communicates with thousands of
other nerve cells. This complexity
allows the brain to interpret the
rich sensory input that it
receives from the five senses
and to react accordingly.

### NEUROANATOMY

Although nerve cells from
different regions of the nervous
system can look very dissimilar,
they all contain the same three
basic elements: dendrites, a cell
body and an axon:
■ Dendrites (from the Greek
'dendros', meaning tree) are
branch-like protrusions of the
cell membrane which provide
a large surface area to receive
neurotransmitters released from
other neurones. The dendrites
transduce (convert) this chemical
information into small electrical
impulses, which are then
conveyed to the cell body.
■ The greater part of a neurone
is made up of the cell body
which, like the majority of
the body's cells, contains a
nucleus. A region of the cell
body called the axon hillock
collates all the small nervous
impulses generated by the
many dendrites and initiates
action potentials (nerve
impulses) accordingly.
■ The axon of a neurone carries
nerve impulses from the cell body
to the synaptic terminals –
specialized endings which release
neurotransmitters to communicate
with other neurones.

## Anatomy of a nerve cell (neurone)

*Although neurones differ
a great deal in shape,
they all contain the same
main elements: dendrites,
a cell body containing a
nucleus and an axon.*

**Dendrite**
The 'input' side of
the neurone; it is
responsive to chemical
messengers released
from other neurones

**Cell body**
Like all the body's
cells, neurones
contain organelles
such as mitochondria

**Nucleus**
Contains the
neurone's 23 pairs
of chromosomes

**Axon hillock**
'Adds up' the
information received
from the dendrites and
generates nerve
impulses accordingly

Direction of action potential

**Axon**
Carries nerve
impulses from the
cell body towards
the synaptic terminals

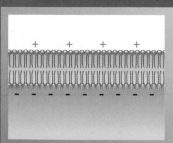

*This neurone (a Purkinje cell
from the cerebellum) has a large
number of dendrites, allowing it
to receive information from a
large number of other neurones.*

**Synaptic terminals**
These release
neurotransmitters
(chemical messengers)
into the space
outside the cell

## What makes neurones different from other cells in the body?

*Unlike neurones, the majority
of the body's cells do not have
protein pores which can open
and close in response to a pre-
determined signal.*

The chemical composition of
the fluid inside a cell (called the
cytosol) is different from the
composition of the fluid outside
the cell (extracellular fluid).
   Compared to the extracellular
fluid, the cytosol has fewer
positive charges and more
negative charges; this means that
the inside of the cell is slightly
negative compared to the outside
of the cell. This electrical charge
across the membrane is called
the membrane potential, and in
most cells is about minus 70
millivolts (thousandths of a volt).

What makes neurones so
special is that they can alter the
electrical charge across their
membrane to generate nerve
impulses. They can do this
because their cell membrane
contains gated protein pores
which allow electrically charged
ions (sodium, potassium, calcium
or chloride ions) to cross it
transiently, so altering the
neurone's membrane potential.
Other cells do not have these
protein pores and so their
membrane potential stays
relatively constant.

*Neurones are able to generate
nerve impulses because their
membrane contains gated
channels that respond either
to chemical messengers (left)
or to a change in voltage (right)*

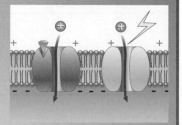

# How nerve impulses are generated

Neurones generate nerve impulses by altering the charge across their membrane. If this is reduced (e.g. by cooling) production of impulses is decreased.

A neurone can only generate an action potential when it has been adequately stimulated. Neurotransmitters (chemical messengers), released from nearby neurones, cause receptor proteins in the dendritic membrane to open. This allows positive sodium ions to flow into the dendrite, causing the membrane potential to become slightly less negative.

### THE 'UPSHOOT' OF AN ACTION POTENTIAL
If sufficient sodium ions enter the neurone to raise the membrane potential to the 'threshold potential', other voltage-dependent protein pores open, which allows even more positive sodium ions to enter the neurone.

*An electroencephalogram (EEG) records the electric fields generated by the billions of action potentials that the brain generates every second.*

Action potentials are not graded in amplitude (that is, they do not vary in 'strength'). Rather, when the threshold potential is reached the membrane potential suddenly rockets to its maximum level.

By analogy, in order to flush a toilet, sufficient pressure has to be applied to the handle to open the valve that connects the cistern with the toilet bowl. However, once the water starts flowing, it is not possible to stop the cistern emptying.

### ACTION POTENTIAL RECOVERY
When the membrane potential reaches its maximum level, the sodium channels close and other channels, which are permeable to positive potassium ions, open in response to the high membrane potential (the potassium channels only open in response to a high voltage). The positive potassium ions flow out of the cell, bringing the membrane potential back towards its resting value.

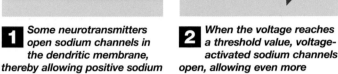

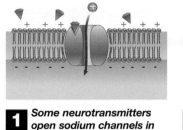

**1** *Some neurotransmitters open sodium channels in the dendritic membrane, thereby allowing positive sodium ions to flow into the cell.*

**2** *When the voltage reaches a threshold value, voltage-activated sodium channels open, allowing even more positive ions to enter the cell.*

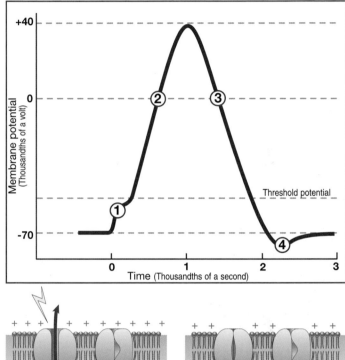

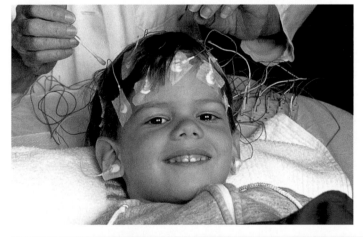

**3** *Sodium channels close and potassium channels open, allowing positive potassium ions to leave the cell; both these events act to lower the voltage.*

**4** *Eventually, both the sodium and potassium channels inactivate – at this point the neurone is at rest and no further action potentials can occur.*

## Speed of nerve impulses

Each axon transmits nerve impulses at a constant speed. However, there is a wide degree of variability in the speed at which different axons conduct action potentials.

### NERVE DIAMETER
For example, conduction speeds can vary between about 0.5 and 120 metres per second. The speed depends on the diameter of the nerve (nerves with large diameters conduct quicker than nerves with small diameters) as well as the degree to which the nerve is insulated; conduction speed is increased in those

nerve fibres that are wrapped in a fatty insulating substance called myelin.

### EFFECT OF TEMPERATURE
Furthermore, the speed of nerve impulse transmission varies according to temperature. For example, cooling a twisted ankle with an ice pack dulls the pain because it reduces the number of action potentials along the nerve.

*Placing an ice pack on a swollen ankle eases the pain by slowing down the transmission of the nerve impulses.*

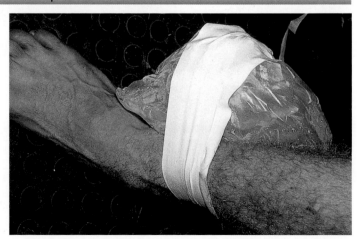

# How nerve cells communicate

Nerve cells communicate with each other by releasing chemical messengers called neurotransmitters. Both therapeutic and illicit drugs act by altering the effectiveness of these transmitter molecules.

Nerve cells do not make direct contact with each other. Rather, there is a very small gap, called the synaptic gap, which separates the nerve cell sending the information (the pre-synaptic neurone) from the neurone receiving the information (the post-synaptic neurone).

This gap means that an electrical nerve impulse cannot flow directly from one neurone to the next. Instead, when a

*This transmission electron micrograph shows a presynaptic neurone (left) containing vesicles (blue) in synaptic contact with a post-synaptic neurone (right).*

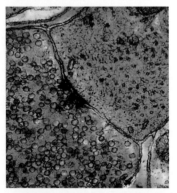

nerve impulse reaches the synaptic terminals, the sudden change in voltage causes calcium ions to flow into the pre-synaptic cell.

## RELEASE OF NEUROTRANSMITTERS

Calcium ions cause vesicles (small membrane-bound sacs containing chemical messengers called neurotransmitters) to move towards, and dock with, the pre-synaptic cell membrane, releasing their contents into the synaptic gap.

The neurotransmitter molecules diffuse across to the post-synaptic cell and activate receptor proteins located within its membrane. This can have the effect of either exciting or inhibiting the post-synaptic cell (depending on the neurotransmitter and its associated receptor), increasing or decreasing the likelihood of an action potential being generated respectively.

*Neurotransmitter molecules diffuse across the synaptic gap and bind to receptors in the post-synaptic membrane.*

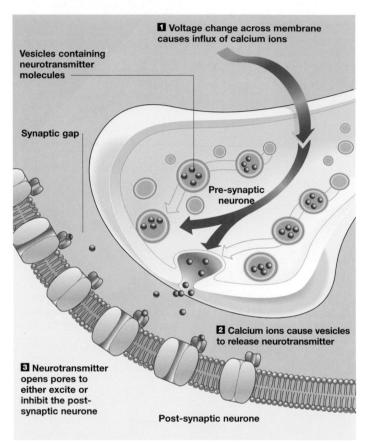

**1** Voltage change across membrane causes influx of calcium ions

Vesicles containing neurotransmitter molecules

Synaptic gap

Pre-synaptic neurone

**2** Calcium ions cause vesicles to release neurotransmitter

**3** Neurotransmitter opens pores to either excite or inhibit the post-synaptic neurone

Post-synaptic neurone

## Nervous control of muscle

Some nerves project from the spinal cord to serve muscle. When a nerve impulse arrives at a 'neuromuscular junction' it causes a neurotransmitter called acetylcholine to be released from the nerve endings.

*A micrograph showing a neuromuscular junction. The nerve (black) can be seen innervating the pink muscle.*

Acetylcholine diffuses across the synaptic gap and binds with receptors in the muscle tissue. This initiates a sequence of events that results in the contraction of the muscle fibres.

In this way, the central nervous system controls which muscles contract at a given moment. This is essential for complicated movements such as walking.

## Neurotransmitter effects

After a neurotransmitter has bound with, and activated, its receptor on the post-synaptic membrane, it rapidly disengages and is either broken down by enzymes floating in the synaptic gap, or is taken up into the pre-synaptic terminal, where it is repackaged into another vesicle. This ensures that the effect of the neurotransmitter on a receptor molecule is short-lived.

Some illegal drugs, such as cocaine, as well as some prescription drugs, work by preventing the neurotransmitter

(dopamine in the case of cocaine) from being reabsorbed; this prolongs the time that the neurotransmitter can activate receptors in the post-synaptic membrane leading to a much greater stimulatory effect.

*Cocaine works by inhibiting the uptake of the neurotransmitter dopamine. This allows the dopamine molecules to activate their receptors for longer.*

# Neural processing

The brain is an incredibly complex structure; each of its neurones is connected to thousands of others located throughout the nervous system.

Since nerve impulses do not vary in strength, information is encoded in the frequency of nerve impulses (that is, the number of action potentials that a neurone generates per second), in a similar way to Morse code.

One of the big problems that neuroscientists face today is to try to understand how this relatively simple encoding system produces; for example, the emotional responses that we feel when a friend or relative dies, or the ability to throw a ball with such accuracy that it hits a target 20 metres away.

In this regard, it is clear that information is not transmitted from one neurone to another in a linear fashion. Rather, a single neurone is likely to receive synaptic inputs from many other neurones (called convergence) and be able to influence a large number (up to 100,000) of other neurones (called divergence).

Indeed, it has been calculated that the number of possible routes for nerve impulses to take through this vast neural network is greater than the number of sub-atomic particles contained in the entire universe!

*This scanning electron micrograph shows many pre-synaptic neurones (blue) synapsing with a post-synaptic neurone (orange).*

*Information transfer does not occur in a linear fashion. A single neurone can thus influence and be influenced by thousands of other such cells.*

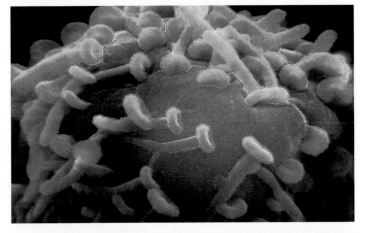

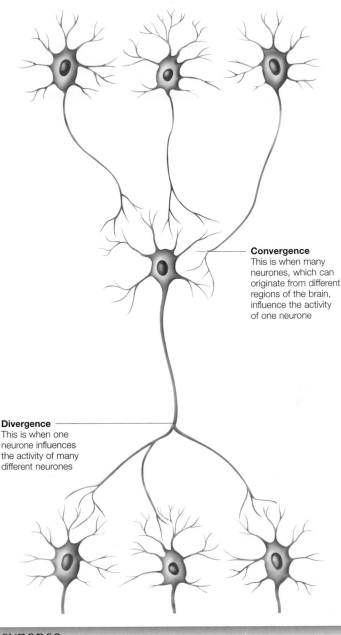

**Convergence**
This is when many neurones, which can originate from different regions of the brain, influence the activity of one neurone

**Divergence**
This is when one neurone influences the activity of many different neurones

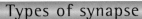

## Types of synapse

**Axo-somatic synapse**
Inhibitory synapses are often of this type – they reduce the likelihood of a nerve impulse being generated

**Axo-dendritic synapse**
The vast majority of synapses are of this type

**Axon of post-synaptic neurone**
This carries nerve impulses away from the cell body towards the synaptic terminals

*Synapses are named based on their constituent parts. For example, in an axo-dendritic synapse an axon makes synaptic contact with a dendrite.*

**Axo-axonic synapse**
This type of synapse is relatively rare

There are two main types of synapse: those that cause the post-synaptic neurone to become excited, and those that cause it to become inhibited (this depends to a large degree on the type of neurotransmitter that is released). A neurone will only fire a nerve impulse when the excitatory inputs outweigh the inhibitory ones.

### STRENGTH OF SYNAPSES
Each neurone receives a large number of both excitatory and inhibitory inputs. Each of the synapses present will have a greater or lesser effect in determining whether an action potential is initiated.

For example, synapses that have the most powerful effect are generally those close to the nerve impulse-initiating zone in the cell body (soma).

# The role of water

Without water, human beings could not survive as it is essential for hydration and certain bodily processes, and is a vital source of minerals. If fluid intake is insufficient, dehydration can occur.

Of all forms of nourishment, water is the most vital. A person can survive for up to several weeks without food, but without water they would perish in a matter of days.

The reason for this is that a very large percentage of the body is actually made up of water. Most body cells consist of approximately 80 per cent water, while plasma (the liquid component of blood) consists of 92 per cent water.

### SOURCES OF WATER
It is essential that water intake is sufficient to meet the body's needs. Most foods contain some water; meat ranges from 40–75 per cent water, and vegetables can consist of as much as 95 per cent water. Surprisingly, even dry foods, such as bread and cereal, can contain as much as 30 per cent water.

It is vital, however, that food is supplemented with regular drinks of water in order for the body to gain optimum levels of hydration. As a rough guideline, people should drink around two litres (about eight to 10 glasses) of water per day.

### FLUID TYPE
Unfortunately, most people do not drink enough fluid, and those who do often fail to drink the right type of fluid.

For many people, the bulk of fluid intake comes from drinks such as tea, coffee or cola drinks. Despite the fact that these drinks do contain water, they also contain caffeine – a diuretic – which actually serves to deplete the body of valuable water by increasing urine production. Drinks containing alcohol also serve to dehydrate the body.

*Water is essential for survival, as it makes up a large proportion of the body. People should ideally drink around two litres of water every day.*

---

## Benefits of water

The benefits of drinking water are often overlooked despite the fact that a lack of water can have a serious impact on health. As well as quenching thirst, water is essential to a number of body processes: it helps to maintain body temperature, acts as a lubricant, enables a variety of chemical reactions to take place and serves as a mixing medium.

### BODY TEMPERATURE
Water has what is known as a high specific heat, which means, in effect, that it takes a relatively large amount of energy to raise its temperature. Consequently, water within the body helps it to resist great fluctuations in body temperature. In addition, water in the body enables it to be cooled in high temperatures or during physical exertion. This occurs through the evaporation of water in the form of sweat.

### PROTECTION
Water acts as a lubricant to prevent friction within the body. For example, tears produced by the lacrimal glands prevent the surface of the eye from rubbing against the eyelid. Water also forms a cushion within joints and between organs to protect them from trauma, as seen, for example, in the cerebrospinal fluid around the brain.

### CHEMICAL REACTIONS
The chemical reactions that take place in the body could not occur without water. This is because molecules must be dissolved in water to form ions (electrically charged atoms)

*Cerebrospinal fluid is watery fluid that surrounds the brain and spinal cord. It cushions the brain from contact with the skull when the head is shaken.*

before they can react. For example, when sodium chloride is dissolved in water, it splits to form separate sodium and chloride ions, which are then free to react with other ions.

In addition, cell membranes rely on water for the movement of enzymes into and out of cells. Enzymes are essential to cell function and so, without sufficient water, these reactions could not occur.

### MIXING MEDIUM
Water mixes with other substances to form a solution (for example, when sodium chloride is dissolved in water to form sweat), a suspension (for example, red blood cells in plasma), or a colloid (a liquid that contains non dissolved materials that do not settle out of the liquid, for example the water and protein within cells).

The ability of water to mix with other substances enables it to act as an effective medium for the transport of nutrients, gases and waste products throughout the body in body fluids such as plasma.

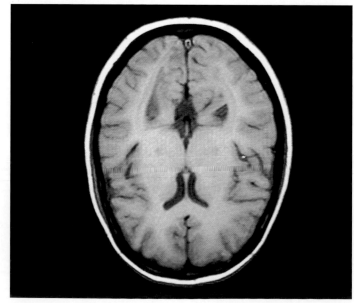

## Loss of water

A number of regulatory mechanisms ensure that body fluids are kept within fine limits (homeostasis). This balance may be upset by extreme temperatures or illness, however, when dehydration may occur due to extreme water loss.

### THREE ROUTES

Water is lost from the body through three main routes:
■ Perspiration – fluid loss through sweat depends upon a number of factors, such as environmental temperature, humidity and the degree of physical exertion.

The volume of sweat lost by a person at rest in a cool temperature is negligible. When exercising in elevated temperatures, or during a fever, however, the volume of water lost through sweat increases substantially. A person working outdoors in the summer, for example, could lose up to five litres of sweat

■ Urination – the amount of fluid ingested usually exceeds the body's needs; the excess is eliminated by the kidneys in the form of urine. Drugs or medical conditions that cause increased urination can cause dehydration

■ Defecation – only a small portion of body fluids is lost through defecation, since water is reabsorbed in the colon. However, this is not true in the case of diarrhoea. Diarrhoea occurs when increased waves of movement in the intestinal tract

cause faecal matter to pass through the colon too rapidly for water reabsorption to occur. This can cause a great deal of fluid to be lost from the body.

### DEHYDRATION

Loss of body fluids can lead to dehydration, which is potentially fatal and must be treated promptly. The young and the old (the sense of thirst tends to dim with age) are most at risk of developing dehydration.

Symptoms of dehydration include raised body temperature, fatigue, nausea, extreme thirst, the passing of small amounts of dark urine, headaches and confusion.

Severe dehydration is defined as fluid loss of more than 1 per cent in body weight. For example, a person weighing 70 kg would have to lose 700 grams of fluid to be considered seriously dehydrated. Affected individuals can experience low blood pressure, loss of consciousness, severe cramping of the arms, legs, stomach and back, convulsions, heart failure, sunken eyes, inelasticity of the skin, and deep, rapid breathing.

Dehydration is treated by replacing lost fluids, as well as the electrolytes (salts) contained within them. In mild cases, this can be achieved by taking oral

*In the developing world, education programmes help to prevent dehydration. Mild dehydration can be treated by the use of oral rehydration salts.*

rehydration salts (a sachet of powder which is mixed with water to replace both water and salts such as salt and glucose). Severe cases are treated with an intravenous infusion of saline solution to restore the patient's fluid levels rapidly.

Sadly, in the developing world, where uncontaminated water supplies are limited and hospital facilities are not always available, many people die from dehydration every day.

## The thirst mechanism

*When the thirst centre within the hypothalamus is stimulated, it triggers a sensation of thirst. As water is drunk in response, the body's 'problem' is solved.*
The body requires a fairly constant water balance. This means that the water lost, mainly through sweating and urination, must be replaced. Certain circumstances, such as excessive heat or exercise, use of diuretics, or a high-salt diet, can result in a rapid depletion of water.

### Maintaining the balance

The body monitors water levels constantly, by checking blood volume and concentration. If the volume becomes low, and/or the concentration high, it registers the need both to conserve water and to increase intake via drinking. This is mainly controlled by the hypothalamus within the brain.

The hypothalamus sends 'instructions' to the kidneys to

*The level of water in the body affects blood concentration and volume. The brain will trigger the thirst sensation when these need correction.*

decrease the amount of urine passed, while its thirst centre initiates the sensation of thirst. This triggers an impulse to drink. The thirst centre is also activated by a dry mouth, whether caused by diet, drugs or nervousness.

# How DNA works

DNA is the genetic material of all organisms, located in the nucleus of every cell. The discovery of its chemical structure revolutionized the biological sciences and our understanding of human genetics.

The chemical properties of DNA (deoxyribonucleic acid) allow it to carry out two very important functions:

■ It provides the body's cells with the 'recipes' needed to build proteins from the 20 essential amino acids found in proteins

■ It is able to make copies of itself, and so provides the means by which these protein 'recipes' can be transmitted from one generation to the next; this means that characteristics such as eye colour or facial features can be passed from parent to child.

*In humans, DNA is packaged within 23 pairs of chromosomes. These 'X' shaped structures replicate during cell division.*

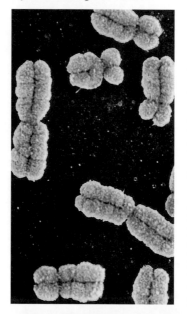

## CHROMOSOMES

The vast majority of human DNA is packaged into 23 pairs of chromosomes, which are stored within the cell's nucleus; one set of 23 chromosomes is inherited from the father and one set is inherited from the mother.

The exceptions to this rule are sperm cells and egg cells, which contain only one set of 23 chromosomes; and red blood cells, which contain no chromosomes at all.

## GENES

Useful DNA (as opposed to so-called 'junk' DNA – see below) is packaged within the chromosomes into what are known as genes, of which there are thought to be around 100,000 in the human body. Each of these genes provides the 'recipe' which tells the cell how to make a specific protein.

However, while each of the body's cells contains a copy of every protein recipe, not all of these recipes are 'switched on'. This is what differentiates a heart cell from, for example, a liver cell – each produces its own set of proteins.

## 'JUNK' DNA

Most DNA is so-called 'junk' DNA, which serves no known purpose in the human body. Much of this DNA is inherited from our distant ancestors and their parasites, dating back to when life on earth began around four billion years ago.

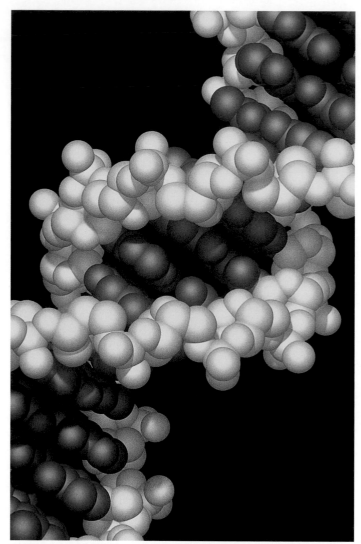

*DNA is composed of two strands of nucleotides (shown here as yellow and blue) which curl around each other in a helical manner (called a double helix).*

## Mutations in DNA

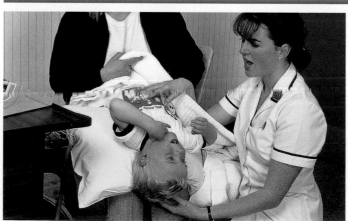

If the set of instructions (that is, the DNA sequence) detailing how to make a specific protein becomes altered in even the smallest way, a 'mutation' is said to have occurred; this may result in a defective protein, or no protein at all, being made.

The consequences of this can be quite severe; for example cystic fibrosis is the result of a

*Cystic fibrosis sufferers have a mutated gene that produces a faulty protein. The result is that lungs become clogged with mucus.*

mutation at a single point in one of the DNA molecules in an affected individual.

Mutations are not necessarily harmful, though, and occur spontaneously throughout our lifetimes. However, certain chemicals increase the rate of mutation, one example being agent orange, a defoliant used in the Vietnam war. Nuclear radiation can also have a mutating effect. If a large number of mutations occurs, the chances of one being harmful are statistically higher, so these mutagens are harmful to humans.

## Structure of DNA

The ability of DNA to make copies of itself is the direct result of its chemical structure. A molecule of DNA consists of two interlinked strands of nucleotides, which are exact

*James Watson (left) and Francis Crick (right) were awarded a Nobel Prize for their contribution to the discovery of DNA structure.*

mirror images of each other, and which run in opposite directions.

These two strands are each made up of a sugar-phosphate 'backbone', to which are attached specialized molecules, called bases. These bases are: adenine, guanine, cytosine and thymine (abbreviated to the letters A, G, C and T). What gives DNA its special properties is that the four bases will only pair off in the following combinations: A with T and G with C. Thus a strand of DNA with the sequence of 'TGATCG' will only bind with a complementary strand with the sequence 'ACTAGC'.

*DNA is made of two strands, which run in opposite directions. The two strands are joined by special molecules called bases.*

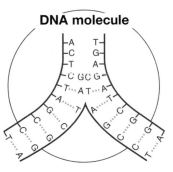

**DNA Strand 1**    **DNA Strand 2**

**Bases**

Phosphate — Sugar—A···T—Sugar — Phosphate

Phosphate — Sugar—C···G—Sugar — Phosphate

Phosphate — Sugar—G···C—Sugar — Phosphate

Phosphate — Sugar—T···A—Sugar — Phosphate

## How DNA makes copies of itself

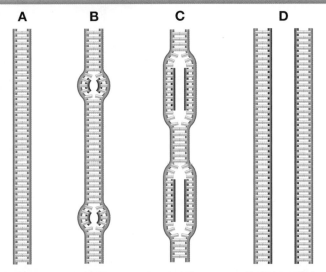

**A**    **B**    **C**    **D**

DNA makes a copy of itself during a process called replication. First, the original double helix 'parent' DNA is unwound, so separating and exposing the base pairs. Since each base will only bind with

one of the three others (such as A with T, but not with G or C), a complementary strand can then be built up on each of the parent strands. Thus one DNA double helix becomes two identical double helices.

*DNA (A) is simultaneously unwound at a number of points (B). A new strand (red) is built on each parent strand (B and C) forming two DNA molecules (D).*

*The two strands of a DNA molecule are separated from each other and a new strand is built onto each one. Thus, two identical strands can be made from the original.*

**DNA molecule**

## DNA as a recipe book for proteins

In many ways DNA is similar to a language; however, unlike the English language there are only 64 three-letter 'words' that can be formed using the four letters A, G, C and T. Geneticists call these 'words' codons as each codes for a specific amino acid, the building blocks of proteins.

Proteins are made on structures called ribosomes in the cytoplasm. However, since DNA is unable to leave the nucleus, first of all one strand of DNA is 'transcribed' onto a single-stranded messenger molecule, with a very similar structure to a DNA strand, called messenger RNA (mRNA), which can cross the nuclear membrane. The mRNA is then 'translated' on the ribosomes in the cytoplasm so that the correct amino acids are joined together in the correct order.

*Proteins are built from amino acids according to a template copied from DNA. This process occurs in subcellular structures called ribosomes, which are found inside the cell.*

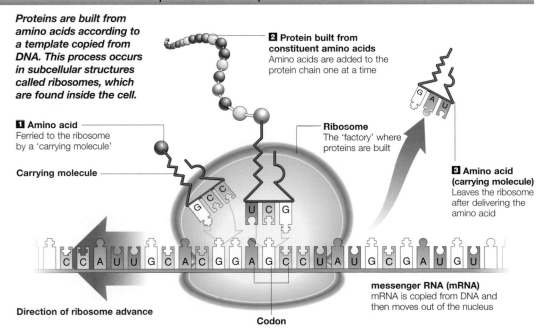

**1 Amino acid**
Ferried to the ribosome by a 'carrying molecule'

**Carrying molecule**

**2 Protein built from constituent amino acids**
Amino acids are added to the protein chain one at a time

**Ribosome**
The 'factory' where proteins are built

**3 Amino acid (carrying molecule)**
Leaves the ribosome after delivering the amino acid

**messenger RNA (mRNA)**
mRNA is copied from DNA and then moves out of the nucleus

**Direction of ribosome advance**

**Codon**

# How our genes can affect us

Faulty genes do not always lead to disease. It is possible for people who are normal to carry abnormal genes. Such people often only learn of the problem when they have an affected child by another, equally normal carrier.

An observable characteristic in a person is called a phenotype. This could be a disease, a blood group, eye colour, nose shape or any other such attribute. The genetic information that gives rise to a phenotype is known as the genotype.

A gene locus is the site on a chromosome at which a gene for a particular trait lies. The different forms of a gene that may be present at a gene locus are called alleles. If there are two alleles – 'A' and 'a' – for a given gene locus, then three genotypes may be formed. These are: 'AA', 'Aa' or 'aa'. 'Aa' is known as a heterozygote and 'aa' and 'AA' are homozygotes.

If the 'A' allele is dominant, it will mask the effects of the

*In these family trees, the parents have a dominant allele 'A' and recessive allele 'a'. If 'A' represents the phenotype of brown eyes, and 'a' represents blue eyes, only those with the 'aa' genotype will have blue eyes. Otherwise, the dominant 'A' allele dictates the phenotype.*

recessive 'a' allele, and produce a recognizable phenotype in a heterozygous (Aa) individual. Recessive alleles only result in a recognizable phenotype in the homozygous state (aa).

If both alleles are recognized in the heterozygous state (Aa), they are designated co-dominant. The expression of the ABO blood groups is a example of the effects of co-dominance.

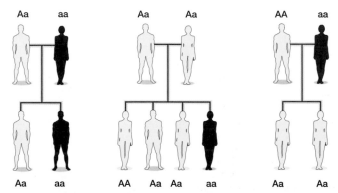

## Autosomal dominant conditions

Affected individuals (male or female) who carry a dominant abnormal gene have a 50 per cent chance of producing affected offspring with a normal partner. Only people who inherit a copy of the gene will be affected. Achondroplasia (dwarfism) is an autosomal dominant condition.

> **KEY**
>
> Normal male and female
>
> Affected male and female

*An individual is either normal or affected by an autosomal dominant condition. When their partner is unaffected there is a 50 per cent chance that a child will be affected.*

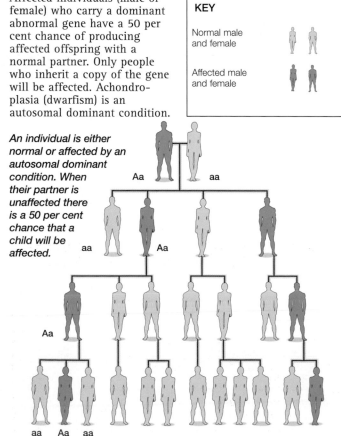

*Conditions such as achondroplasia (pictured here) result from the inheritance of an affected gene from either the mother or father.*

## Autosomal recessive conditions

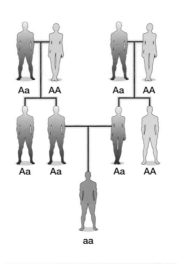

Aa AA Aa AA

Aa Aa Aa AA

aa

Unaffected individuals of either sex may be carriers. When two carriers (Aa; heterozygotes) have a child, there is a one in four (25 per cent) risk that the child will be affected. An example of an autosomal recessive condition is sickle-cell disease, a disease of the blood that mainly affects people of African ancestry.

**KEY**

Normal male and female

Carrier male and female

Affected male and female

*Sickle-cell disease affects haemoglobin, causing red blood cells to distort into a distinctive sickle shape. The condition occurs when an individual inherits the sickle-cell gene from both parents.*

## Sex-linked conditions

In these conditions, the abnormal trait is carried on the sex chromosomes (X and Y). Males only have one X chromosome, therefore all daughters inherit their father's X chromosome. They will also inherit one of the two X chromosomes from their mother. A son will inherit his father's Y chromosome and one of his mother's two X chromosomes.

If one of the two X chromosomes from the mother contains a gene that can give rise to a disorder, she is referred to as a 'carrier'. Half the sons of a carrier female are likely to be affected. Half the daughters will be carriers for the gene. Males are clinically affected because they carry only one X chromosome, while females are unaffected because they have two X chromosomes. Affected males can only inherit the gene through a female line.

A well known example of an X-linked disorder is the haemophilia that affected Queen Victoria's family line. Baldness can also be X-linked. Y-linked traits include genes for sex determination and male development. Father-to-son transmission is only possible in Y-liked traits as the Y chromosome is only inherited by sons.

*This family tree shows the sex-linked recessive inheritance of haemophilia in the royal families of Europe. All affected individuals can trace their inheritance back to Queen Victoria in the 19th century, who was a carrier of the disease. The current British royal family is unaffected as they are descended from an unaffected individual (Victoria's son, King Edward VII).*

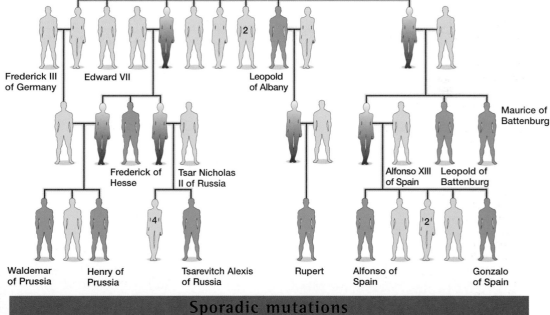

Figures represent multiple siblings

Queen Victoria

Frederick III of Germany    Edward VII    Leopold of Albany    Maurice of Battenburg

Frederick of Hesse    Tsar Nicholas II of Russia    Alfonso XIII of Spain    Leopold of Battenburg

Waldemar of Prussia    Henry of Prussia    Tsarevitch Alexis of Russia    Rupert    Alfonso of Spain    Gonzalo of Spain

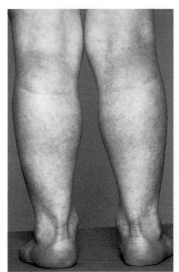

*Sex-linked (Duchenne) muscular dystrophy is an example of a severe X-linked recessive condition. It produces progressive muscle weakness, beginning in early childhood.*

## Sporadic mutations

Mistakes can be made during the normal process of DNA duplication. These are known as new mutations. Only a few of the mutations that occur are in areas of the DNA that lead to an alteration of phenotype. Most occur in regions that are not concerned with gene function.

Achondroplasia (dwarfism) has been shown to arise through new mutations in some families. The mutation then continues to be inherited in subsequent generations in an autosomal dominant fashion.

*Achondroplasia occurring as a new mutation is subsequently inherited by offspring in an autosomal dominant manner. That is, a child has a 50 per cent chance of being affected if one parent has the condition.*

# How we smell

The nostrils carry air towards specialized cells located just below the front of the skull. These cells are able to detect thousands of different types of odours at very low concentrations.

Our sense of smell is in many ways similar to our sense of taste. This is because both taste and smell rely on the ability of specialized cells to detect and respond to the presence of many different chemicals.

The olfactory (smell) receptors present in the nose 'transduce' (convert) these chemical signals into electrical signals which travel along nerve fibres to the brain.

## OLFACTORY RECEPTORS

Odours are carried into the nose when we inhale, and dissolve in the mucus-coated interior of the nasal cavity. This mucus acts as a solvent, 'capturing' the gaseous odour molecules. It is continuously renewed, ensuring that odour molecules inhaled in each breath have full access to the olfactory receptor cells.

A small patch of mucous membrane located on the roof of the nasal sinuses, just under the base of the brain, contains around 40 million olfactory receptor cells. These are specialized nerve cells which are responsive to odours at concentrations of a few parts per trillion. The tip of each olfactory cell contains up to 20 'hairs', known as cilia, which float in the nasal mucus; these greatly increase the surface area of the cell, thereby enhancing its ability to detect chemicals.

When odour molecules bind to receptor proteins on an olfactory cell they initiate a series of

### The olfactory system

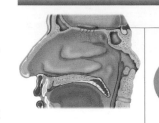

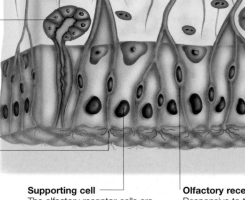

**Olfactory bulb**
A collection of nerve cells which receive information from olfactory receptor cells

**Mucous gland**
Secretes mucus into the nasal cavity

**Cilia of the olfactory receptors**
Microscopic hairs that protrude into the nasal cavity

**Supporting cell**
The olfactory receptor cells are embedded in supporting cells

**Nerve fibre of olfactory tract**

**Cribriform plate of ethmoid bone**

**Nasal cavity**

**Olfactory receptor cell**
Responsive to the presence of odour molecules

nerve impulses. These impulses travel along the cell's axon (a nerve fibre which projects from the nerve cell body), which projects through the cribriform plate, the thin layer of skull immediately above the olfactory epithelia. The olfactory cells in turn communicate with other nerve cells, located in the olfactory bulb, which carry information, via the olfactory nerves (also known as cranial nerve I), to the rest of the brain.

*Odour molecules dissolve in mucus secreted into the nasal cavity. Specialized receptors respond to odour molecules by sending nervous impulses to the brain via a structure called the olfactory bulb.*

### Dimensions of odour

Receptors in the retina at the back of the eye are responsive to three colours (red, blue and green). Taste receptors respond to seven modalities. In contrast, there are thought to be hundreds (if not thousands – scientists are not entirely sure) of different types of olfactory receptor.

However, since most of us can differentiate between around 20,000 different odours, it seems unlikely that there is an individual receptor dedicated to

*An experienced wine taster can distinguish between numerous odours. Even an untrained nose is thought to be able to detect 20,000 different smells.*

each odour molecule. Rather, it is thought that an odour molecule activates many different types of receptor with varying degrees of success; some receptors are very responsive to a specific odour, whereas other respond only weakly. This pattern of activity is interpreted by the brain to represent a specific smell.

When an odour molecule binds to an olfactory receptor, a complex cascade of chemical reactions is initiated inside the olfactory cell. This has the effect of amplifying the original signal; thus the brain can become aware of odours at remarkably low concentrations.

## Memory, emotions and smells

The way the brain interprets smell is different from the way it interprets other senses (for example, vision) – some branches of the olfactory nerves project directly to the areas of the brain which control emotions and memory, without first travelling to the cortex, the region responsible for the development of conscious experience.

In contrast, visual input is first relayed to the visual cortex, an area involved in the conscious perception of vision, before being relayed to the emotion and memory areas.

### EFFECT ON MEMORY

The neuroanatomy of the olfactory pathway means that smells can have a very profound effect on our memory. Re-exposure to an odour that was first smelt during childhood, for example, can bring back a flood of memories of that period.

*This PET scan of the brain shows olfactory (smell) activity. Areas of low activity are purple; highly active areas are yellow.*

*Smells first experienced during childhood can evoke strong and intense memories when they are re-encountered in later life.*

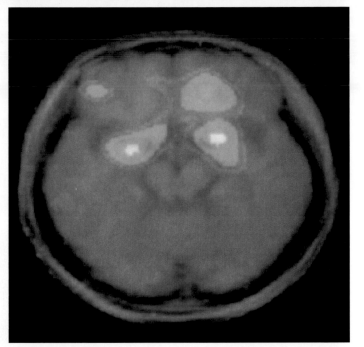

## The role of pheromones

Some animals release special types of chemicals, called pheromones, into the air, water or ground in order to influence the behaviour or physiology of other members of their species. There is currently much debate as to the degree that humans use pheromones to unconsciously communicate with each other.

Research suggests that humans do respond to pheromones to some degree. For example, one study showed

*It has been suggested that humans unconsciously react to pheromones released by potential sexual partners, but no firm evidence exists to prove this.*

that some mothers are able to discriminate between a T-shirt worn by their child and one worn by another child of the same age.

### MENSTRUAL SYNCHRONY

Over the past 30 years, a research group in the US has provided much evidence to suggest that the menstrual cycles of female flat-mates tend to converge with time.

A recent study, in which underarm body odour was collected on cotton pads from female donors and then wiped under the noses of recipient women, demonstrated that this is because women are responsive to each others' pheromones.

## How good is our sense of smell?

Compared to other animals, humans have very poor smell. To take an extreme example, a dog has 25 times as many olfactory cells as a human, with 30 per cent of its cortex devoted to smell, compared to only five per cent in humans. This explains why trained sniffer dogs can detect odours at concentrations 10,000 times weaker than we can smell.

*The evolution of a bipedal gait, which resulted in the nose being raised far from the ground, may have reduced Homo sapiens' reliance on olfaction.*

Our sense of smell seems to have been blunted during the process of evolution. One possible explanation for this is that the development of a bipedal gait led to the nose being raised further from the ground; thus there was less advantage, evolutionarily speaking, in having a large area of the cortex

devoted to detecting odours.

The development of higher cognitive functions, such as language – which require considerable cortical processing power – may have also contributed to the reduced reliance on olfaction.

### Losing smell

Anosmia ('without smell') is a term used to describe the sudden loss of the sensation of smell. It often occurs after a blow to the head injures the olfactory nerves, but may also be the result of a nasal infection affecting the olfactory receptors.

Disorders of the brain can also affect the sense of smell. For example, some epileptics may experience an 'olfactory aura' before they have a seizure. Other disorders include olfactory hallucinations in which the affected individual experiences a specific odour, which is usually unpleasant.

# How we sneeze

Sneezing is a defence mechanism, designed to protect the respiratory tract from irritant materials. The explosive exhalation that occurs during sneezing serves to clear the upper airway.

The nose is the major route for air to enter the respiratory apparatus. It acts as a very effective air filter, preventing dust and large airborne particles from entering the lungs, and allowing incoming air to adjust to body temperature before passing further down into the lungs.

### DEFENCE MECHANISM

Sneezing, a sudden, forceful, involuntary burst of air out through the nose and mouth, is one of the body's many defence mechanisms.

It is designed primarily to protect the respiratory system from irritant particles which could otherwise pass further into the breathing apparatus, causing significant harm. Sneezing also serves to dislodge accumulated particles in the nose, preventing congestion of the nose's filtering system.

### EXPLOSIVE REACTION

A sneeze is a blast of air that is forced out of the lungs under pressure through the airway to the mouth and nose. Most of the compressed air of a sneeze escapes through the mouth, but a percentage is directed by the soft palate to flush out the nose.

The speed of the outgoing blast of air in a sneeze can reach up to 160 km/hr (100 miles per hour) – equivalent to the wind-speed of a major typhoon.

A sneeze may carry as many as 5,000 droplets, which may contain infectious material, and be propelled as far as 3.7 metres from the nose.

## The sneezing mechanism

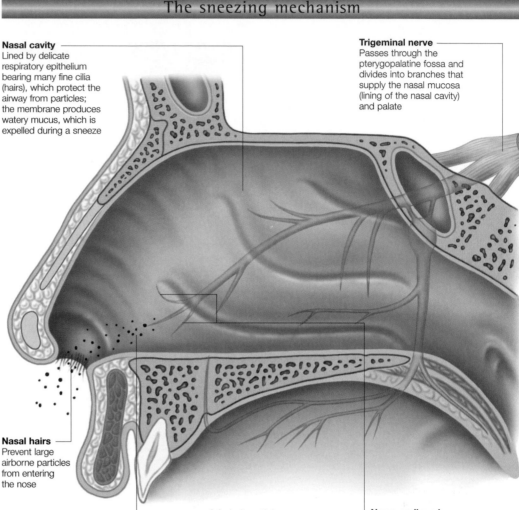

**Nasal cavity**
Lined by delicate respiratory epithelium bearing many fine cilia (hairs), which protect the airway from particles; the membrane produces watery mucus, which is expelled during a sneeze

**Trigeminal nerve**
Passes through the pterygopalatine fossa and divides into branches that supply the nasal mucosa (lining of the nasal cavity) and palate

**Nasal hairs**
Prevent large airborne particles from entering the nose

**Inhaled particles**
Stimulate nerve endings within the nasal cavity and trigger the sneeze reflex that clears the nasal passages of obstruction

**Nerve endings in the nasal cavity**
When these are stimulated, the sneeze reflex is triggered in the brain

*A sneeze is an involuntary reflex designed to protect the body's respiratory system. It ensures that irritant particles are expelled from the nose.*

## Common triggers of sneezing

While sneezing can be a classic symptom of the nasal congestion that accompanies a common cold, there are many stimuli which trigger this reflex reaction. The most common include:
■ Inhalation of fine particles in the atmosphere, such as dust, hair, smoke and aerosol sprays

*Sneezing is triggered by various stimuli. For example, hay fever sufferers react to the allergen pollen, causing them to sneeze frequently.*

■ Allergy to mould, triggered by the inhalation of airborne spores
■ Inhalation of skin and scalp cells (dander), either human or animal
■ Hay fever (allergy to pollen) and house dust mite
■ Upper respiratory tract infections
■ Nasal polyps
■ Looking at bright light, particularly the sun
■ Changes in environmental temperature
■ Inhaled cocaine withdrawal.

# What happens when we sneeze

Sneezing occurs as a result of a reflex reaction, triggered by the sensory nerve endings in the lining of the nasal cavity. The voluntary part of the brain is bypassed during this reaction, causing an automatic and involuntary response.

Sneezing occurs when the sensory nerve endings within the mucous membranes lining the nasal cavity are stimulated by triggers such as inhaled dust. This gives rise to the ticklish sensation which often precedes a sneeze. A reflex reaction follows, whereby the secretory cells of the mucous membrane are stimulated to produce watery mucus (sneezing cannot take place through a dry nose).

### NERVE IMPULSE

Simultaneously, the sensory nerve fibres within the mucous membrane transmit nerve impulses to the respiratory centre of the brain (the medulla oblongata – located at the base of the brain).

The brain relays these nerve impulses to the respiratory muscles, triggering them to contract. This causes the body to inhale, close the airways and squeeze the chest, and then exhale rapidly.

The air in the lungs 'explodes' upward and outward, expelling the excess secretion along with its trapped particles through the nose and mouth.

The voluntary part of the brain is not involved in this automatic reaction, which is why we have no control over sneezing.

*The rapid exhalation brought about by sneezing causes watery mucus to be expelled forcefully. A sneeze cannot be consciously controlled.*

## Sneezing as a reaction to light

About 25 per cent of people sneeze when exposed to bright lights, such as the sun. This phenomenon has been recognized for at least 40 years, and is often referred to as the 'photic sneeze reflex'.

It is not known exactly why this happens, although it may reflect a crossing of reflex pathways in the brain. In any reflex, a sensory nerve signal directed towards the brain communicates directly with an outgoing neural response pathway bypassing the

*Many people sneeze as a reaction to looking at a bright light, especially the sun. The reason for this reaction is unknown.*

conscious part of the brain.

Normally, reflex pathways take different and separate routes through the nervous system. In the case of the photic sneeze reflex, it is possible that neural signals cross over between the normal reflex of the eye in response to light and the sneezing reflex. In this situation exposure to bright light simultaneously triggers constriction of the pupil and a sneeze. There is no apparent benefit from 'sun-sneezing', and it is probably a vestigial (redundant) evolutionary trait.

Other unexplained triggers of sneezing include combing hair, plucking eyebrows, and rubbing the inner corner of the eye.

131

# How taste buds work

We have approximately 10,000 taste buds, located mainly on the surface of the tongue and the soft tissues of the mouth. Their sensitivity and distribution means that we are able to discern between food flavours to savour and those to reject.

## CHEMICAL SENSE

Taste is, together with smell, a chemical sense. It is reliant on the binding of chemicals from food to receptors located in specific cells, the taste buds, which then transmit via nerves to the brain for interpretation as 'tastes'.

The tongue is, of course, the main organ of taste, as food that the body takes in must pass through the mouth. The tongue's upper surface is covered in numerous small projections called papillae, and it is around these structures that most of the taste buds are clustered. However, a few are found elsewhere in the mouth, such as on the pharynx, the soft palate and the epiglottis.

## PAPILLAE

There are three major types of papillae (the word papilla literally means a nipple-shaped protuberance). In increasing order of size, these are filiform (cone-like), fungiform (mushroom-shaped) and circumvallate (circular). In humans, most taste buds are found in these last two. Fungiform papillae are distributed all over the tongue, with a higher number along the sides and the tip. Circumvallate papillae are the largest – there are between 7 and 12 towards the rear of the tongue, arranged in a shallow inverted 'V' form. Taste buds are found in the sides of the circumvallate papillae and on the upper surfaces of the fungiform papillae.

## CELLULAR STRUCTURE

Each taste bud is made up of 40 to 100 epithelial cells, which make up the epithelium, the layer that covers the entire external surface of the body and its hollow structures. In the taste buds, there are three types of these: supporting, receptor and basal cells. Receptor cells are also called the gustatory or taste cells, which give rise to taste sensations. The supporting cells form the major part of the taste bud and separate the receptor cells from each other. Taste bud cells are replaced continually – the typical lifespan is about 10 days.

## Parts of the tongue

**Epiglottis**
Small numbers of taste buds located here, even as far down as the upper oesophagus (start of the digestive tract)

**Lingual tonsil**

**Palatine tonsil**
One of a pair; some taste buds are present in the supporting soft tissue

**Circumvallate papillae**
Round in shape, form an inverted 'V' at back of tongue

**Midline groove**

**Fungiform papillae**
Mushroom-shaped; mostly found at sides and tip of tongue

**Filiform papillae**
Conical projections, mostly in the lateral folds of the tongue

## Gustatory pathway

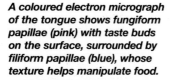

*A coloured electron micrograph of the tongue shows fungiform papillae (pink) with taste buds on the surface, surrounded by filiform papillae (blue), whose texture helps manipulate food.*

From each gustatory cell fine, sensitive, gustatory hairs project through the layers of epithelial cells to the surface, where they are washed in the saliva in which the substance to be tasted has dissolved. The hairs are sometimes referred to as receptor membranes, in recognition of their role in initially transmitting taste.

Sensory nerve cells form coils around the gustatory cells, and it is from here that the taste impulses start being sent to the brain. This transmission of impulses from the taste cells to the brain is called the 'gustatory pathway'.

*Circumvallate papillae in cross-section reveal the taste buds which open through a gustatory pore onto the sides of each projecting structure.*

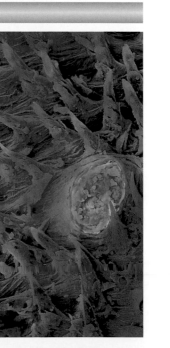

*The gustatory pore leads through to a taste bud under the surface. This one is surrounded by lingual papillae, which have a sensory and tactile function.*

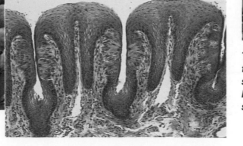

# The tasting mechanism

Once food is dissolved by saliva in the mouth, the taste buds on the tongue's surface are stimulated. Gustatory cells then convert the chemical reaction into nerve impulses. When the information reaches the brain, the taste information can be analysed.

When a food chemical binds to a gustatory cell, nerve impulses are sent to the thalamus, the part of the brain that receives sensory information. The thalamus processes the impulses and categorises similar functions together. Subsequently, the thalamus transmits them to the part of the brain associated with the sense of taste – the gustatory or taste cortex. The thalamus is unable to discern to any great extent whether the taste experience is good or bad. This is the job of the more sensitive gustatory cortex.

### GUSTATORY CORTEX
The gustatory cortex identifies the food as good or bad and judges whether to continue eating or not. For a substance to be tasted it must be dissolved in saliva and come into contact with the gustatory hairs. From there, nerve impulses are set up to transmit impulses to the brain.

A branch of the facial nerve transmits impulses from the taste buds in the front two-thirds of the tongue, and the lingual branch of the glossopharyngeal nerve serves the rear third of the tongue. It would appear that there is a two-way flow of information to the brain regarding taste and the need to eat certain foods to satisfy the body's requirements.

The gustatory cells in the different regions of the tongue have different thresholds at which they are activated. In the bitter region of the tongue the cells can detect substances such as poisons in very small concentrations. This explains how the apparent disadvantage of its location is overcome and how its 'protective' nature works. The sour receptors are less sensitive and the sweet and salty receptors are the least sensitive of all. The taste receptors react rapidly to a new sensation, usually within three to five seconds.

What is often called taste depends to a great extent on our sense of smell. Taste is about 80 per cent smell, which explains why when we have a heavy cold food never tastes very good. The mouth also contains other receptors which can accentuate the taste sensation. Spicy foods can add to the pleasure of eating by exciting the pain receptors in the mouth.

## Taste bud structure

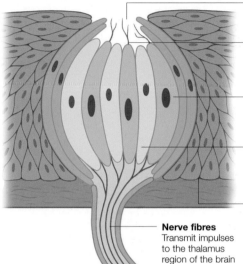

**Pore**

**Gustatory hair (microvilli)**
Sensory receptor of taste cell, bathed by saliva

**Gustatory cell**
Also known as a taste or receptor cell

**Supporting cells**
Insulate taste cells from each other and from tongue epithelium

**Epithelial cells**
Form the epithelium (outer layer) of the tongue

**Nerve fibres**
Transmit impulses to the thalamus region of the brain

## Papilla cross-section

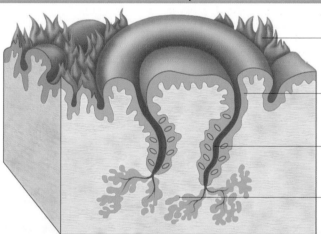

**Lingual papillae**
No taste function, but detect food and provide an abrasive surface

**Taste buds**
Clustered in groups at the base of papillae

**Furrow**
The furrow base opens into the Glands of Ebner

**Glands of Ebner**
Serum secreting glands at the base of the furrow

## Which part of the tongue tastes what?

**Bitter**

**Sour**

**Centre of tongue**
Fewer taste receptors

**Salty**

**Sweet**

Taste sensations can be grouped into four main categories. These are: sweet, sour, salty and bitter. Different parts of the tongue are more sensitive to different taste sensations, although there is no structural difference between the taste buds in the different areas.

The tip of the tongue is most sensitive to sweet and salty tastes, the sides of the tongue is most sensitive to sour tastes and the back of the tongue tastes bitter flavours most strongly. However, these differences are not absolute, as most taste buds can respond to two or three – and sometimes all four – taste sensations. Certain substances seem to change in flavour as they move through the mouth: saccharin, for example, tastes sweet at first, but goes on to develop a bitter aftertaste.

Many natural poisons and spoiled foods have a bitter flavour. It is perhaps likely, therefore, that bitterness receptors are located at the back of the tongue as a protective measure. In other words, the back of the tongue screens for 'bad' food and rejects it.

# How we speak

All spoken languages are constructed from a number of separate speech sounds, or phonemes. In English, these phonemes all result from the expulsion of air from the lungs.

All the speech sounds produced when speaking the majority of languages are the direct result of expelling air from the lungs. In the first instance, air travels from the lungs, via the trachea, into the larynx (the voice box).

The larynx acts as a valve, sealing off the lungs from harmful irritants during coughing, for example. The opening in the larynx is called the glottis, and this is covered by two flaps of retractable tissue called the vocal folds (the term 'vocal cords' is incorrect because they are not cords at all).

### VOCAL FOLDS

As air rushes through the glottis, the vocal folds resonate, producing a buzzing sound. The pitch of this buzz is determined by the tension and position of the vocal folds. However, not all speech sounds rely on the 'voicing' produced by the vocal folds; for example, the sound 'sssss' lacks voicing, whereas the sound 'zzzzzz' requires the vocal folds to vibrate.

### EXPULSION OF AIR

The vibrating air then moves up through the pharynx (throat) before leaving the head by travelling either over the tongue and through the mouth, or behind the soft palate and through the nose.

## Organs of speech

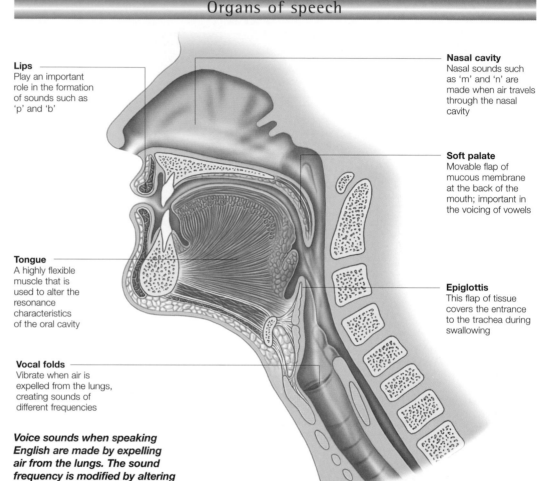

**Lips**
Play an important role in the formation of sounds such as 'p' and 'b'

**Tongue**
A highly flexible muscle that is used to alter the resonance characteristics of the oral cavity

**Vocal folds**
Vibrate when air is expelled from the lungs, creating sounds of different frequencies

**Nasal cavity**
Nasal sounds such as 'm' and 'n' are made when air travels through the nasal cavity

**Soft palate**
Movable flap of mucous membrane at the back of the mouth; important in the voicing of vowels

**Epiglottis**
This flap of tissue covers the entrance to the trachea during swallowing

*Voice sounds when speaking English are made by expelling air from the lungs. The sound frequency is modified by altering the shape of the cavities that the sound passes through.*

## Looking at the vocal folds

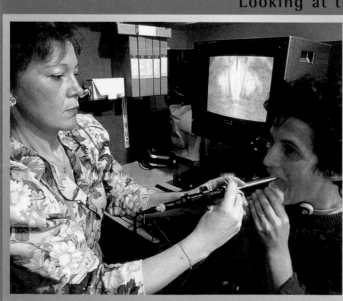

During speech, the mucosa over the vocal folds vibrates at between 120 and 250 times per second. In order to see this vibration directly, the movement is slowed down using a strobe light. A rigid laryngoscope is introduced over the back of the tongue and the vocal folds are inspected while the person vocalizes.

*Laryngoscopy can be used to examine the vocal folds. The laryngoscope relays the image to a TV monitor.*

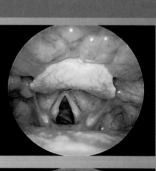

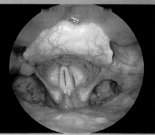

*Top: This laryngoscope image shows the human vocal folds at rest; note that the folds appear separated.*
*Bottom: This image shows the vocal folds during speech.*

# Voice sounds

Each of the chambers that air from the lungs passes through is of a different size and shape; the wavelength of the sound is altered as it travels through these chambers, resulting in a modified sound emitted through the mouth or nose.

### VOWELS

Vowel sounds are produced when air is able to travel freely from the larynx to the outside. These vowel sounds are generated by altering the dimensions of the chambers the sound has to pass through.

For example, when you repeat the vowel sounds in 'bet' and 'but' alternately you should be able to feel the body of your tongue move backwards and forwards. This motion alters the resonance characteristics of the mouth cavity, altering the sound produced.

The lips are also important (note the difference in the lip position when pronouncing the vowel sounds in 'loot' and 'look') in determining the final sound, as is the soft palate (the fleshy flap at the back of the roof of the mouth). If the soft palate is opened, air will be able to flow out through the nose, as well as through the mouth, producing a 'nasal twang'.

### CONSONANTS

In contrast to vowels, consonants are produced when a barrier is put in the way of the passing air. When the sound 'sssss' is made, the tip of the tongue is brought up just behind the teeth; this narrows the passage that the air can flow through, producing a hissing sound. Sounds like this are called 'fricatives' because they are created by the friction of moving air. Other fricative sounds include 'sh', 'th' and 'f', which are all produced by creating turbulence in the airflow.

Other consonant sounds are made by stopping the flow of air

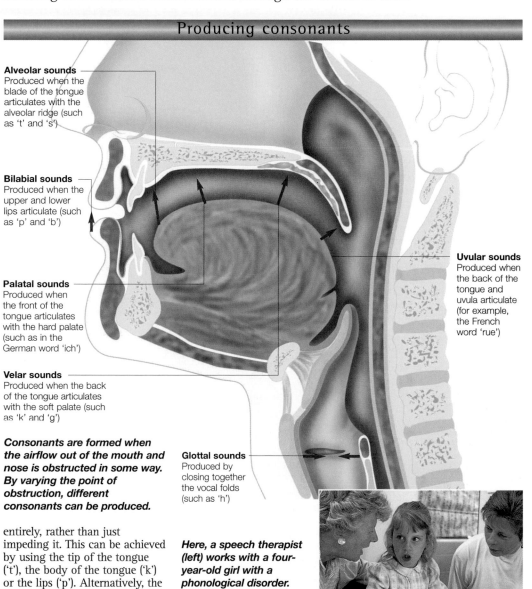

## Producing consonants

**Alveolar sounds**
Produced when the blade of the tongue articulates with the alveolar ridge (such as 't' and 's')

**Bilabial sounds**
Produced when the upper and lower lips articulate (such as 'p' and 'b')

**Palatal sounds**
Produced when the front of the tongue articulates with the hard palate (such as in the German word 'ich')

**Velar sounds**
Produced when the back of the tongue articulates with the soft palate (such as 'k' and 'g')

**Uvular sounds**
Produced when the back of the tongue and uvula articulate (for example, the French word 'rue')

**Glottal sounds**
Produced by closing together the vocal folds (such as 'h')

*Consonants are formed when the airflow out of the mouth and nose is obstructed in some way. By varying the point of obstruction, different consonants can be produced.*

entirely, rather than just impeding it. This can be achieved by using the tip of the tongue ('t'), the body of the tongue ('k') or the lips ('p'). Alternatively, the passage of air out through the mouth can be blocked, while opening the soft palate to produce sounds like 'm' and 'n'.

*Here, a speech therapist (left) works with a four-year-old girl with a phonological disorder. The girl's mother (right) is encouraged to join in so that she can continue the practice back at home.*

## Other speech sounds

*South African singer Miriam Makeba is a native speaker of Xhosa. Many of her popular songs contain a large number of 'click consonants'.*

Every word in the English language is pronounced based on a set of 40 distinct sounds, called phonemes. However, not every language uses the same set of sounds. Indeed, it has been estimated that the number of phonemes utilized by all the world's languages is in the thousands.

While English speech sounds are made by expelling air from the lungs, other languages often use different techniques:
■ Click sounds are sharp suction sounds made using the tongue or lips (what we might write as 'tut tut', for example) and are widely used in non-European languages
■ Glottalic sounds are made by using the glottis (the space between the vocal folds) to create turbulent air movement. These sounds can be created by moving air inwards (implosive sounds) or outwards (ejective sounds).

# How the eye focuses

Sight is the principal human sense, and we rely on our relatively small eyes for all our visual information. Despite their size, we can focus on a distant star or a speck of dust, and see in bright sunlight or near-darkness.

The human eye works like a camera. Light rays from an object pass through an aperture (the pupil) and are focused by a lens on to the retina, a light-sensitive layer at the back of the eye. The optical quality and versatility of the eye are much better than any camera.

The retina – the eye's equivalent of camera film – is a light-sensitive membrane composed of layers of nerve fibres and a pigmented light-sensitive membrane. It contains two kinds of light-sensitive cells: cones and rods.

### CONES AND RODS
Cones are sensitive to either red, green or blue light, and their signals enable the brain to interpret a colour image. They also give the eye acute vision.

Rods are extremely sensitive to low light but cannot differentiate between colours, which is why objects appear to lose their colour at night. The rods and cones are linked to the brain by nerve cells which all pass out of the back of the eye via the optic nerve.

To see objects clearly, the muscles of the eye must pull on the lens and focus light on the retina. If this process is faulty, or the lens or eye is the wrong shape, the image will appear blurred, and spectacles, or even surgery, will be needed.

**Tendons of the rectus muscles**
Connective tissue joining the eye and the rectus muscles, which control the movement of the eye

**Vitreous body**
Chamber filled with jelly-like vitreous humour

**Lens**
Transparent crystalline structure that fine-tunes the focusing of images on to the retina

**Pupil**
Opening in the iris through which light enters

**Cornea**
Round transparent window in the front of the eye. Refracts light entering the eye on to the lens

**Fovea**
Shallow depression in the retina where light is most accurately focused

**Optic nerve**
Bundle of nerves, about 25 mm long, that send signals from the retina to the brain

**Sclera**
Outer fibrous coating that gives the eye its shape

**Choroid**
Middle layer of the eye wall. Supplies blood and oxygen to the retina

**Retina**
Innermost wall of the eye consisting of layers of nerve fibres and a light-receptive membrane. Where light entering the eye is focused

**Ciliary body**
Connects the lens – via suspensory ligaments – to the choroid. Contains muscles which control the shape of the lens

**Aqueous humour**
Fluid in front of the lens

**Iris**
Muscular ring in front of the lens. Controls the amount of light entering the eye

**Suspensory ligaments**
Ligaments between the lens and ciliary muscle. They pull on the lens, thus changing its shape, when the ciliary muscles contract

## Muscles of the eye

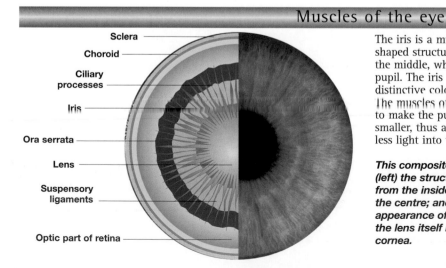

Sclera
Choroid
Ciliary processes
Iris
Ora serrata
Lens
Suspensory ligaments
Optic part of retina

The iris is a muscular, ring-shaped structure with a hole in the middle, which is called the pupil. The iris contains a distinctive coloured pigment. The muscles of the iris are used to make the pupil larger or smaller, thus allowing more or less light into the eye according

**This composite picture shows (left) the structure of the eyeball from the inside, with the lens in the centre; and (right) the outer appearance of the eye, where the lens itself is covered by the cornea.**

to the conditions that the person is trying to see in.

The iris muscles are to be found in the ciliary body, which is the part of the eye connecting the choroid (middle layer of the eye wall) with the iris.
The ciliary body consists of three parts:

■ The ciliary ring, adjoining the choroid
■ The ciliary processes, 70 radial ridges around the ciliary body
■ The ciliary muscle, which controls lens curvature

# Focusing on the retina

Light entering the eye passes through the cornea and the aqueous humour, both of which cause refraction (bending) of the light rays inwards.

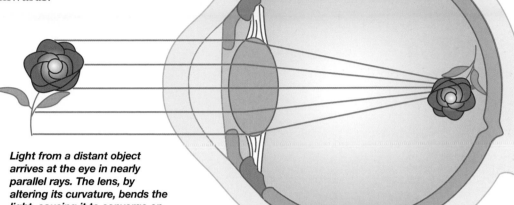

The cornea refracts most of the incoming light, and it is the task of the lens to 'fine tune' the focusing of the rays so that the image falls accurately onto the retina. The lens is a crystalline structure, made up of several layers. It is attached to the muscular ciliary body by suspensory ligaments. Movements of the ciliary muscle alter the shape of the lens, according to whether the eye needs to focus on a distant or nearby object. The diagrams below (viewing the eye from inside and from the side respectively) demonstrate how the shape of the lens is adjusted as necessary.

*Light from a distant object arrives at the eye in nearly parallel rays. The lens, by altering its curvature, bends the light, causing it to converge on the retina. This results in an inverted image on the retina, but the brain is able to process the information so that the image is 'seen' the right way up.*

## Looking at close objects

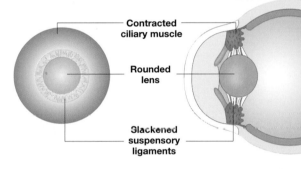

Contracted ciliary muscle

Rounded lens

Slackened suspensory ligaments

Light rays from a nearby object are more diverged, needing greater refraction. The ciliary muscle contracts, reducing the tension on the suspensory ligaments, and the lens gets more rounded. As the light rays pass through the rounded lens they are sharply converged on the back of the eye.

## Looking at distant objects

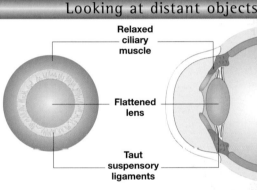

Relaxed ciliary muscle

Flattened lens

Taut suspensory ligaments

Light rays from a distant object are more parallel when they reach the eye, so require less refraction by the lens. The ciliary muscle relaxes and the tension on the suspensory ligament pulls the edges of the lens outwards, thus making it thinner and flatter. The rays are focused on the back of the eye.

## Common eye defects

Two common defects of the eye are short-sightedness (myopia) and long-sightedness (hypermetropia).

**Short-sightedness** is the inability to focus on distant objects. It is usually the result of the eyeball being slightly too long, which means that the sharpest image from a distant object is formed in front of the retina.

**Long-sightedness**, on the other hand, occurs when the eyeball is too short, with the result that the focus point of light from a nearby object lies behind the retina.

Short-sightedness is corrected by wearing spectacles (or contact lenses) that place a diverging (concave) lens in front of the eye; long-sightedness is corrected by

using spectacles with a converging (convex) lens.

Another common eye defect is **far-sightedness** (presbyopia), which is an inability of the eye to focus on nearby objects as a result of the lens losing its elasticity. The defect occurs naturally as people get older – often in early middle age – and is corrected by the use of converging lenses. This is often the first time that a person needs spectacles to correct a problem with their vision.

**Astigmatism** is the result of the eyeball being slightly misshapen, causing the image of an object to become distorted. This can be corrected by wearing spectacles with cylindrical lenses which cancel out the distortion caused by the eye itself.

**SHORT-SIGHTEDNESS**
*Parallel light rays are brought to a focus in front of the retina, resulting in distant objects being perceived as blurred. A concave lens diverges the light rays falling on the lens, correcting the vision.*

**LONG-SIGHTEDNESS**
*Light rays from an object focus beyond the retina when the muscles that control the focusing of the lens are relaxed. Greater degrees of hypermetropia result in a blurring of near vision.*

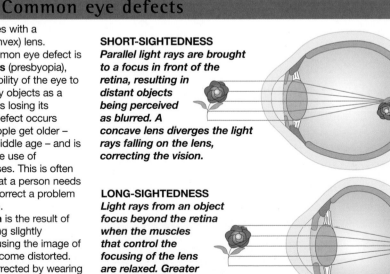

# How the retina works

The retina, located at the back of the eye, contains specialized cells called photoreceptors which are sensitive to light of different colours. These allow us to see in both the light and the dark.

The eye has adapted through evolution to be extremely sensitive to light. However, the bulk of the eye tissue is not responsive to light. Rather, the muscles which surround the eyeball, as well as the iris, cornea and lens, all act to focus light on to the retina, a relatively small area at the back of the eyeball which contains photoreceptors.

## STRUCTURE OF THE RETINA

At its simplest level, the retina consists of four layers of cells:

■ At the back of the retina is the outer, pigmented layer – these epithelial cells absorb light (but do not 'detect' it), so preventing it from scattering in the eye

■ Next are aligned a layer of photoreceptors, which are able to convert light energy into electrical energy

■ The electrical potentials the photoreceptors generate are transmitted to the 'bipolar cells'

■ The bipolar cells in turn communicate with 'ganglion cells'; the axons (nerve fibres) of the latter converge and make a right-angled turn before leaving the eye through the optic nerve, which carries information on the visual scene to the brain.

Thus light has first to travel through the ganglion and bipolar cells before it reaches the light-sensitive photoreceptors at the back of the retina. This apparently 'back-to-front' arrangement does not hinder photoreceptors from detecting light.

## Structure of the retina

**Ganglion cell**
These nerve cells send axons (nerve fibres) through the optic nerve to the brain

**To the brain via optic nerve**

**FRONT OF RETINA**

**Retina**

**Optic nerve**

**Bipolar cell**
These nerve cells receive information from photoreceptors which they pass on to ganglion cells

**Rod photoreceptor**
Rods are very sensitive to light and are involved in night vision

**Cone photoreceptor**
Cones vary in sensitivity to light of different colours

**Pigmented cell**
These cells absorb light and prevent it from scattering in the eye

**Light direction**

**BACK OF RETINA**

## Visual acuity

### Demonstration of the blind spot

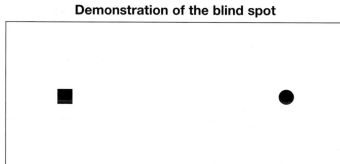

*Close your left eye and focus on the square. The circle should disappear when the page is held about six inches away because its image falls on the optic nerve.*

*This electron micrograph shows the fovea, a crater-like depression in the retina. This area has the greatest visual acuity of the whole of the retina.*

There are two main types of photoreceptors: rods, which operate in dim light and provide low acuity vision in scales of grey; and cones, which operate in bright light and provide high acuity, colour vision.

### DISTRIBUTION

The relative distribution of the two types of photoreceptor varies throughout the retina. For example, the peripheral

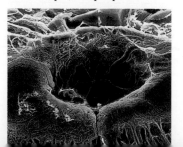

regions contain mainly rods, with relatively few cones. In contrast, at the centre of the retina, directly behind the middle of the lens, is a region the size of a pin head called the fovea which contains entirely cones.

The fovea is the only part of the retina which has cones at sufficient density to provide us with highly detailed colour vision. This is why only one thousandth of our visual field can be in hard focus at any one time; we have to move our eyes continuously in order to comprehend a rapidly changing visual scene, for example when driving along.

# Rods and cones

There are two types of photoreceptors: rods, which are sensitive to low levels of light, and cones, which are responsive to light of different colours.

Rods are the most numerous of the two types of photoreceptor; it has been estimated that there are 120 million rod cells compared to only six million cones. Furthermore, rods are about 300 times more sensitive to light than cones.

### NIGHT VISION
This sensitivity, coupled with their relative abundance, makes rods ideal for seeing in the dark when light levels are low.

*An electron micrograph of a group of rod cells (green). Rod cells are very sensitive to light and so are mainly used for vision in the dark.*

However, rods provide the brain with only low acuity vision in scales of grey. This is because a rod cell makes connections with more than one bipolar cell, which, in turn, sends electrical impulses to the brain via many ganglion cells. Thus a ganglion cell – which leaves the eye through the optic nerve – provides the brain with information gathered from a large number of rod cells. This explains why vision seems to be made of lots of large grey dots when a person is out at night.

### DAY VISION
In contrast to rods, cones operate primarily in strong light and provide the brain with high acuity, colour information on the visual scene. This is aided by the fact that each individual cone cell has a 'direct line' to the brain; one cone cell is in contact with only one bipolar cell, which in turn communicates with only one ganglion cell. Thus a neuron in the brain can receive information on the activity of a single cone photoreceptor.

*Rods and cones have a similar shape. The main difference between them is the photopigment that they contain.*

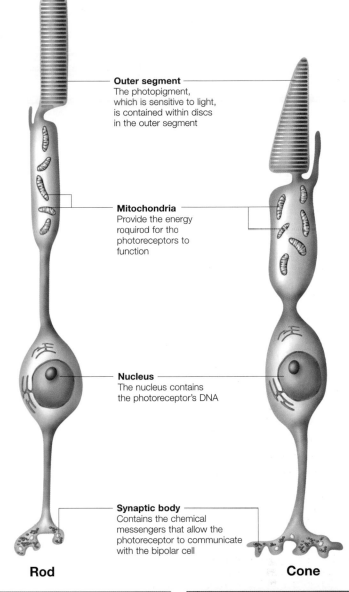

**Outer segment**
The photopigment, which is sensitive to light, is contained within discs in the outer segment

**Mitochondria**
Provide the energy required for the photoreceptors to function

**Nucleus**
The nucleus contains the photoreceptor's DNA

**Synaptic body**
Contains the chemical messengers that allow the photoreceptor to communicate with the bipolar cell

**Rod**          **Cone**

## Colour vision

We are able to see in colour because there are three different types of cone, each of which is sensitive to light of different wavelengths (colours).

The three cone types each contain a different photopigment; a photopigment is a molecule which is responsive to light of specific wavelengths and which can change the electrical excitability of the photoreceptor cell.

The three cones are called blue, green and red cones. It should be pointed out that these names do not necessarily correspond to the colour of light that activates them best. For example, green cones are the best of the three groups of cells at responding to green light, though they are activated the most by yellow light.

### COLOUR DIFFERENTIATION
We are able to distinguish between different colours because light of a specific wavelength will activate blue, green and red cones to different degrees. The cones send impulses to the brain at a rate proportional to the degree they are activated – the brain interprets the ratio of the nerve impulses arising from the three types of cone as representing a specific colour.

*There are three types of cone photoreceptors, each being responsive to a different range of colours.*

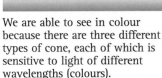

Blue cone     Green cone   Red cone

Sensitivity to light

Colour type

## Colour blindness

Red-green colour blindness is a relatively common inherited condition that affects one in 12 men and one in 100 women. Affected individuals have a deficiency in either red or green cones, which makes it impossible for them to differentiate between red and green and between orange and yellow.

*Colour-blind people will be unable to see the 'L' in this colour blindness test because the red and green dots appear the same.*

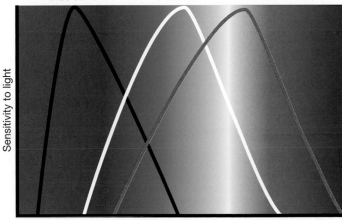

# How tears are produced

The eyes are highly complex and delicate structures. The constant secretion of fluid from the lacrimal glands above each eye lubricates the eyes and protects them from foreign bodies and infection.

The eye is the organ of visual perception – our dominant sense. It relays vital information to the brain about our surroundings, and plays a crucial role in communication.

### MOVEMENT OF THE EYES
In order for us to have a large field of vision, the eyeball is designed to move around within the orbit by fine muscular control.

To facilitate this movement, each eye produces lacrimal secretions. These secretions moisten the conjunctiva (the membrane that covers the eye) and lubricate the eye, allowing it to move more efficiently within the eye socket.

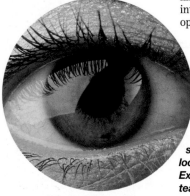

*The eyeball is designed to move within the eye socket. The secretion of lacrimal fluid moistens and lubricates the eye, facilitating this movement.*

Lacrimal fluid is produced, distributed and carried away by the lacrimal apparatus.

### ANATOMY OF THE LACRIMAL APPARATUS
The lacrimal apparatus consists of the lacrimal gland (where lacrimal secretions are produced) and the ducts that drain the excess secretions into the nasal cavity.

Each lacrimal gland lies within the orbit (the eye socket) just above the outer aspect of the eye and is the size and shape of an almond.

These specialized glands are responsible for the constant production of lacrimal secretion, the salty solution otherwise known as tears. Tears are secreted into the eye via several tiny openings in the lacrimal gland.

*Tears are produced and secreted by the lacrimal gland, located just above the eye. Excess fluid drains through the tear ducts into the nasal cavity.*

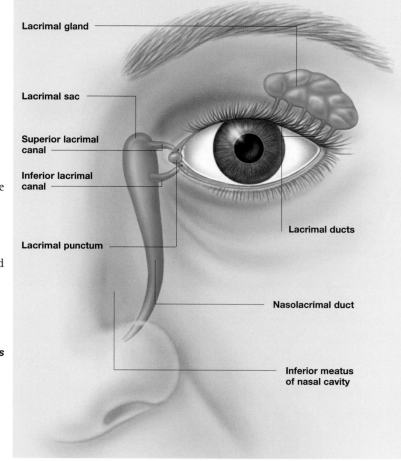

Lacrimal gland

Lacrimal sac

Superior lacrimal canal

Inferior lacrimal canal

Lacrimal punctum

Lacrimal ducts

Nasolacrimal duct

Inferior meatus of nasal cavity

## Production and drainage of lacrimal fluid

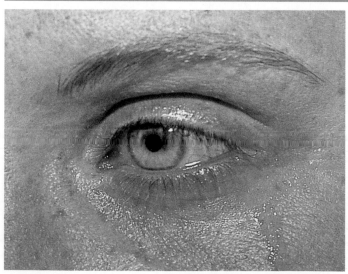

*Lacrimal fluid washes across the eyeball before draining into the lacrimal canal. From here the fluid is drained into the nasal cavity via the nasolacrimal duct.*

As the eye blinks (around every two to ten seconds) lacrimal fluid is spread downwards, across the eyeball.

Normal amounts of tears washing down over the front of the eyeball are prevented from spilling out onto the cheeks by the oil that the lid glands deposit on the margins of the lids.

Most of the fluid produced by the lacrimal glands evaporates from the surface of the eye, but some collects in the inner corner of the eye.

### FLUID DRAINAGE
The excess fluid that collects in the inner corner of the eye enters the lacrimal canals via two tiny openings called the lacrimal puncta. These appear as tiny red dots on the inner margin of each eyelid – adjacent to the bridge of the nose.

From the lacrimal canals, fluid drains into the lacrimal sac, and thence into the nasolacrimal duct, which is an extension of the lacrimal sac. The fluid is then released into the nasal cavity.

It is estimated that the average person produces around 0.75 to 1.1 ml of lacrimal fluid every day, which serves to keep the eyes moist and free from infection.

# Tear production

Teardrops are produced when the lacrimal glands are stimulated to secrete increased amounts of fluid. This may be in response to irritants or emotional upset.

When lacrimal secretion increases substantially, the excess spills over the eyelids and drips from the corners of the eyes, forming characteristic drops of fluid that run down the cheeks as teardrops. An excess of lacrimal fluid also fills the nasal cavities, causing congestion and the characteristic sniffling that accompanies tears.

### REFLEX REACTION
One trigger of this excess secretion of lacrimal fluid is the presence of foreign bodies such as grit in the eye. When a foreign body enters the eye the lacrimal glands are stimulated to produce increased amounts of lacrimal fluid. This excess fluid irrigates the eye and flushes out the foreign body. In this way, the eye is protected from damage or infection.

In the case of potentially harmful irritants such as noxious chemicals, increased production of lacrimal fluid serves to dilute and wash away the irritating substance.

An example of this mechanism is seen when we chop an onion. The onion releases pungent chemicals into the atmosphere which dissolve in the moisture present on the surface of the eyes, releasing an acid which stings the eyes.

The lacrimal glands are

*The pungent chemicals released from a chopped onion stimulate increased production of lacrimal fluid. The excess fluid washes the potentially harmful irritant from the eyes.*

stimulated to produce an increased amount of lacrimal fluid, which spills across the eyes, diluting the irritant, and flushing it out of the eyes. As there is an excess of lacrimal fluid it drips from the eyes, giving the appearance of crying.

### TRIGGER MECHANISM
Tears are secreted as part of a reflex response (automatic and involuntary) to a variety of stimuli. Examples include irritants to the eye and lining of the nose, as well as hot or peppery foods coming in to contact with the mouth and tongue. Tear flow also occurs in association with vomiting, coughing and yawning.

In each case the reaction is controlled autonomously by a region of the brain known as the hypothalamus.

When receptors in the eye are stimulated, nerve impulses are transmitted to the hypothalamus via the facial nerves supplying the lacrimal glands, and a reflex arc occurs whereby the lacrimal glands are stimulated to produce more tears.

## Crying

*Little is understood about the mechanism that triggers crying in response to emotional upset. However, it is certain that tears play a vital role in communication.*

The production of tears as a result of emotional upset is known as crying or psychical weeping, and is a different kind of response. Research has shown that even if the nerves which cause reflex production of tears to take place are severed, the emotional response of crying can still occur.

### EMOTIONAL UPSET
The significance of emotionally induced tears is poorly understood. The discovery that lacrimal secretions contain encephalins (natural opiates) and the fact that only humans shed emotional tears suggest that crying may play a role in reducing stress. This is perhaps why crying is accompanied by a feeling of relief.

Crying is also an effective way of communicating our pain or anguish to others.

## Composition of tears

Lacrimal fluid contains mucus, antibodies, and lysozyme, an enzyme that destroys bacteria. The function of this fluid is to cleanse and protect the eye surface as well as moistening and lubricating it.

Some medical conditions such as keratoconjunctivitis sicca (dry-eye) result in impaired lacrimal function, and the eyes become dry and infected. In such cases, patients require artificial saline solution (such as that used by contact lens

wearers) to help lubricate the eye and ward off infection.

As we grow older the lacrimal glands become less active, and the eyes tend to become less moist. Consequently the eyes are more prone to infection and irritation during the later years of life.

*Antibodies present in tears help to ward off infection. As the lacrimal glands become less active with age the eyes are more prone to infection.*

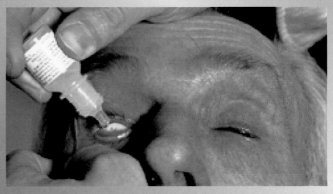

# How the ear controls our balance

The ear not only facilitates hearing, but is also responsible for maintaining balance when everyday tasks are performed, from climbing the stairs to rollerblading. The intricately designed structures of balance are in the inner ear.

Olympic skiers can maintain their balance at speeds in excess of 50 mph. This is possible because of the structures of the ear.

The ear is made up of three parts. The outer, visible part of the ear (the pinna and auditory canal) gathers and focuses the sound waves. In the middle ear, the eardrum vibrates, and the three ossicles (small bones) transmit these vibrations to the inner ear. The inner ear performs two functions: the cochlea receives the sound waves and helps to transmit them to the brain, where they are interpreted as sound, and the non-auditory or vestibular labyrinth detects changes in the body's position.

### BONY LABYRINTH

The part of the inner ear concerned with balance is the bony labyrinth. Within this are the vestibule, the semicircular canals and the membranous labyrinth. The membranous labyrinth is surrounded by a fluid called perilymph. Another fluid, endolymph, is contained in the membranous labyrinth. These fluids do not just fill space; they are a vital part of the whole equilibrium system.

The individual parts of the bony labyrinth are sensitive to movement, rotation and orientation of the head.

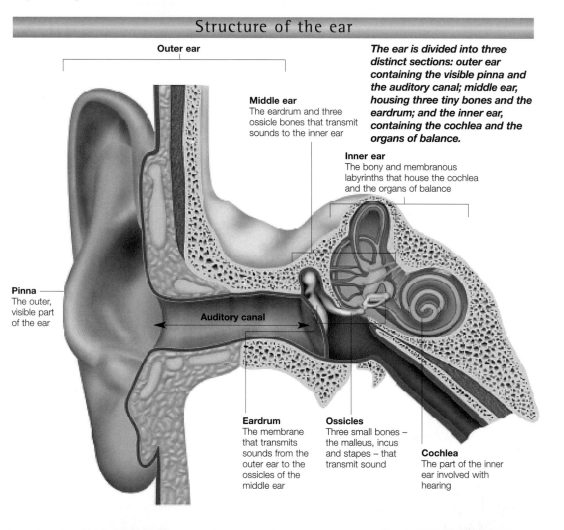

## Structure of the ear

*The ear is divided into three distinct sections: outer ear containing the visible pinna and the auditory canal; middle ear, housing three tiny bones and the eardrum; and the inner ear, containing the cochlea and the organs of balance.*

**Outer ear**

**Middle ear**
The eardrum and three ossicle bones that transmit sounds to the inner ear

**Inner ear**
The bony and membranous labyrinths that house the cochlea and the organs of balance

**Pinna**
The outer, visible part of the ear

**Auditory canal**

**Eardrum**
The membrane that transmits sounds from the outer ear to the ossicles of the middle ear

**Ossicles**
Three small bones – the malleus, incus and stapes – that transmit sound

**Cochlea**
The part of the inner ear involved with hearing

*An Olympic slalom skier travels at high speeds and at acute angles, but he is still aware of his body's position thanks to the in-built sense of equilibrium provided by the inner ear.*

## Loss of balance

When you are stationary, the fluid in the canals and chambers of the ear are in equilibrium. When the head is moved, the fluid moves in the opposite direction, and the brain senses the change in position. The size of this change is different in each ear (depending on which way you turn), but the system remains in equilibrium. However, if the vestibular system of one ear is damaged, the activity of the other ear causes a false sense of turning (vertigo) towards the unaffected side.

If the vestibular function of both ears is damaged, posture and gait can be seriously affected, causing vertigo and disorientation. If our environment changes, as it does when we fly or go to sea, the vestibular system may also react, resulting in air or sea sickness. A similar effect results from drinking too much alcohol.

Recently, space scientists have been studying the effects of weightlessness on the vestibular system. Some astronauts have had minor vestibular symptoms upon return. No disturbances have been permanent.

# Parts of the ear that control balance

The tubes and chambers of the bony labyrinth protect the membranous tubes and chambers of the membranous labyrinth, with their fluids and sensors.

## SEMICIRCULAR CANALS

The semicircular canals are three bony tubes in each ear that lie roughly at right-angles to each other. Because of their position and structure they are able to detect movement in three-dimensional space and are the parts sensitive to rotation.

Each canal has an expanded end called the ampulla, and is filled with endolymph. There are receptor cells located in the ampulla of each canal which have fine hairs that project up into the endolymph. When we move, these projecting hairs are displaced by the movement of the endolymph. This stimulates the vestibular nerve which sends signals to the cerebellum of the brain.

When we move, a reflex called nystagmus (the back and forth movement of the eyes), helps to prevent dizziness. The eyes move slowly against the direction of the rotation, which allows us to concentrate on a fixed point.

## MEMBRANOUS LABYRINTH

The vestibule contains two membranous sacs called the utricle and the saccule. These are known as the otolith organs, and they respond to our orientation. On the inner surface of each sac is a 2mm-wide patch of sensory cells – a macula – which monitors the position of the head.

The utricle maculae lie horizontally and provide information when our heads move from side to side. Less is known about the saccular maculae, but because they are arranged vertically they probably respond to backward and forward tilting of the head. Together, they allow the detection of all the possible positions of the head.

The sensory organs (particularly in the utricle) play an important role in controlling the muscles of the legs, trunk and neck to keep the body and head in an upright position.

### The inner ear

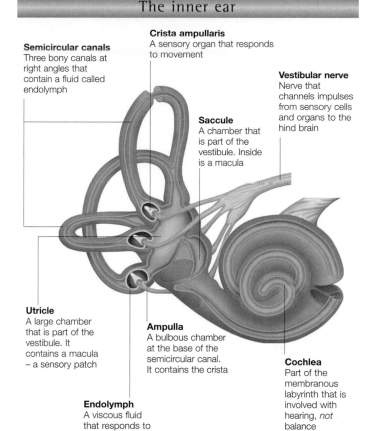

**Semicircular canals**
Three bony canals at right angles that contain a fluid called endolymph

**Crista ampullaris**
A sensory organ that responds to movement

**Vestibular nerve**
Nerve that channels impulses from sensory cells and organs to the hind brain

**Saccule**
A chamber that is part of the vestibule. Inside is a macula

**Utricle**
A large chamber that is part of the vestibule. It contains a macula – a sensory patch

**Ampulla**
A bulbous chamber at the base of the semicircular canal. It contains the crista

**Cochlea**
Part of the membranous labyrinth that is involved with hearing, *not* balance

**Endolymph**
A viscous fluid that responds to head movement

## How the maculae work

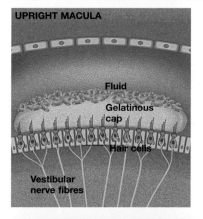

**UPRIGHT MACULA**

Fluid
Gelatinous cap
Hair cells
Vestibular nerve fibres

Each macula consists of a layer of tissue known as the neuroepitheliam. In this layer are sensory cells called hair cells that send continuous nerve impulses to the brain.

The hair cells are covered by a gelatinous cap that contains small granular particles that weigh against the hairs. When the hair bundles are deflected – because of a tilt of the head, for example – the hair cells are stimulated to alter the rate of nerve impulses being sent.

Hair cells near the centre are rounded, and those on the periphery are cylindrical. This may increase sensitivity to a slight tilting of the head.

*The macula within the utricle is a horizontal gelatinous cap with tiny hairs embedded in it.*

*When the head tilts, endolymph fluid and gravity pull the cap down, stimulating the hair cells.*

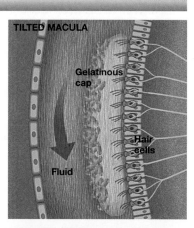

**TILTED MACULA**

Gelatinous cap
Hair cells
Fluid

## What happens to the crista within the ampullae

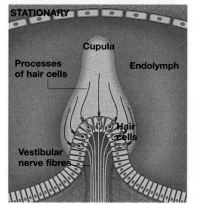

**STATIONARY**

Cupula
Processes of hair cells
Endolymph
Hair cells
Vestibular nerve fibres

The crista is a cone-shaped sensory structure within the ampulla – the swollen base of each semicircular canal. There are six cristae in each ear. Each crista is surrounded by a fluid called endolymph.

Each crista responds to changes in the rate of movement of the head, passing information along the vestibular nerve to the brain.

Sensitive hair cells are embedded in a gelatinous cone called the cupula. Any kind of head movement causes fluid to swirl past the cupula, bending it and activating the hair cells.

*Hair processes in the jelly-like cupula are connected to hair cells and nerve fibres. When the head is stationary, the cupula does not move.*

*As the head moves, endolymph fluid displaces the cupula, stimulating the hair processes. These send signals to the brain, which registers movement.*

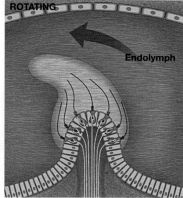

**ROTATING**

Endolymph

# How the brain processes sound

Sound hitting the inner ear is converted into neuronal (nerve) signals. This is a complex and subtle process, which enables the brain to interpret and understand a wide range of sound.

The cochlea – the organ of hearing located in the inner ear – is a coiled bony structure containing a fluid-filled system of cavities.

The central cavity, or cochlear duct, contains the specific structure for hearing, called the spiral organ of Corti. Located on the basilar membrane, this spiral organ contains the thousands of sensory hair cells that convert mechanical movement (caused by sound vibrations resonating through the fluid) into electrical nerve impulses which are then transmitted to the brain.

## PATHWAYS TO BRAIN
The neuronal pathways of the auditory system are composed of sequences of neurones arranged in series and parallel. The impulses begin in the organ of Corti and ultimately reach the auditory areas of the cerebral cortex known as the transverse temporal gyri of Heschl.

## TRANSIT STATIONS
As neuronal activity is transmitted towards the brain it goes through several 'transit stations'. Certain of these transit stations respond in particular ways to various aspects of the auditory signal thus giving the brain more context to the sound. For example, some cochlear neurones have a sharp burst of activity at the start of a sound, called a primary-like response pattern; this informs the auditory cortex of the start of a sound sequence.

The neurones, transit stations and various brain auditory centres are found on both sides of the body. The auditory centres in the brain receive sound from the opposite ear.

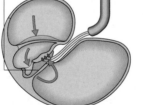

**Spiral organ of Corti**
Contains vibration-sensitive hair cells that transmit signals via auditory nerve

*This cross-section of the cochlea shows how vibrations are transmitted across membranous divisions between the chambers to the organ of Corti hair cells.*

## Pathway of signals to the brain

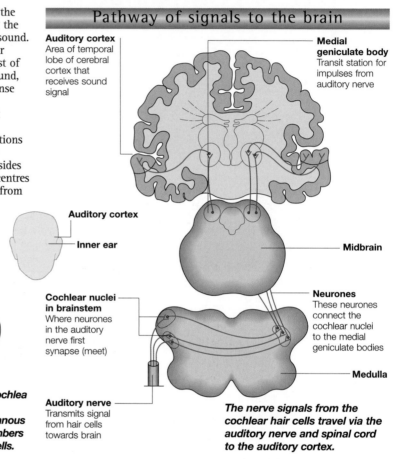

**Auditory cortex**
Area of temporal lobe of cerebral cortex that receives sound signal

**Medial geniculate body**
Transit station for impulses from auditory nerve

**Auditory cortex**

**Inner ear**

**Midbrain**

**Cochlear nuclei in brainstem**
Where neurones in the auditory nerve first synapse (meet)

**Neurones**
These neurones connect the cochlear nuclei to the medial geniculate bodies

**Medulla**

**Auditory nerve**
Transmits signal from hair cells towards brain

*The nerve signals from the cochlear hair cells travel via the auditory nerve and spinal cord to the auditory cortex.*

## Interpreting pitch of sound

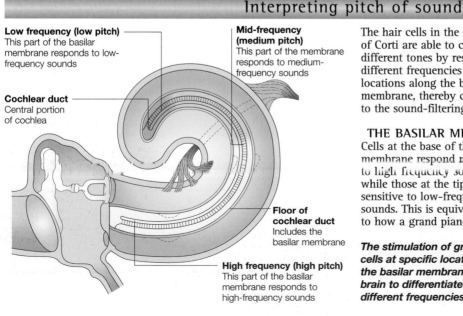

**Low frequency (low pitch)**
This part of the basilar membrane responds to low-frequency sounds

**Mid-frequency (medium pitch)**
This part of the membrane responds to medium-frequency sounds

**Cochlear duct**
Central portion of cochlea

**Floor of cochlear duct**
Includes the basilar membrane

**High frequency (high pitch)**
This part of the basilar membrane responds to high-frequency sounds

*The stimulation of groups of hair cells at specific locations along the basilar membrane allows the brain to differentiate sounds of different frequencies or pitch.*

The hair cells in the spiral organ of Corti are able to convey different tones by responding to different frequencies at different locations along the basilar membrane, thereby contributing to the sound-filtering process.

## THE BASILAR MEMBRANE
Cells at the base of the basilar membrane respond more readily to high frequency sound waves, while those at the tip are more sensitive to low-frequency sounds. This is equivalent to how a grand piano emits sounds, with one end producing high notes and the other low ones.

However, there are additional subtleties used to transduce the different tones.

Imagine a tuning fork that emits the note 'A' is struck. The sound waves reaching the cochlea will all resonate at a frequency of 440 cycles per second (Hertz). This triggers the basilar membrane to vibrate at 440 times a second. However, there is a particular section of the basilar membrane, which is constructed in such a way that it will vibrate with the largest amplitude at 440 times a second. This will then set the neurones from that region signalling at 440 times a second.

# How the brain interprets sound signals

Once nerve impulses are transmitted to the auditory cortex, several areas of the brain are responsible for interpreting the signals.

There is still much to be learned about how the brain interprets sound and language. We know that there are several areas of the temporal lobe on both sides of the brain responsible for interpreting different aspects of sound. We also know that these areas receive a lot of additional contextual information from the various staging posts as the basic neuronal signals make their way to the auditory cortex.

### IDENTIFYING SOUNDS
The brain identifies sounds by recognizing essential features of each sound – such as volume, pitch, duration, and intervals between sounds. From those elements, the brain creates a unique acoustic 'picture' of each sound, in much the same way that a colour television can reproduce the whole spectrum of colours on a screen using dots of just three colours.

The auditory cortex also has to separate many different sounds arriving at the same time, filtering and analysing them to produce meaningful information. Of course, the brain uses the context in which sound is received to make certain assumptions about what it it will hear. For instance if the visual cortex tells it that a young girl is speaking it will expect speech of a certain pitch to arrive.

### AUDITORY ASSOCIATION CORTEX
The auditory association cortex is used to process complex sounds whereby many sound waves arrive at the same time. This is particularly important in language recognition, and damage to this area results in a person detecting sounds without being able to distinguish between them.

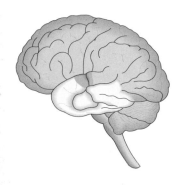

*The auditory cortex (pink) recognizes and analyses sounds. The association cortex (yellow) acts to distinguish more complex features of the sounds.*

*The visual cortex influences the context in which sound is interpreted. When using a phone we have no visual clues and rely solely on auditory input.*

## Locating sound

### Listening to sound from behind

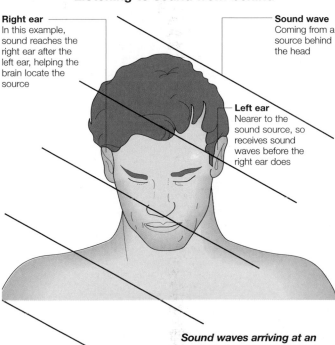

**Right ear**
In this example, sound reaches the right ear after the left ear, helping the brain locate the source

**Sound wave**
Coming from a source behind the head

**Left ear**
Nearer to the sound source, so receives sound waves before the right ear does

*Sound waves arriving at an angle to the head will reach each ear at a different time. This allows us to detect the direction from which the sound is coming.*

The brain is very accurate at integrating information to locate sound.

The two main ways it does this are by picking up the minute difference in timing and intensity of the sound reaching the two ears.

A sound wave will reach the ear that is closer to the source of the sound a fraction of a second before it reaches the other ear. The brain can interpret the time difference to distinguish the direction of the sound.

In addition to this, if sound is coming from the side, the head causes a 'sound shadow' screening one ear, such that it receives less sound than the other ear. Often, our response is to turn our head in the direction of the sound, evening up the sound to both ears.

However, even with only one ear we would still be able to locate a sound source. This is because small details of the sound we hear, caused by waves deflecting off the irregular surface of the pinna, vary with the angle at which the sound approaches the ear. As we develop, we learn that particular sound differences are associated with particular directions, and from this can detect the direction of a sound source.

*From an early age, babies learn to recognize typical details of sounds coming from different directions. They can then use the information as a reference.*

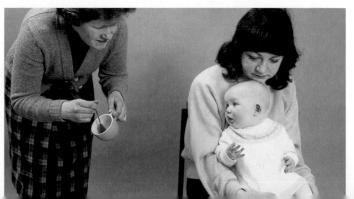

# How the body feels pain

Pain is not just a signal that certain tissues in the body have been damaged – it also alerts the sufferer to danger. Painkillers can bring relief, but the body also has its own built in pain inhibition system.

Any event that causes a degree of damage to the tissues of the body – be it mechanical (from pressure or a wound), chemical (exposure to acid, for example) or thermal (extreme heat or cold) – brings about the release of large amounts of chemicals, such as serotonin and histamine.

As well as producing reactions within the tissues, such as swelling and redness, these chemicals are detected by special sensory cells, called free nerve endings, which are found in the superficial layers of skin as well as in some of the internal organs. They are also known as nociceptors, because they react to noxious substances.

### PAIN IMPULSES

In response to the chemical changes within the tissues, the sensory cells send nerve impulses to relay stations in the spinal cord. From here, they are passed through further relays in the lower part of the brain in the brain stem and the thalamus, and so on to the higher levels of the brain. There, the information is analysed and perceived as pain. In most circumstances, a person will withdraw from the source of the pain.

## Receptors in the skin

**Hair shaft**

**Epidermis**
Outer layer of skin

**Merkel's disc**
Senses continuous touch against the skin; signal is initially strong, then continues weaker

**Dermis**
Inner layer of skin; contains blood vessels, sweat glands and nerves

**Ruffini's corpuscle**
Located deeper in the skin; signals heavy, prolonged pressure

**Free nerve endings**
Pain receptors which are widespread in the skin and certain other tissues

**Meissner's corpuscle**
Elongated nerve ending; sensitive touch receptor, found especially in the lips and fingertips

**Pacinian corpuscle**
Detects the rapid movement of tissues

## Classifying pain

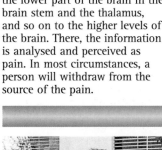

There are two types of pain, distinguished according to the speed with which the sensations are felt. The first, which is felt as soon as tissue damage is sensed, is sharp and stabbing and is known as acute pain. Its impulses travel extremely quickly to the brain along special nerve fibres, called A-fibres, that have myelin sheaths to speed the impulses along.

The purpose of acute pain is to bring about an immediate, subconscious, reaction, to

remove the body from the danger; A-fibre impulses cause a hand to be moved out of a flame, for example.

After some time, acute pain dies down and is replaced by the second type: the dull, throbbing, aching, persistent feeling that characterizes chronic pain. The impulses of chronic pain come from sensory receptors deeper in the tissues, and they travel 10 times more slowly that those of acute pain along unmyelinated nerve fibres called C-fibres.

*People suffering from serious chronic pain, such as this cancer patient, may need intravenous painkilling drugs. These work by suppressing the C-fibre impulses.*

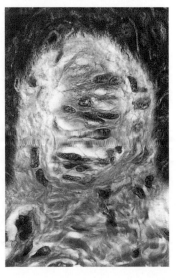

*Meissner's corpuscles, one of which is shown here, transmit signals along myelinated nerve fibres. Acute pain signals also travel along myelinated fibres.*

# Pain inhibition

The body has three pain relief systems: each depends on
preventing nerve impulses from reaching the higher levels of the brain
by blocking them at the spinal relays or lower brain levels.

The first, and most simple, pain relief system is best summed up as 'rubbing it better'. However, this phrase disguises a complex sequence of events.

Two nerves join at the relay station in the spine, the junction of the two being called a synapse. One nerve carries signals from the sensory nerve endings, and the other carries them up the spine to the brain. Neurologists think of the synapse as a gate: normally it is shut, but strong impulses, as in acute pain can force it open.

However, the synapse is only open to one type of pathway at a time. This is why A-fibre impulses, which travel faster, reach the synapse before C-fibre

impulses and block them out until they have themselves died down. But if a painful area is rubbed vigorously, A-fibre impulses are generated, and again they reach the synapse first, blocking out the slower C-fibre impulses. As a result, the aching, chronic pain is relieved.

## CHEMICAL BLOCK
The second system depends on blocking the passage of nerve impulses by chemical means. In response to pain signals, the brain produces chemicals called endorphins. These are the body's own painkillers, and they block receptors in the brain stem and thalamus, and block the gates in the spinal relays. Heroin and morphine are painkillers because they block the same receptors.

## SUPPRESSION
Finally, the brain can send impulses down the spinal cord to suppress pain signals at the spinal relay. This is most apparent when pain is extreme, when, for example, a soldier is fighting for his life or an athlete is pushed to the limits.

## PAIN TOLERANCE
How much pain is felt is determined by the quantity of endorphins (pain-relieving chemicals in the brain). Exercise increases endorphin levels, as does relaxation, a positive mental outlook and

*This second-degree burn was caused by boiling fat. Pain from such injuries is acute at first, becoming chronic for several days afterwards.*

sleep. In contrast, fear, depression, anxiety, lack of exercise and concentrating on pain all reduce endorphin levels. The fewer endorphins there are, the more pain is felt.

*A natural and subconscious response is to rub a painful area, particularly when muscles are affected. Physiologically, the action of rubbing works effectively to ease discomfort.*

## Referred pain

Sometimes pain is felt in an area that is not in fact the source of the pain, and in such cases the sensation is called referred pain. Examples of this include pain from the area of the diaphragm, which can be felt at the tip the shoulder, and pain from the heart – as in angina – which is felt across the chest, in the neck and along the inner side of the arm.

There are two explanations for this phenomenon. First, tissues which originate

*Referred pain that affects the ear is very common. The cause is often found to be tooth-related, such as abscesses or impaction, or associated with the larynx or pharynx (tonsillitis, for example).*

from the same embryological building block – that is, they come from the same area of basic tissue in a fetus as it develops inside the uterus – often share the same spinal relays, so activity in one part of the relay triggers activity in another part of the same relay. Second, there can be so many nerve impulses from an internal organ that they flood the pathways normally reserved for other areas of the body.

Doctors often check for referred pain as part of the diagnosis of a disorder that affects the internal organs. This is often somewhat of a surprise to the patient, who perhaps cannot understand why the main source of their discomfort (that is, the source of the pain) is being ignored during an investigation.

# How memory works

Memory is the brain's ability to store and access information.
Short-term memory stores only small amounts of information, while
greater amounts of data are kept in long-term memory.

Memory is the ability to store and retrieve information. Remembering is a vital function, since learning, thought and reasoning could not occur without it. We learn not to touch hot objects, for example, from a very early age as we remember that they burn us, causing pain. In addition, our memories, the sum of our experiences, play a huge part in the development of our personalities.

### BRAIN
Memory is regarded as a function of the brain, often likened to the way in which a computer stores and processes information.

Whereas a computer can only store one billion bits of information, however, the brain can store up to 100 trillion. Moreover, the word 'store' is misleading, as, unlike a computer, there is no single centre in which memories are filed away. Remembering appears to be a function of many parts of the brain, rather than any one structure.

### MEMORY INPUT
The storage of memory is very complex, and our sensory experiences suggest that there may be many different kinds of memory: visual (sight), auditory

(hearing), olfactory (smell), gustatory (taste) and tactile (touch).

Information is never presented in one simple form, but tends to be embedded in a complex context – we know from daily experience how important context and associations are for effective memorizing. For

example, a single item of information conveyed to us by speech will be set in the context of other data such as the speaker's face, voice and displays of emotion.

### TWO FORMS
There are two forms of memory: short-term and long-term. Short-term memory stores small

*Individuals carry with them a huge amount of information which has been amassed over the years. This data is stored in the long-term memory.*

amounts of information and the contents are quickly lost. Long-term memory stores larger quantities of information.

## Short-term memory

Research has shown that the short-term memory is able to hold around five to seven items at a time for a maximum of one minute.

For example, you are able to remember a telephone number while you dial the number. However, if the number is engaged and you redial, you will have to look up the number again – the result of having no memory trace for it in the brain.

The reason for this inability to remember in the short term is that complex data cannot be stored the moment it is perceived. It appears that some

*If an individual is dialling a telephone number for the first time, they remember it only briefly. Short-term memory can only store a few items at a time.*

form of analysis and selection process is necessary for the brain to determine which information is assimilated, and which is discarded. It seems that this process cannot occur without first storing the data temporarily.

### CONSOLIDATION
To last, a memory has to be recorded via the short-term memory first, before being consolidated. This process requires repetition or study, and usually classification (organization into a category of related items).

Consolidation moves a fact from the short-term memory to long-term storage. Consolidation is believed to result in an alteration in the structure of the brain, as a memory trace is formed.

# Long-term memory

Large amounts of information are carried in the long-term memory. This data is stored and accessed through large collections of nerve cells located within the brain – the amygdala and hippocampus.

Every individual carries an immeasurable amount of data, often preserved for life in the long-term memory. It is now known exactly where in the brain sensory data must pass in order to be stored in the memory.

### CEREBRAL HEMISPHERES
The interface circuits, through which long-term memory is recorded and recalled, are located in large structures on the inner surfaces of the temporal lobes of each cerebral hemisphere of the brain.

These huge collections of nerve cells are known as the amygdala and the hippocampus, and together they make up the limbic system. Both structures are connected to all the sensory areas of the cortex (outer layer of the brain), and damage to these structures, for example

through a stroke or brain trauma, will lead to profound memory loss.

### MEMORY SITES
The exact physical basis for the long-term memory is unknown. There is evidence, however, that the sites of memory are the same as the areas of the brain in which the corresponding sensory impressions are processed in the cortex.

It appears that, during recall, the amygdala and the hippocampus play back the neurological activity that occurs during sensory activity to the appropriate part of the cerebral cortex.

*The amygdala and hippocampus are structures in the brain associated with memory. They convert new information into long-term memories.*

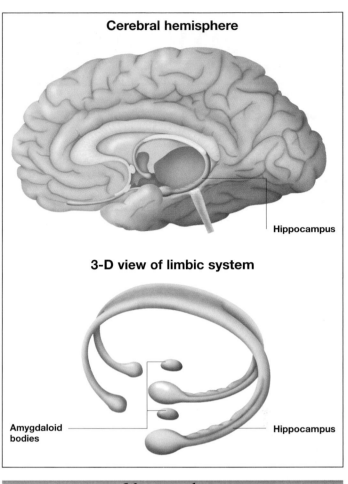

**Cerebral hemisphere**

**Hippocampus**

**3-D view of limbic system**

**Amygdaloid bodies**

**Hippocampus**

---

## Amnesia

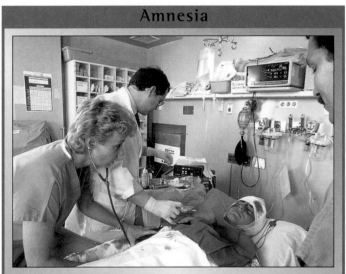

Amnesia is a failure to remember recent or past events. Most cases are caused by physical damage to the brain, although in rare instances it may be induced by emotional trauma, whereby an experience is too painful to remember.

### Two types
Amnesia may take one of two forms:
■ Retrograde amnesia – this is most commonly caused by a blow to the head. The patient fails to remember what happened several hours prior to the accident, as the brain did

*Patients with head injuries may experience amnesia. This can affect memories before (retrograde) or after (anterograde) the incident.*

not have the chance to process that information.
■ Anterograde amnesia – this is caused by damage to the hippocampus, whereby memory of events occurring after the injury is impaired. Memory of the past remains intact, but everyday life becomes very difficult since the patient has no recollection of events from one moment to the next.

## Memory loss

Most of us have no recollection of the first few years of our lives, after which time memories are fragmented and vague until we reach the age of around 10. This is probably because, in the first few years of life, the brain is not yet developed enough to process and store information.

### DEGENERATION
Likewise, in the latter years of life, the brain undergoes a natural degeneration, and so memory may become impaired.

Interestingly, in older people, it is the short-term memory that is usually affected. For example, an older person may be able to

remember the exact details of a journey made 50 years before, but may be unable to recall what they did yesterday. This is because the ability to process new information often declines with age due to physical and chemical changes in the brain. Moreover, the regular recollection of long-term memories sharpens them, leaving a permanent memory trace in the brain.

*Older people often have a good memory for past events, but have trouble recalling more recent memories. This is due to age-related changes in the brain.*

# How we feel emotion

External stimuli received through the senses arrive in the brain as nervous impulses. Their emotional significance is determined by the limbic system before producing a physiological response.

Experiencing an emotion involves a combination of physical and mental processes, which produce both physiological and psychological sensations.

### RESPONDING TO STIMULI
To a large extent emotion is produced in response to external stimuli. The emotion experienced depends on the nature of stimuli and the individual's interpretation of those stimuli.

The physical aspects of emotional experience can be divided into two main elements:
■ The neurological processes produced by environmental or psychological stimuli
■ The physiological arousal that results from the stimuli.

### ROLE OF THE AMYGDALA
Nervous impulses from the senses arrive in the brain at the thalamus, a mid-brain structure, where they are processed and passed on in a number of ways. Their emotional significance is believed to be determined by the limbic system within the brain, and in particular by the amygdala, an almond-shaped structure near the brainstem.

The amygdala assigns emotional content and value to incoming stimulus to provide a rapid initial assessment of its significance. This helps to determine quickly whether something is dangerous. The stimulus of encountering someone unexpectedly in a dark room, for instance, is labelled by the amygdala as a potential threat, and so produces an initial emotional response of fear.

### ROLE OF THE CORTEX
Higher brain centres in the cortex can override the amygdala, integrating data from other sources, such as memory and context, to make a more accurate and considered determination of emotional significance.

In the example above, the cortex uses memory to identify the encountered person as a friend, and overrides the initial amygdala-produced emotion.

*Emotional reactions may be complicated by culture or context. Emotions stimulated by fictional events, as in the theatre, produce real physical responses.*

## Physiology of emotion

*A lie detector test operates on the presumption that telling lies produces a stress response in the person talking. This can be identified by physical changes.*

Physiological processes are responsible for what are known as the visceral sensations involved in emotion. These include responses such as dry mouth, dilated pupils or unsettled stomach.

One purpose of emotion is to elicit an active response, and these visceral sensations are part of the process by which emotion readies the body for a physical response. For example, a stimulus that causes fear will also prepare the body to act on that fear.

### THE ENDOCRINE SYSTEM
The level and type of physiological arousal is determined by the autonomic nervous system (ANS). This in turn is regulated by the endocrine system as it releases hormones in response to emotional triggers. These hormones produce many of the visceral sensations associated with emotion. Two of the most important hormones in this context are adrenaline and noradrenaline, which set up the sympathetic division of the ANS for a 'fight or flight' response.

### PATTERNS OF AROUSAL
Hormones produce widespread physiological sensations that are common to different types of emotion. Specific emotions, however, produce more specific patterns of physiological arousal according to their effect on another type of chemical messenger: neurotransmitters.

These work in conjunction with hormones to produce a range of distinctive response patterns, each with its own heart rate, finger temperature, galvanic skin response (electrical conductivity of skin) and so on.

# Psychological and cultural factors

**More complex emotions, such as shame, involve input from brain centres that control learning and memory. Cultural factors also affect the final response.**

Emotion involves more than just visceral sensations. As a subjective experience, emotion is as much psychological as it is physiological. Experiments show that drugs or hormones can produce the physiological correlates of emotional arousal, without producing the conscious sensation of emotion.

In particular, more complex, less visceral emotions, such as guilt, involve more input from higher brain centres and processes such as learning, memory and self-image.

## CONTEXT AND CULTURE

Factors that influence the psychology of emotion include context and culture. For instance, in the context of a theme-park ride, 'scary' stimuli can produce a mixture of terror and pleasure.

Cultural influence on emotions includes culture-specific emotions, such as the Chinese 'sad love'. Whereas in the West love is characterized as a positive emotion, in China love is not always positive and can be a negative or mixed emotion.

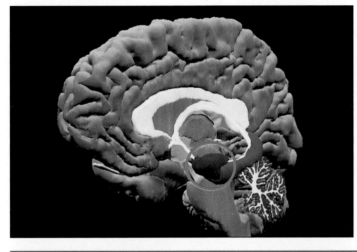

*Nervous impulses send external stimuli from the senses to the brain. Part of the limbic system, the amygdala (circled), then determines the response.*

*A roller-coaster ride produces a variety of emotional responses. Our higher brain centres intervene to determine whether the experience is fun or terrifying.*

## Expression of emotion

It has long been believed that some emotions are physically linked to the way they are expressed, especially in terms of the muscular activity of facial expression. To put it simply, some emotions and facial expressions are 'hard-wired' together.

This has led in turn to the belief that the process can be reversed, and that adopting an expression can induce a particular emotion.

For example, it has been found that smiling primes individuals to interpret stimuli as more positive. Suggested mechanisms to explain this finding include:
■ Smiling induces the release of endorphins (naturally occurring mood-enhancing opiates)
■ Some sort of feedback effect occurs with smiling that primes the brain centres involved with happiness and positive emotions.

**Brain hemispheres**
The two hemispheres of the brain play different roles in the recognition of faces, facial expressions and even the recognition and experience of positive and negative emotions.
For instance:
■ Some areas of the left hemisphere are specialized for the recognition and processing of positive emotions, such as happiness
■ Some areas of the right hemisphere are specialized for negative emotions, such as sadness and fear.

*The face on the left is a mirror image of that on the right but is perceived as happier. This is because of the way that the hemispheres process emotion.*

Brain damage can impair the experience of some emotions and exaggerate others. Left-hemisphere damage can produce excessive fear or depression, while on the right, damage can produce uncontrollable laughter or mania. Clinically depressed people may show reduced function in the left frontal lobe.

This hemispheric lateralization can be demonstrated by looking at the picture below. Which face looks happier?

Most people choose the left-hand picture. This is because in the left-hand picture the smiley face appears in the left visual field of the observer, and is therefore processed primarily by the right hemisphere, where recognition of expression primarily occurs. The faces are actually mirror images of each other.

# How laughter occurs

Laughter is the body's response to happiness and comprises both gestures and sound. Although laughter is not essential to survival, it is thought to act as a type of relief mechanism.

Laughter is a physiological response to happiness and humour and appears to be a distinctly human response. It consists of two components: a set of gestures and the production of sound. When a person finds something humorous, the brain triggers both of these responses to occur simultaneously, at the same time causing changes to occur throughout the body.

### FACIAL MUSCLES
Laughter involves the contraction of 15 facial muscles as well as stimulation of the zygomatic major muscle, which causes the upper lip to lift. Meanwhile, the epiglottis partially blocks the larynx, resulting in irregular air intake and causing a person to gasp. In extreme cases the tear ducts may be activated, causing tears of laughter to stream down the face. A person may even turn red in the face as they continue to gasp for air.

### RANGE OF NOISES
A range of characteristic noises, which range from a gentle giggle to a loud guffaw, accompanies this response. In fact, research into the sonic structure of laughter (the pattern of sound waves produced when a person laughs) shows that all human laughter consists of varying patterns of a basic form, which is short vowel-like notes repeated every 210 milliseconds. It has also been revealed that laughter triggers other neural circuits in the brain, which in turn generate more laughter. This explains why laughter can be contagious.

*The average person laughs around 17 times a day. Laughter clubs (one in Bombay shown) encourage people to get together and laugh.*

## The role of laughter

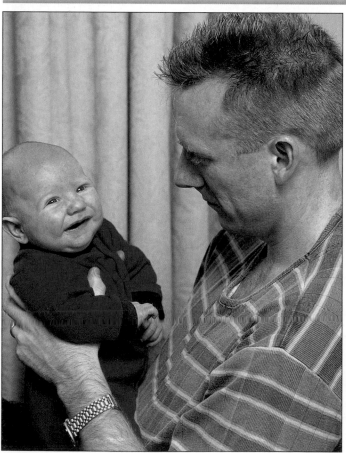

*Smiling and laughter may be a sign of trust in a friend or relative. Babies often communicate with their parents by smiling and laughing.*

As with much of human behaviour, it is difficult to determine the exact purpose of laughter, although there appear to be a variety of physical and psychological benefits. Many theories suggest that laughter may have evolved as a relief mechanism, whereby our ancestors would use laughter as a gesture of shared relief at the passing of danger. What is more, because laughter inhibits the 'fight or flight' response – designed to protect the body in danger – laughter may also indicate trust in a companion.

### COMMUNICATION
In this way, many scientists believe that the purpose of laughter is one of communication, a social signal that strengthens human connections. Research by cultural anthropologists demonstrates that people tend to laugh together when they feel comfortable with each other, and that the more people laugh together, the greater the bonding between them. Interestingly, research shows that people are 30 times more likely to laugh in a group than when alone and that even the use of nitrous oxide (laughing gas) elicits less laughter when taken in solitude.

### RESULTS OF STUDIES
Studies have also shown that laughter conforms to a social hierarchy whereby dominant individuals tend to use humour more than their subordinates; for example, when a boss laughs it is not uncommon for all his or her employees to laugh too. By controlling the emotional climate of the group, the boss exercises power.

In fact, it appears that laughter, like most human behaviour, has evolved as a means of influencing the behaviour of others. Studies have shown that in an embarrassing or threatening situation, laughter may serve as a conciliatory gesture and a means to deflect anger. If a threatening person can be made to laugh, then the risk of confrontation is reduced.

## The role of the brain in laughter

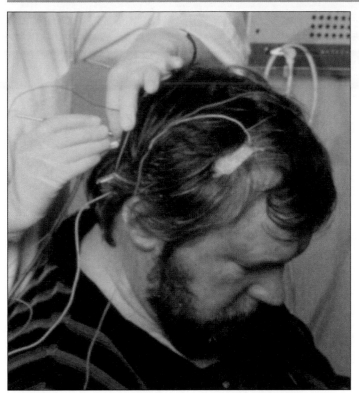

Gelotology is the study of the physiological responses that occur during laughter, and much research has been conducted to work out how laughter is triggered. While other emotional responses seem to be confined to one part of the brain (frontal lobe), laughter appears to involve a circuit running through several brain areas.

### EEG RESEARCH
This has been demonstrated by research in which human subjects were connected to an electroencephalograph (EEG) (an instrument that allows the electrical activity of the brain to be measured). The subjects were then told a joke and the consequent electrical activity of their brains was observed.

*An EEG can help to study response to laughter. When subjects are connected to an EEG and told a joke, the brain's electrical activity is measured.*

Within less than a second, a wave of electrical activity was seen to pass through the cerebral cortex (the largest part of the brain). It was found that if this wave had a negative charge then laughter resulted, but if it was positive, laughter did not occur.

### ELECTRICAL ACTIVITY
The electrical activity of the brain during laughter appears to take the following path:
**1** The left side of the cortex (the layer of cells that covers the surface of the forebrain) is stimulated as the structure of the joke is analysed
**2** The frontal lobe, usually involved with emotional responses, is activated
**3** The right hemisphere of the cortex is stimulated – intellectual analysis of the joke occurs here, determining whether or not the joke is funny
**4** The sensory processing area of the occipital lobe (the area located at the back of the head that is associated with the processing of visual signals) is activated as nerve impulses from the right hemisphere are interpreted and converted into a sensory response

**5** Various motor sections (responsible for movement) of the brain are stimulated causing a physical response to the joke.

### THE LIMBIC SYSTEM
As with any emotional response, the limbic system in the brain appears to be central to laughter. The limbic system is a network of complex structures that lies beneath the cerebral cortex, and controls behaviour that is essential to survival.

While this area of the brain in other animals is heavily involved in defending territory and hunting, in humans it has evolved to become more involved in emotional behaviour and memory.

### EMOTIONAL RESPONSE
Indeed, research has shown that the amygdala. which controls anxiety and fear, and the hippocampus, which plays a role in learning and memory, seem to be the main areas of the brain involved with emotional responses.

The amygdala interacts with the hippocampus and thalamus (the part of the brain that relays information from the senses to the cortex), playing a key role in the expression of emotions.

In addition, the hypothalamus has been identified by researchers as a major contributor to the production of loud, uncontrollable laughter.

## The benefits of laughter

*Laughter is more than an expression of happiness; it can actually promote health. Here, a stroke patient and speech therapist laugh together.*

While people have always known that laughter makes them feel good, there is now scientific evidence that it promotes health in a number of ways.

**Health benefits**
Laughter has many benefits for the general health of an individual. These include:
■ Immune system – laughter inhibits the 'fight or flight' response, by reducing levels of certain stress hormones responsible. This is beneficial to health since these hormones suppress the immune system and raise blood pressure. Laughter actually boosts the immune system by causing an increase in white blood cells
■ Blood pressure – laughter lowers the blood pressure, while increasing vascular blood flow and oxygenation of the blood. This in turn aids healing
■ Saliva – laughter leads to increased production of salivary immunoglobulin A, which helps to prevent pathogens (disease-causing organisms) invading the body via the respiratory tract
■ Exercise – it has been estimated that laughing 100 times is the equivalent of 15 minutes' workout on an exercise bike. Laughter exercises the diaphragm and abdominal, respiratory, facial, leg and back muscles, which explains why people often feel exhausted after laughing a lot
■ Mental health – laughter provides a way for negative emotions, such as anger or frustration, to be released. Ever since the pioneering work of Patch Adams (a physician who recognized the benefits of humour when treating patients) doctors have become increasingly aware of the therapeutic benefits of laughter.

# How we sleep

The body enters an altered state of consciousness during sleep.
While it used to be believed that the sole function of sleep was rest,
studies show that the brain is far from inactive during this time.

Sleep is defined as a state of relative unconsciousness and reduced body movement. Unlike coma, subjects can be aroused from sleep by external stimulation. Relatively little is known as to the exact function of the phenomenon of sleep, despite the fact that the average person spends around a third of their lifetime asleep.

### RESTORATIVE FUNCTION
In the past it was believed that sleep served a restorative function only. More recently however, sleep studies with electroencephalography (using electrodes attached to the head which measure the electrical activity of the brain) suggest otherwise. While motor activity is inhibited by sleep, it seems the brain is far from inactive during this time. Although the functioning of the conscious part of the brain is depressed, brain stem functions such as control of respiration, heart rate, and blood pressure are maintained.

### PHYSIOLOGICAL CHANGES
While sleeping, humans close their eyes, and adopt a sleeping posture – typically lying down. Hormonal changes cause heart, respiration, and breathing rates to slow down. In addition, digestive activity is reduced and urine concentrated to allow a period of uninterrupted sleep.

*In sleep the sensory part of the brain is depressed. However, we are still aware of external stimuli which is why we can be woken.*

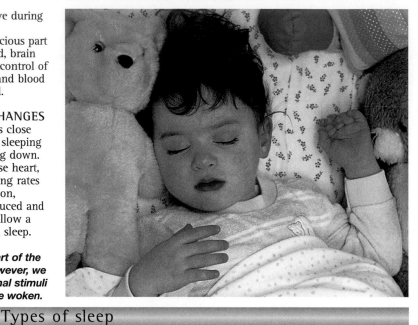

## Types of sleep

By monitoring brain activity, scientists have identified two states of sleep. These are referred to as non-rapid eye movement (NREM) sleep and rapid eye movement (REM) sleep. These alternate throughout the night and serve very different roles.

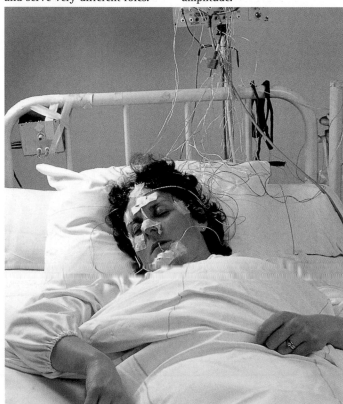

### NREM SLEEP
During the first 45 minutes of sleep, the body passes through four stages of deeper and deeper NREM sleep. This is seen as a decline in the frequency of brain waves, but an increase in their amplitude.

The four stages of NREM sleep are:
■ First stage – the eyes are closed and relaxation begins. Conscious thoughts begin to drift. At this stage arousal is immediate if the body is stimulated
■ Second stage – the EEG becomes more irregular, and arousal becomes more difficult
■ Third stage – as the body slips into this stage the skeletal muscles begin to relax and dreaming is common
■ Fourth and final stage – (slow wave sleep) the body relaxes completely and arousal is difficult. Bedwetting and sleepwalking may occur during this stage.

### REM SLEEP
Around an hour after sleep begins the EEG pattern changes, becoming irregular and more frequent, indicating the onset of REM sleep. This change in brain activity is accompanied by an increase in body temperature, heart rate, respiratory rate and blood pressure and a decrease in digestive activity.

The brain pattern seen during

*Studies of brain activity during sleep reveal two main stages. During REM sleep the brain is very active, and respiration rates increase.*

this stage of sleep is more typical of the awake state, although the body actually respires more oxygen during this phase of sleep, than when awake.

Typically during this phase, the eyes move rapidly beneath the eyelids, although the rest of the body muscles are inhibited and go limp, resulting in a temporary paralysis designed to prevent us from acting out our dreams. REM sleep makes up around 20 per cent of adult sleep.

### DREAMS
Most dreaming occurs during REM sleep. It is hardest to wake somebody during this stage of sleep, although sleepers can wake spontaneously during this time – and will be more likely to remember the details of their dream if they do so.

### CHEMICAL MESSENGERS
In addition to changes in brain wave patterns during sleep, there are changes in levels of neurotransmitters (the chemical messengers secreted by the brain). Noradrenaline levels decline and serotonin levels rise. This is because noradrenaline is responsible for maintaining alertness, while serotonin is thought to function as a sleep neurotransmitter.

# The role of sleep

Sleep allows the skeletal muscles to relax and our energy levels to be replenished. The amount of sleep the body requires differs among individuals.

The most obvious role of sleep appears to be physical restoration. While we sleep, our muscles relax, allowing them to rest. The body requires more sleep after great physical exertion, or illness.

### BRAIN ACTIVITY
Slow wave sleep appears to be the restorative stage of sleep, when most neural mechanisms wind down. Sleep deprivation studies, in which subjects are woken each time they reach a certain stage of sleep, reveal that when continually deprived of REM sleep, subjects become moody and depressed, and exhibit personality disorders.

Many theories exist regarding the function of brain activity during sleep. The most likely theory is that REM sleep gives the brain the opportunity to analyse the day's events, discarding useless information, processing useful information and working through emotional problems in dream imagery.

*During REM sleep, brain activity increases considerably. This is thought to be a time when the brain assimilates useful information learnt that day.*

## Sleep requirements

Sleep requirements and patterns change throughout our lives. While a baby can require as much as 16 hours sleep every day, the average adult will only require seven hours.

In old age, the amount of sleep required declines considerably, with people over 60 years requiring shorter spells of sleep, although these tend to be taken more frequently. Elderly people are more likely to take naps during the day.

### SLEEP PATTERNS
Sleep patterns also change throughout life: the amount of REM sleep declines from birth, and often disappears completely in people over 60.

This is the reason why many older people sleep more lightly and commonly wake up more frequently in the night. This is because they are not able to attain the profound depths of REM sleep.

*Sleep requirements vary from person to person, and with age. Elderly people require shorter, more frequent spells of sleep, and often nap during the day.*

## Sleep disorders

Although the exact role that sleep fulfils is not entirely known, it is clearly essential to our mental and physical well-being.

#### Insomnia
Insomniacs suffer from an inability to obtain a sufficient amount or quality of sleep needed to function adequately during the daytime. With prolonged lack of sleep, insomniacs show signs of fatigue, impaired ability to concentrate and carry out everyday tasks and, in some cases, paranoia.

Insomnia can be caused by unfavourable surroundings (noisy neighbours or an uncomfortable bed); physical ailments, such as those causing breathlessness or pain; or an irregular sleep pattern (caused by jet lag or working night shifts). The most common cause of insomnia, however, is psychological disturbance such as anxiety, or depression.

#### Narcolepsy
Narcolepsy is the complete opposite of insomnia. Sufferers have little control over their sleep patterns, and can lapse into deep sleep spontaneously during waking hours. These episodes of unconsciousness last between 5 and 15 minutes and can occur without warning at any time.

This condition can be very hazardous, for example when the sufferer is taking a bath, or operating machinery. The cause of narcolepsy is not understood, although it seems to arise from an inability to inhibit REM, or dreaming sleep. Most people sleep for some time before falling into a deep sleep, but narcoleptics appear to enter REM as soon as they close their eyes.

*Insomnia is a condition in which the sufferer does not have enough quality sleep. The cause is often psychological.*

# How we dream

Around a fifth of time asleep is spent dreaming, although many people claim not to remember their dreams. The mental activity involved in dreaming is very different from that of waking thought.

Although many people claim not to dream, sleep studies have revealed that the average adult spends around 20 per cent of their sleep in a state of dream activity.

### WHAT ARE DREAMS?
Dreams result from a form of mental activity that is very different from waking thought.

A dream is a series of images, thoughts and sensations conjured up by the mind during sleep. Dreams can take the form of pleasant fantasies, everyday scenarios or terrifying nightmares.

### DREAM STUDIES
In-depth studies, in which subjects are monitored throughout sleep and woken during dreaming phases and questioned about their dreams, reveal much about the nature of dream activity.

It appears that most dreams are perceptual rather than conceptual – meaning that things are seen and heard rather than thought. In other words, in our dreams we often appear to be an onlooker witnessing events as opposed to conducting them and reflecting upon them.

### SENSORY EXPERIENCE
In terms of the senses, visual experience is present in almost all dreams and auditory (hearing) experience in around 40 to 50 per cent of dreams. In comparison the remaining senses – touch, taste and smell – feature in only a small percentage of dreams.

### EMOTIONS
The overriding feature of all dreams tends to be a single and strong emotion such as fear, anger or joy, rather than the integrated range of subtle emotions experienced during the waking state.

Most dreams are composed of interrupted stories, partly made up from memories and fragmented scenes. Dreams can range from the very mundane to the truly bizarre.

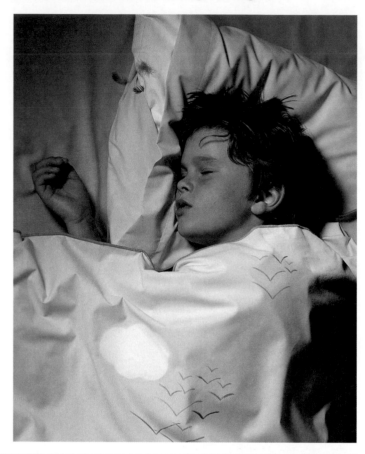

*During sleep the brain conjures up the scenarios we know as dreams. They tend to be composed of vivid visual images and, often, strong emotions.*

## When do dreams occur?

Research in recent years has revealed that two clearly distinguishable states of sleep exist: non-rapid eye movement sleep (NREM) and rapid eye movement sleep (REM).

NREM sleep makes up the greater part of our sleeping time, and is associated with a relatively low pulse and blood pressure and little activation of the autonomic nervous system.

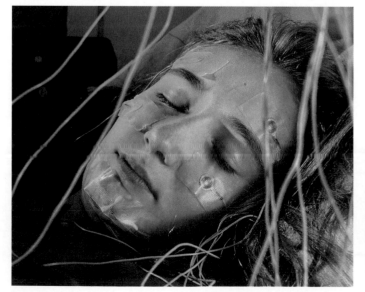

Very few dreams are reported during this state of sleep, and tend to be more like thoughts rather than vivid images.

REM sleep occurs cyclically during the sleep period and is characterized by increased conscious brain activity, the eyes moving rapidly from side to side

*Sleep studies reveal that most dreams occur during the REM stage of sleep. This stage is associated with rapid movement of the eyes beneath the lids.*

beneath the eyelids, and frequent reports of dreams.

Typically a person will have four or five periods of REM sleep during the night, although usually only a single dream may be remembered the following morning if at all.

REM sleep occurs at intervals of about 90 minutes and makes up around 20 per cent of the night's sleep. Evidence from dream studies suggests that dream periods last for around 5 to 20 minutes.

## Sleepwalking

When we sleep, our muscles become very relaxed, with the result that the body becomes temporarily paralysed. This is designed to prevent the body from acting out our dreams.

In some people this mechanism does not work quite so effectively and sleepers can become active while dreaming, sometimes to the point of walking in a semi-conscious state. This phenomenon is known as somnambulism, or sleepwalking.

Sleepwalkers can often perform tasks and even hold conversations. Very often they will have no recollection at all of what happened during the night.

# Brain activity while dreaming

When we dream, the limbic system (the part of the brain associated with emotions, senses and long-term memory) is active, while the forebrain (associated with short-term memory and intelligence) is inactive. This may explain the nature of our dreams.

Recent studies using positron emission tomography (PET) scanning, which can be used to measure blood flow to the brain, indicate that different parts of the brain are active when we dream and when we are awake.

### PREFRONTAL CORTEX
During the normal waking state the prefrontal cortex – the front part of the brain – is the most active (indicated by increased blood flow to this area on a PET scan). This part of the brain is responsible for our conscious thought, intelligence, reasoning and short-term memory.

### LIMBIC SYSTEM
Studies show that during REM sleep the prefrontal cortex of the brain is completely inactive, while the limbic system – the part of the brain that controls emotions, senses and long-term memory – is most active.

It appears that this could account for the heightened emotions experienced during REM dreams, as well as the retrieval of long-term memories (often our dreams can transport us back to events that occurred some time ago).

The fact that short-term memory is de-activated may also account for the bizarre content of dreams – the scene changes, fragmented narratives, and people's identities which seemingly melt into one another.

It may also account for the fact that many people cannot remember their dreams once they awake.

### VISUAL IMAGES
PET studies have also revealed that the primary visual cortex – the part of the brain used to see when we are awake – is inactive during sleep. Instead a different visual area, called the extrastriate, is active.

The extrastriate is the visual area that is responsible for the recognition of complex objects like faces and emotions. This could explain the vivid visual images typical of most dreams.

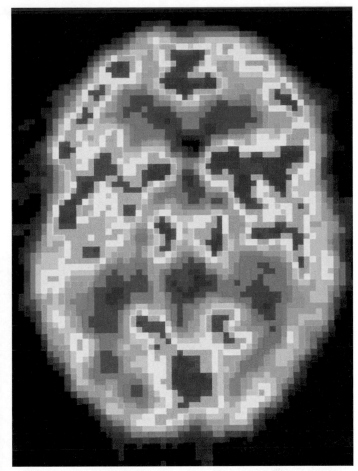

*The content of our dreams often seems utterly disconnected from the real world. We dream about situations and scenarios that could never occur in real life.*

*PET studies reveal that different parts of the brain are active during dreaming and when awake. This may explain the strange nature of many dreams.*

## Role of dreams

Throughout history the role of dreams has attracted many different theories. Ancient cultures placed much importance on dreams, believing that they were spiritual in origin and could even predict the future.

**Subconscious expression**
The psychologist Sigmund Freud believed that dreams represented a 'road to the subconscious' and were an expression of repressed (usually sexual) desires.

Today, many psychoanalysts use the recounting of dreams as a part of clinical treatment.

*It has long been thought that dreams are an expression of the subconscious. Analysis of dreams is often used as a technique by psychoanalysts.*

Dreams may express important wishes or fears of the dreamer, and the analysis of dreams can provide great insight into a person's mental functioning.

**Dreams and brain function**
A more recent theory suggests that dreams are directly linked to the long-term memory system. Research has been carried out in which subjects who were deprived of REM sleep found it more difficult to learn new information, which appears to support this theory.

Also some studies show that REM sleep increases when we are trying to learn a new or difficult task. This suggests that information in the short-term memory is transferred to the long-term memory as we dream.

# How the body responds to exercise

During exercise, the body's physiological needs change in certain characteristic ways. Exercising muscle requires an increase in the supply of oxygen and energy, which must be met by the body.

The body needs energy for everyday activities. This energy is produced as the body burns food. However, when exercising, the muscles of the body require more energy than at rest.

To exercise for a brief period, a sprint to the bus stop for example, the body is capable of increasing the supply of energy to the muscles quickly. The body can do this because it has a small amount of stored oxygen and is able to respire anaerobically (producing energy without using oxygen).

The need for energy increases when exercising for a longer period. Muscles must be supplied with more oxygen to allow aerobic respiration (producing energy by using oxygen).

## CARDIAC ACTIVITY

Our heart beats about 70 to 80 times a minute at rest; this can rise to 160 beats per minute after exercise, the heart also beating with a greater force. Thus, a normal person can increase their cardiac output a little over fourfold, while a trained athlete can increase output about sixfold.

## VASCULAR ACTIVITY

At rest, blood flows through the heart at a rate of about five litres a minute; during exercise, blood circulates at a rate of 25 or even 30 litres a minute.

This bloodflow is directed towards active muscle, which needs it most. This is achieved by reducing the supply of blood to areas of the body with less need, and by widening blood vessels to allow greater bloodflow to active muscles.

## RESPIRATORY ACTIVITY

Circulating blood must be fully oxygenated (saturated with oxygen), so the rate of breathing must also increase. The lungs fill with more oxygen, which can be passed to the blood.

During exercise, the rate at which air enters the lungs increases to as high as 100 litres a minute. This is vastly greater than the six litres per minute which we breathe at rest.

*A marathon runner achieves 40 per cent greater cardiac output than an untrained person. Through training, heart mass and chamber size increase.*

## Changes in the heart's activity

### Effects of exercise on the heart

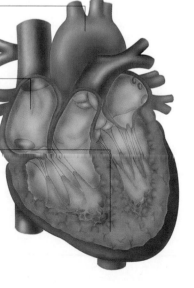

**Aorta**
Supplies blood to all muscles; supply to heart muscle must also increase

**Right atrium**
Volume and pressure of blood returning to the heart from the veins increases

**Ventricular muscle**
Stimulated via nerves to the heart's pacemaker to pump more rapidly

*Strenuous exercise causes a number of circulatory changes. It is very demanding on the heart muscle itself.*

During exercise, the heart rate (beats per minute) and cardiac output (volume pumped per minute) increase. This is due to increased activity of the nerves that supply the heart causing the heart to beat more quickly.

### INCREASED VENOUS RETURN

The amount of blood returning to the heart increases due to:
■ Reduced resistance of vessels in the muscle bed due to dilation
■ Muscle action (contraction and relaxation), which pumps more blood back to the heart
■ Chest movements of rapid

*Much research has been done into circulatory changes during exercise. This research shows that the more we exercise, the greater these changes will be.*

breathing, which also have a pumping effect
■ Constriction of the veins, forcing blood back to the heart.

As the ventricles in the heart become increasingly full, the muscular walls of the heart are stretched and work with greater power. Thus, a higher volume of blood is expelled from the heart.

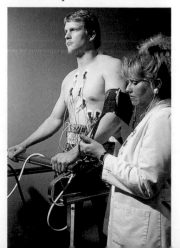

# Circulatory changes

When we exercise, our body experiences an increase in the bloodflow to the muscles. This ensures a ready supply of oxygen and other essential nutrients.

Even before muscles begin to contract in exercise, the bloodflow to them can be increased through brain signals.

### DILATION OF VESSELS
Nerve signals, carried by the sympathetic nervous system, cause blood vessels in the muscle bed to dilate (widen), allowing more blood to flow to muscle cells. However, to keep the vessels dilated, after this initial change, local changes occur. These include decreased levels of oxygen and a rise in carbon dioxide and other waste products of respiration in muscle tissue.

Increased temperature, caused by excessive heat produced by active muscles, also leads to vessel dilation.

### CONSTRICTION OF VESSELS
In addition to these changes in the muscle bed, blood is diverted from other tissues and organs of the body which have less need for blood during exercise activity.

Nervous impulses cause vasoconstriction (narrowing of the blood vessels) in these areas, particularly the gut. This causes blood to be redirected to those areas where it is most needed, making it available to be fed into muscles in the next cycle of circulation.

*The increased bloodflow to muscles during exercise is particularly dramatic in fit young adults. The increase can be more than 20-fold.*

## Respiratory changes

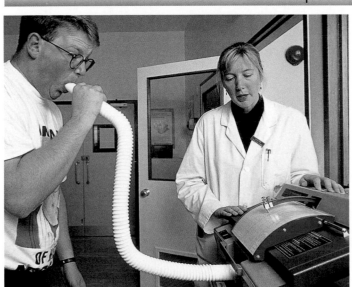

During exercise the body uses far more oxygen than it normally would, and the respiratory system must respond to the need by increasing the rate of ventilation. Although our breathing rate increases rapidly with the onset of exercise, the precise mechanism is uncertain.

As the body uses up more oxygen and produces more carbon dioxide, receptors in our bodies, which can detect changes in blood gas levels, may stimulate breathing. However, our reaction occurs

*In order to meet the demands of increased muscular activity, the body will require more oxygen. For this reason, exercise leads to an increased breathing rate.*

far earlier than any chemical change that can be detected. This indicates that it is a learned response which causes us to send a signal to our lungs to increase the rate of breathing, whenever we begin exercise.

### RECEPTORS
Some experts suggest that the small increase in temperature which occurs almost as soon as our muscles start working, is responsible for triggering more rapid and deep breathing. However, fine control of breathing, which allows us to match our breathing with the amount of oxygen needed by our muscles, is controlled by chemical receptors in the brain and main arteries.

## Body heat during exercise

In order to dissipate the heat produced during exercise, the body uses mechanisms similar to those it would employ on a hot day in order to cool down.

These mechanisms include:
■ Vasodilation at the skin – to allow loss of heat from the blood to the environment
■ Increased sweating – sweat evaporates on the skin using heat energy to do so
■ Increase in ventilation – this acts to dissipate heat via exhaled warm air from the lungs.

Oxygen consumption by the body can increase as much as 20-fold in a well-trained athlete, and the amount of heat liberated

in the body is almost exactly proportional to the oxygen consumption.

If the sweating mechanism cannot eliminate heat on a hot and humid day, a dangerous and sometimes even lethal condition called heatstroke can develop easily in an athlete. Under these conditions, the main aim should be to reduce the body temperature as rapidly as possible by artificial means.

*The body employs several mechanisms to cool itself during exercise. An increase in sweating and ventilation helps to rid the body of excess heat.*

# How the body responds to stress

When we perceive a threat our sympathetic nervous system triggers a widespread response known as 'fight or flight'. The role of this reflex is to enable the body to react effectively to danger.

The autonomic nervous system regulates the body's basic processes (such as heart rate and breathing) in order to maintain homeostasis (normal functioning of internal bodily processes).

Humans have no voluntary control over this aspect of the nervous system, although certain events, such as emotional stress or fear, can bring about a change in the level of autonomic activity.

### OPPOSING EFFECTS

The autonomic nervous system is divided into two parts: the sympathetic and parasympathetic nervous systems. Both generally serve the same organs, but cause opposite effects. In this way, the two divisions counterbalance each other's activities to keep the body's systems operating smoothly.

Under normal circumstances, the parasympathetic nervous system stimulates activities such as digestion, defecation and urination, as well as slowing heart rate and respiration.

The sympathetic nervous system, on the other hand, functions to produce localized adjustments (such as sweating) and reflex adjustments of the cardiovascular system (such as an increase in heart rate).

### 'FIGHT OR FLIGHT'

Under conditions of stress – such as those caused by fear or rage – however, the entire sympathetic nervous system is activated. This produces an immediate, widespread ('fight or flight') response. The overall effect is to prepare the body to react effectively to danger, whether to defend itself or to flee from a dangerous situation.

*The sympathetic nervous system exerts control over a number of organs. In stressful conditions, all of these organs are stimulated simultaneously.*

## The sympathetic nervous system

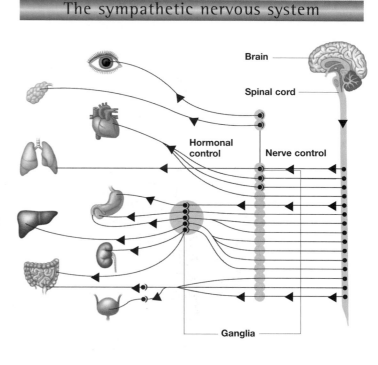

Brain

Spinal cord

Hormonal control

Nerve control

Ganglia

## Role of chemical messengers

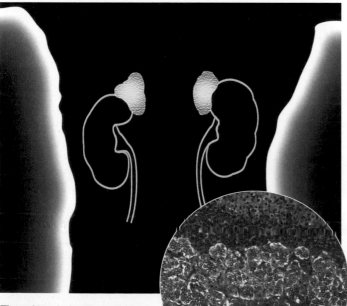

*The adrenal glands are located on the upper surface of each kidney. In stressful situations these glands are stimulated to produce a surge of hormones.*

*The medulla of the adrenal gland, seen on this micrograph, secretes adrenaline and noradrenaline. These hormones are vital for 'fight or flight'.*

The sympathetic nervous system exercises control over the organs via a series of nerves which extend to ganglia (collections of nerve cells) on either side of the spinal cord.

Nerve cells from the ganglia project to target tissues such as glands, smooth muscles or cardiac muscle.

### NORMAL RESPONSE

Under normal circumstances, nerve impulses from the brain stimulate the ends of the sympathetic nerve fibres to secrete the chemical messengers adrenaline and noradrenaline.

These hormones stimulate the target organs, and in this way act as chemical mediators for conveying the nerve impulses to the target organs.

### STRESSFUL STIMULI

In stressful situations, the whole of the sympathetic nervous system is activated at once. Adrenaline and noradrenaline are immediately secreted from the adrenal medulla (inner portion of the adrenal gland). These hormones are carried in the bloodstream, reinforcing the effects of the sympathetic nervous system.

Meanwhile, the hypothalamus (part of the forebrain) stimulates the pituitary gland to secrete adrenocorticotrophic hormone (ACTH). This triggers the adrenal cortex (outer portion of the adrenal gland) to release the hormone cortisol into the bloodstream.

Cortisol prepares the body for danger, by stabilizing membranes and increasing blood sugar. Stored amino acids are rapidly transported to the liver and converted into glucose, the fuel necessary for the production of energy.

# Response to fear

The sympathetic nervous system triggers the characteristic symptoms of fear. These enable the body to achieve a heightened performance under stress.

The surge in levels of adrenaline and noradrenaline from both the nerve endings and the adrenal medulla causes an immediate reaction throughout the body, giving rise to a number of responses which are characteristic of fear.

The aim of these responses is to enable the body to respond effectively to danger, whether it be to run, see better, think more clearly or to stay and fight.

### BODY RESPONSES

Fear responses include:
■ Rapid, deep breathing – the airways enlarge and breathing becomes more efficient to allow an increased intake of oxygen

*Under stressful situations, such as during an examination, there is an increase in blood flow to the brain. This enables us to think more clearly.*

into the body
■ Pounding heart – the heart beats harder and faster and blood pressure rises considerably.

Vasodilatation (increase in diameter of blood vessels) occurs within the vessels of those organs essential for emergency reaction, such as the brain, heart and limbs. This allows more blood to reach the organs, providing more oxygen and essential nutrients necessary for heightened performance
■ Pale skin – the effects of the sympathetic nervous system cause vasoconstriction (contraction in the walls of the blood vessels supplying the skin). As a result, blood flow is greatly reduced. This means that blood loss from superficial wounds is decreased should the body be required to fight. It also explains why people can literally go white with fear
■ A surge in energy – the body's metabolism is increased by as much as 100 per cent in order to maintain heightened responses. To compensate, the liver produces more glucose, which is rapidly respired to produce extra energy. This explains why a cup of sweet tea

may be helpful after a stressful event
■ Increased physical strength – as a result of increased blood flow and energy levels, the strength of muscular contraction increases. This is the reason why people can perform great feats of strength when they are in danger, for example lifting a very heavy weight, such as a human body
■ Resistance to pain – the secretion of endorphins (natural painkillers) from the brain increases the body's resistance to pain, enabling an individual to remain active despite injury
■ Hair shafts – hairs stand on end as part of a primitive reflex,

*Stressful stimuli, such as a confrontation with danger, activates the entire sympathetic nervous system. This triggers a number of fear responses.*

similar to hair ruffling in cats and dogs
■ Pupils dilate – this sharpens the vision
■ Sweating of the skin – perspiration increases to keep the body cool
■ 'Butterflies' in the stomach – this is caused by decreased blood flow to the stomach (in favour of the vital organs). Urinary tract mobility is also suspended as blood is diverted away from the kidneys.

## Effects of long-term stress

*Prolonged stress can be damaging to health. The effects can render individuals more susceptible to infection and stress-related illness.*

The fear responses are designed to help the body in threatening situations, such as those of immediate and physical danger.

### Relaxation
As soon as a threat has passed, the body gradually reverts back to normal as the parasympathetic nervous system is activated.

The muscles begin to relax, heart rate and blood pressure decrease, breathing becomes more regular and deeper, and the stomach relaxes as blood flow returns. The emotional state changes from one of anger and

fear to a more calm and peaceful condition.

### Prolonged stress
However, in stressful conditions that are socially generated, such as those caused by a heavy workload or financial worries, the fear response can exist on a long-term basis – in other words, there is no relaxation in the body's response to stress.

If there is no outlet for this tension, the effects of stress can have a detrimental effect on the body. An individual may suffer symptoms such as headaches, abdominal pain, tissue wasting (due to the constantly raised metabolic rate), fatigue and high blood pressure, which may lead to damage to the heart, blood vessels and kidneys.

# How alcohol affects the body

Alcohol is appreciated in modern society for the pleasurable effects it can have on the body. In excess however, alcohol is an intoxicating substance and may be detrimental to health.

Alcohol (otherwise known as ethyl alcohol, or ethanol) has long been exploited for its pleasurable effects on the body. Historical archives record the use of alcohol in ancient civilizations, in a number of religious and social rituals.

## FERMENTATION
Alcohol is an organic substance, produced by a natural process known as fermentation.

Sugars present in fruits or grains undergo a reaction with enzymes to form alcohol – a process exploited artificially by breweries and distilleries worldwide.

## ALCOHOL CONCENTRATION
The concentration of alcohol varies with different drinks, from around four per cent in most beers and 12 per cent in wine, to 40 per cent in spirits such as

vodka or whisky.

Today the consumption of alcohol plays a major role in society, and still features in many religious practices.

## DETRIMENTAL EFFECTS
Ever since ancient times however, the perils of this intoxicating substance have been preached about, and strict laws exist in order to regulate alcohol consumption.

Although in moderation the effects of alcohol on the body are negligible, it is an addictive substance and excessive intake, particularly for prolonged periods, can have a serious impact upon health.

*Alcohol plays an important role in social gatherings. People drink together in pubs and bars, enjoying the relaxing effects that alcohol can have.*

---

## Path of alcohol through the body

The route taken by alcohol during its passage through the body includes the alimentary canal and several organs, in the following order:

**1** Mouth – alcohol may be diluted by saliva before it is swallowed

**2** Stomach – alcohol passes via the oesophagus into the stomach where it is further diluted by gastric juices. Some alcohol is absorbed into the bloodstream here, but most passes into the small intestine. The rate of absorption will depend upon the strength of the alcohol and the presence of food in the stomach

**3** Small intestine – this is supplied by a dense network of small blood vessels, and is the site of most of the absorption of alcohol into the bloodstream

**4** Bloodstream – once in the bloodstream, alcohol is circulated around the body and

*Alcohol is absorbed into the bloodstream as it passes down the alimentary canal. Once it reaches the liver, alcohol is metabolized to release energy.*

taken up by the cells of various tissues

**5** Brain – once alcohol reaches the brain it has an immediate intoxicating effect. Alcohol acts on many sites of the central nervous system including the reticular formation (responsible for consciousness), the spinal cord, cerebellum and cerebral cortex

**6** Liver – absorbed alcohol quickly passes to the liver, where it is metabolized to water, carbon dioxide and energy at a rate of around 16 grams of alcohol (two units; for example two small glasses of wine) per hour. This rate varies however, depending upon the build of the individual.

## OTHER SITES OF EXCRETION
A small proportion of alcohol goes to the lungs, and is excreted in exhaled air (allowing levels of intoxication to be calculated by the use of a breathalyzer). Some alcohol is disposed of in the urine, and a tinier amount still is excreted in the sweat.

# Effects of alcohol

Once absorbed into the bloodstream, alcohol has an immediate effect on the central nervous system. This results in symptoms characteristic of drunkenness.

In general, alcohol reaches the bloodstream within five minutes of ingestion.

### IMPAIRED JUDGEMENT
The most immediate effect of alcohol is that drinkers become relaxed and more sociable.

After a single unit of alcohol, the activity of the brain is slowed down, with the result that judgement may be impaired and reaction times slower.

### LOSS OF CO-ORDINATION
Muscle co-ordination is increasingly reduced as the relevant control centres of the brain become intoxicated. This can result in clumsiness, staggering and slurred speech.

As the levels of alcohol in the blood rise, the pain centre of the brain is numbed, and the body becomes desensitized.

If the individual continues to drink, their vision may become blurred as the visual cortex is affected.

### DRUNKEN BEHAVIOUR
A person is said to be 'drunk' when they no longer have control over their actions.

If sufficient alcohol is consumed the individual may fall into a deep sleep, or even lose consciousness. Extreme quantities of alcohol effectively anaesthetize certain centres of the brain, causing breathing or heart beat to cease, resulting in death.

### MEMORY LOSS
Excessive measures of alcohol can affect the short-term memory, and thus actions carried out when drunk may not be recalled the following day.

*As blood alcohol levels rise, the brain becomes increasingly intoxicated. The drinker may lose consciousness as certain brain centres are affected.*

## Long-term effects

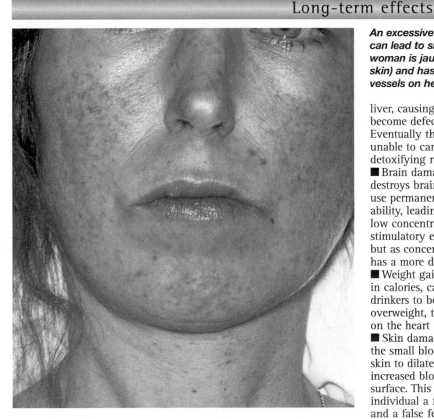

If the body is subjected to excessive alcohol intake for prolonged periods, the effects can be extremely serious. These include:
■ Tissue damage – as an irritant, alcohol, especially in purer forms, damages the tissues of the mouth, throat, gullet and stomach, causing increased susceptibility to cancer
■ Loss of appetite – large quantities of alcohol affect the stomach and appetite; thus heavy drinkers tend to neglect their diet. Alcohol is calorific but it does not contain any useful nutrients or vitamins
■ Liver damage – excessive quantities of alcohol damage the

*An excessive intake of alcohol can lead to skin changes. This woman is jaundiced (yellowed skin) and has tiny broken blood vessels on her face and neck.*

liver, causing it to shrink and become defective (cirrhotic). Eventually the organ will be unable to carry out its detoxifying role
■ Brain damage – as alcohol destroys brain cells, prolonged use permanently reduces mental ability, leading to dementia. At low concentrations alcohol has a stimulatory effect on the brain, but as concentrations increase it has a more depressant effect
■ Weight gain – alcohol is rich in calories, causing heavy drinkers to become bloated and overweight, thus putting a strain on the heart
■ Skin damage – alcohol causes the small blood vessels in the skin to dilate, resulting in increased blood flow to the skin surface. This will give the individual a flushed appearance, and a false feeling of being hot. The capillaries in the skin eventually rupture, giving the skin a permanently ruddy and unsightly appearance
■ Accidental injury – fatal injury is more likely in heavy drinkers. Alcoholics are seven times as liable to be victims of serious accidents as non-alcoholics.

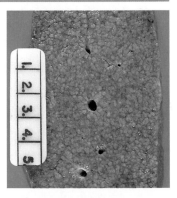

*Alcohol is an addictive substance. Long-term abuse can lead to serious health problems such as cirrhosis of the liver (shown here).*

### Withdrawal

Heavy drinking may be followed by a headache, nausea and fatigue, otherwise known as a hangover. This is due to the dehydrating effect of alcohol, which effectively starves the body's cells of water.

Prolonged alcohol abuse can lead to dependence, and so withdrawal may result in DTs (or delirium tremens), causing shaking, loss of appetite, inability to digest food, sweating, insomnia and seizures. In severe cases, people may hallucinate.

# How smoking affects the body

Tobacco contains a number of harmful compounds which are drawn in to the lungs during smoking. Tens of thousands of people die every year in the UK from this addictive and deadly habit.

The practice of inhaling smoke produced by burning tobacco leaves was introduced to the Western world by European explorers in the early 17th century. They had observed this custom in native Indians, who used tobacco in a number of rituals and believed it possessed medicinal properties.

### ADVERSE EFFECTS
Before long, smoking became a fashionable pastime. Lung cancer, once comparatively rare, began to increase dramatically in the 20th century and research into the effects of smoking on the body began.

Today, despite the fact that a clear correlation has been made between smoking and a range of diseases, the number of people who smoke continues to increase. In developed countries, smoking leads to around three million deaths a year, and is the main cause of death in people under 65.

*Smoking is favoured by many for its stress-relieving properties. In reality nicotine is a stimulant and has harmful effects.*

### GAS COMPOSITION
When a cigarette is lit, the burning tobacco gives off a pungent smoke, which is drawn into the lungs through inhalation. Cigarette smoke consists of both a gas and a particle phase. The particle phase (the smoke we see) consists of around 4000–5000 different particles of unburnt tobacco. Among these are chemicals that can cause cancer, poison cells, alter cell structure, suppress the immune system and alter neural activity in the brain.

The gas phase consists mainly of carbon dioxide, carbon monoxide and nicotine.

Carbon monoxide (the noxious gas in car exhaust fumes) combines with the blood pigment haemoglobin that is responsible for the transport of

oxygen to vital organs and tissues. This means that less oxygen can be carried in the blood, reducing the availability of oxygen to the tissues.

Nicotine affects the central

nervous system, constricting blood vessels and increasing heart rate and blood pressure. Many smokers are addicted to nicotine and have withdrawal symptoms when they stop.

## Effect on the cardiovascular system

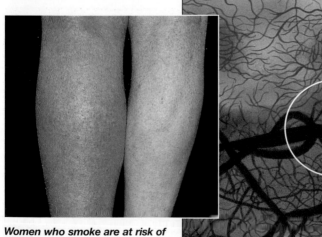

*Women who smoke are at risk of developing a blood clot in a deep vein in the leg. This causes pain and swelling in the calf, and can travel to a lung.*

*Smoking can lead to narrowing of the arteries; a blockage of the coronary artery can be seen right (circled). This is a common cause of fatal heart attacks.*

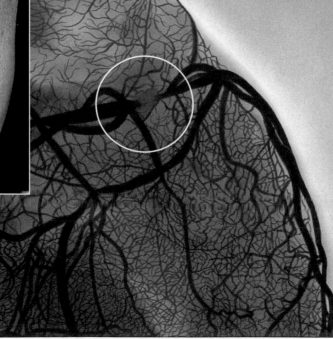

Smoking is a greater cause of death and disability than any single disease.

In particular, smoking has a grave impact upon the cardiovascular system and has been linked to around one in four deaths from cardiovascular disease.

### NARROWING OF ARTERIES
Nicotine and carbon monoxide present in cigarette smoke encourage the narrowing of arteries, a disorder known as atherosclerosis. This increases the risk of stroke and other cardiovascular disorders.

Coronary artery disease is one example of a cardiovascular disorder, whereby the blood supply to the heart is restricted, increasing the risk of a fatal heart attack.

Women who smoke are also at a far greater risk of developing deep vein thrombosis and stroke, particularly if they take the oral contraceptive pill.

# The effect of smoking on the lungs

With time, the effects of smoking reduce the capacity of the lungs and impair their defence mechanisms, exposing the body to attack by diseases.

As well as having a serious effect on the cardiovascular system, smoking is detrimental to the lungs.

### THE LUNGS

The two lungs lie beneath the rib cage, and surround the heart. They function like bellows, drawing air into the airways, so that oxygen can pass from the lungs into the blood. Oxygen is then delivered throughout the body, and waste products such as carbon dioxide are returned to the lungs and exhaled.

In order to prevent foreign bodies, such as dust or pollen, from entering the lungs, the airways are are lined with specialized cells covered in cilia (hair-like projections). These cells maintain a constant wave-like motion, so that any potentially harmful particles are wafted up the airways and out of the lungs into the throat. The mechanism of coughing also serves to remove any foreign particles from the lungs.

### IMPAIRED FUNCTION

Smoking inhibits the lungs' protective mechanisms. First, it reduces the body's response to smoke, so that people do not cough when smoking a cigarette as they normally would when inhaling pungent smoke.

Secondly, the ciliated cells beat much more slowly as they become paralysed by toxins in the tobacco. For this reason harmful substances contained in cigarettes are able to settle in the lungs, reducing the overall capacity of these vital organs, and compromising the entire body.

As harmful substances settle, the mucous membrane of the lungs produces more and more mucus (otherwise known as phlegm). Tar, ash and phlegm accumulate in the tiny air sacs of the lungs, reducing their capacity, and causing severe shortness of breath.

### IMMUNE RESPONSE REDUCED

Smoking also damages the white blood cells that would normally scavenge and remove dirt and bacteria from the lungs. This means that the lungs are more prone to infection.

In this way, smoking causes the body to be exposed to a greater number of harmful foreign bodies, while the normal defence mechanisms for combating disease are severely impaired.

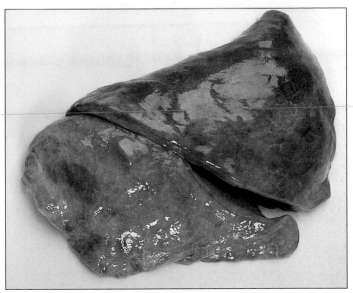

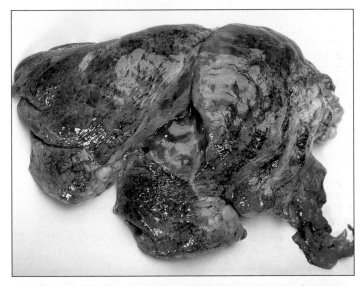

*Shown here is a healthy lung (top) and the diseased lung of a smoker (below). Tar contained in tobacco smoke has severely discoloured the smoker's lung.*

## Nicotine addiction

Everybody is aware of the hazards of smoking, but most smokers fail to give up. This is partly due to habituation to the stimulatory effects of nicotine, but also due to routine and social convention.

### Stimulatory effect

Nicotine stimulates neurons in the brain, increasing attentiveness, decreasing appetite and irritability, and relaxing muscles. Indeed, many smokers find that smoking regulates their mood and they associate cigarettes with a pleasant sensation. In reality the body has no physiological need for nicotine.

*Nicotine patches allow nicotine to be absorbed into the blood. This reduces the craving for cigarettes, avoiding the harmful effects of smoking.*

### Tobacco substitutes

There are a number of products available that act as a substitute for cigarettes, supplying nicotine without the effects of smoking.

These include nicotine patches, inhalers and gum. The idea is that if the body is receiving nicotine the smoker will no longer crave cigarettes. Eventually the dose of nicotine is reduced until it is no longer required by the body.

A drug known as Zyban has also been developed in recent years, which removes cravings for nicotine by interfering with the same chemical messengers in the brain that nicotine disrupts.

Acupuncture and hypnotherapy are also reputed to be helpful in smoking cessation. It is worth bearing in mind that the risks of developing smoking-related diseases decreases dramatically with time after giving up smoking.

# How caffeine affects the body

Caffeine, found in a range of products, has a powerful stimulant action on the body. As a result, it can adversely affect sleep patterns and may become addictive in the long term.

Caffeine is the most widely used drug in the world – most people consume it in some form every day. Although caffeine is usually associated with coffee, it actually occurs naturally in many plants, including tea leaves and cocoa nuts, and is contained in many drinks. In fact, many people consume up to a gram of caffeine a day without even knowing it.

## SOURCES
The most common sources of caffeine include:
- Fresh coffee – a single cup can contain up to 200 mg
- Tea – a cup of tea can contain as much as 70 mg of caffeine
- Cola – a can may contain around 50 mg
- Chocolate – milk chocolate can contain up to 6 mg per 28 g. Dark chocolate contains more

cocoa and therefore more caffeine
- Painkillers – certain headache tablets can contain as much as 200 mg per tablet.

## STIMULANT
Recreationally, caffeine is enjoyed by many people who find that it gives them an energy boost and a feeling of heightened alertness. Many people drink coffee to help them wake up in the morning or to remain alert during the day.

Medically, caffeine (or trimethylxanthine) is used as a heart stimulant and a diuretic (it increases urine production).

*Coffee beans are the seeds of coffee fruits. Coffee contains caffeine, which is a stimulant, boosting energy and increasing mental activity.*

## Short-term effects

Adenosine is a chemical secreted by the brain. Levels of this chemical build up throughout the day and bind to specialized adenosine receptors in the brain, causing nervous activity to slow down, blood vessels to dilate and drowsiness to occur.

In terms of its chemical make-up, caffeine looks very similar to adenosine. Caffeine is thus able to bind to the same receptors in place of adenosine. However, caffeine does not slow down the activity of a nerve cell as adenosine would, but has the

opposite effect, causing nerve cell activity to speed up.

Moreover, because caffeine blocks the ability of adenosine to dilate blood vessels, the blood vessels of the brain constrict. This is the reason why some headache tablets contain caffeine (constriction of the brain's blood vessels can help to relieve certain types of headache).

## ADRENALINE
When a person takes caffeine, the pituitary gland responds to the increased brain cell activity. It does this by acting as though the body were facing an emergency situation, and releases hormones that stimulate the adrenal glands to produce adrenaline.

The release of adrenaline (the 'fight or flight' hormone) has the following effects, explaining why, after a cup of coffee, a person might experience tense muscles, cold, clammy hands

*A dose of caffeine has an instant effect on the nervous system. Brain cell activity is increased, resulting in release of the hormone adrenaline.*

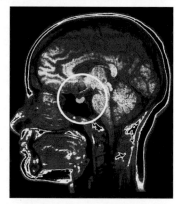

*Caffeine stimulates the pituitary gland in the brain, shown on this scan circled. The gland triggers the releases of 'fight and flight' hormones from the adrenals.*

and a feeling of excitement:
- Pupils and airways dilate
- Heart rate increases
- Blood pressure rises, as blood vessels close to the surface of the skin constrict
- Blood flow to the stomach is reduced
- The liver releases sugar into the bloodstream to provide extra energy.

# Addictive properties

Many people become addicted to caffeine. Not only is it a stimulant, but it raises the levels of dopamine in the brain, which increases feelings of pleasure.

Caffeine is an addictive drug. It belongs to a drug group known as stimulants, so called because of their excitatory effect on the brain. Other stimulants include amphetamines and cocaine.

### BRAIN CHANNELS
Although the effects of caffeine are less powerful than those of other stimulants, the drug operates in a similar way and, because it manipulates the same channels in the brain, it is just as addictive.

In the short term, caffeine is a harmless substance, but the long-term consumption of caffeine can be a problem. Once the adrenaline released by ingesting caffeine wears off, a person may feel tired and mildly depressed and so may reach for

another cup of coffee.

It is in this way that many people become addicted to caffeine without even realizing it. It is not healthy for the body to be in a constant state of emergency and many people become jumpy and irritable.

### PLEASURE
Like other stimulants, caffeine raises levels of dopamine, a neurotransmitter that activates the pleasure centre of the brain. It is suspected that this action is a contributory factor to the addictive nature of caffeine.

*For years, scientists have studied the behaviour of neuro-transmitters – chemicals in the brain. Caffeine raises the level of the neurotransmitter dopamine.*

## Effect on sleep

Caffeine has a significant effect on sleep. It takes around 12 hours for caffeine to leave the body's system. This means that if a person has a cup of coffee containing 200 mg of caffeine at around 4 pm, then by 10 pm there will still be 100 mg of caffeine in their bloodstream.

### LACK OF DEEP SLEEP
Although the person may be able to fall asleep, they will not be able to attain the deep sleep that the body requires. As a result, they will wake feeling tired, and may instinctively pour themselves a cup of coffee to help wake them up. And so the

cycle continues. If a person tries to break this cycle, they may find that they feel very tired and mildly depressed. They may also experience headaches due to dilation of the blood vessels in the brain.

▶ *Caffeine may hinder deep sleep. A person is therefore likely to wake feeling tired and repeat the cycle by drinking coffee to help them wake up.*

◀ *It takes around 12 hours for caffeine to leave the body after consumption. If caffeine remains in the bloodstream, it can adversely affect sleep patterns.*

## Decaffeinated drinks

With increasing awareness of the harmful effects that caffeine can have on the body, decaffeinated drinks are growing in popularity. These provide the taste of coffee, tea and cola, but without the detrimental effects.

### Filtration
Decaffeination of coffee involves treating the coffee beans with a solvent that absorbs the caffeine. This is then filtered from the solution, leaving only the coffee oils (vital to flavour). This solution is then added back to the coffee beans, which are roasted and processed as normal.

Research has shown that

*Decaffeinated coffee, which has no harmful effects, is very popular. Removing caffeine from coffee beans, however, is a complex process.*

people suffering from hypertension benefit from cutting caffeine out of their diets.

# How drugs work on the body

Drugs used to prevent or treat diseases work by causing biochemical or physiological changes in the body, or by alleviating symptoms. Some drugs affect specific cells while others act on the whole body.

## TYPES OF DRUGS

Drugs exert their action in a variety of ways. A drug's effects may be described according to the changes that it causes, or with reference to the clinical symptoms it is intended to relieve or prevent. In general, drugs may be classified into those that:

- Artificially moderate or regulate the activity of specific body cells, tissues or organs
- Combat virulent organisms invading the body (bacteria that cause infections, for example)
- Act in place of substances occurring naturally within the body
- Have an effect on abnormal or malignant cells or tissues.

## CELL-REGULATING DRUGS

Certain drugs affect the activity of the body's cells by influencing the maintenance of normal cell function. Cell-regulating drugs (artificial moderators) can act either on cells throughout the entire body (systemically) or only upon those located within certain tissues or organs.

Some of these artificial moderators enhance or inhibit substances in the cell necessary for energy production, synthetic reactions or other normal cell functions.

Such drugs often work on enzyme (biological catalyst) activity, either by inhibiting or enhancing it. One specific example is allopurinol, which is used to treat gout because it prevents the formation of uric acid. Gout occurs when joints become painfully swollen because uric acid salts collect around them.

Drugs acting at the cellular level may be specific to certain organs or they may have wide-ranging (systemic) effects. For example, the drug hydralazine is an antihypertensive, used to lower blood pressure. It causes the small arteries around the body to widen, increases the heart-rate and elevates cardiac output.

Therefore, hydralazine works at two levels: the effects on blood circulation are exerted at the cellular level, while those on the heart are exerted at the organ function level.

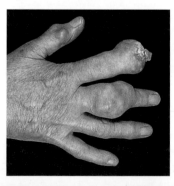

*Gout is an inflammation of the joints caused by a failure in the meabolism of uric acid. Drugs prevent uric acid from forming and then collecting in joints.*

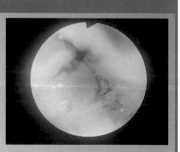

*A Novopen is used to administer a metered doses of insulin to a patient with diabetes. The insulin is needed to regulate the patient's glucose metabolism.*

## Multi-drug management

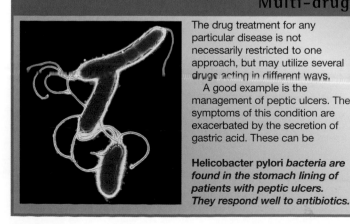

The drug treatment for any particular disease is not necessarily restricted to one approach, but may utilize several drugs acting in different ways.

A good example is the management of peptic ulcers. The symptoms of this condition are exacerbated by the secretion of gastric acid. These can be alleviated, and ulcer healing promoted, by a range of drugs acting locally in the stomach (using antacids), or by reducing gastric acid secretion (perhaps with an H2-receptor antagonist such as ranitidine), or by enhancing mucosal protection (for example, with carbenoxolone). In addition, since the bacterium *Helicobacter pylori* has been implicated in gastric ulceration, antibiotic treatment may also be initiated. Any combination of these approaches may be adopted.

*Helicobacter pylori bacteria are found in the stomach lining of patients with peptic ulcers. They respond well to antibiotics.*

*This endoscope image shows a peptic ulcer. Multi-drug therapy can reduce gastric acid and act against the bacteria involved.*

## Anti-infective drugs

Some drugs exert their effects on invading organisms (infections) or abnormal body cells (such as cancers). The specific activity of anti-infectives, including antibiotics, antifungals, and antimalarials is generally due to the intrinsic differences between the cells of the infecting agent (for example, the bacterium) and those of the host. An effective and safe antimicrobial preparation is one that is toxic to the infecting organism, but not to the host.

Some of these drugs merely arrest the growth of the susceptible organism, whereas others kill the organism, but these effects may depend on the dose taken.

The means by which anti-infective drugs exert their toxicity are diverse, and are frequently related to the drug's chemical structure. Some anti-infectives (such as gentamicin and erythromycin) interfere with the synthesis of bacterial protein, while others (penicillins, for example) interfere with bacterial cell wall synthesis, or cell function.

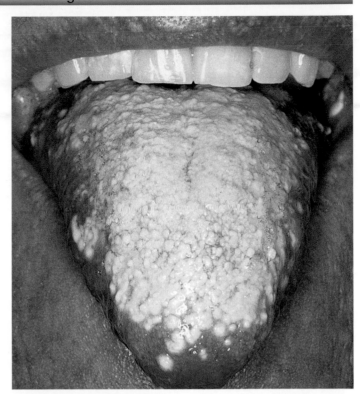

*The fungus Candida albicans can cause oral candidiasis on the tongue. Antifungal preparations may treat the condition by killing the fungus or slowing its growth.*

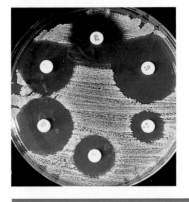

*Antibiotic drugs are tested on a culture of a strain of bacteria to see which is the most effective. The drug must do as little harm as possible to human cells.*

## Drugs that replace natural substances

The treatment or prevention of some diseases involves the administration of a substance that, under normal circumstances, occurs naturally within the body.

An example is the use of insulin in the treatment of Type 1 (insulin-dependent) diabetes mellitus. In patients with Type 1 diabetes, the administered insulin compensates for the lack of insulin secreted by the pancreas cells and acts by enhancing the transport of glucose into cells, thus restoring normal function.

Similarly, oestrogenic and progestogenic hormones are used as hormone replacement therapy in post-menopausal women, to alleviate post-menopausal symptoms and to prevent osteoporosis. These hormones exert actions comparable to the actions of naturally occurring hormones prior to the menopause.

Oral contraceptive pills contain oestrogen and progestogen preparations. These suppress ovulation by mimicking the effects of the woman's own hormones on the pituitary and hypothalamus.

Other substances that act in place of naturally occurring substances are vitamin and mineral preparations used to treat or prevent deficiency states.

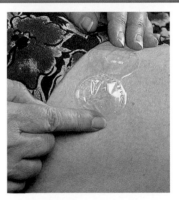

*Transdermal patches, as used in hormone replacement therapy, deliver hormones through the skin. They release a set amount of the drug every hour.*

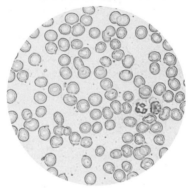

*Anaemia (iron deficiency) is evident in this blood smear. Two white blood cells (purple) serve to fight infection. Anaemia may be treated by iron supplements.*

## Antimalignancy drugs

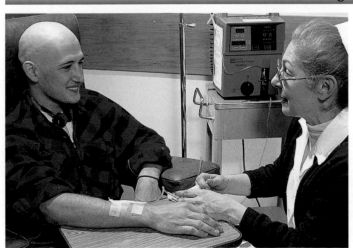

Cytotoxic (or antineoplastic) drugs are used in the treatment of malignant disease, either in instead of or as well as surgery or radiotherapy.

The actions of such drugs are often not specific to the cancerous cells, and they therefore affect healthy cells in the body. However, the ability of such drugs in targeting malignant cells is generally attributable to the different

*Cytotoxic drugs used in cancer chemotherapy may be given intravenously. They often act to prevent tumour cells dividing, but may also affect normal cells.*

characteristics shown by malignant and normal cells. For example, malignant cells undergo cell division at a more rapid rate than is usually seen in normal cells. Alkylating agents (such as cisplatin) exploit this feature, and arrest cell division in rapidly dividing cells.

Some normal body cells (including bone marrow cells) divide rapidly and are therefore prone to toxicity from these drugs. Some newer anticancer treatments aim for greater specificity for malignant cells by using antibodies that bind selectively to the malignant cells and not normal cells.

# How anaesthetics work

Anaesthetic drugs work by stopping the conduction of pain sensations through the body's nervous system. There are different types of drug that can be given by different routes, but they all act to affect nerve conduction.

### THE NERVE NETWORK
Nerve cells (or neurones) form a comprehensive network throughout the body relaying information from sensory receptors to the brain. The information is processed in the brain (itself a collection of many neurones) which then sends appropriate information, in the form of electrical impulses, via motor neurones

*The synapse (circled) is the point of contact between two nerve cells, where the synaptic bulb of one meets the axon, dendrite or cell body of another.*

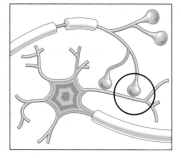

**Normal synapse action**

to move muscles. Anaesthetics work by interfering with the transmission of these impulses between nerve cells.

### NERVE CELL STRUCTURE
Unlike other cells, neurones can be very long – up to 100 cm – in order to conduct electrical impulses over long distances. The longest projection from a neurone is called the axon.

The nervous system forms an elaborate circuit throughout the body; however, nerve cells are not physically connected to each other. Instead, nerves connect to other nerves (or muscles) via gaps called synapses.

When an impulse has reached the end of a nerve cell (the synaptic bulb), chemicals called neurotransmitters are actively transported across the synapse. When they bind to receptors on the adjoining cell, they trigger an impulse which can then continue along the length of the adjoining cell.

Cell membranes are largely

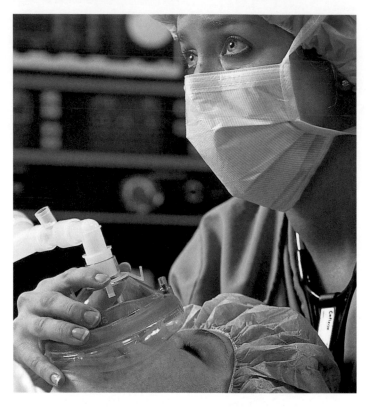

made up of adjoining layers of lipid (fat) molecules. Proteins embedded in the membrane act as channels, specifically controlling entry and exit of chemicals into and out of the cells.

*During major operations, the anaesthetist's role is vital. Gaseous anaesthetic mixed with oxygen may be administered via a mask (as here) or an endotracheal tube, which is inserted into the windpipe.*

**Neurotransmitter molecules**
These are released when the nerve impulse has reached the end of the neurone

**Lipid bilayer**
The outer membrane of the cell

**Protein channel**
Neurotransmitter chemicals bind to protein channels on adjoining cells, causing them to open

**Synaptic cleft**
Gap between nerve cell and adjacent cell (which may be a muscle, gland, or another nerve cell)

**Charged particles**
Opening of protein channel allows their entry, enabling the nerve impulse to continue

*When an impulse reaches the end of a nerve cell, chemicals called neurotransmitters are transported across the synapse (gap) where they bind to the adjoining cell. This allows the entry of charged particles which continue the impulse.*

## Anaesthetic effect at the synapse

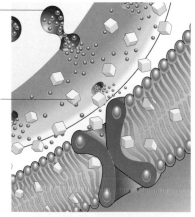

**Synaptic vesicle**
Sac which contains the neurotransmitter molecules

**Anaesthetic agent**

*It is believed that anaesthetics block the protein channel in the cell membrane or alter its ability to open as normal. Other researchers believe that anaesthetics can act on other sites, as the affected sites vary between different anaesthetics.*

# Where anaesthetics operate

Although the exact effect of anaesthetic agents is unclear, it is known that they act in the region of the synapse. This is the gap through which impulses are transferred between nerve cells, and between nerve cells and muscle fibres.

## NERVE IMPULSES

The conduction of nerve impulses along the axon is achieved by the rapid entry and exit of ions through the protein channels, causing a small electrical current that spreads down the nerve. If these ions are prevented from passing through the protein channels, nerve conduction is impaired.

The exact mechanism by which drugs cause anaesthesia is still unknown, but because different types of molecules can all cause anaesthesia, it is thought that several molecular sites may be involved.

## MOLECULAR SITE OF ACTION

Early studies suggested that the site of action of anaesthetic drugs is within the membrane of the cell, because the potency of inhaled anaesthetic drugs was proportional to their solubility in oil, a substance which closely resembles the membrane lipids. The assumption is that by inserting into the lipid bilayer, anaesthetic drugs may change the properties of the membrane – the membrane is a fluid structure and embedded structures are able to move freely within it. If the membrane was less fluid, this would affect the conduction of impulses.

Further studies suggested that anaesthetic drugs in the lipid bilayer cause the cell membrane to expand. Once a critical volume is reached, nerve conduction is impaired. A rise in pressure is thought to reduce the expansion of the cell membrane.

## Types of anaesthetic

■ **Local anaesthetic**
Used for minor operations, such as stitching a wound, when a specific area (a local nerve) needs to be numbed. This may be done by injection, topical cream or eye-drops.

■ **Regional anaesthetic**
Numbs larger areas (often a limb), and operates in a similar way: a series of local anaesthetic injections is made around a nerve or a number of nerves to render them unresponsive to pain.

■ **General anaesthetic**
Renders the patient totally unconscious by the injection of drugs into the bloodstream, or by inhalation of gas; often both are combined. The drugs affect the brain to cause loss of consciousness and to prevent the sensation of pain.

Other drugs may be given during general anaesthetic to control post-operative pain, and in some cases to induce paralysis (neuro-muscular blockers) so that the muscles are relaxed during surgery.

*As well as keeping the patient fully anaesthetized, the anaesthetist is responsible for monitoring their state throughout the operation. Equipment will measure blood pressure, heart rate and respiration.*

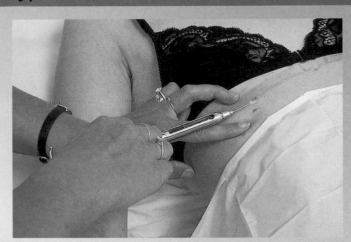

*A local anaesthetic injection is used prior to the removal of a malignant melanoma (tumour of the skin's pigment cells). The patient is fully aware of what is going on but feels no pain.*

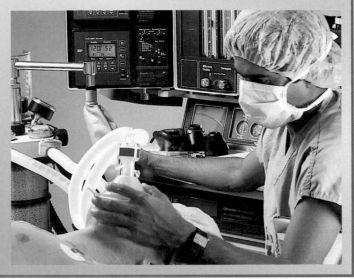

*Premedication is commonly administered before major surgery to sedate the patient. Often, another drug is given to control lung secretions, which could otherwise be inhaled under anaesthesia.*

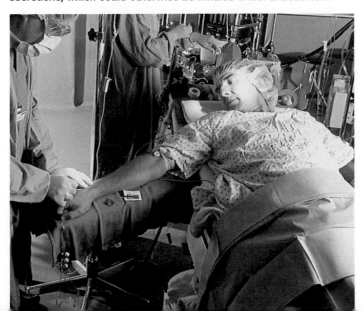

## Other sites of anaesthetic action

As well as the actions on the nerve cell membrane and within the lipid bilayer, anaesthetic drugs may well affect other sites involved with nerve impulse conduction.

### SYNAPSES AND AXONS

When the nerve impulse arrives at the end of the nerve cell, this causes specific channels to open. These channels allow the passage of calcium ions into the nerve cell. This in turn causes neurotransmitter chemicals to be released – in sacs called vesicles – into the synapse.

Anaesthetic drugs may affect these calcium channels, preventing their normal opening and reducing the release of the neurotransmitter vesicles.

There is also evidence that some anaesthetic drugs bind to proteins on the surface of the adjoining nerve cell, impairing the binding of acetylcholine, an important neurotransmitter. In theory, this would reduce the nerve impulse that is triggered.

### HIGHER NEURONAL CIRCUITS

The reticular activating system is a region of the brain involved in regulating consciousness.

General anaesthetic drugs may cause loss of consciousness by blocking the processing of sensory information as it passes through this area.

# How infection occurs

Although the body is a natural host to a huge number of
bacteria, infection does not usually arise unless the body's defences
are damaged. Infections are generally acquired from other people.

The body is exposed to a myriad of micro-organisms every day. In fact, it plays host to millions of bacteria, all living in a state of co-existence.

Most bacteria are harmless as long as they stay in protected places such as the surface of the skin, intestines, nose, mouth or vagina. However, if these surfaces become damaged through injury or disease, and micro-organisms are allowed to enter the normally sterile internal tissues of the body, infection can occur. The large intestine, for example, is home to numerous bacteria which do not usually cause any harm, but if they were to enter the abdominal cavity, serious infection would occur.

### PROTECTIVE BARRIERS
The body, fortunately, has a number of protective barriers, which act as a first line of defence against infection,

including:
■ The skin – this provides a physical barrier to pathogens (disease-causing organisms), helping to maintain a sterile internal environment
■ The nose – this contains sticky mucus and hairs to trap potentially harmful micro-organisms, while the sneezing mechanism expels any irritants
■ Saliva – this contains antibodies that combat pathogens
■ Tears – these contain antibodies to prevent infection of the eyes
■ Throat – this is protected by the reflex reaction of coughing
■ Stomach – this produces a strong acid that destroys any ingested pathogens.

*Coughing is a reflex action by which micro-organisms in the airway are expelled. This is one of the body's defence mechanisms against infection.*

## Local infection

If pathogens manage to breach the body's first line of defence, they can multiply in the tissues, causing infection. The body's response to this is to produce inflammation, an important reaction that prevents the spread of infection.

### REDNESS
If a sufficient number of pathogens invade the body, they will release harmful toxins or cause enough damage to cells for local blood vessels to dilate, resulting in an increased blood

flow to the affected area. This gives rise to the redness and warmth typical of an inflamed area. In addition, a watery fluid leaks out of the blood vessels, causing the surrounding area to swell visibly.

The increase in blood flow enables cells of the immune system, including phagocytes (a

*In some infections, a wall of fibrous tissue may form around the inflamed area. Pus can then build up within this wall to form an abscess.*

form of white blood cell that engulfs and destroys pathogens) to reach the area and attack the organisms present. This is usually sufficient to prevent infection spread, and the swelling eventually subsides as the pathogens are destroyed.

If the infection is particularly severe, then the body will also

form a wall of fibrous tissue around the infected area. This wall serves to keep the infection localized while it is brought under control by the immune system. Within the fibrous walls, a build-up of pus may occur; this contains dead white cells, body cells and bacteria, and cell debris.

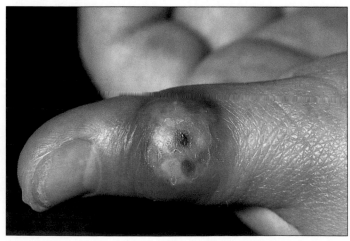

## Incubation period

After a pathogen has invaded the body, there is an interval of time before there is any evidence of disease. This is because all pathogens undergo an incubation period during which they multiply. Once there are sufficient pathogens, they will cause noticeable effects or symptoms in the patient.

### Variable length
Incubation periods vary greatly, from only a few hours to some years. Cholera, for example, can develop within a couple of hours of drinking contaminated water, but AIDS may not develop until many years after the HIV virus has been acquired.

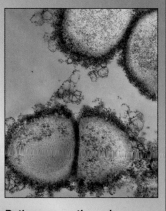

*Pathogens go through an incubation period in which they multiply in the body. Here, Streptococcus bacteria are dividing (lower centre).*

# Systemic infection

Some micro-organisms enter the bloodstream and spread quickly to engulf the whole body. Common signs of systemic infection are a fever or rash.

In some cases, infecting organisms, or the toxins they produce, enter the bloodstream and rapidly spread throughout the entire body. This is known as systemic infection and can lead to some characteristic symptoms, such as fever or rash.

### FEVER
Fever occurs when the immune system cells are damaged by invading pathogens, causing them to release substances called cytokines. These affect the body's 'thermostat' (controlled by the brain), effectively adjusting it to a higher setting. As a result, the normal body temperature is perceived by the brain to be too low, causing

shivering to occur, which automatically produces extra heat. This causes the body temperature to rise to a level that is fatal to most invading micro-organisms.

### RASH
Skin rashes in systemic infection are caused by multiple areas of skin damage as a result of the micro-organisms or their toxins. Rashes indicate that similar damage may be occurring within the body.

*Sometimes, infections affect the whole body. Such systemic infections are serious and cause characteristic symptoms, such as fever or a rash.*

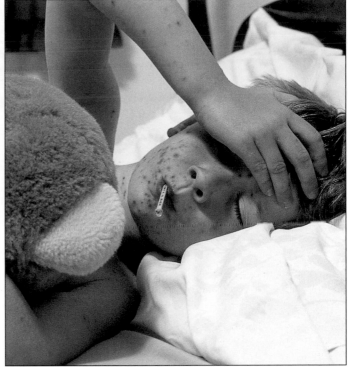

## Spread of infection

The majority of infections are acquired, directly or indirectly, from other people, and may be spread in the following ways:
■ Skin-to-skin contact – if the dose of micro-organisms is large or virulent enough, skin infections may be spread by contact. Some organisms, such as staphylococci, penetrate the sweat glands and hair follicles, causing pustules and boils. For example, impetigo, a bacterial skin infection, can very easily be spread through contact with infected skin
■ Transfer to eye – pathogens may be spread from the fingers to the eye, causing infections such as conjunctivitis. This may be spread from one eye to the next, and may even be transmitted by infected towels or

*If the water supply is contaminated, infection spreads easily. Washing cooking pots in polluted rivers can lead to diseases such as typhoid.*

make-up products
■ Transfer to nose – pathogens are often picked up by the fingers and spread to the nose through rubbing. In fact, the rhinoviruses that cause the common cold are more readily transmitted by hand-shaking than by sneezing
■ Inhalation – a number of infections are spread through the inhalation of airborne droplets released during coughing or sneezing. Some infective agents are inhaled in the form of dried spores contained in dust, for example Q fever (an influenza-

type infection)
■ Ingestion – although stomach acid destroys the majority of ingested pathogens, some manage to survive and pass through to the intestines. The consumption of contaminated food or water can spread infection in this way, such as in gastroenteritis. Food poisoning can also be caused by food contaminated with material from the infected hands of food handlers. This can contain a virulent toxin produced by staphylococci bacteria, which causes severe illness
■ Faecal contamination – this is a common cause of infection, since faeces can contain pathogens that are transmitted to food prepared by a person who has not washed their hands (such as in salmonella poisoning). Certain viruses (enteroviruses) can be spread by the ingestion of faecal traces, for example the viruses that cause polio and hepatitis A
■ Pregnancy – infection can be spread directly from mother to baby during pregnancy via the placenta, for example toxoplasmosis. During birth, babies may also contract infections such as herpes or syphilis through contact with an infected vagina
■ Blood – pathogens in blood

*The saliva of a particular female mosquito contains the parasite responsible for malaria. This disease is one of a number spread by insects or animals.*

can be transmitted by the use of an infected syringe, or through tattooing and ear-piercing with unsterilized needles. HIV can be spread in this way
■ Sexually-transmitted infection – some diseases (such as herpes) can be spread during sexual activity due to intimate contact and exchange of bodily fluids.

### ANIMAL CONTACT
A few infections are contracted through contact with animals and insects. Some, such as rabies, may be acquired from infected animals; others, such as malaria, may be picked up from insects which act as vectors for a disease, but do not actually have it themselves.

# Common allergies

Allergies can be caused by anything from peanuts and bee stings, to penicillin and jewellery. Immunologists have divided these allergic, or hypersensitive, responses into four types.

## Type I – Immediate, allergic responses

*Allergy to peanuts is an increasingly recognised problem, that can lead to life-threatening anaphylactic shock.*

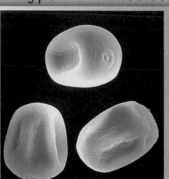

*Hay fever, an allergic reaction to pollen grains, is the most common example of a Type I, atopic allergy.*

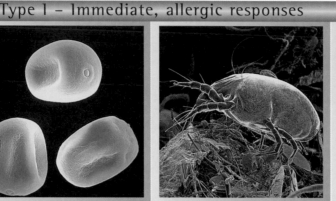

*The faeces of the house-dust mite, which lives in bedding, carpets and furniture, are a common allergen.*

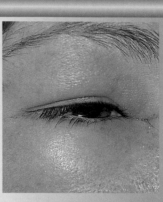

*This young boy has had a severe anaphylactic reaction to a bee sting, causing oedema – fluid accumulation around the eye.*

Type I hypersensitivity is an immediate response, beginning within seconds of exposure.

The commonest examples are hay fever, childhood eczema and extrinsic asthma. About 10 per cent of the population have a tendency to develop such a reaction, called atopy.

Upon encountering an allergen, instead of making a normal immune response, the body produces a class of antibody molecule called IgE. These bind to mast cells, which are especially prevalent in the skin, respiratory passages and gastrointestinal tract, and cause the release of a number of inflammatory chemicals, including histamine.

Histamine causes blood vessels to dilate and become 'leaky', and is the main cause of typical allergic reactions - runny nose, watery eyes and itchy, red skin. Symptoms also depend upon where the allergen enters the body. An inhaled allergen causes the airways to constrict, causing asthma symptoms; if ingested, symptoms include cramp, vomiting and diarrhoea.

A second, more dramatic, reaction can occur if an allergen enters the bloodstream. This is called anaphylactic shock. The airways constrict (and the tongue may swell) making breathing difficult, and the sudden dilation of blood vessels and loss of fluid may cause circulatory collapse. This is typically triggered in susceptible individuals by bee stings and spider bites, injection of a foreign substance (for example penicillin, or other drugs) or certain foods, such as peanuts. Susceptible individuals may have to carry syringes of adrenaline (epinephrine) to administer in an emergency. Fortunately, reactions such as these are rare.

## Type II – Reactions against 'foreign' cells

Type II hypersensitivity is caused by the binding of antibodies to 'self' molecules on the surface of cells. This does not generally cause damage, but may trigger a number of further responses.

One example of this may occur in mismatched blood transfusions. Another involves incompatibility between blood groups. All blood is either rhesus positive (Rh$^+$) or negative (Rh$^-$), depending on whether a certain protein is present on the surface of a person's blood cells. If a Rh$^-$ woman is pregnant with a Rh$^+$ fetus, it is possible for fetal blood to enter the mother's bloodstream during delivery, or following abortion.

Upon a subsequent pregnancy with a Rh$^+$ fetus, antibodies may cross the placenta, enter the fetal bloodstream and cause a number of detrimental effects. Injection of antibodies shortly after birth of an incompatible child will destroy fetal red cells in the mother's circulation.

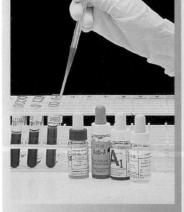

*Accurate blood typing is crucial in preventing serious immune reactions in transplants. This occurs in both of the two blood matching systems.*

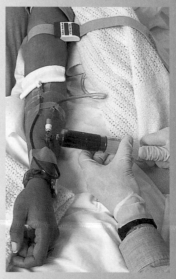

*If a mismatch occurs in a blood transfusion (such as a Rh+ patient receiving Rh-), host defences cause destruction of the 'foreign' blood.*

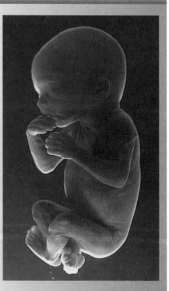

*A mother may form antibodies to her own fetus's blood, if she comes into contact with it. This can lead to immune reactions in subsequent pregnancies.*

## Type III – Reactions against antibody-antigen complexes

Type III hypersensitivity results when allergens are distributed throughout the body. The body produces antibodies, which form insoluble antibody-antigen complexes. The body is unable to clear these, and a large inflammatory response develops.

Examples of such allergies include farmer's lung, which is caused by the inhalation of mould growing on hay, and mushroom grower's lung, caused by inhaling the spores produced by mushrooms.

A number of microorganisms can trigger immune complexes. Streptococcal throat infection may be exacerbated by the formation of these immune complexes, as can the organisms that cause malaria, syphilis and leprosy. Drugs can also have the same effect.

These responses are also involved in autoimmune disorders, when the body's defences attack host tissue. Examples are systemic lupus erythematosus (SLE) and rheumatoid arthritis.

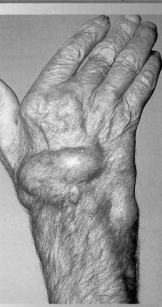

*Rheumatoid arthritis is an autoimmune disorder, in which the body's defences attack host tissues. In this case, it is the lining of the joints that are affected, causing erosion and damage, leading to deformity.*

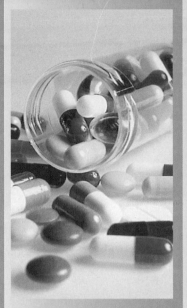

*A number of drugs are known to cause allergic responses. For instance, penicillin in the body can bind to the protein albumin (the protein also present in egg white) and provoke a significant immune reaction.*

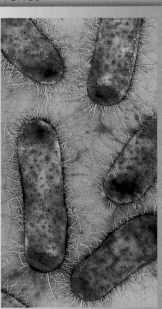

*In microbial infections causing malaria, syphilis and leprosy, amongst others, the surface of the microorganism can trigger a Type III response. The complex of antibodies and bacteria can be harmful.*

## Type IV – Delayed reactions

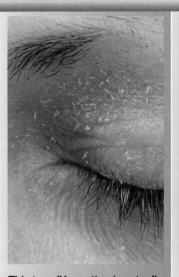

*This type IV reaction is actually a reaction to nail varnish. These allergic reactions can occur some distance from the site of the original allergen – in this example, dermatitis has occurred on the eyelid.*

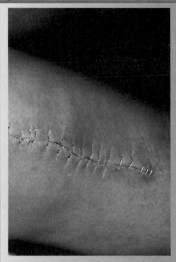

*This sore has been caused by an allergic response to sticking plaster on the skin, used to cover a wound. Such reactions are caused by the release of chemicals called lymphokines from T-cell white blood cells.*

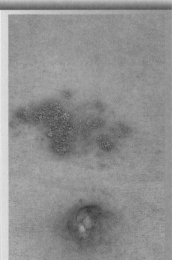

*Here a patient has suffered a large wound, running across his knee. The red allergic patches which surround the trauma result from a hypersensitivity to the metal surgical sutures used to close up the wound.*

*Contact dermatitis in an 18-year-old woman, caused by a reaction to nickel in jewellery. The nickel is absorbed into the skin, where it binds to body proteins and becomes 'foreign' to the immune system.*

Type IV reactions are known as delayed hypersensitivities. They appear much more slowly and are caused by the actions of a number of white blood cells. The main effects are caused by a class of immune cell called T-cells. Inflammatory responses are caused by the release of chemicals from T-cells called lymphokines. Therefore antihistamines are not effective against these allergies.

A well-known manifestation of a Type IV reaction is allergic contact dermatitis. This results from skin contact with, for example, nettles, poison ivy, heavy metals (such as lead and mercury), cosmetics and deodorants. These substances are often too small to evoke an immune response, but upon absorption through the skin, they bind to body proteins and become recognized as 'foreign' (this is utilized in the Heaf test for tuberculosis, in which the bacterial proteins are 'punched' beneath the skin surface).

Nickel and copper in jewellery may cause contact dermatitis, and in these cases, the cause is obvious. A wide number of potential allergens exist, and careful questioning of the patient's circumstances and relevant patch tests can establish the cause. Rashes can be chronic (long-term), patchy and some distance from the allergen. For example, allergy to nail varnish may manifest itself as a rash on the face or neck.

# How allergies occur

An allergy is an inappropriate response by the body's immune system to a normally harmless substance. Allergies vary from hay fever and asthma to life-threatening anaphylactic shock.

An allergy is a hypersensitivity of the body to a particular substance. If the body comes into contact with this substance, unpleasant and even life-threatening symptoms may occur.

### IMMUNE REACTION
Allergies occur when the immune system – the body's defence against infection – misidentifies an innocuous substance as being harmful and overreacts to it. This can result in mildly inconvenient symptoms such as a rash or runny nose or, in some cases, life-threatening shock. Allergies can be caused by anything, but typical allergens are pollen, wasp sting venom, penicillin, latex, peanuts and shellfish.

The main components of the body's immune system are lymphocytes (white blood cells). B-cells are a form of lymphocyte that are able to identify foreign particles (antigens) and form appropriate antibodies

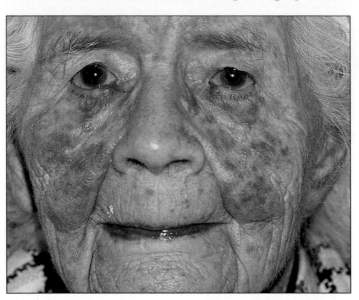

(immunoglobulins) specifically engineered to fight them. There are five basic types of antibodies: IgA, IgD, IgE, IgG and IgM. The immunoglobulin responsible for allergic reaction is IgE.

Allergies tend to be inherited, whereby the gene responsible for producing the protein that enables lymphocytes to distinguish between threatening and non-threatening proteins is faulty. This means that in a

*Skin allergies are usually caused by direct contact with an allergen. Here, an elderly woman has developed a rash in response to a particular bubble bath.*

person allergic to shellfish, for example, a B-cell is unable to recognize that a protein ingested as part of a meal containing shellfish is not invading the body. As a result, the B-cell produces large quantities of IgE antibodies.

### SENSITIZATION
These antibodies subsequently attach themselves to basophils (a type of white blood cell) and mast cells (found in connective tissue) in the body, causing the body to become sensitized to the allergenic protein.

Basophils and mast cells both produce histamine, an important weapon in the body's defence against infection. When released in extreme quantities, histamine can have a devastating effect upon the body.

## The allergic cascade

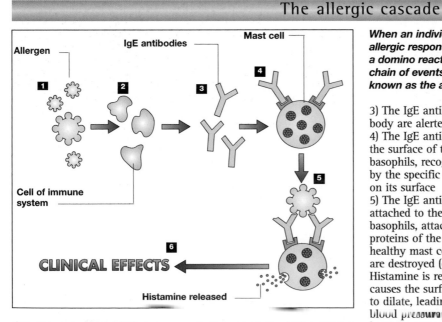

**Allergen**

**IgE antibodies**

**Mast cell**

**Cell of immune system**

**CLINICAL EFFECTS**

**Histamine released**

*When an individual develops an allergic response to a substance, a domino reaction occurs. A chain of events is set in motion, known as the allergic cascade.*

3) The IgE antibodies within the body are alerted
4) The IgE antibodies, bound to the surface of the mast cells and basophils, recognize the allergen by the specific protein markers on its surface
5) The IgE antibodies, still attached to the mast cells and basophils, attach to the surface proteins of the allergen. The healthy mast cells and basophils are destroyed (degranulation). Histamine is released, which causes the surface blood vessels to dilate, leading to a drop in blood pressure; the spaces between surrounding cells fill with fluid
6) Depending on the allergen, and where the reaction occurs, this may result in immediate symptoms. For example, if the reaction occurs in the mucous membrane of the nose, it may cause symptoms of hay fever, such as sneezing.

### NON-ALLERGIC REACTION
In a normal person, the allergic cascade fails to progress because the allergen is destroyed. A group of around 20 proteins that are present in the blood bind, one by one, to the allergen/antibody site. When the string of proteins is complete, the allergen is destroyed.

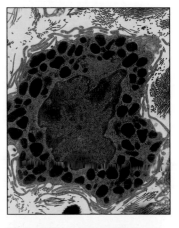

*Mast cells are large cells found in connective tissue. Histamine (which helps the body to fight infection) is produced in the cells' granules (shown in black).*

Over a period of around 10 days from initial exposure to the allergen, all the body's basophils and mast cells are primed with IgE antibodies and the body becomes sensitized to that allergen. If the body then comes into contact with the allergen for a second time, it will be prepared to attack immediately and a cascade

reaction occurs, in which a domino effect is triggered.

### ALLERGIC CASCADE
The allergic cascade occurs as follows:
1) The body and the allergen come into contact
2) The cells of the immune system are stimulated

# Anaphylaxis

Anaphylactic shock is an extreme allergic reaction that affects the whole body. Without treatment with adrenaline, the condition may be fatal.

In some cases, an allergic reaction can involve the entire body; this is known as a systemic reaction. During this reaction, histamine is released throughout the body, causing capillaries in many tissues to dilate. Anaphylaxis occurs when the reaction is so severe that the blood pressure becomes dangerously low. In extreme cases, the blood pressure drops so low that the body goes into shock. This is known as anaphylactic shock, and is often a fatal condition.

### SEVERE REACTION
Anaphylaxis develops very suddenly and presents in a number of ways. A person may rapidly develop a rash and the throat may swell as cells release fluid into surrounding tissue, causing breathing difficulties. A dangerous and rapid drop in blood pressure accompanies this as the blood vessels throughout the body dilate. The brain and other vital organs become

*A severe allergic reaction can cause localized swelling, known as oedema, in the tissues. This man has been stung by a bee on his lip resulting in inflammation.*

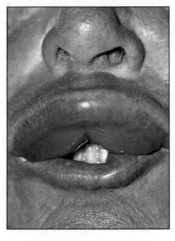

starved of oxygen and, within a matter of minutes, the person may die. Even if the victim survives this form of allergic reaction, the brain and kidneys may be permanently damaged.

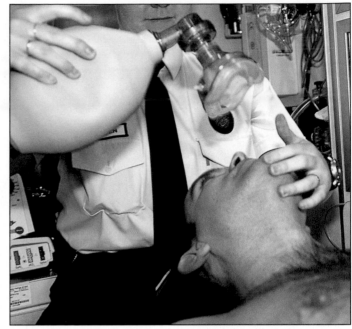

*Anaphylactic shock can be a life-threatening event. In extreme cases, a person can suffer a respiratory and cardiac arrest and need resuscitation.*

### ADRENALINE
The only effective treatment for anaphylaxis is an intramuscular injection of adrenaline, a hormone naturally produced by the adrenal glands.

Adrenaline counteracts the symptoms caused by excess histamine by constricting the body's blood vessels and opening the airways. It is vital that the injection is administered correctly at the onset of symptoms for it to be effective.

People who are aware of a serious allergy usually carry an injection for self administration.

## Treatment for allergies

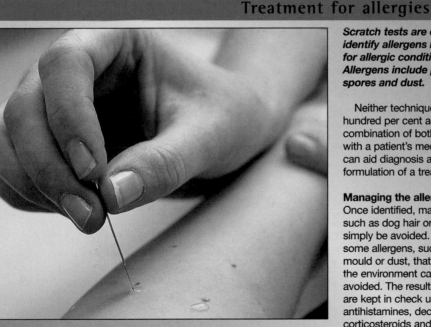

If a person suspects that they have an allergy, they can request tests to determine its exact nature. The scratch test is a common means of determining the cause of an allergy. This involves applying a diluted extract of a possible allergen to the skin (usually of the forearm) and then scratching the skin under the allergen with a needle. If swelling

or redness develops in the scratched area, it indicates that IgE antibodies to that allergen are present.

Blood tests may also be used to diagnose an allergy, especially in young children, since exposing a child to even minute amounts of allergen during a scratch test could trigger an anaphylactic reaction.

*Scratch tests are often used to identify allergens responsible for allergic conditions. Allergens include pollen, fungal spores and dust.*

Neither technique is one hundred per cent accurate, but a combination of both tests along with a patient's medical history can aid diagnosis and the formulation of a treatment plan.

**Managing the allergy**
Once identified, many allergens, such as dog hair or shellfish, can simply be avoided. However, some allergens, such as pollen, mould or dust, that are present in the environment cannot be avoided. The resulting allergies are kept in check using antihistamines, decongestants, corticosteroids and, in the case of anaphylaxis, adrenaline.

**Immunotherapy**
For people with severe allergies that cannot be avoided or managed with medication, immunotherapy may be their only hope of leading a normal life. This involves a number of injections of the specific allergen, starting with a very weak dilution and building

up to a higher dose that can be maintained over time.

These injections allow the immune system to adjust and desensitize to the allergen over time, so that it produces fewer IgE antibodies. Immunotherapy also stimulates the production of IgG antibodies, which block the effects of IgE. The treatment is expensive, time-consuming and entails risk (such as severe allergic reaction).

*Some people may choose to consult a homeopath. Here, a vegetative reflex test for allergies is measuring substances in the body.*

# Adapting to changes in atmospheric pressure

Changes in atmospheric pressure are experienced when we are above or below sea level. The body can adapt, within limits, to changes in the concentration of oxygen when pressure is raised or lowered.

The body depends upon oxygen, a major component of air, for survival. Oxygen ($O_2$) is transferred by red blood cells, from the lungs to body tissues, where it is exchanged for the waste product carbon dioxide ($CO_2$), which is exhaled. This process is essential to the production of energy necessary for the body to function.

### ATMOSPHERIC PRESSURE

Oxygen accounts for 20.96 per cent of volume of the air. Atmospheric pressure determines how dense the air is and thus the amount of oxygen in the air we inhale.

Humans are designed to thrive at around sea level, at which pressure the air is dense enough to ensure that oxygen is present in adequate concentrations in every breath taken.

### PHYSIOLOGICAL CHANGES

The further we move away from sea level, for example when climbing a mountain, or deep-sea diving, the atmospheric pressure changes. To survive, the body must adapt by undergoing physiological changes. This is known as acclimatization, or acclimation.

*The amount of oxygen inhaled with each breath depends on ambient pressure. As pressure changes, the body must adapt itself or be artificially aided.*

## Surviving high pressure under water

Water represents a high-pressure medium to which humans are not adapted. The main obstacle to survival is, of course, an inability to extract oxygen from the water for long-term survival.

In addition, gaseous exchange within the lungs is compromised by the increased ambient pressure that occurs with increasing depth.

### DIVING REFLEX

Although humans are poorly adapted to an aquatic environment, they do have some reflexes to prevent drowning and to conserve oxygen. These include inhibition of breathing, slowing down of the heart (bradycardia), constriction of the peripheral blood vessels, and reduced peripheral blood flow.

### ADAPTATIONS

Experienced divers are able to exploit these reflexes, enabling them to remain underwater for longer periods of time.

Through practice, lung capacity is increased so that a greater amount of oxygen can be stored before surfacing. Also, the employment of techniques such as hyperventilation, whereby a greater concentration of oxygen is taken into the lungs, enables

*Self-contained underwater breathing apparatus enables divers to breathe underwater. Increased pressure can have adverse effects on the body.*

divers to remain below the surface for longer than would normally be possible.

### DEEP-SEA DIVING

There are limitations to the body's ability to stay underwater, however, and for deeper diving an artificial supply of oxygen is required.

Modern equipment provides divers with a supply of oxygen, the pressure of which is constantly equalized to that of the lungs. This allows divers to remain underwater for greater lengths of time, reaching profound depths, although this in itself can be hazardous.

## Decompression sickness

Although nitrogen (which forms 79 per cent of air) normally has little effect on the body, prolonged exposure to high pressure can cause it to concentrate in the body tissues, giving a narcotic effect. As a result, divers can become dizzy and appear drunk.

With gradual ascent, the dissolved nitrogen gas dissipates slowly. If a diver surfaces too quickly, however, the rapid decrease in pressure causes the dissolved nitrogen to form bubbles of gas in the blood which can develop emboli (clots) that may be fatal or cause paralysis (when bubbles migrate to the brain) and evoke acute musculoskeletal pain (commonly referred to as 'the bends').

Treatment should be carried out immediately, which involves recompression (hyperbaric therapy) of the body in a compression chamber, before gradual decompression.

# Coping with low pressure

At high altitudes, atmospheric pressure becomes lower and oxygen more scarce.
The body is able to compensate for the lack of oxygen using certain mechanisms;
however, altitude sickness may occur if a climber ascends too high or too quickly.

With an increase in altitude there is a decrease in pressure and the air becomes less and less dense as the oxygen molecules spread out. As a result, each breath taken will contain less oxygen.

### DECREASED OXYGEN

Under these challenging conditions there are noticeable effects on respiration. The body therefore adapts to the decrease in partial pressure of oxygen in the lungs by employing a number of compensatory mechanisms.

In the short term, the decrease in available oxygen will be compensated for by an increase in the rate and volume of air inspired. The respiratory centre of the brain causes deeper breaths to be taken in order to inhale greater volumes of air and therefore more oxygen.

The scarcity of oxygen at high altitudes also stimulates an increase in the production of

haemoglobin and red blood cells, helping to increase the blood's oxygen-carrying capacity. In addition, heart rate and blood pressure are increased to maximize the amount of oxygen transported throughout the body.

For prolonged periods at high altitudes body tissues develop more blood vessels, increasing the efficiency of gaseous exchange. In addition the size of muscle fibres decreases, shortening the diffusion path of oxygen.

### ACCLIMATIZATION

These acclimatizing physiological changes are effective, but not spontaneous, and acclimatization must occur progressively. Ascending to altitude too quickly or climbing too high will result in the body not being able to adapt quickly enough, if at all, and the body will be unable to cope with the oxygen depletion.

*Most aircraft are pressurized to counteract low atmospheric pressure at high altitudes. Oxygen masks are available in case of emergency.*

*The Sherpas are people renowned for their ability to survive in the high Himalayan mountains. They are adapted to living at a very low atmospheric pressure.*

## Altitude sickness

*At extreme heights, or if ascent is too rapid, the body is unable to cope with the low pressure. Altitude sickness occurs due to an inadequate oxygen supply.*

Altitude sickness occurs when the altitude is simply too high for the body to cope with, or the decrease in pressure is too rapid.

Because there is so little oxygen, the body must work harder to pass more air through the lungs, while the increased breathing rate requires even more energy expenditure. Breathing becomes laboured and irregular, and as oxygen concentrations

reaching the body tissues become inadequate, a state of hypoxia is reached. The climber experiences confusion, light-headedness, headache and nausea.

Treatment for this condition is gradual descent and, in some cases, drug therapy. Severe forms of altitude sickness are extremely dangerous and can give rise to brain haemorrhage and fluid accumulation in the lungs.

The body is unable to function unaided beyond 6,400 metres (21,000 feet). Mount Everest is 8,840 m (29,000 ft) high, meaning that climbers normally require oxygen to complete the ascent.

# Counteracting the effects of space travel

Space travel has some dramatic effects on the body. In order to counteract these effects, astronauts need to undergo specialized training, and rely on increasingly sophisticated equipment.

From the minute the space shuttle takes off, the astronaut's body is subject to dramatic environmental changes.

### ADJUSTING TO SPACE

Immediately, the gravitational pull of the shuttle taking off puts the body under immense pressure. As the shuttle accelerates, the *g*-forces increase to three times normal gravity, causing chest compression, breathing difficulties and an extreme feeling of heaviness. Within minutes, the shuttle is in orbit and weightlessness occurs.

The body will then have to adjust all over again on return to Earth. In order to cope with all the extreme changes brought on by space travel, astronauts have to undergo rigorous training and must be in excellent health.

*As the shuttle takes off, the body is subject to gravitational forces three times greater than normal. This puts immense pressure on all the systems within the body.*

*On take-off, astronauts experience a feeling of extreme heaviness. Within a matter of minutes this gives way to a sensation of weightlessness.*

## In-flight precautions

When in space, it is essential that astronauts follow a strict exercise programme (up to two hours a day) to counteract the wasting of muscle, bone and the heart.

Without this exercise, the body would be too weak to survive a return to the Earth's atmosphere.

The combination of confined space and weightlessness means that astronauts have to rely on exercise machines such as treadmills to prevent the muscles from wasting. They also use large rubber bands (bungee cords) and shoulder weights to hold themselves down, producing a sensation similar to weight.

### Fluid loss

One way to deal with fluid loss is the use of a lower body negative pressure (LBNP) device. This involves the use of a vacuum-cleaner-like suction below the waist to keep fluids in the legs.

The LBNP device might be attached to an exercise machine, such as a treadmill. By spending around 30 minutes every day using this device, astronauts can keep their circulatory system in near-Earth condition.

Just before returning to Earth astronauts drink large volumes of water or electrolyte solutions to help replace the fluids lost. Without this measure the astronaut would be likely to faint when first standing up on return to Earth.

### Monitoring

Constant monitoring of body changes on each mission is an

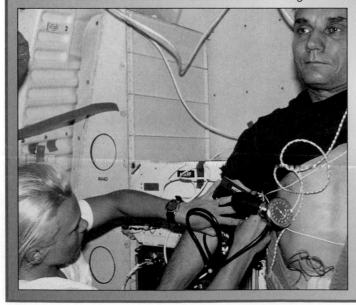

*Astronauts exercise every day on machines such as treadmills. This counteracts the muscle wasting that would otherwise occur in space.*

*Astronauts constantly monitor body changes in space. This provides vital data for research into the effect of space travel on the body.*

extremely important part of the astronaut's role. These measurements are essential since they allow any abnormal changes to be detected, as well as providing vital data for research into the effect of space travel on the body.

# Creating a safe micro-environment

Space represents a hostile environment for the body. Beyond the spacecraft, astronauts would perish within seconds without the aid of a spacesuit.

Although astronauts have successfully landed and walked on the moon, this would be impossible without extremely specialized equipment.

### HOSTILE ENVIRONMENT

If an astronaut were to leave the security of the spacecraft without a spacesuit, they would instantly perish for a number of reasons:
■ A lack of oxygen means they would lose consciousness within 15 seconds
■ There is little or no air pressure in space, which would cause the blood and other body fluids to boil instantly
■ Extreme temperatures ranging from 120°C in sunlight, to –100°C

in the shade would be fatal
■ The body would be exposed to deadly levels of radiation from cosmic rays and charged particles emitted from the sun.

In addition, astronauts face the hazard of fast-moving rock particles and satellite debris bombarding the site, creating a dangerous environment.

For this reason, increasingly sophisticated equipment is required to create a safe micro-environment.

*Spacesuits provide astronauts with a temperature- and pressure-controlled environment. They also protect them from radiation and space debris.*

---

## Spacesuits

Spacesuits allow astronauts to leave the safety of the spacecraft by providing the following:

■ A pressurized atmosphere – this is vital for keeping the body's fluids in a liquid state. Spacesuits operate below normal atmospheric pressure, while the space cabin operates at normal air pressure. For this reason, an airlock is operated between the cabin and the exterior so that pressure can be reduced before astronauts put on their suits, to prevent nitrogen building up in the blood (causing the 'bends').

■ Oxygen supply – spacesuits provide pure oxygen for breathing, supplied either from the spacecraft (via an 'umbilical cord') or from the astronaut's specialized backpack. As the shuttle has a normal air mixture (simulating Earth's atmosphere), astronauts must breathe pure oxygen for some time before putting on their spacesuits.

This eliminates nitrogen from the astronaut's blood and body tissues, minimizing the risk of it entering the blood and causing the 'bends'. The spacesuit is also designed to eliminate carbon

*Astronauts enter an airlock compartment before putting on their spacesuits. This allows their body to adjust to the lower atmospheric pressure.*

dioxide, which would otherwise build up and poison the body.

■ Insulation – spacesuits are designed to maintain the optimum temperature for the body, despite strenuous activity, and prevent exposure to extreme temperatures.

Spacesuits are heavily insulated with layers of sophisticated fabrics that allow the body to breathe, but maintain temperature. Heat produced by the body during strenuous activity is dissipated by a fan or water cooler, to prevent excessive sweating and subsequent dehydration. It has been known for astronauts to lose several pounds during a single space walk due to fluid loss.

■ Protection – spacesuits are made up of many layers of durable fabric which protect the body from flying debris and prevent the suit from tearing.

■ Defence against radiation – spacesuits offer only limited protection from radiation, so

spacewalks are always planned during periods of low solar activity.

■ Easy mobility – joints in the fabric of the spacesuit enable astronauts to move easily.

■ Clear vision – visors are made of clear material, designed to reflect sunlight and reduce glare. Fitted lights enable the astronaut to see in the shadows

■ Communication – spacesuits are equipped with radio transmitters and receivers to allow communication.

*Space is a hostile environment for human life. Spacesuits create optimum conditions for the body, enabling astronauts to explore new frontiers.*

# How biorhythms occur

Many of the of the body's important physiological processes take place in cycles, known as biorhythms. These cycles occur at specific intervals, and are controlled by an internal biological clock.

Many of the physiological processes that take place within the body are timed to occur at specific intervals. The onset of puberty, for example, is a physiological event triggered by a form of timing mechanism to occur in early adolescence.

Many of the body's physiological processes are controlled by hormones that fluctuate in cycles known as biorhythms.

### MONTHLY CYCLE
One example of a biorhythm is the female menstrual cycle. The uterine lining develops, degenerates and is shed in a cycle that begins approximately every 28 days.

This cycle suggests that the hormones responsible for menstruation are controlled by a form of internal clock.

Different types of biorhythms occur over varying intervals of time. They include:
■ Pulses – hormones may be secreted in spurts every few minutes, for example insulin, or over every hour
■ Circadian rhythms – regulated over a 24-hour period, for example the hormones that control the sleep-wake cycle
■ Monthly cycles – for example, the fluctuations of the hormones that control the menstrual cycle
■ Seasonal – levels of thyroid hormones decrease in winter while melatonin levels increase.

*Many physiological processes occur in cycles. These biorhythms appear to be synchronized by external factors such as light and dark.*

---

## Circadian rhythms

Many of the biorhythms exhibited by humans appear to be linked to environmental rhythms.

Biorhythms that occur in 24-hour cycles (roughly corresponding with the solar or light-dark cycle) are referred to as circadian rhythms (literally meaning 'about a day').

### SLEEP-WAKE CYCLE
An obvious example of a circadian biorhythm is the sleep-wake cycle. In general, adults tend to wake around 7 am and become sleepy around 10 pm.

Likewise, body temperature fluctuates over a 24-hour period; it is at its lowest in the middle of the night, and tends to reach a peak during mid-afternoon.

The levels of many hormones are seen to correspond with this circadian pattern.

### HORMONES
The production of the hormone cortisol by the adrenal glands is one such hormone. If levels of cortisol are monitored over a 24-hour period, a distinct pattern can be seen. Production of cortisol rises when we wake, peaking at around 9 am. Levels of this hormone reach their lowest around midnight.

### THYROID-STIMULATING HORMONE
The production of thyroid-stimulating hormone from the pituitary also follows a circadian rhythm. Thyroid hormones act directly on almost all the body cells, controlling their rate of metabolism. Levels of this hormone reach a peak around 11 pm, and are at their lowest around 11 am.

The production of other hormones, such as endorphins and sex hormones, also vary in a circadian manner.

*The sleep-wake cycle is one example of a circadian rhythm. Our levels of alertness appear to be synchronized with the 24-hour light-dark cycle.*

---

## Light-dark cycle

Studies reveal that when subjects are placed in isolation chambers (with no indication of time) they continue to follow a regular sleep-wake cycle, although it is closer to 25 hours. With time, therefore, subjects lose synchronization with day and night.

**Synchronization**
If subjects are once again exposed to light-dark cycles the body soon reverts to the circadian cycle.

This demonstrates that the natural period of the body clock is not caused by the day-night cycle, but is simply synchronized by it.

*In the absence of external cues, humans continue to follow a regular sleep-wake cycle. Our natural cycle is slightly longer than 24 hours however.*

# The biological clock

Biorhythms appear to be regulated by a self-sustaining timing mechanism or biological clock. Research indicates that this clock is synchronized with the light-dark cycle through interaction between the hypothalamus and pineal gland.

Light entering the eye reaches the retina (the densely innervated area at the back of the eye) stimulating the visual cortex of the brain.

Some of the retinal nerve fibres however, are connected to the suprachiasmatic nuclei, two tiny structures located within the hypothalamus of the brain.

### PINEAL GLAND
Stimulation of the suprachiasmatic nuclei causes the hypothalamus to send signals to the pineal gland (a small oval gland located immediately above the brainstem). This gland is often referred to as the 'third eye' since it is triggered by levels of light and dark.

### MELATONIN
The pineal gland secretes the hormone melatonin in response to the signals it receives from the retina (mediated by the hypothalamus).

In darkness, the pineal gland secretes melatonin, while the presence of light suppresses it. Research shows that melatonin influences the activity of a number of endocrine glands.

Melatonin plays an important role in the regulation of the sleep cycle, as increased levels lead to sleepiness and fatigue.

Research indicates that there is a relationship between the activity of the pineal gland and seasonal affective disorder (SAD).

The presence of melatonin also reduces the activity of the suprachiasmatic nuclei.

### LOST RHYTHMS
It has long been known that damage to the suprachiasmatic nuclei, for example following surgery to remove a brain tumour, causes circadian rhythm to be lost. Likewise, diseases of the hypothalamus cause disorders of normal patterns such as sleep.

### RESEARCH
Although research continues, it certainly seems that synchronization of the body with the day-night cycle involves the stimulation of the suprachiasmatic nuclei to activate the clock, and the action of the pineal gland to turn it off.

Together these specialized areas of the brain regulate the timing of events such as sleeping, waking, times of eating, and body temperature.

*The pineal gland is located immediately above the brainstem. This gland secretes melatonin in response to signals from the hypothalamus.*

## The pineal gland

**Pineal gland**
Secretes melatonin in response to signals received from the hypothalamus

**Brainstem**

**Hypothalamus**
The suprachiasmatic nuclei are located within this region

## The effects of jet lag

Rapid travel across time zones gives rise to a phenomenon commonly referred to as jet lag.

**Disrupted biorhythms**
As the body is thrown into a different time zone, its biological clock does not corresponds with that of the time zone it is actually in, with the result that circadian rhythms no longer synchronize with the light-dark cycle.

Consequently, the normal circadian rhythms of sleeping, waking, eating and drinking become disrupted. This can lead to insomnia, fatigue during the day, light-headedness, malaise and reduced mental and physical performance.

*Travel across time zones, can interfere with the body's natural cycles. Circadian rhythms, such as eating patterns, can become very disrupted.*

These effects do not only occur as a result of air travel, but are also experienced by people translocated to extreme environments, as in space travel, or expeditions to the arctic or antarctic, where light-dark cycles are markedly different.

**Travelling east**
The effects of jet lag tend to be worse when travelling east due to the hours lost. As the body's natural cycle is around 25 hours long, it is easier for the body to adjust to a lengthened day when flying west.

Interestingly, if a person were to travel the entire circumference of the globe in a day and return to their original time zone, they would not suffer from jet lag.

Research into the effects of melatonin in resynchronizing the body with the 24-hour cycle after long distance travel is underway.

# How the body ages

Ageing is the gradual degeneration of the body with time.
Biological processes, such as cardiovascular system functions,
become less efficient until they can no longer fulfil their role.

Ageing is the term used to describe the physiological changes that take place in the body as it slowly degenerates with time. This process occurs gradually over a number of years, beginning in the third decade of life (age 20–30).

### LIFE EXPECTANCY
The longest lifespan recorded by the *Guinness Book of Records* is currently 122 years. With advances in lifestyle, medicine and sanitation, however, this record is likely to be broken. On average in the UK, life expectancy is 74 years for men and 79 years for women.

### 'STOPPING THE CLOCK'
Extensive research has been carried out into the biological mechanisms behind ageing, in an attempt to delay its effects, and even reverse the process.

Though much progress has been made in our understanding of the ageing process, what holds true is that ageing is an inevitable biological state and is as much a part of life as infancy, childhood and adolescence.

*Ageing occurs gradually, over a period of many years. Medical advances have helped to ensure that people are living longer today than ever before.*

## Cell ageing

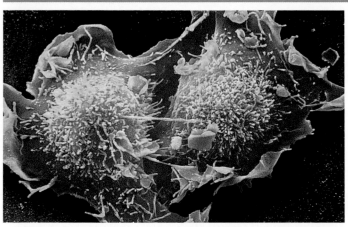

In order to understand the ageing process, it is necessary to investigate the biological mechanisms that occur at the cellular level. Cells are the individual building blocks, functioning together, that form the tissues which make up the body. These cells are replenished through the process of replication (cell division).

*Cells divide a finite number of times before dying. It is likely therefore that cellular genes are programmed to stop functioning at a predetermined time.*

### CELL DEATH
Research has shown that cells divide a finite number of times before undergoing apoptosis (programmed cell death). In addition, the remaining cells may not function as efficiently as those in the young.

Certain cellular enzymes may be less active, so more time may be required for chemical reactions to occur that are essential to the basic functioning of the cell. As the cells fail to reproduce, the organ becomes less efficient, until it can no longer fulfil its biological role.

## External changes

Ageing is most commonly characterized by the external changes that take place in the body.

### HAIR CHANGES
Perhaps the most obvious change that takes place during the ageing process is the alteration in hair colour. Around the age of 30, grey or white hairs often begin to appear as the hair follicles lose their source of pigmentation. This greying becomes increasingly obvious as pigmented hairs are shed and replaced by grey hairs.

In both sexes, the hair thins considerably, and many men may experience balding.

### SKIN CHANGES
The skin loses its elasticity with age, and wrinkles develop. This is due to changes in collagen (a structural protein) and elastin (the protein that gives the skin its elastic quality).

### CHANGES IN STATURE
Middle age is often associated with an increase in weight as the metabolism slows, followed by a significant decrease in weight as old age progresses.

Muscle tissue may be replaced by fat, particularly around the trunk, while the arms and legs generally become thinner.

Older people tend to shrink in height, owing to compression of the spinal vertebrae.

*As the body ages, the hair loses its colour and turns grey. The skin becomes less elastic and wrinkles develop due to changes in collagen and elastin.*

# Internal changes

Physiological studies reveal that the performance of many of the body's vital organs – such as the heart, kidneys and lungs – declines with age.

Changes associated with ageing also take place internally. Many internal organs, such as the liver, kidneys, spleen, pancreas, lungs and liver, shrink in size and function less efficiently, as the cells which comprise them gradually degenerate.

The circulation of blood by the heart is also affected by ageing. The heart's pumping action is greatly reduced and the body's response to exercise or stress by increasing the heart rate is much more extreme. The blood vessels (veins, arteries and capillaries) throughout the body lose some elasticity and tend to become convoluted.

The bones become more brittle, as the calcium content decreases, making older people more liable to fractures, even after relatively minor falls.

There is a general decline in the body's regulating mechanisms, resulting in the body being less adaptable to external changes. Older people are more sensitive to extremes of temperature, and may take longer to recover from illness.

The gradual decline of the immune system also means that older people are more vulnerable to infection and disease.

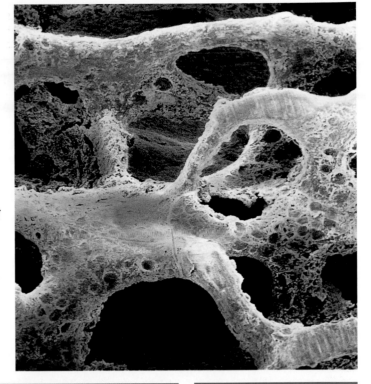

*Calcium and protein are progressively lost from the bones with age. This can lead to the condition osteoporosis, in which the bones become brittle.*

## Changes in the nervous system

The ageing brain undergoes a gradual loss of neurones (brain cells), which are not replaced.

### MENTAL ABILITY
However, although the number of brain cells decreases throughout life, this represents only a small percentage of the total number of cells in the brain. There is no conclusive evidence that intelligence deteriorates with age, rather that it is closely associated with education and lifestyle.

### AGE-RELATED DISEASE
Brain cells are extremely sensitive to oxygen deficiency. It is likely that, when deterioration of the brain does occur, it is caused not by ageing itself, but by age-related diseases, such as arteriosclerosis.

Such diseases affect the cardiovascular system and

*Mental stimulation plays a part in countering the effects of ageing on the brain. Activities such as doing crosswords help to keep the brain active.*

reduce oxygen supply to the brain. The efficiency of the brain is therefore reduced, and there may be a decline in intellectual performance. Logic, mental agility and the ability to grasp new ideas can all be affected.

### BRAIN FUNCTION
Functions related to the brain also lose their efficiency. Reflexes and physical movements become slower and the memory may deteriorate, especially for recent events.

### SENILE DEMENTIA
In severe cases, this can lead to senile dementia. This condition is characterized by a loss of memory, childlike behaviour, incoherent speech and a lack of awareness.

## Senses

There is a gradual deterioration of the senses with age:
■ Vision – beyond the age of around 20, there is a decline in visual acuity, which deteriorates at an even greater rate after age 50. The size of the pupil also reduces with age, with the result that night vision is affected. The eyes are also increasingly susceptible to disease
■ Hearing – there is a gradual reduction in the ability to hear tones at higher frequencies. This can interfere with the identification of individuals by their voices, and with following group conversations
■ Taste – the number of taste buds is gradually reduced, and the sense of taste is dulled
■ Smell – this may deteriorate with age, also affecting the sense of taste.

## Genetics of ageing

Medical advances have served to increase the average life expectancy, although they have not yet extended the maximum lifespan.

Laboratory research has shown that cells replicate themselves a certain number of times before dying, and that the quality of each cell gradually deteriorates. This suggests that human beings may

*The rate at which a person ages is determined by both genetic and environmental factors. Taking regular exercise can help to delay the effects of time.*

be programmed to age and die at some pre-determined point and that genes may carry instructions to cease functioning at a certain time.

**Environmental factors**
In reality, how a person ages is determined not solely by genes, but by environmental factors such as lifestyle and diet.

A person who smokes, has a generally poor diet and does not take any exercise is more likely to age more quickly, become ill and die before their genetically determined time.

# Index

# Picture Credits

Apart from those images listed below, all of the pictures in this book, including the back cover, were originally sourced for the part-work *Inside the Human Body*, produced by Bright Star Publishing plc.

**Front cover:** Photos.com
**Getty Images:** 6 (Geoff Brightling/Iconica)
**Corbis:** 7 (Howard Sochurek), 8 (Visuals Unlimited), 9 (Clouds Hill Imaging Ltd.)